iOS 11 Swift Programming Cookbook

Solutions and Examples for iOS Apps

Vandad Nahavandipoor

Beijing · Boston · Farnham · Sebastopol · Tokyo

iOS 11 Swift Programming Cookbook

by Vandad Nahavandipoor

Printed in the United States of America.

Published by O'Reilly Media, Inc., 1005 Gravenstein Highway North, Sebastopol, CA 95472.

O'Reilly books may be purchased for educational, business, or sales promotional use. Online editions are also available for most titles (*http://oreilly.com/safari*). For more information, contact our corporate/institutional sales department: 800-998-9938 or *corporate@oreilly.com*.

Editor: Rachel Roumeliotis	**Indexer:** Ellen Troutman-Zaig
Production Editor: Nicholas Adams	**Interior Designer:** David Futato
Copyeditor: Kim Cofer	**Cover Designer:** Karen Montgomery
Proofreader: Rachel Head	**Illustrator:** Rebecca Demarest

December 2017:   First Edition

Revision History for the First Edition

2017-12-04:   First Release

See *http://oreilly.com/catalog/errata.csp?isbn=9781491992470* for release details.

978-1-491-99247-0

[LSI]

Table of Contents

Preface

Swift 4 is an incremental release of Swift: a *tock* in Apple's usual tick-tock release cycle, where the tick is a major release and the tock is a follow-up release with bug fixes and some additions and improvements. Two of the biggest additions to Swift 4 are the `Decodable` and `Encodable` protocols, which together form the `Codable` protocol. These protocols allow you, with just a bit of configuration, to define, encode, and decode JSON objects, a task that you either previously did on your own or used a library to accomplish.

Another welcome addition to Swift is the ability to extend typed arrays. For instance, you can now add a function to arrays that contain `Int` instances, but not to any other arrays. This way you could, for instance, define a `sum()` function that returns the sum of all integers in the array. Such a function wouldn't make sense for an array of `String` objects, and therefore it's best placed inside an extension to arrays that contain numeric data, such as an array of `Int`.

We all have had moments when we wished Xcode's source editor would be rewritten in order to properly function, and that's exactly what Apple has done with Xcode 9. We have a whole new state-of-the-art source editor with built-in GitHub integration. Xcode Server is also now built into Xcode itself, and you don't have to install macOS server in order to take advantage of it. We have a whole chapter dedicated to Xcode Server, so you will get to know it better soon.

The previous edition of this book focused primarily on what's *new* in iOS 10, but this version takes a more holistic look at iOS 11 and what can make a great iOS developer, including knowledge of continuous integration, snapshot testing, Swift 4, and Xcode 9.

Audience

I assume that you are comfortable writing iOS apps, at least know your way around Xcode, and can work with the simulator. This book is *not* for beginners. If you have never programmed in Xcode before for iOS, it will be tough to learn iOS programming only from this book, so I suggest that you complement your skills with other online resources. The intended audience for this book is intermediate and advanced users.

I also assume that you have written a little bit of Swift code. In this book, I use Swift 4 and will teach you some of the concepts, but if you don't know Swift, this is not the right place to start. If you're just starting out, pick up Apple's book on Swift programming first; once you've read through it and are a bit more comfortable with Swift, come back to this book and I'm sure you'll learn a lot of new things, even about Swift 4.

Organization of This Book

Here I'll explain what each chapter is about so that you'll get a feeling for what this book is going to teach you:

Chapter 1, Continuous Integration and Delivery
> Continuous integration (CI) and continuous delivery (CD) are both popular and the subject of some very deep discussions at the organizational level of development teams, sometimes with some developers being entirely against them and others enthusiastically for them. If you are lucky, you will work in an organization where everyone in the team has *some* knowledge of CI and CD, but if you are unlucky, you might be the only person in your team who is responsible for your CI servers. In this chapter, we will dive deep into Travis and Xcode Server as our CI servers, and also have a look at fastlane as our CD tool.

Chapter 2, Snapshot Testing
> Snapshot testing is a modern way of testing your user interface in order to detect sudden and unwanted changes, such as unwanted changes to a font that can affect certain UI components. With snapshot testing, we will capture the state of our UI when we are sure of it being correct, and use this captured state as a reference to compare future states with. Should anything have changed compared to the original and correct state, the snapshot test will fail, triggering the development team to look for the bug. In this chapter, we will focus on Facebook's snapshot testing iOS library and how we can leverage its power to make UI testing easier than ever before.

Chapter 3, SiriKit

Since its introduction, Siri has been an integral part of iOS and how people interact with the operating system. However, because it was a closed technology, we developers couldn't integrate our apps into Siri. That's not the case anymore. Now you can write your own app extensions that integrate into Siri and allow you to interpret various "intents" that come from Siri into your applications. For instance, you can create a financial application that allows the user to send and receive money from various sources, all driven through Siri. In this chapter, you will see how to create one of these extensions and learn the different entry points from Siri into your application.

Chapter 4, Measurements and Units

This chapter is dedicated to the new series of classes and structures that Apple has provided to developers to convert between various measurements and units.

Chapter 5, Core Data

Core Data is without a doubt the standard and best way to store large amounts of data and structure your data object models in an iOS application. In this chapter we will focus on the fundamentals of Core Data and how you can leverage its power to not only store your data, but also search for it using queries and retrieve it as managed objects.

Chapter 6, Swift and Cocoa Touch

Swift 4 brought with it a lot of great new features, such as built-in JSON parsing and typed array extensions. In this chapter we will have a look at what's new in Swift 4 and some functionalities introduced in Cocoa Touch.

Chapter 7, Xcode 9 and Interface Builder

In this chapter, we take a look at a lot of new stuff in Xcode and Interface Builder (IB). Apple has brought us refactoring features for Swift in Xcode 9. We can also debug our iOS applications wirelessly on iOS devices, so you can finally build that iOS test farm that you have been dreaming about for years. We will look at some of these cool new features, plus GitHub integration right inside Xcode.

Chapter 8, The User Interface

Apple tends not to release a piece of technology until it knows that the implementation is really well thought out. One of the features lacking from iOS since the beginning was a built-in drag-and-drop functionality that would have allowed intra-app drag and drop on iPads, or even inter-app drag-and-drop functionality on iPhone devices. As of this year, we can now implement drag and drop in our iOS apps, thanks to the new SDK. In this chapter, you will learn about 3D Touch, drag-and-drop features, font scaling, named colors, and much more.

Chapter 9, Document-Based Apps

We've had the ability to develop apps that take advantage of iCloud data storage for a while now, but never have developers been able to present an iCloud document browser to their users, allowing them to create documents right in iCloud from within this system UI. We now have a view controller that functions as a built-in document browser that is easy to use in and integrate with our application. User can now open and create iCloud documents without ever leaving your applications. In this chapter you will learn all about the document browser view controller and how you can harness its power to create document-based applications.

Chapter 10, Apple Watch

This year Apple didn't focus as much on watchOS. However, there are exciting new ways of interacting with watchOS, which we will discuss in this chapter.

Chapter 11, Contacts

The contacts APIs will be discussed in this chapter. You'll learn how to use the Contacts framework to add new contacts to the user's device, remove contacts, edit them, or even allow the user to pick a contact from the list so that you can perform your tasks on it—all without having to fiddle with low-level C APIs.

Chapter 12, Extensions

The Safari Content Blocker extension allows developers to create apps that get installed as extensions in the user's Safari browser and allow us to block various elements of web pages that the user views. For instance, you can now block pictures or other unwanted elements in the websites that you specify in your app, and you can share these content blockers with those who use your app. This chapter is all about these extension points that you can add to your apps.

Chapter 13, Web and Search

Apps can provide content to iOS for indexing in the device's search engine. iOS will then index this content and allow the users to search for it right within Spotlight on their devices. Your content can also be indexed globally on Apple's servers so even those who don't have your app can see your content on their devices. Intrigued? Read this chapter, then!

Chapter 14, Multitasking

In iOS, we have the ability to provide Picture in Picture (PiP) to our users. Your app can provide a video player to iOS and allow the user to minimize your whole app into that video player while she works with other apps. It's really cool, in my opinion!

Chapter 15, Maps and Location

With new additions to the Core Location and MapKit frameworks, you can, for example, display an ETA for transit between two locations or display your custom view inside the annotation of a pin on the map. You will also learn how to cluster similar pins into a group to avoid cluttering your map view. Another welcome addition to the map view is the ability to remove system buttons from it and instead display those system buttons somewhere else on your user interface, where it fits your UI best. You will learn all about that and more in this chapter.

Chapter 16, UI Testing

We will discuss Apple's UI Testing framework in this chapter. I'll show you how to write native Swift code to do UI testing.

Chapter 17, Core Motion

Core Motion is also available on watchOS. In this chapter, you'll learn some of the things that you can do with this framework, including reading cadence information from sensors on the device.

Chapter 18, Security

When a user registers for your service on your website on their iOS device and saves the password with which she registered her account, this password ends up in the user's iCloud Keychain, if she has enabled it. In your iOS app, you now have the ability to ask iOS for these credentials should the user be able to authenticate herself in your app with Touch ID. Application Transport Security in iOS forces all requests to go through HTTPS. If you build your project with the latest Xcode and iOS SDK, all your network requests will go through HTTPS by default, protecting your content—but possibly breaking a few things if you don't support HTTPS in your web services. Read this chapter to learn more.

Chapter 19, Multimedia

iOS includes great ways for apps to interact with Siri's voice, and you can read about them in this chapter.

Chapter 20, UI Dynamics

There are some amazing effects that you can achieve in your user interface with UI dynamics, including the ability to create turbulence or magnetic fields. In this chapter, we'll review some examples that show these effects in action.

Chapter 21, iMessage Stickers and Apps

Sticker packs are extensions that you can distribute either as part of your iOS applications or as standalone applications. They allow you to add interactions to messages being sent and received in iMessage conversations. In this chapter, we will discuss different types of these extensions and how you can create interactive sticker pack applications for iMessage.

Conventions Used in This Book

The following typographical conventions are used in this book:

Italic

> Indicates new terms, URLs, email addresses, filenames, and file extensions.

`Constant width`

> Used for program listings, as well as within paragraphs to refer to program elements such as variable or function names, databases, data types, environment variables, statements, and keywords.

`Constant width bold`

> Shows commands or other text that should be typed literally by the user.

`Constant width italic`

> Shows text that should be replaced with user-supplied values or by values determined by context.

> This element signifies a note, tip, or suggestion.

> This element indicates a warning or caution.

Additional Resources

This book is not for beginners, so I assume you have already gotten a grip on Swift and can do basic things with it. You can find Apple's documentation on Swift by doing a quick web search. You can read it in your browser, as a PDF, or via iBooks.

Also check this book's GitHub repository in order to get the most up-to-date code, as I update the code to ensure it works with the latest Swift and Xcode versions.

Using Code Examples

Supplemental material (code examples, exercises, etc.) is available for download at *https://github.com/vandadnp/iOS-11-Swift-Programming-Cookbook*.

This book is here to help you get your job done. In general, if example code is offered with this book, you may use it in your programs and documentation. You do not need to contact us for permission unless you're reproducing a significant portion of the code. For example, writing a program that uses several chunks of code from this book does not require permission. Selling or distributing a CD-ROM of examples from O'Reilly books does require permission. Answering a question by citing this book and quoting example code does not require permission. Incorporating a significant amount of example code from this book into your product's documentation does require permission.

We appreciate, but do not require, attribution. An attribution usually includes the title, author, publisher, and ISBN. For example: "*iOS 11 Swift Programming Cookbook* by Vandad Nahavandipoor (O'Reilly). Copyright 2018 Vandad Nahavandipoor, 978-1-491-99247-0."

If you feel your use of code examples falls outside fair use or the permission given above, feel free to contact us at *permissions@oreilly.com*.

O'Reilly Safari

Safari (formerly Safari Books Online) is a membership-based training and reference platform for enterprise, government, educators, and individuals.

Members have access to thousands of books, training videos, Learning Paths, interactive tutorials, and curated playlists from over 250 publishers, including O'Reilly Media, Harvard Business Review, Prentice Hall Professional, Addison-Wesley Professional, Microsoft Press, Sams, Que, Peachpit Press, Adobe, Focal Press, Cisco Press, John Wiley & Sons, Syngress, Morgan Kaufmann, IBM Redbooks, Packt, Adobe Press, FT Press, Apress, Manning, New Riders, McGraw-Hill, Jones & Bartlett, and Course Technology, among others.

For more information, please visit *http://oreilly.com/safari*.

How to Contact Us

Please address comments and questions concerning this book to the publisher:

O'Reilly Media, Inc.
1005 Gravenstein Highway North
Sebastopol, CA 95472
800-998-9938 (in the United States or Canada)
707-829-0515 (international or local)
707-829-0104 (fax)

We have a web page for this book, where we list errata, examples, and any additional information. You can access this page at *http://bit.ly/ios-11-swift-prog-cookbook*.

To comment or ask technical questions about this book, send email to *bookquestions@oreilly.com*.

For more information about our books, courses, conferences, and news, see our website at *http://www.oreilly.com*.

Find us on Facebook: *http://facebook.com/oreilly*

Follow us on Twitter: *http://twitter.com/oreillymedia*

Watch us on YouTube: *http://www.youtube.com/oreillymedia*

You can also check the author's blog (*https://vandadnp.wordpress.com*) and YouTube channel (*https://www.youtube.com/c/iosdevcafe*).

Acknowledgments

Thank you to:

Rachel Roumeliotis

For always having trust in me and knowing that I stick to my words when I promise to write a whole new book in a short period of time with quality material. Your trust means a lot to me and I hope this book will make you proud, as much as it makes me.

Andy Oram

The editor that anybody would dream about, Andy has been by my side editing this book nonstop since I started. His relentless efforts have allowed me to relax while he craftily worked his way through the book, making it even more understandable for readers. I would not have been able to write this book without Andy's help.

CHAPTER 1

Continuous Integration and Delivery

Continuous integration, or CI as it will be referred to from here on, is an ecosystem of software, usually more than one package, that allows you to test and deploy your iOS apps with minimal manual involvement, sometimes even none. Once you commit your code to a source control repository, such as Git, your code will automatically be built and run by a CI server and then perhaps deployed to TestFlight, eventually reaching the point where you can send it to Apple for review.

Every iOS developer needs to know about CI to some extent. You might not need to be very involved with CI on a day-to-day basis, but should you wish to find work in a company where you have to work with other iOS engineers, chances are that you will have to work with a CI system of some sort, whether that be Xcode Bots or Travis mixed with fastlane.

In this chapter we will talk about two CI systems:

- Xcode Bots running on macOS
- Travis plus fastlane

 Xcode Bots, Travis, and fastlane are not the only CI and CD systems out there. You have a choice from many service providers, some easier than others to implement, and each with its own advantages and disadvantages. The three systems I have chosen to cover in this chapter are very popular, and are the ones you are most likely to encounter if you decide to work in a larger team of developers.

Xcode Bots are tiny integration points that are installed on macOS running Xcode. They use Xcode's capabilities on that server to check out your code from Git (or

SVN), build that code for you, and test it on your behalf. They may even create an Xcode archive for you, ready to be sent to the App Store.

Travis is a distributed public service that easily integrates with GitHub and can access your source code (should you grant access to it) and build and distribute your products on your behalf, without you having to press a single button.

These are the systems most often used for iOS CI. Granted, you might sometimes stumble on a company using another popular CI, such as Jenkins, and there are many references online where you can learn about those systems. Should you go through this chapter to learn about Xcode Bots and Travis, you will already have learned how CI works and will be able to work with Jenkins without a problem. The purpose of all CI systems is the same, although their interfaces and functionalities differ. As we'll see, Xcode Bots and Travis/fastlane show several differences.

1.1 Setting Up Xcode Server

Problem

You want to be able to run Xcode Bots, which require an Xcode Server.

Solution

Follow these steps:

1. Designate a computer that runs macOS in your network to become the server that runs your Xcode Bots. This machine has to have quite a lot of disk space to dedicate to builds, and also quite good processing power to run concurrent builds.
2. Open Xcode on this server machine.
3. On the server machine, in Xcode, press Cmd-, on your keyboard to open Xcode's preferences screen.
4. In the Server & Bots tab, enable Xcode Server.
5. You will then be asked to provide a username on the server machine under which Xcode builds run, using that user's credentials. It's best to use an administrator account, as recommended by Xcode.
6. Follow the steps on screen to enable Xcode Server.

Discussion

Xcode Bots run on a server that you will connect your local Xcode to (as you will later see). On that server machine, which needs to run macOS, you will need to install Xcode and enable Xcode Server. There is no special Xcode Server application! Xcode Server merely means an instance of Xcode that you designate as your server.

You should also register some development devices with Xcode Server in case you want to run some UI tests on it. You can do that by simply connecting an iOS device with a cable to the computer that is your designated server machine running macOS. (That could be your current computer, if you are just testing things out!)

You might be wondering whether you even need a server machine to host your Xcode Bots. The answer depends on the scale of your development. If you are working alone as the sole iOS developer, and have no QA members dedicated to testing your apps, you can simply live with setting up and running the Bots locally on your own computer. More complex development environments need a dedicated server to run the Bots: a server that is accessible by all your designated team members. This could occur in a company where you would like Bots to be distributed across the team and run remotely and on a schedule, perhaps every night, typically running your unit and UI tests, building your app, and submitting it to TestFlight.

See Also

Recipes 1.2, 1.3, and 1.4

1.2 Connecting Local Xcode to Xcode Server

Problem

You have set up your Xcode Server on a server machine and now want to ensure that all those in your development team that need CI access are connected to your Xcode Server.

This recipe assumes that both the development machine and the Xcode Server are on the same network.

Solution

Follow these steps in order to connect each development machine to your Xcode Server:

1. On the server, ensure that the Xcode service is turned on.
2. Open Xcode on the developer machine, ensuring that the machine is on the same network as the server hosting your Xcode Server.
3. Press Cmd-, on your keyboard when Xcode opens to go to Xcode's preferences.
4. Click the Accounts tab.

5. Press the + button on the bottom of the screen and in the little menu that appears, choose Add Server....

6. In the Choose Server dialog that appears, choose the server that hosts your Xcode Server and press the Next button (see Figure 1-1).

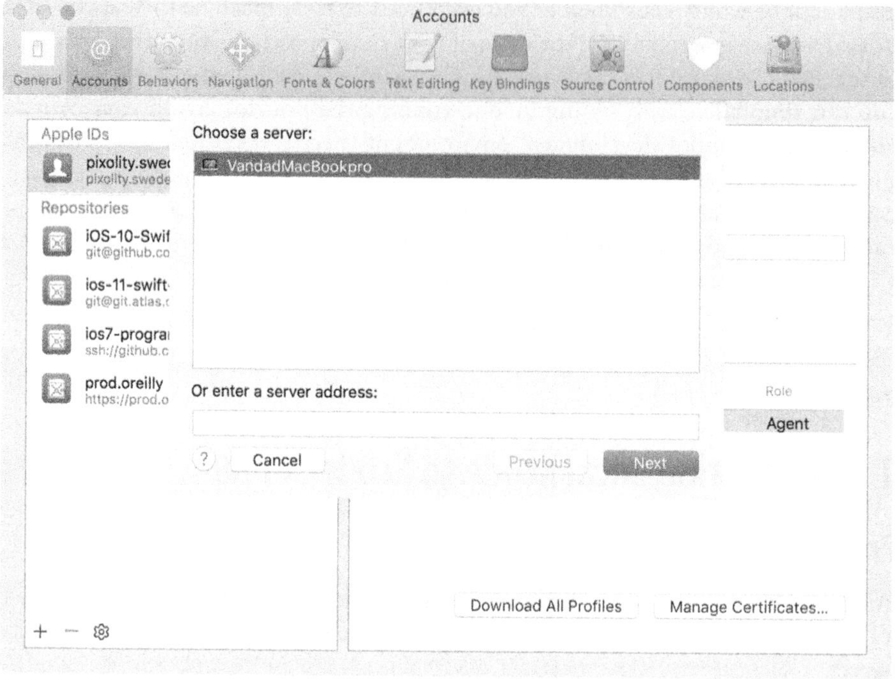

Figure 1-1. Choosing your server

> If you don't see your server in the list, it might not have the Xcode Server service enabled, or it might not be accessible to your local development machine. If you are setting all this up at work, contact your network administrator.

7. On the next screen, you will be asked for the account to use to log in to the server. You know this account information better than I do, so provide that information here and continue to the next step.

If everything went as expected, you should now see your Xcode Server in the list of accounts on your local development machine (see Figure 1-2).

Figure 1-2. The Xcode Server successfully added to the development machine

Discussion

Every development machine that wants to run Xcode Bots on your Xcode Server needs to have direct access, through Xcode, to your Xcode Server. This brings you many advantages, including direct integration of Xcode Bots into your local Xcode IDE.

If you have followed the steps in the Solution section of this recipe, you should have now created the bridge between your local machine and the remote server hosting your Xcode Server. The next step is to start creating and running (integrating) Xcode Bots to do your work on your behalf.

See Also

Recipe 1.1

1.3 Archiving Your Apps with Xcode Bots

Problem

You want to create an Xcode Bot that can create an Xcode archive of your application. This can be done periodically, manually (triggered by you), or automatically at specific times.

Solution

Follow these steps:

1. Ensure that your Xcode project is hosted in a version control system such as Git, perhaps on GitHub.
2. Make sure that your Xcode Server has credentials to also check out (clone) the application's repository. (This requires setting up your SSH keys and related administrative tasks on a server, a topic that is outside the scope of this book. If you are on GitHub for version control, you can read about the tasks using the GitHub website.)
3. While you have your project open in Xcode, from the Product menu, choose Create Bot.
4. A new dialog appears on the screen asking you to specify a name for your Bot (Figure 1-3). Call it *archive-my-app*. When you are done, press the Next button.

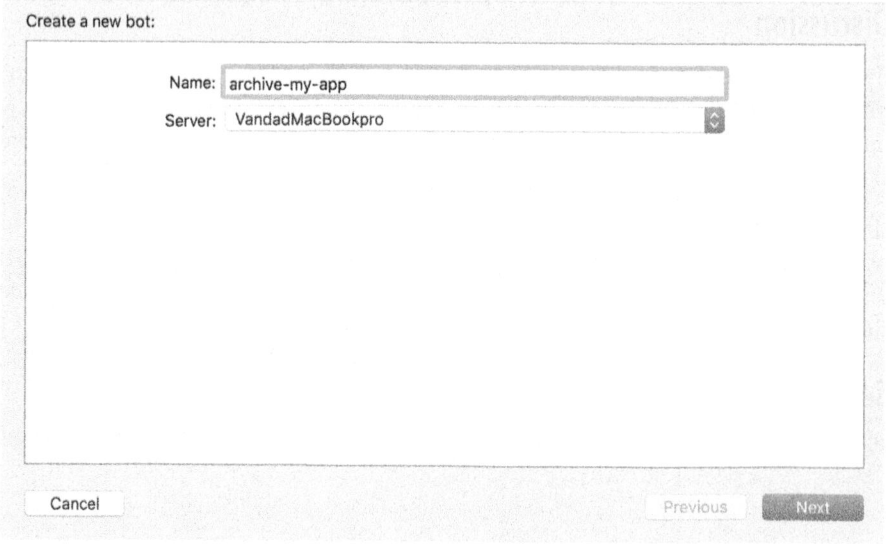

Figure 1-3. Provide a name for the Xcode Bot that will be responsible for archiving your application

5. If this is the first Xcode Bot you are setting up, you will have to provide a way for your Xcode Server to connect to GitHub on your behalf, either using your own account (if you are developing privately at home) or using Xcode Server's own dedicated account that has access to clone your repository (perhaps an Active Directory account, if you are in an organization).

6. At this stage, you will see a screen similar to Figure 1-4. On this screen, press the Sign In... button.

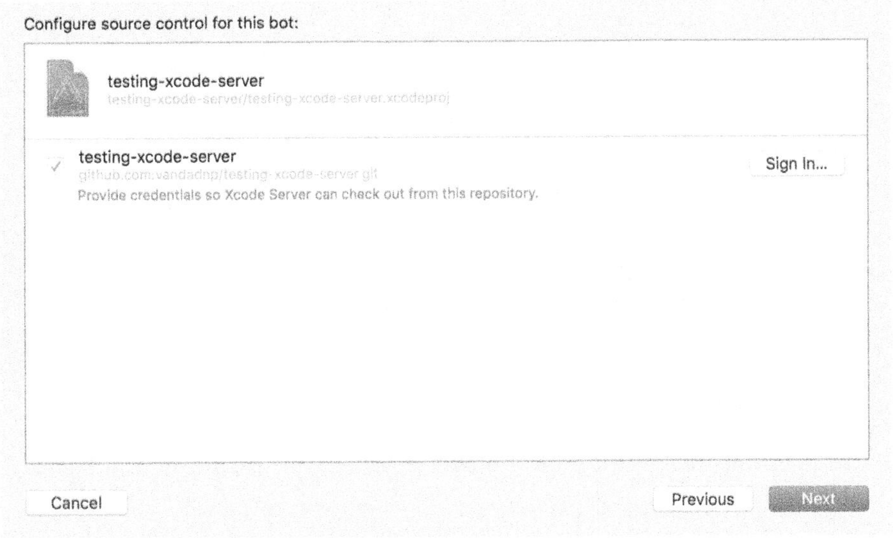

Figure 1-4. Xcode Server reports that it has problems cloning the repository and communicating with GitHub in general

7. In the dialog that appears (Figure 1-5), choose the way that suits you best for your Xcode Server to connect to GitHub on your behalf and clone your repository in order to be able to build the app. I have Xcode Server locally, so I can simply share my SSH keys with this local installation of the server. If you are setting up macOS and Xcode Server in an organization, you probably have a separate account through which your server can connect to GitHub. In this dialog, therefore, choose an appropriate method of connection to GitHub based on your situation. Once you are done, press the OK button.

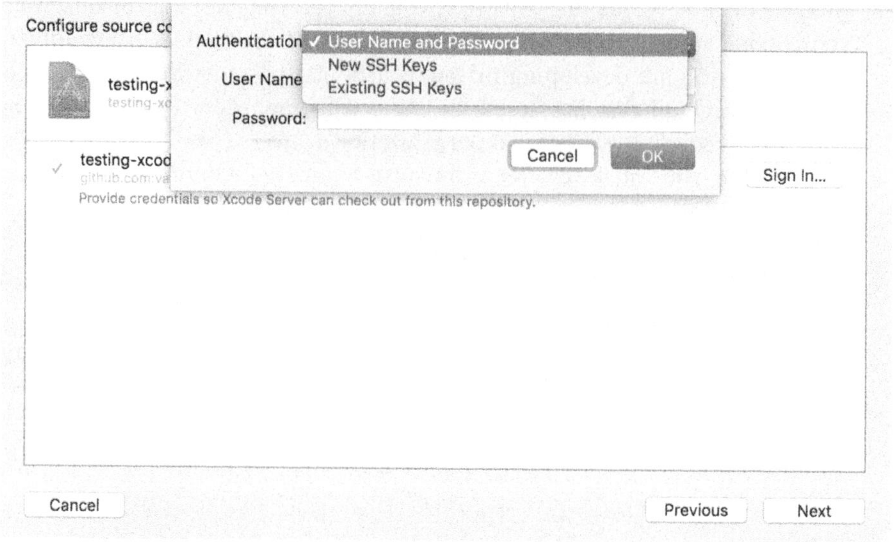

Figure 1-5. Specify a way for Xcode Server to connect to GitHub on your behalf and clone your repository

8. If your Xcode Server now succeeds in connecting to GitHub, you should be able to press the Next button on the dialog where you had previously landed (see Figure 1-6).

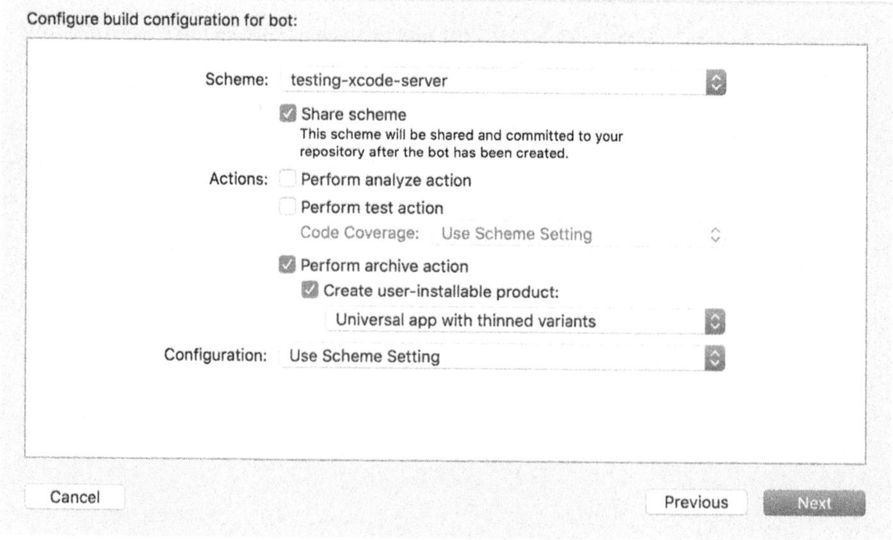

Figure 1-6. Configure the Xcode Bot to archive your application

9. In this dialog shown in Figure 1-6, you will see the main settings related to your Xcode Bot. Here you can specify that your Xcode Bot has to build, analyze, or even test and archive your application. For now, choose only to archive the application. Once you are done in this dialog, press the Next button.

10. In the next step (see Figure 1-7), you can choose to integrate (run) your Xcode Bot when specific events happen, such as at a specific time of the day or when new commits are available. For now, choose to manually integrate the Bot whenever it is requested, so that I can show you how to integrate an Xcode Bot whenever you need it instead of having to wait for a certain event to occur. Then, in the Clean drop-down, choose Always. This ensures that the project artifacts from the previous archiving action get deleted before the new build is created. Once you are done, press the Next button.

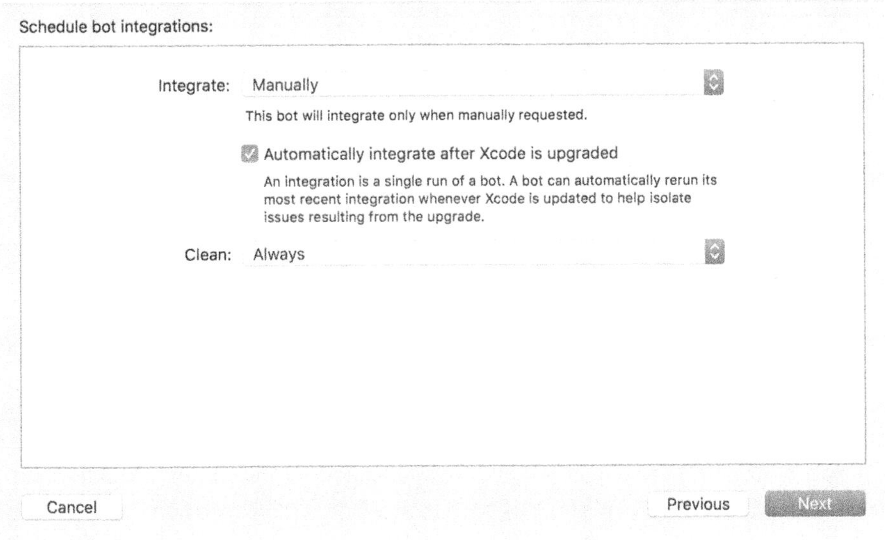

Schedule bot integrations:

Integrate:	Manually
	This bot will integrate only when manually requested.
	☑ Automatically integrate after Xcode is upgraded
	An integration is a single run of a bot. A bot can automatically rerun its most recent integration whenever Xcode is updated to help isolate issues resulting from the upgrade.
Clean:	Always

Cancel   Previous   Next

Figure 1-7. Configure the Xcode Bot so that you can integrate (run) it whenever you need to

11. In the next dialog, you will be able to pass environment variables to your Xcode build if you want. Leave this page empty for now and press the Next button.

12. On the next page, you can create triggers for your build. Triggers occur when an event happens during the Bot's life, such as success in creating an archive or a failure to run all UI or unit tests. You can also add pre- and post-integration scripts to your Xcode Bot so that the Bot runs your scripts before and after every integration. Leave this page empty as well for now, and press the Create button.

Discussion

Once you are back in Xcode, after the creation of your first Xcode Bot, press the Cmd-8 keys on your keyboard to go to the Report Navigator. On this page, you can see the events that your Xcode Bots have triggered. You have one Xcode Bot right now that is supposed to archive your application whenever you integrate the Bot, so let's go to that page and see what has happened (Figure 1-8).

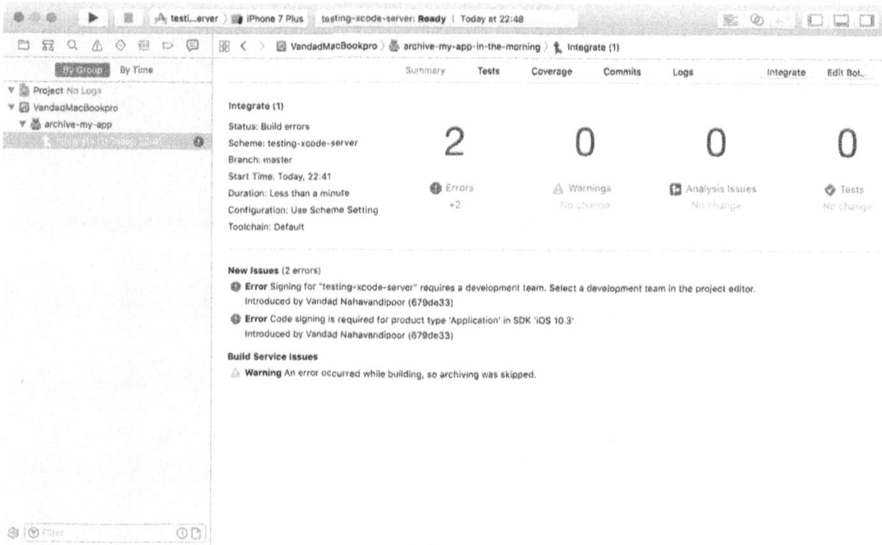

Figure 1-8. The first Xcode Bot failed to integrate due to code-signing issues

This is a typical error that you might get when starting to work with Xcode Bots, and that's why I wanted to show you this particular error. The way to solve this problem is to go to your project settings in the General tab and ensure that Xcode is set up to automatically handle your signing certificates, by choosing a development team for it.

> After you have solved your code-signing issues, ensure that you have checked in your fixes *and* pushed them to GitHub (or any other service that you might use for version control). Otherwise, your Xcode Bot will not be able to access the fresh changes that you have just made to the project.

Once you have fixed your code-signing issues in Xcode for your project, go back to the Report Navigator by pressing the Cmd-8 keys on your keyboard. On the lefthand side, choose the *archive-my-app* Xcode Bot, and press the Integrate button in the top-right corner of the screen to run the Bot again (see Figure 1-9).

Figure 1-9. The second integration of the Bot, after fixing the code-signing issues, appears to be running as expected

If everything went according to plan (see Figure 1-10), you should have your second integration of the Xcode Bot returning successfully with your archived application.

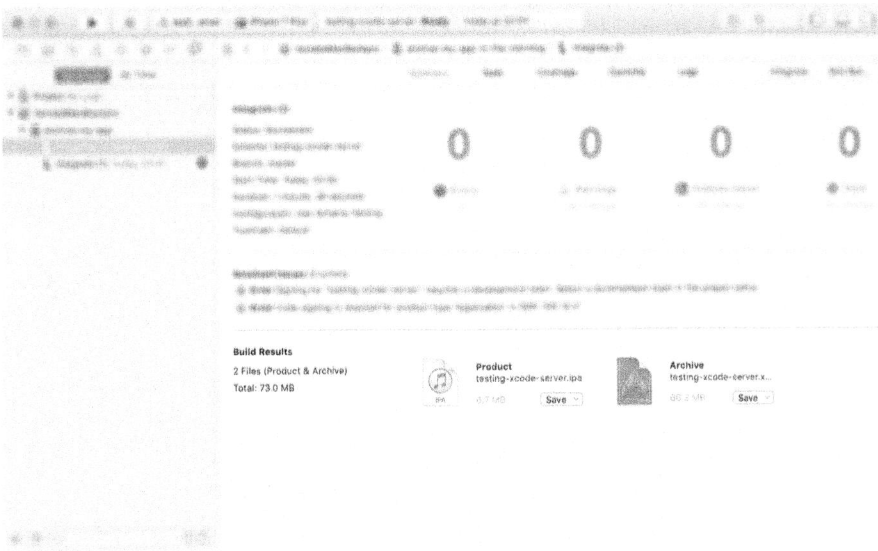

Figure 1-10. The Xcode Bot successfully archived the application!

See Also

Recipe 1.5

1.4 Running Your Tests Automatically with Xcode Bots

Problem

You have some unit tests that you've written for your application and you want to run them whenever there are new commits on your *master* branch.

 I'm taking the *master* branch as an example. You can set up Xcode Bots on any branch of your choice in your repository.

Solution

Follow these steps:

1. While you have your project (with unit tests previously written for it) open in your own Xcode instance, select the Product menu and under that choose Create Bot.
2. In the dialog that appears, for the name of the Bot, provide the name of *running-tests*. Ensure you are connected to the right server, and press the Next button.
3. On the next screen (see Figure 1-11), ensure that your Xcode Server can log in to your application by following the same steps that we talked about in the previous recipe (Recipe 1.3). When you are done, press the Next button.

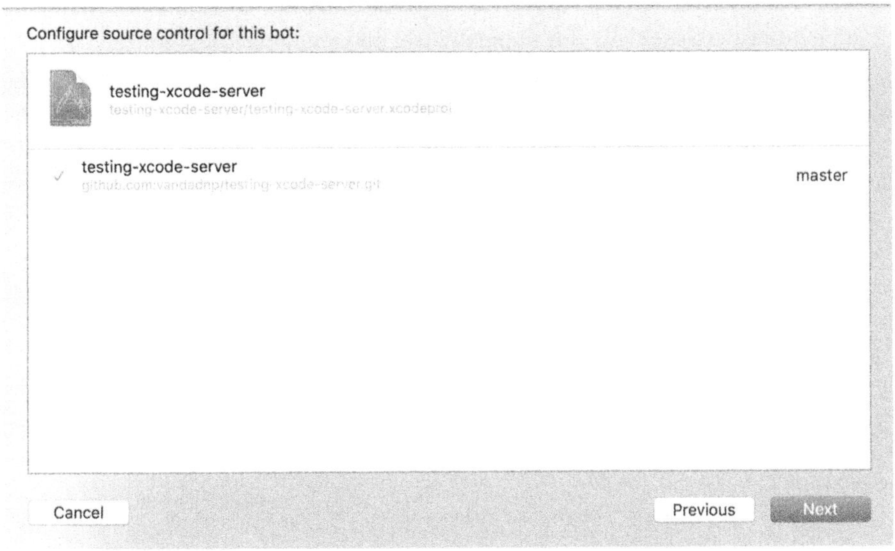

Figure 1-11. Now your Xcode Server can connect to your repository

4. In the next dialog (see Figure 1-12), ensure that your Xcode Bot tests only your target, and does nothing else. After you are done, press the Next button.

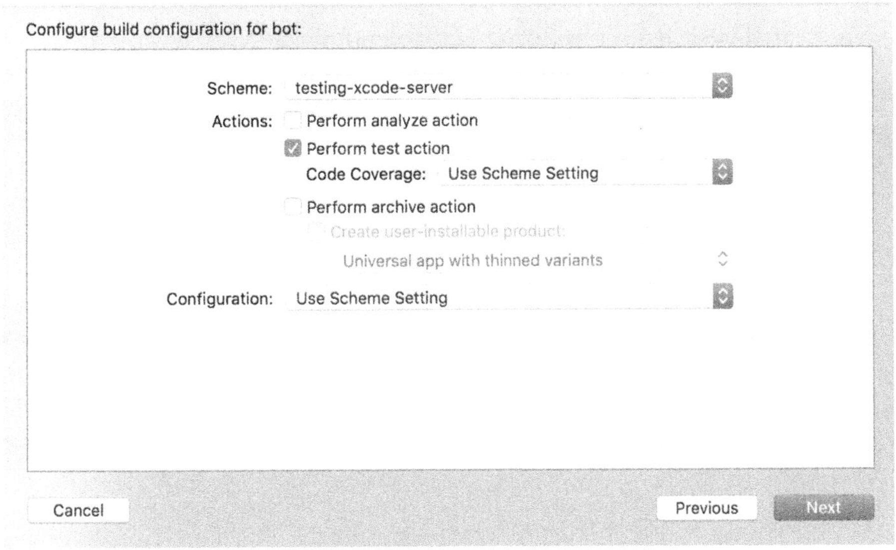

Figure 1-12. Set up this new Xcode Bot so that it only tests your project, nothing else

5. On the next screen (see Figure 1-13), in the Integrate field, choose Manually so that you can trigger this Bot manually whenever you need to. For the Clean field, choose "Once a day." This makes sure that Xcode performs a clean build (by cleaning up its build artifacts cache) once a day. This is good general practice because cached project resources can sometimes cause issues where old resource files creep into the new binary and cause undesirable effects. Once you are done, press the Next button. You can leave in place the default option that automatically integrates this Bot as soon as it is created, in order to ensure that it works as expected.

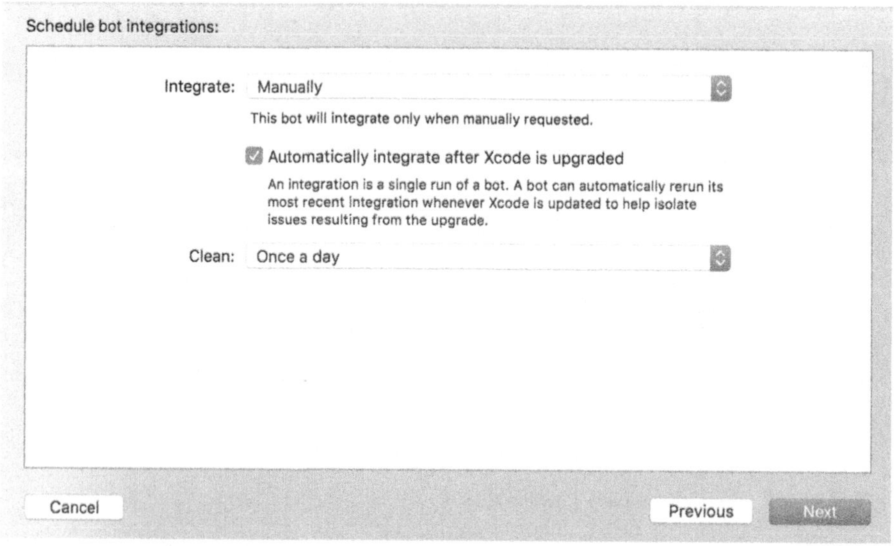

Schedule bot integrations:

Integrate: Manually

This bot will integrate only when manually requested.

☑ Automatically integrate after Xcode is upgraded

An integration is a single run of a bot. A bot can automatically rerun its most recent integration whenever Xcode is updated to help isolate issues resulting from the upgrade.

Clean: Once a day

Cancel   Previous   Next

Figure 1-13. You will run your testing Xcode Bot manually and ensure that it cleans up build artifacts once a day

6. On the next screen (see Figure 1-14), you can choose to test your project on all available simulators and devices, on all devices (but no simulators), on all simulators (but no actual devices), or on a specific mixture of devices and simulators that you configure. For the sake of being able to run the tests fast, I am choosing to run the tests on only one simulator. Once you are done, press the Next button.

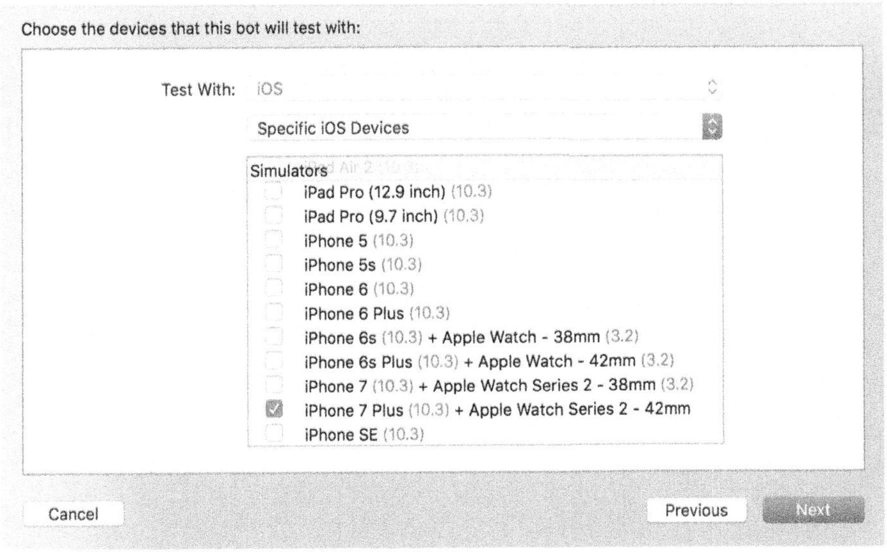

Figure 1-14. Set up the new Xcode Bot so that it runs the tests on a specific iOS simulator

7. Leave the next screen, where you can enter new environment variables, empty and press the Next button.

8. On the Triggers screen, leave the screen empty and press the Create button to create your Bot.

Discussion

If you went through the steps provided in the Solution section of this recipe, you should now be able to navigate to the Report Navigator panel of Xcode by pressing Cmd-8, scroll down in the left panel to the *running-tests* Xcode Bot, and expand it so that you can see the integrations (runs) of this Bot that have taken place since you created it. So far, we have only one run (Figure 1-15).

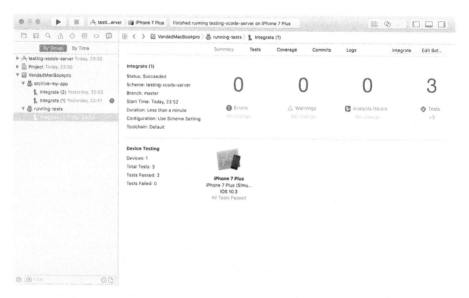

Figure 1-15. The new Xcode Bot has run our unit and UI tests together and reported the results back

You can connect physical devices to the machine that runs your Xcode Server if you can reach that machine physically. These physical devices can then be used by Xcode Server to run and test your applications on. Gaining physical access to the server may be difficult if you are in an organization with many people sharing a server.

Starting from Xcode 9, you can wirelessly debug your applications on iOS devices as well. So if you are in the mood, physically connect your iOS 11 device to your server machine, pull up the device information panel in Xcode, and choose to enable network debugging (wireless). Once you have done that, you can disconnect the device from your server machine, but ensure that it stays on the same network as your server machine. You will now have access to this remote iOS device to run your tests on it, as long as you choose to execute your tests with the help of your server.

See Also

Recipe 1.5

1.5 Performing Analysis of Your Code Using Xcode Bots

Problem

You want to perform periodic analysis of your code (for unused methods, unused function return values, etc.) using Xcode Bots and see the results right in your machine's instance of Xcode.

Solution

Follow these steps to set up an Xcode Bot that analyzes your code:

1. While in Xcode on your own machine, go to the Product menu and from there choose Create Bot.
2. In the Name field, enter *code-analysis-bot* and press the Next button.
3. On the next screen, ensure that your Xcode Bot can access your repository. Every Bot needs its own SSH keys. If you are setting up your Xcode Bot on a server that is inside your organization but not on your own machine, you will need to create a new pair of SSH keys for your new Bot. The public key can then be copied to the server. (For instance, if you are using GitHub to host your projects, it provides a field where you can paste in the key.) If you are setting up this Bot on your machine, you can use your existing SSH keys on your machine. Once you are done, press the Next button.

   Figure 1-16 demonstrates creating a new public key for the Bot. The Bot will use it to connect to your repository and clone it. When the public key is provided to you in this dialog, you need to copy it and paste it into your SSH keys section of GitHub or whatever service you are using. This public key is linked to the private key that is already on the server instance.

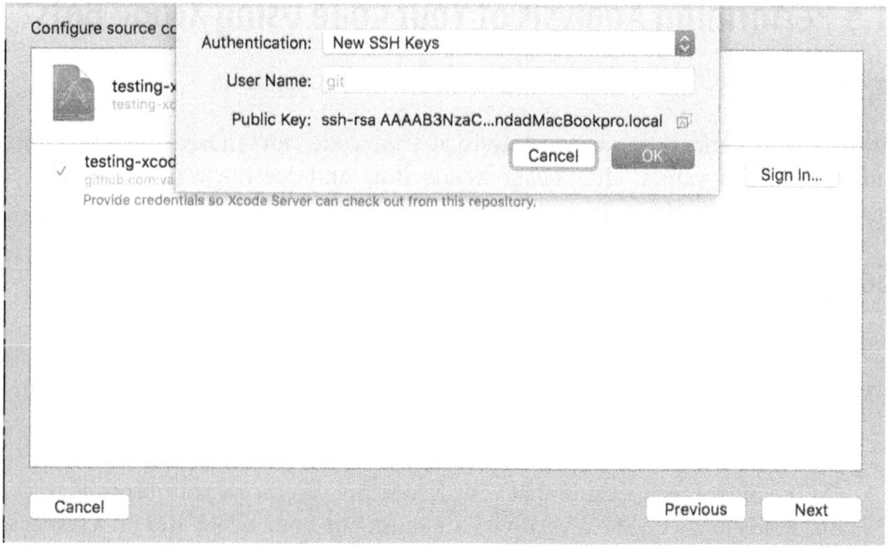

Figure 1-16. Creating a new public key for the Bot

4. On the next screen (see Figure 1-17), choose only the "Perform analyze action" option from the list and then press the Next button.

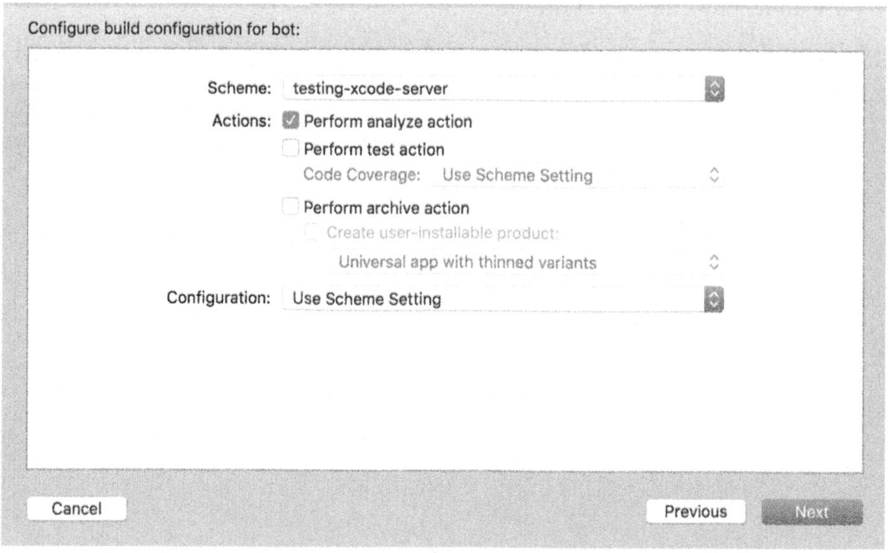

Figure 1-17. The only thing this Xcode Bot is going to have to do is to analyze your code for warnings and problems

5. On the next screen, choose to integrate your Xcode Bot manually. In the Clean field, choose to always clean the project before every analysis. Once you are done, press the Next button.
6. On the Environment Variables screen, do not add any variables, but simply press the Next button.
7. Leave the Triggers screen empty again and simply press the Create button.

Discussion

For the sake of discussion, I've created a function in my *AppDelegate.swift* file where I return a simple integer object like this:

```
func returnSomeInteger() -> Int{
  return 10
}
```

And then, when the application starts, I just call this function without using its return value, like so:

```
func application(
  _ application: UIApplication,
  didFinishLaunchingWithOptions launchOptions:
  [UIApplicationLaunchOptionsKey: Any]?) -> Bool {

  returnSomeInteger()

  return true
}
```

Calling a function and not using its return value (if the function is not marked as @discardableResult) causes Xcode's analyzer to trigger a warning about unused function results.

Go to your own Xcode and press Cmd-8 in order to go to the Report Navigator and then integrate your *code-analysis-bot*. The Xcode Bot should run, analyze the project, and report its results (see Figure 1-18). You can see the warning reported by the Xcode Bot.

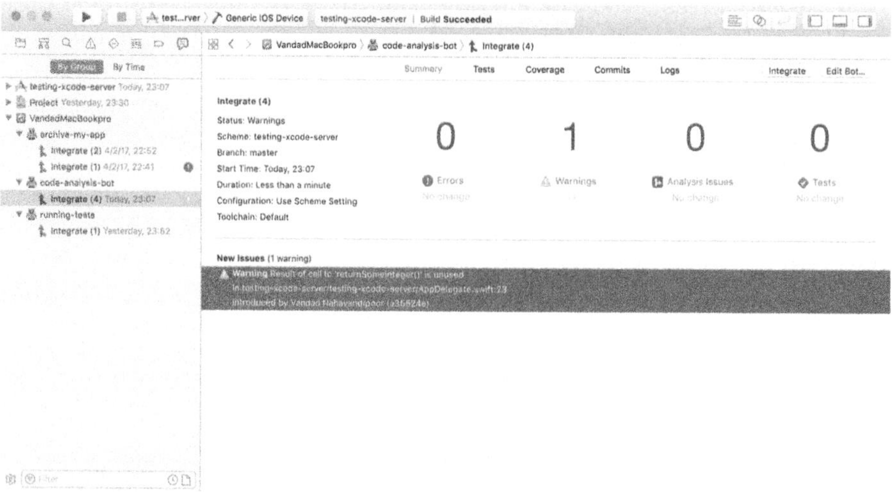

Figure 1-18. The unused function results are reported as a warning that you can read in your Xcode instance

See Also

Recipes 1.4 and 1.7

1.6 Integrating GitHub Projects with Travis

Problem

You have an iOS project hosted on GitHub (either on GitHub.com or enterprise Git-Hub) and you would like to integrate it with Travis so that you can build your projects there.

Solution

Follow these steps:

1. Go to the Travis CI website (*https://travis-ci.org*).
2. Sign in to Travis CI with your GitHub credentials.
3. You will be asked for permission (see Figure 1-19) to allow Travis to access your repositories. Press the "Authorize application" button to proceed.

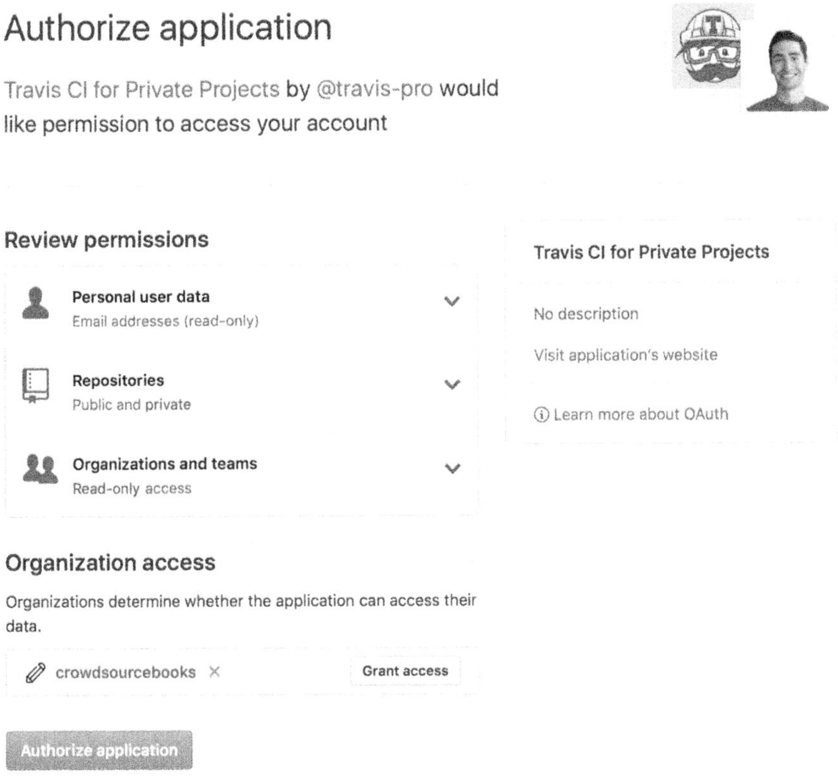

Authorize application

Travis CI for Private Projects **by** @travis-pro **would like permission to access your account**

Review permissions

Travis CI for Private Projects

👤 **Personal user data** ⌄
Email addresses (read-only)

No description

Visit application's website

📕 **Repositories** ⌄
Public and private

ⓘ Learn more about OAuth

👥 **Organizations and teams** ⌄
Read-only access

Organization access

Organizations determine whether the application can access their data.

✏️ crowdsourcebooks ✕   Grant access

Authorize application

Figure 1-19. Authorizing Travis CI to access your repositories in GitHub for integration purposes

4. You will now be sent to Travis CI's landing page. On this page, click your name on the top righthand side in order to integrate Travis with your projects.

5. On the page that comes up now, you should be able to see all your public repositories. If you don't see them, click the Sync button so that Travis CI reconnects to GitHub to find all your public repositories.

6. Find your iOS project's repository name in the list of fetched repositories and then flick the little switch (see Figure 1-20) to the *on* state (all switches are turned off by default).

7. Right next to the switch that you just turned on, you should be able to see a gear button that sends you to the Travis settings for your project. Click that button.

Figure 1-20. Turn Travis on for your repository

8. In Travis's settings page for your project, turn on the switch that says "Build only if .travis.yml is present."

Discussion

After you successfully perform the steps in the Solution section, you can test that things are working as expected by going to GitHub (either the public site or your enterprise GitHub), navigating to your project's GitHub page, and clicking Settings. Then, in the Integration & Services section (see Figure 1-21), make sure that Travis CI is present under the Services heading on the right.

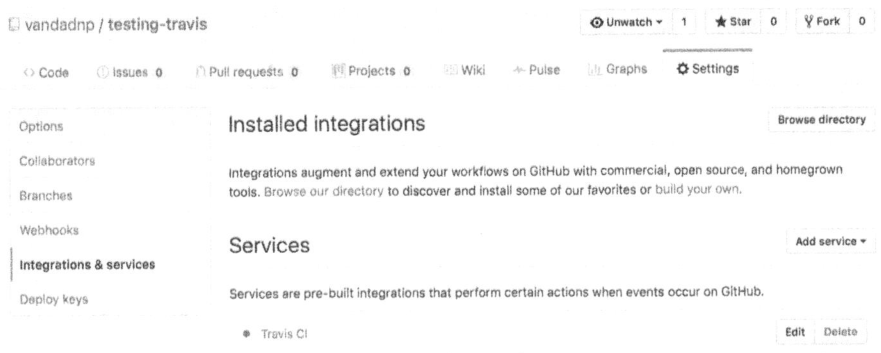

Figure 1-21. Confirming that Travis CI is successfully integrated into your GitHub project

See Also

Recipe 1.1

1.7 Installing the Travis CLI

Problem

You want to be able to control your Travis builds from your own command line.

Solution

Follow the instructions provided at GitHub's site for installing the Travis CI Client (*https://github.com/travis-ci/travis.rb#installation*).

Discussion

Usually the status of your builds can be controlled by going to Travis's website. However, you can also use the Travis CLI to control and manipulate the status of your builds.

After installing the Travis CLI, you need to complete the installation process using your command line, so issue the following command at your command-line prompt:

```
travis version
```

The command will then prompt you with the following question:

```
Shell completion not installed. Would you like to install it now? |y|
```

Answer **Y** (for yes) and then press the Enter key.

Now if you issue the same command as before (`travis version`), you should get a reply from the Travis CLI as expected. A few more settings have to be in place before you can fully use the Travis CLI, however. Assuming that you are currently inside a repository directory that is integrated with Travis (see Recipe 1.6), you can issue the following command to see your build history on Travis:

```
travis history
```

If this is the first time you are doing this, you will get a reply similar to that shown here:

```
Detected repository as vandadnp/testing-travis, is this correct? |yes|
```

 The name of the repository here is *vandadnp/testing-travis*. For you it may be something different but similar.

In answer to this prompt, just press the Enter key on your keyboard to continue.

Now you need to add the *.travis.yml* file to your project so that your builds can trigger a Travis build when they are pushed over to GitHub. This file will contain your build script and configurations. To create this file, issue the following command to the Travis CLI:

```
travis init
```

Travis will then ask you about the language you've chosen for your project. To this, you can reply `obj-c` (for Objective-C, even though your project is in Swift) and then press the Enter key. Travis will then reply to you as shown here:

```
travis init
Main programming language used: |Ruby| obj-c
.travis.yml file created!
not logged in, please run travis login --org
```

You can see that you need to give Travis the right to access your GitHub repository on your behalf in order to see your build and integration status. Travis.org is directly connected to free and public GitHub repositories, and it needs your permission to get into your repository. To do that, provide a personal access token to Travis by following these instructions:

1. In your browser, navigate to your Personal access tokens (*https://github.com/ settings/tokens*) page (logging in to GitHub if you are not already logged in).
2. Press the "Generate new token" button.
3. In the "Select scopes" section, check the repo box, which in turn checks the entire repo section for you.

4. In the "Token description" field, type "Travis" or similar text that describes to you who this token belongs to.
5. Once you are done, press the "Generate token" button.

You should land on a page that shows the token that was generated for you. Copy this token to your clipboard, go back to your terminal, and issue the following command:

```
travis login --org --github-token XXX
```

where *XXX* is the token that you just copied to your clipboard (in other words, in place of *XXX* just press Cmd-V on your keyboard to paste in the copied token). Once you're done, press the Enter key. If everything goes fine, you should see a message similar to this:

```
Successfully logged in as ABC!
```

where *ABC* is your username on GitHub. Now to ensure that everything is working as expected, issue the following command in your terminal:

```
travis settings
```

This should go to the Travis servers, fetch your repository's settings for you, and print the results out to the console:

```
[+] builds_only_with_travis_yml   Only run builds with a .travis.yml
[+] build_pushes                  Build pushes
[+] build_pull_requests           Build pull requests
  0 maximum_number_of_builds      Maximum number of concurrent builds
```

See Also

Recipe 1.1

1.8 Running Your Unit Tests with Travis

Problem

You have your unit tests all ready to go and you want to run them with Travis.

Solution

Follow these steps:

1. Make sure that your unit tests are all written, saved inside your project, and pushed to GitHub.
2. Hold the Alt key down on your keyboard and then click the Run button in Xcode.
3. On the screen that pops up, press the Manage Schemes... button.

4. Next to the scheme that you want Travis to run your tests on, ensure that the Shared checkbox is ticked and then press the Close button.

5. In your *.travis.yml* file, ensure that you have specified your project name (or your workspace name if you have one), plus your scheme to run the tests on. Additionally, you will need a script to run xcodebuild with xcrun to run your tests, as shown here:

```
language: objective-c
osx_image: xcode9

xcode_project: TestingTravis.xcodeproj
xcode_scheme: TestingTravis

script: xcrun xcodebuild test -project TestingTravis.xcodeproj \
        -scheme TestingTravis -sdk iphonesimulator -destination \
        'platform=iOS Simulator,name=iPhone 7,OS=10.3'
```

As highlighted by Apple in its Technical Note TN2339 (*http://apple.co/2jaNOfk*), the xcrun tool allows you to run any tool that is executable within your Xcode's installation folder, without you having to find the path to that tool. Shortcuts for some tools are already created for you in your */user/bin* folder, but other tools are hidden deep within Xcode's installation folder. The Xcode tools that have a shortcut in the aforementioned folder are called *shims*, and all you need to know to run these tools is their names, not their paths. xcrun is one of these shims. This makes command-line execution of Xcode tools a pleasant experience indeed.

I am using the \ line break here to ensure that the text fits inside the page width of this book. When you are writing your scripts to run on Travis, make sure you remove these line breaks, as they are known to cause issues on Travis images.

Discussion

If you have already issued the `travis init` command in Terminal in your project directory (see Recipe 1.7), you should have a file called *.travis.yml* in your project's root folder.

In order for Travis to run your tests, you need to satisfy three requirements:

- Specify your Xcode project's name in your *.travis.yml* file using the xcode_project key.
- Specify the scheme that you want to be used to test your project, with the xcode_scheme key.

- Write a script in your *.travis.yml* file to actually run your tests.

Once you have made all these changes and committed them to your repository, ensure that you push your changes to GitHub. Also make sure to install the Travis CLI (see Recipe 1.7) on your computer. After that, you can simply monitor your build's status on Travis with the `travis history` command in your terminal. The result of this command will be similar to that shown here:

```
#4 created:    master Updated the travis file
#3 failed:     master Added the travis file
#2 passed:     master testing still
#1 errored:    master testing still
```

See Also

Recipes 1.1 and 1.2

1.9 Building and Archiving Your Project with Travis

Problem

You want to build your project and create an *.ipa* archive of your project with Travis.

Solution

Follow these steps:

1. Create a distribution profile, certificate, and private key for your project and export them to disk.
2. Write a script that creates a keychain and saves your private key and certificate into it.
3. Compile and sign your project with `xcodebuild` inside a script.
4. Using your *.travis.yml* file, execute that script while your build is being executed on a Travis node.

Discussion

There are many steps involved in creating an *.ipa* archive. They should be done in order:

1. Compile the source code and all resources.
2. Produce the *.app* folder with the compiled source code and resources.
3. Sign the *.app* folder with the correct profile and certificate.
4. Zip up the signed *.app* folder plus a *plist* file into the *.ipa* archive.

Follow these steps to build and archive your project with Travis. Uploading to TestFlight will be discussed in another recipe.

Xcode has an automatic code-signing setting that creates certificates and profiles for you. But because this process hides all the details of creating a certificate from you, you will not know where your private and public keys are, how certificates are created, or where profiles come into play. In this section I will focus on doing this work together with you manually so that you can see how certificates and private keys are created, in the hope of making your life easier later on when you have to export your private keys and certificates to be used on a Travis machine:

1. TestFlight needs a distribution certificate, which you'll create in your developer portal. So, head over to your Apple developer account (*http://apple.co/2zV7s9M*) and follow the guides that Apple provides to create your new production certificate (or distribution certificate, as it's also called).
2. The previous step created a certificate for you. The private key for this certificate was also created for you when you created the certificate request (as outlined in the instructions by Apple). Import this certificate into your keychain to link it to its private key by double-clicking it and importing it into the login keychain (see Figure 1-22).

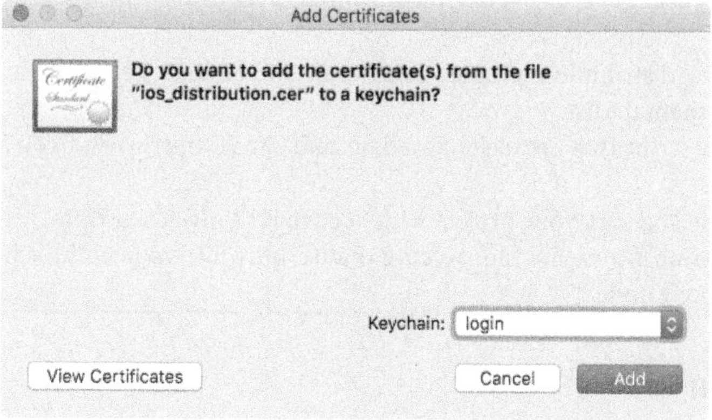

Figure 1-22. Import the certificate that you downloaded from Apple into the login keychain on your computer

3. Right-click the certificate and choose to export the certificate.
4. In the dialog that appears (Figure 1-23), in the File Format drop-down, choose "Certificate (.cer)." Then set the name of the file to *cert.cer* and save the file in the root folder of your project. Once you are done, press the Save button.

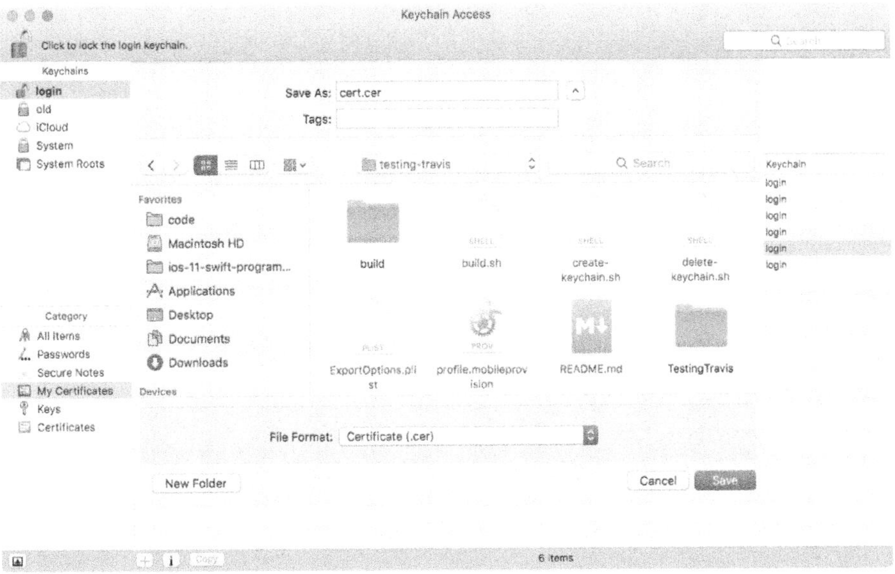

Figure 1-23. Save your distribution certificate into a file and place it in the root folder of your project

5. Now expand the certificate in Keychain Access to see the private key associated with it, right-click the key, and choose the export option to export it.

6. In the dialog that appears (see Figure 1-24), navigate to the root folder of your project, choose "Personal Information Exchange (.p12)" in the File Format drop-down, and enter *key.p12* as the name of the file. Once you are done, press the Save button. You are now prompted to assign a password to this private key. Enter *travis* as the password and then press the OK button to export the private key.

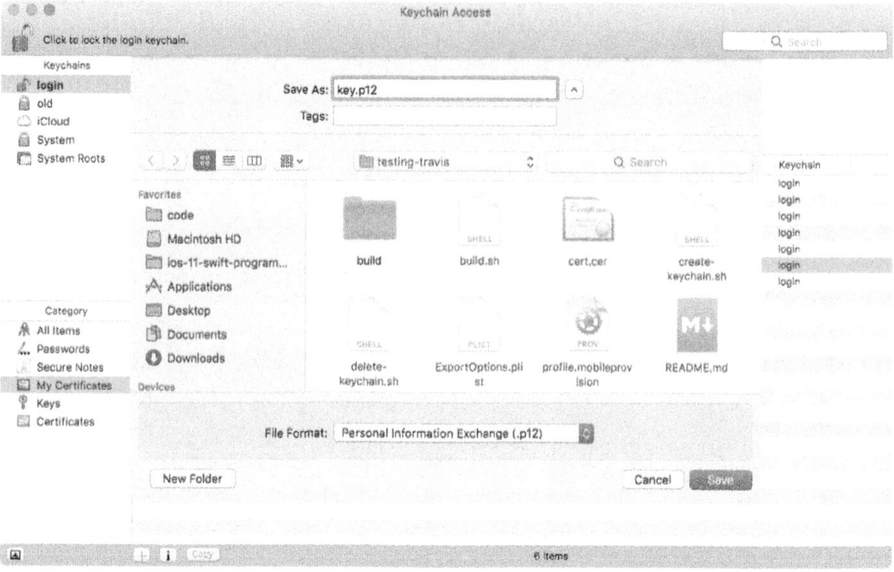

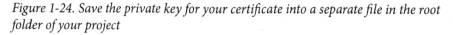

Figure 1-24. Save the private key for your certificate into a separate file in the root folder of your project

7. You still need one more certificate to sign an iOS application into an *.ipa* file: the *Worldwide Developer Relations Certificate Authority*. When you are signed into your developer account, you can download this certificate from the website at the bottom of the certificate page (*http://apple.co/2i0ZQrt*).

8. Once you have downloaded this certificate, save it into your project's root folder as *apple.cer* (see Figure 1-25).

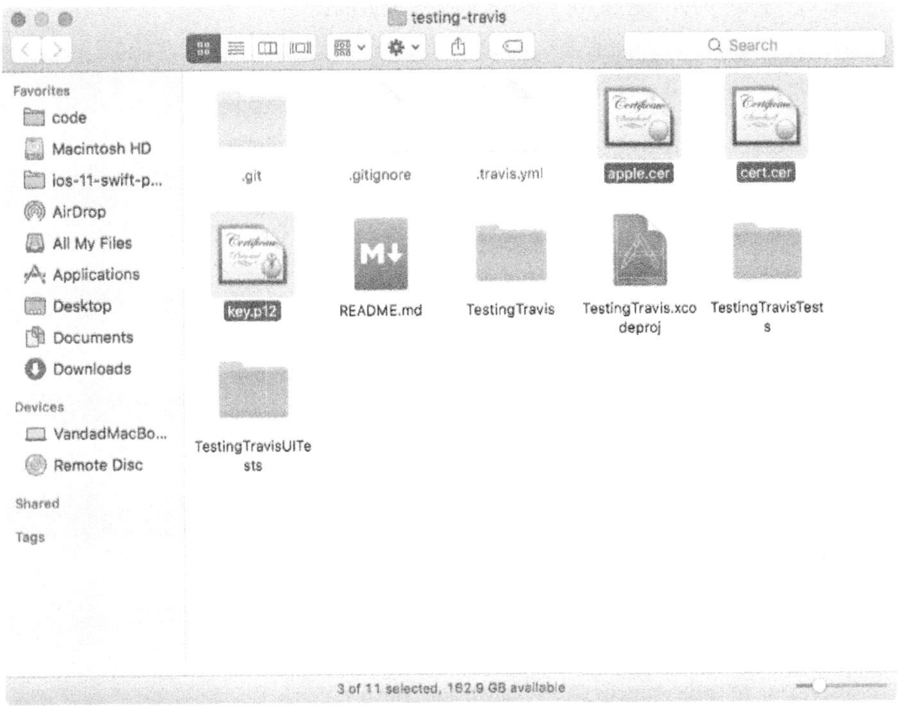

Figure 1-25. You should now have the three highlighted files in the root folder of your project under the exact same names as shown here

9. Head over to the developer portal and create an application ID for your app.

10. Then head over to the provisioning profiles section of the developer portal and create a new distribution profile for App Store distribution that is linked to your newly created certificate and application ID. Save the profile in the root folder of your project under the name *profile.mobileprovision*.

11. You then need to create a script in the root folder of your project that creates a keychain on the Travis machine on which your project is built. The script must also import your certificates into that keychain for code signing. So, create a file in the root folder of your project called *create-keychain.sh* with the following contents:

```bash
#!/bin/bash

KEY_PASSWORD=travis

# Create the keychain with a password
security create-keychain -p travis ios-build.keychain

# Make the custom keychain default, so xcodebuild will use it for signing
```

```
security default-keychain -s ios-build.keychain

# Unlock the keychain
security unlock-keychain -p travis ios-build.keychain

# Add certificates to keychain and allow codesign to access them
security import ./apple.cer -k ~/Library/Keychains/ios-build.keychain -A
security import ./cert.cer -k ~/Library/Keychains/ios-build.keychain -A
security import ./key.p12 -k ~/Library/Keychains/ios-build.keychain -P \
    $KEY_PASSWORD -A

security set-key-partition-list -S apple-tool:,apple:,codesign: -s \
    -k travis ~/Library/Keychains/ios-build.keychain
```

12. In Terminal, give execute rights to this file with the `chmod u+x create-keychain.sh` command.

13. When you create a keychain like this on the fly, it's in your best interest to delete it once you are done, since your distribution certificate and private key are saved inside it. So, create a file called *delete-keychain.sh* in the root folder of your project, with the following contents:

```
#!/bin/bash

security delete-keychain ios-build.keychain
security default-keychain -s login.keychain
```

14. Give this file execution rights as well, with the `chmod u+x delete-keychain.sh` command.

15. Now you need a script that can actually build your project. Create a file called *build.sh* in the root folder of your project with the following contents:

```
#!/bin/bash

security list-keychains -s ios-build.keychain

rm  ~/Library/MobileDevice/Provisioning\ Profiles/profile.mobileprovision
mkdir -p ~/Library/MobileDevice/Provisioning\ Profiles/
cp profile.mobileprovision ~/Library/MobileDevice/Provisioning\ Profiles/

xcrun xcodebuild -project TestingTravis.xcodeproj -scheme TestingTravis \
    -archivePath TestingTravis.xcarchive archive

xcrun xcodebuild -exportArchive -archivePath TestingTravis.xcarchive \
    -exportPath . -exportOptionsPlist ExportOptions.plist
```

16. Give this file execution rights as well with the `chmod u+x build.sh` command.

17. As required by xcodebuild, your build script uses a file called *ExportOptions.plist* that tells Xcode whether the project should be built as an ad hoc build, an App Store build, or a development build. We are building an App Store application

---

now. So in the root folder of your project, create a file called *ExportOptions.plist* (you can use Xcode to create a *plist* file if you want), with the following contents:

```
<?xml version="1.0" encoding="UTF-8"?>
<!DOCTYPE plist PUBLIC "-//Apple//DTD PLIST 1.0//EN"
  "http://www.apple.com/DTDs/PropertyList-1.0.dtd">
<plist version="1.0">
<dict>
        <key>method</key>
        <string>app-store</string>
</dict>
</plist>
```

18. Now you need to change the contents of your *.travis.yml* file so that it executes your scripts properly:

```
language: objective-c
osx_image: xcode9

xcode_project: TestingTravis.xcodeproj
xcode_scheme: TestingTravis

before_script: ./create-keychain.sh

script: ./build.sh

after_script: ./delete-keychain.sh
```

Once you are done with all of this, commit and push your changes to GitHub in order to see how Travis does with your build. Remember that you can monitor the status of your builds using the `travis history` command if you have installed the Travis CLI on your computer (see Recipe 1.7).

See Also

Recipe 1.5

1.10 Installing and Setting Up fastlane

Problem

You want to start using fastlane to streamline your building, testing, and distribution process.

If you are looking for a reason as to why you would even want to use fastlane, the answer is simple: to save time and energy and let the dedicated team of developers who work on fastlane fix any issues related to continuous delivery and integration. For instance, if you use the gym command in fastlane, you will be building your application and producing some form of a binary application that is submittable to Apple. This command is really as simple as that; just run `fastlane gym` and fastlane will figure out itself how to build your project. If you want to do the same thing manually, you will need a deeper knowledge of how the `xcrun` and `xcodebuild` commands work and their nightmare-like lists of parameters.

Solution

To use fastlane, you need to have a Ruby environment set up on your computer (with the Ruby installation utility *gem*), and you need to install fastlane. fastlane is a set of Ruby scripts maintained as an open source project on GitHub and backed by Google. In order to install fastlane, execute the following command in your Terminal:

```
sudo gem install fastlane -NV
```

You will be asked for your local computer account's password. After providing that password, if everything goes according to plan, you should see a message similar to `49 gems installed` in your Terminal. Obviously the number there depends on how many Ruby gems were installed in the process of installing fastlane.

After fastlane is installed on your computer, you will need to set it up for your project. fastlane needs to have some information about your project, such as its bundle identifier and profiles that it uses to build the project, in order to integrate with your project.

Follow these steps to set up fastlane for your project:

1. Open Terminal and navigate to where your project is saved.
2. Run fastlane in Terminal.
3. You will be asked if you want to integrate your project with fastlane. Answer **y** to this question.
4. You will then be asked to enter your Apple ID. Enter your Apple ID and then press the Enter key on your keyboard.
5. You should now be asked to enter your Apple ID password. This is so that fastlane can log in to iTunes Connect on your behalf and access your profiles. This password will be saved to your keychain locally on your computer.

When you integrate fastlane with Travis, you can pass your iTunes Connect password to fastlane using the `FASTLANE_PASS WORD` environment variable and encrypt this password in your *.travis.yml* file using Travis's own CLI. More about this later.

6. fastlane then presents the detected information about your project to you. If this information is correct, enter **y** to continue.

If everything went according to plan, you should now have a folder in your project called *fastlane* with the following contents (issue the `ls fastlane` command in Terminal to see this folder's contents):

```
ls fastlane
Appfile    Deliverfile Fastfile    metadata    screenshots
```

Discussion

While Travis is a tool for continuous integration, fastlane is used for continuous delivery. In other words, Travis builds your projects, while fastlane is the tool with which it builds them. fastlane can also help you upload your builds to iTunes Connect and generally makes the process of building, testing, and distributing your iOS apps easier than using shell scripts. However, it is a dependency nonetheless, which can be its weak point in that it lags behind official Xcode releases by sometimes days, if not more, and has its own set of bugs that are managed online in GitHub.

fastlane is a set of open source tools maintained by Google. This project started as a hobby project for one developer many years ago, then was bought by Twitter and then bought by Google, where it currently lives. You can read more about it at *https://github.com/fastlane/*.

You need to set up fastlane once for every project and then configure it as you go using the different files that get saved in the *fastlane/* folder inside your project's root folder, as you will see soon!

See Also

Recipe 1.11

1.11 Building Your Apps with fastlane

Problem

You want to use fastlane to build your iOS applications from the command line, instead of having to use your own custom shell script.

Solution

Assuming that you have already followed the instructions in Recipe 1.10 to set up fastlane for your project, all you have to do to build your project with fastlane is:

1. Open the *fastlane/Fastfile* file in your favorite editor.

 Because this file doesn't have an extension, most editors won't be able to color code it for you. If your editor allows you to manually specify a language for the input document, choose Ruby. I personally use Visual Studio Code, a free downloadable tool, for this type of editing.

2. Find the *beta* lane that was created for you by default, by searching the file for its method definition:

```
desc "Submit a new Beta Build to Apple TestFlight"
desc "This will also make sure the profile is up to date"
lane :beta do
  gym(scheme: "TestingTravis")
  pilot
end
```

3. Duplicate all this code and create a new lane called *build* that calls only the *gym* action, and not *pilot*:

```
lane :build do
  gym(scheme: "TestingTravis")
end
```

 The application for which I am demonstrating fastlane's capabilities is called *TestingTravis*, the same app used in previous recipes in this chapter. Remember to change this name in your *gym* action to reflect the name of the project that you are building with fastlane.

4. From Terminal, run the `fastlane build` command.

If you have set up your profiles and certificates correctly in your project and keychain, the result of the `fastlane build` command should be similar to the following:

```
+------+-----------------------------------------+-------------+
|                  fastlane summary                            |
+------+-----------------------------------------+-------------+
| Step | Action                                  | Time (in s) |
+------+-----------------------------------------+-------------+
| 1    | Verifying required fastlane version     | 0           |
| 2    | default_platform                        | 0           |
```

```
|  3   |  gym                                |  29         |
+------+------------------------------------+------------+
```

```
[22:04:25]: fastlane.tools finished successfully
```

Discussion

fastlane employs the idea of a *lane*, a set of instructions to fastlane that indicate how it should react. For instance, when you set up fastlane for the first time for your project, you will be given a lane that is called *beta*. That means that if you run the fastlane beta action from Terminal while in your project's folder, fastlane will go to the *fastlane/Fastfile* file, find the lane called *beta*, and run its instructions.

Every lane in your *Fastfile* is constructed of one or more actions, or instructions, that fastlane understands. These actions are well documented on the GitHub page for fastlane. One of the most important of these actions is *gym*, which builds your application. You can pass many parameters to the action in order to specify how your application has to be built. In order to get a better understanding of which parameters you can pass to the *gym* action, run the fastlane gym help action from Terminal. Here is a short list of some of the most important parameters you can pass to the *gym* action:

workspace
> The name of the workspace that the *gym* action has to use to build your project.

project
> The name of the project file itself inside the root folder of your application. If you are specifying a workspace, you should not use this parameter; use the scheme parameter instead.

scheme
> The name of the Xcode scheme that will be used to build your application.

clean
> A Boolean value that indicates whether your project has to be cleaned before building.

configuration
> The name of the configuration that will be used to build your application.

codesigning_identity
> The name of the code-signing identity that has to be used to build your scheme. This will take precedence over the code-signing identity that you have specified in Xcode for the scheme you want to use for the build. If you don't specify a code-signing identity in *gym*, the code-signing identity that is specified in your project file will be used for the given scheme.

Here is our *build* lane again, extended to take in a few more parameters:

```
lane :build do
  gym(
    scheme: "TestingTravis",
    clean: true,
    configuration: "Release"
  )
end
```

See Also

Recipe 1.10

1.12 Testing Your Apps with fastlane

Problem

You want to perform UI or unit tests with fastlane.

Solution

Execute the *scan* action in your *Fastfile*. By default, when you set up fastlane for your project (see Recipe 1.10), you will get a lane called *test* in your *Fastfile*, which you can execute with the following command in Terminal:

```
fastlane test
```

If everything goes as expected, you should see the command's output in Terminal as shown here:

```
+------+---------------------------------------+------------+
|                  fastlane summary                         |
+------+---------------------------------------+------------+
| Step | Action                                | Time (in s) |
+------+---------------------------------------+------------+
| 1    | Verifying required fastlane version   | 0          |
| 2    | default_platform                      | 0          |
| 3    | scan                                  | 35         |
+------+---------------------------------------+------------+
```

```
[20:49:50]: fastlane.tools finished successfully
```

The default implementation of the *test* lane in your *Fastfile* will probably look like this:

```
desc "Runs all the tests"
lane :test do
  scan
end
```

Discussion

We saw a couple of fastlane's actions in Recipe 1.11; the action we use for testing is *scan*. As its name indicates, it allows you to scan your code for bugs, which it does by running your unit or UI tests, based on which test target you ask it to run.

The *scan* action makes a few assumptions about your project if it is run without any parameters (which is the default setup). It will:

1. Find the first test target in the project and run it.
2. Use the default simulator to run the tests.

 If you want to specify a new target for *scan*, use the scheme parameter. A scheme is bound to a target, so by specifying a scheme, you are implicitly choosing a target.

Some of the most important parameters you can pass to *scan* are:

workspace
> The name of the workspace in which your test target exists, if any.

project
> The name of the project under which your test target exists. You need to specify either a workspace or a project, but not both.

device
> The name of the device to run your tests on, such as 'iPhone 7'.

devices
> A comma-separated array of test devices to run your tests on, such as ['iPhone 7', 'iPad Pro'].

scheme
> The name of the scheme under which to run your tests. Remember that your scheme has to be marked as a *Shared* scheme in order for fastlane to be able to use it from the command line (see Recipe 1.8).

clean
> A Boolean value indicating if all existing and old build artifacts have to be cleaned and the project rebuilt before the tests are run.

configuration

> The name of the configuration that will be used to build and test your project. The default value is `Debug` for the *scan* action, while the same parameter is `Release` for *gym*.

Here is an example of how you can extend the default *test* lane in your *Fastfile* with some of the aforementioned parameters to the *scan* action:

```
desc "Runs all the tests"
lane :test do
  scan(
    project: 'TestingTravis.xcodeproj',
    scheme: 'TestingTravis',
    clean: true,
    configuration: 'Debug',
    devices: ['iPhone 6', 'iPhone 7']
  )
end
```

See Also

Recipe 1.4

1.13 Enabling Slack Notifications in fastlane

Problem

You want to post notifications from fastlane to your Slack channel, regarding:

- Errors found by *gym* when building your project
- Issues found by *scan* while testing your project

> You can ask fastlane to report *any* errors that might occur during the execution of your lanes, using channels such as Slack or email. You do this by defining a function in your *Fastfile* called `error do |lane, exception|`.

Solution

Use the various custom Slack parameters that you can pass to the *gym* and *scan* actions, namely:

slack_url

> The URL to a private webhook into your Slack team. You will learn how to retrieve such a URL later in this recipe.

`slack_channel`
The name of the Slack channel where notifications will be posted.

`slack_message`
A custom message that will be posted alongside the standard message that fastlane posts to Slack.

`slack_only_on_failure`
A Boolean value indicating whether you want Slack messages to be posted only when the build/testing fails.

Here is an example of a *test* lane that uses *scan* to run your unit tests and post the results to Slack:

```
desc "Runs all the tests"
lane :test do
  scan(
    project: 'TestingTravis.xcodeproj',
    scheme: 'TestingTravis',
    clean: true,
    configuration: 'Debug',
    devices: ['iPhone 6', 'iPhone 7'],
    slack_url: 'https://hooks.slack.com/services/id',
    slack_channel: 'fastlane',
    slack_message: 'A custom message from Fastlane',
    slack_only_on_failure: false
  )
end
```

 Your webhook URL will look similar to that provided here; the only difference will be your *id*, a unique string of digits.

And the results, if everything goes fine, will look like Figure 1-26 in Slack.

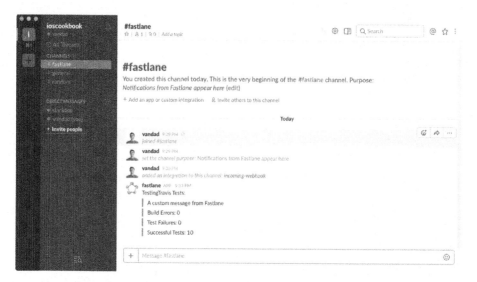

Figure 1-26. Results of the fastlane test command

Discussion

Slack provides webhook URLs that you can use to post JSON payloads. Slack will render the JSON as a nicely formatted message. To create a webhook into your Slack team, you have to have administrator privileges in your team. If you don't have those privileges, you can ask the current administrator for temporary privileges so that you can set up incoming webhooks on Slack, then go back to your regular privileges.

To retrieve a webhook URL in your Slack team, follow these instructions:

1. From the Channel Settings menu in Slack, choose the "Add an app or integration" option.
2. In the search bar that gives you access to the different apps and integrations that you can add to your Slack channel, search for *incoming webhooks* and once it is found, click it.
3. Press the Add Configuration button shown in Figure 1-27.

Figure 1-27. Locating the incoming webhooks plug-in for Slack

4. On the next page, choose the Slack channel in which to create the webhook (see Figure 1-28). You can also create a Slack channel right there and then choose it. In the figure, I have chosen for all fastlane messages to be posted to a Slack channel that is also called *fastlane*. You might want to choose another name or an existing Slack channel in your team.

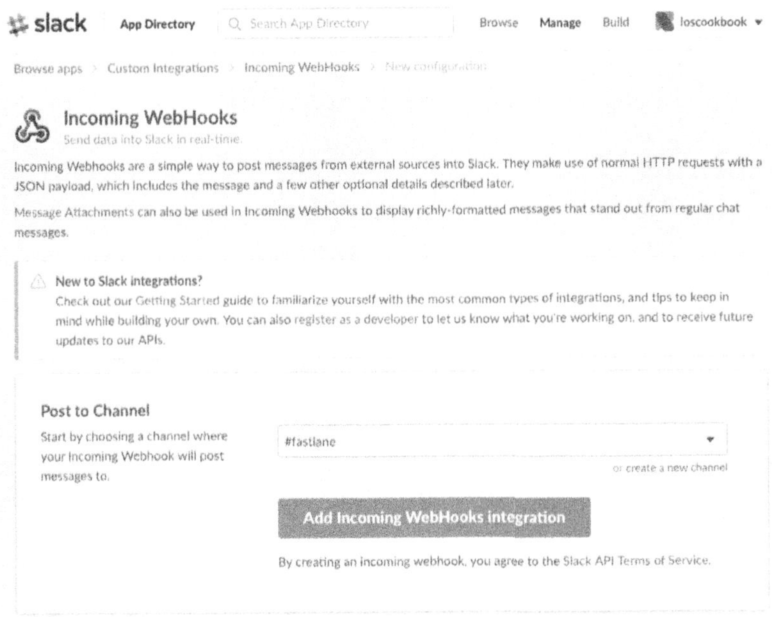

Figure 1-28. Choosing a Slack channel to which fastlane will post messages

5. When you are done, press the "Add Incoming WebHooks integration" button shown in Figure 1-28.

6. On the next page, you will now see your new webhook URL. Copy this value and keep it safe in your computer, because you are going to need it to configure fastlane.

7. In your *Fastfile*, set the `slack_url` parameter of the action generating the notifications (*gym* or *scan*) to the webhook URL that you retrieved in the previous step.

8. In the same file, set the value of the `slack_channel` parameter to the name of the Slack channel for which you created the webhook.

9. Optionally, set the value of the `slack_message` parameter to a message that will be posted alongside every notification from fastlane onto this hook.

10. And last but not least, in the same file, if you want to receive notifications even for successful builds or tests, set the `slack_only_on_failure` parameter to `false`.

Now you can run your tests or make a build with fastlane and test the results in Slack.

If you want to test these things out without polluting your company's Slack channels, you can always create your own Slack team and personal channels (*https://slack.com/create*).

1.14 Archiving Your Apps with fastlane

Problem

You want to create an *.ipa* file with dSYMs and an *.xcarchive* folder containing the original *.app* folder for your iOS app, signed for the App Store, both to submit the application to the App Store and to archive it.

Solution

Use the *gym* fastlane action with the following parameters:

scheme
Provide here the name of the shared scheme that will be used to build your app.

clean
Provide the value of `true` to this parameter to ensure no residual derived data from a previous build will contaminate your App Store archive.

configuration
> Provide the value of `Release` to this parameter. If you have created a custom release configuration, provide its name here.

output_directory
> Provide the value of `./build/` to this parameter, because it's the most common directory to place build artifacts inside your current project folder.

output_name
> Provide the value of `build.ipa` to this parameter so that your output *.ipa* file will be saved as *build.ipa* under your *build* folder.

export_method
> Provide the value of `app-store` to this parameter to ensure that your project gets built for the App Store.

archive_path
> Provide the value of `./build/build.xcarchive` to this parameter so that *gym*, in addition to creating a signed App Store *.ipa* file, creates an *.xcarchive* folder that contains your dSYM files and *.app* folder for archiving purposes.

> The *gym* action uses your target's settings for the code-signing certificate and profile, so ensure that you have set those up properly before running *gym*.

Discussion

Edit your *fastlane/Fastfile* file with your favorite editor and create a new lane named *archive*. Inside this lane, place your *gym* action with the previously mentioned parameters and their corresponding values:

```
lane :archive do

  gym(
    scheme: "TestingTravis",
    clean: true,
    configuration: "Release",
    output_directory: "./build/",
    output_name: "build.ipa",
    export_method: "app-store",
    archive_path: "./build/build.xcarchive"
  )

end
```

Now from Terminal, issue the following command:

```
fastlane archive
```

If everything goes as expected, you should now see the following results printed to Terminal:

```
[20:20:01]: Successfully exported and compressed dSYM file
[20:20:01]: Successfully exported and signed the ipa file:

+------+-----------------------------------------+------------+
|                     fastlane summary                       |
+------+-----------------------------------------+------------+
| Step | Action                                  | Time (in s) |
+------+-----------------------------------------+------------+
| 1    | Verifying required fastlane version     | 0          |
| 2    | default_platform                        | 0          |
| 3    | gym                                     | 23         |
+------+-----------------------------------------+------------+

[20:20:01]: fastlane.tools finished successfully
```

And if you navigate to the *build* folder, you should see:

- dSYM files zipped up together nicely
- An Xcode Archive folder
- A signed *.ipa* file

```
→ testing-travis git:(master) ✗ cd build
→ build git:(master) ✗ ls
archive            build.app.dSYM.zip build.ipa            build.xcarchive
```

See Also

Recipe 1.3

1.15 Uploading Your Apps to iTunes Connect with fastlane

Problem

You want to upload your application to iTunes Connect, from Terminal, using fastlane.

Solution

Follow these steps:

1. Log in to iTunes Connect and create your application template there. You don't have to upload any screenshots or any other information.

---

2. Ensure that your iOS app has all its necessary icons. To do so, open the asset catalogue file that hosts your icons and ensure that all the icons are present. If any icon is missing, iTunes Connect will reject your binary file.
3. Open your *fastlane/Fastfile* and find the *archive* lane that has already been created for you.
4. In that lane, call the *gym* action that will build your application (see Recipe 1.14) followed by the *deliver* action that will actually deliver your app to iTunes Connect. A typical action is:

```
desc "Deploy a new version to the App Store"
lane :release do
  gym(
    scheme: "TestingTravis",
    clean: true,
    configuration: "Release",
    output_directory: "./build/",
    output_name: "build.ipa",
    export_method: "app-store",
    archive_path: "./build/build.xcarchive"
    )
  deliver(force: true)
end
```

5. From Terminal, run the `fastlane release` command.

If everything goes as expected, you should see the following results printed to the console:

```
[21:23:13]: Finished the upload to iTunes Connect

+------+-------------------------------------------+--------------+
|                    fastlane summary                            |
+------+-------------------------------------------+--------------+
| Step | Action                                    | Time (in s)  |
+------+-------------------------------------------+--------------+
| 1    | Verifying required fastlane version       | 0            |
| 2    | default_platform                          | 0            |
| 3    | gym                                       | 22           |
| 4    | deliver                                   | 175          |
+------+-------------------------------------------+--------------+

[21:23:13]: fastlane.tools finished successfully
```

Discussion

fastlane has many actions, including *deliver*. As its name indicates, it is used to deliver your application to the user, through TestFlight and iTunes Connect.

The *deliver* action takes a few parameters, the most important of which are:

force

If the value of this parameter is `true`, fastlane will return immediately after uploading your binary to iTunes Connect, without waiting for your binary to finish processing on iTunes Connect. Every binary that gets uploaded to iTunes Connect goes through a processing stage where iTunes determines whether it follows most of the guidelines set out by Apple, such as including the necessary icons and avoiding the use of private APIs. This process can take a long time, sometimes up to a few hours! You probably don't want your build system to wait until iTunes Connect has finished processing your build; in that case, provide the value of `true` to this parameter.

submit_for_review

By default, *deliver* submits your app to iTunes Connect for TestFlight testing only. Submit the value of `true` to this parameter if you want *deliver* to also send your app to the App Review team at Apple for approval.

automatic_release

Set the value of this parameter to `true` if you want your app to be automatically released to users when it has successfully gone through the App Review team at Apple.

primary_category

This parameter determines the primary category of your application, such as `Entertainment`.

secondary_category

This parameter determines the second category of apps to which your app belongs.

description

This parameter provides information regarding the description of your application in iTunes Connect.

keywords

The value of this parameter is an array of strings that provide the keywords in iTunes with which users can search for your app.

release_notes

You can provide your release notes for this build by providing a value to this parameter.

See Also

Recipe 1.7

CHAPTER 2

Snapshot Testing

Snapshot testing helps you uncover errors that cause unwanted changes to your app's user interface. In this process, you take one view at a time, capture snapshots of that view in different simulators and different resolutions, and record those snapshots as reference images. After you are done recording the "correct" state of your application views, you can then run your snapshot tests in "test" mode instead of "record" mode, in order to compare the output of the new code with the state that you recorded earlier. If the images match (allowing for a certain percentage of mismatch that you set), the snapshot test passes. Otherwise, you get a failure. If any differences are found, you can go through the generated report to find out what has changed in the UI and why.

Snapshot testing allows you to trap unwanted changes to your user interface very effectively. It's important to use if you or your colleagues touch UI code constantly and you risk getting regression bugs on it. That could happen if you are working on a new code base and building it from the ground up, or even if you are working on a well-established code base that has few or no UI tests and a little change to the code could cause unwanted changes to the UI.

Xcode has very powerful built-in UI testing tools, but lacks the ability to do snapshot testing. An example of UI testing is to ask Xcode to press a button, wait x number of seconds, then compare the label of a button that might appear on the screen with a certain value. Xcode's UI testing requires you to anticipate what might change (a label on a button, for example) and explicitly create a test for each change you anticipate. Snapshot testing, on the other hand, finds unanticipated changes.

In this chapter, we will look at Facebook's open source library, iOS Snapshot Test Case, which is available on GitHub (*https://github.com/facebook/ios-snapshot-test-case*) and is being actively developed by developers around the world as well as at Facebook itself. The library ships as a CocoaPod (or simply said, Pod) that you can easily integrate into your project. You will learn all about that, and a lot more, in this chapter.

2.1 Setting Up Snapshot Testing

Problem

You want to start using iOS snapshot test cases but don't know where to begin.

Solution

 I'm going to assume that you are creating a new application from scratch during these steps. If you have an existing application, you just need to ensure that you use the instructions provided here to integrate the Pod for this library and set up your UI tests as mentioned here.

When you believe that the state of your UI is what you want, you will need to ask the Facebook snapshot test library case to generate screenshots of your user interface (recording mode). The next time that you run the tests (not in recording mode), new screenshots will be generated but not saved to disk, and these new screenshots will be compared to the original screenshots. If there are any differences found, these differences will be saved to disk for your future reference.

Follow these steps:

1. If you have not already installed CocoaPods on your computer, do so by following the instructions provided at the CocoaPods website (*http://cocoapods.org*).
2. Create a single view application in Xcode for your iOS project.
3. Enter *SnapshotTesting* as the name of the project (see Figure 2-1) and make sure to check the box that includes unit tests (as opposed to UI tests) in the project.

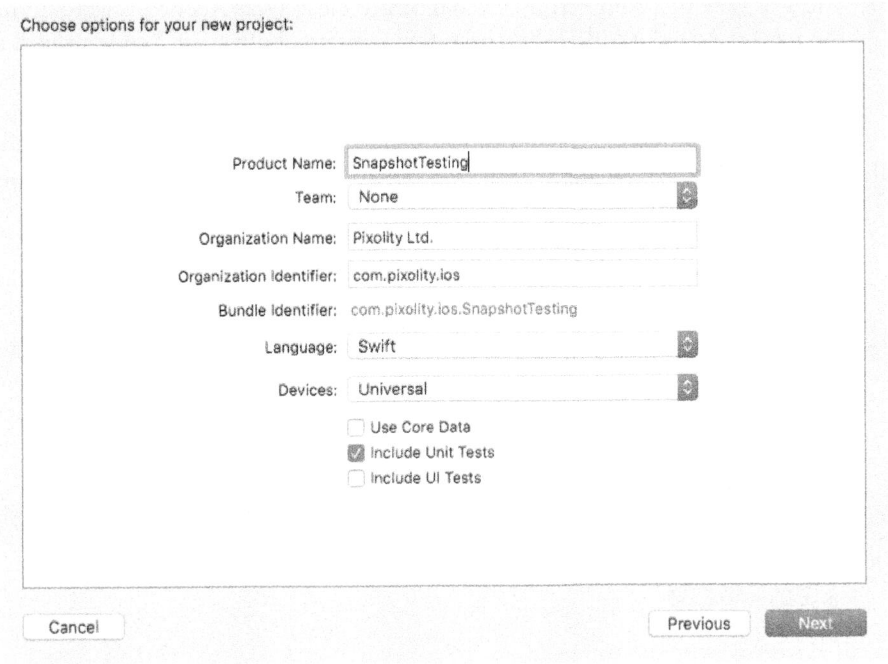

Choose options for your new project:

Product Name: SnapshotTesting

Team: None

Organization Name: Pixolity Ltd.

Organization Identifier: com.pixolity.ios

Bundle Identifier: com.pixolity.ios.SnapshotTesting

Language: Swift

Devices: Universal

☐ Use Core Data
☑ Include Unit Tests
☐ Include UI Tests

Cancel   Previous   Next

Figure 2-1. Creating a new project with a UI test target

4. Open Terminal in the root directory of your newly generated project and issue the following command: `pod init`.
5. Also in Terminal, issue the command `vim Podfile` (or whatever editor you use on plain text files) to start editing your *Podfile*.
6. Add the `FBSnapshotTestCase` Pod to your *Podfile* under the UI test target, as shown in the following excerpt, and then save the *Podfile* and exit Vim:

```
platform :ios, '10.0'

target 'SnapshotTesting' do
  use_frameworks!

  target 'SnapshotTestingTests' do
    inherit! :search_paths
    use_frameworks!
    pod 'FBSnapshotTestCase'
  end

end
```

7. Run the `pod update` command in Terminal to update your repository with all the pods offered on GitHub, and then install the latest snapshot pod in your project.

8. You will now be prompted by CocoaPods to close your Xcode project and open the newly created Xcode Workspace that contains both your Xcode project and the CocoaPods project that was injected into your existing project. Open the workspace file now in Xcode.

9. Press Cmd-B in Xcode to build your project and ensure that it builds successfully.

10. Press Cmd-Shift-U to build your test target and ensure that it goes through as expected.

11. Define where in your scheme CocoaPods will save your snapshot images and the differences between the original and current views by holding down the Alt key on your keyboard and clicking the Play button in Xcode.

12. In the Edit Schemes screen (see Figure 2-2) that opens up now, make sure the *Run* scheme is selected and then click the Arguments tab. You are going to add two new environment variables to that scheme to help your snapshot SDK determine where to save the snapshots.

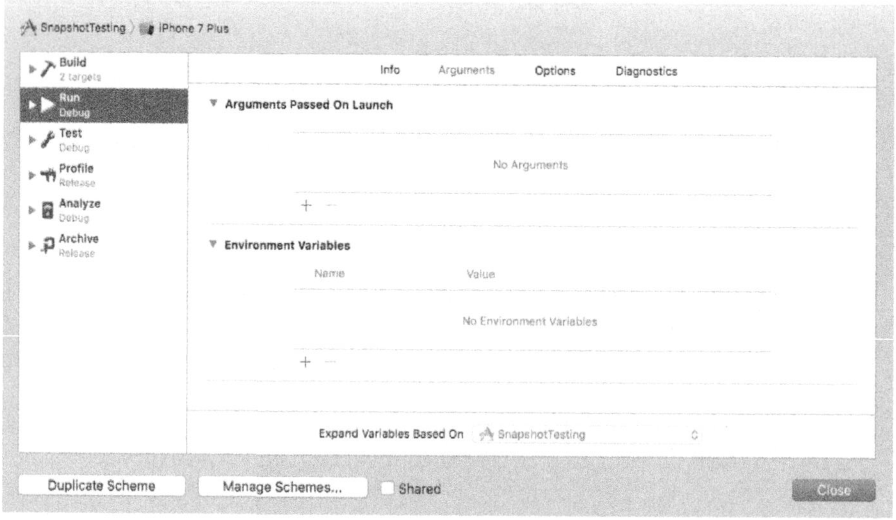

Figure 2-2. Arguments and environment variables for a run

13. Add two keys and values to your environment variables, as shown in Figure 2-3: IMAGE_DIFF_DIR, with a value of $(SOURCE_ROOT)/$(PROJECT_NAME)Tests/Fail ureDiffs, and FB_REFERENCE_IMAGE_DIR, with a value of $(SOURCE_ROOT)/$(PROJECT_NAME)Tests/ReferenceImages.

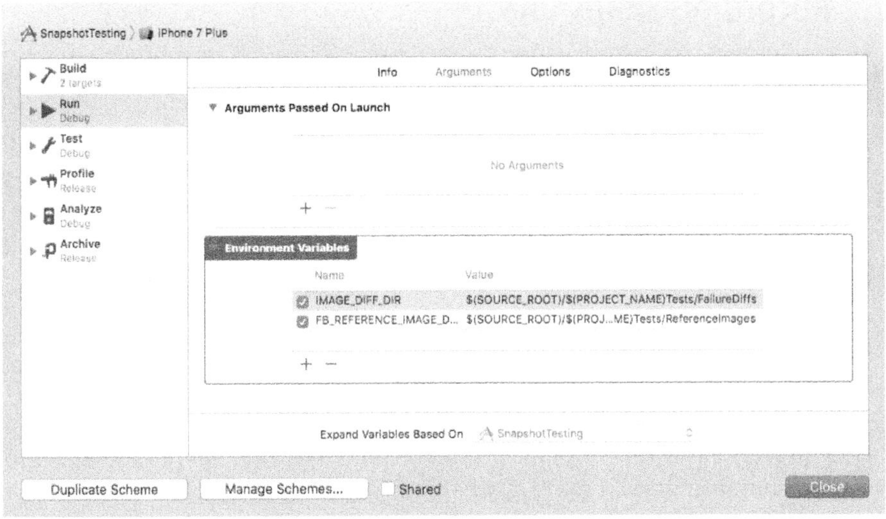

Figure 2-3. Place the two new arguments for snapshot testing in the Run scheme

Discussion

Snapshot testing can be very important if you are working on a modular UI, such as a newspaper application where your article is made out of components such as images, paragraphs, links, and more. A single change in the font, say from 17 points to 18 points, might not be noticeable to a colleague of yours who is a tester, but will be immediately detected by snapshot tests.

Facebook's snapshot test case Pod allows you to run your application in recording mode on any simulator of your choice, or a combination of simulators. In this mode, the snapshot test case Pod will generate screenshots of the parts of your application UI that you specify, and will save those screenshots to disk. Once it's done generating the screenshots in recording mode, you can disable the recording mode by modifying a flag in your test code, as you will see Recipe 2.2). At this point, when you run your snapshot test cases again, new and temporary screenshots will be created for your UI and then compared to the permanently stored screenshots on disk. If there are any differences, they will be saved to disk as images for your future reference.

See Also

Recipe 2.2

2.2 Recording Snapshots

Problem

You want to record a snapshot of a view inside your application while you know it is the right reference image, so that later you can compare the snapshot to any changes that might be made during development, thus catching possible errors.

Solution

Follow these steps:

1. For the sake of this demonstration, create a new class in your application and call it MyView, of type UIView.
2. Write the following code in the app. This code essentially fills the entire view with black and then draws a red ellipse in the middle:

```
import UIKit

class MyView: UIView {

  override func draw(_ rect: CGRect) {

    guard let context = UIGraphicsGetCurrentContext() else {return}

    let backgroundColor = UIColor.black.cgColor

    context.setFillColor(backgroundColor)
    context.fill(rect)

    let middleRect = rect
      .applying(CGAffineTransform(scaleX: 0.5, y: 0.5))
      .applying(CGAffineTransform(translationX: rect.width / 4.0,
                                  y: rect.height / 4.0))

    context.addEllipse(in: middleRect)
    let circleColor = UIColor.red.cgColor
    context.setFillColor(circleColor)
    context.fillPath()

  }

}
```

3. Add a new unit test case class to your unit test target and name your test class MyViewSnapshotTest, of type FBSnapshotTestCase.
4. In your unit test's file, ensure that you have imported FBSnapshotTestCase as a dependency.

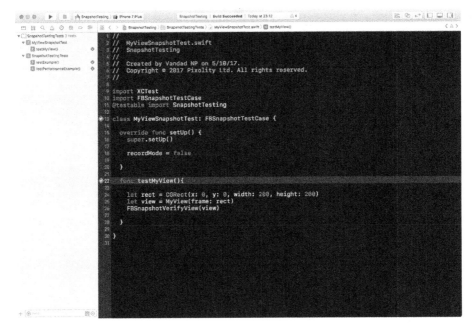

Figure 2-5. After disabling recording mode in the test suite, the tests should pass

To ensure that your test suite is working as expected, go to the *MyView.swift* file and change the background color from black to blue by changing the line let backgroundColor = UIColor.black.cgColor to let backgroundColor = UIColor.blue.cgColor. After you've done this, press the Cmd-Shift-U keys on your keyboard followed by Cmd-U to run your test suite again. You should now receive an error from the snapshot test (see Figure 2-6) telling you that the current state of *MyView* differs from its correct state, which was captured while in recording mode previously.

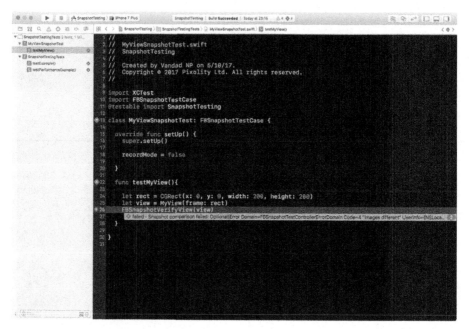

Figure 2-6. The snapshot test is failing

See Also

Recipes 2.1 and 2.3

2.3 Specifying Tolerance in Snapshot Tests

Problem

You have two *almost* identical versions of your view, where a property of your view might change every now and then, but you don't want this slight change to fail your snapshot tests.

Solution

Use the `tolerance` property of the snapshot view to specify a percentage of pixels that can differ while still allowing tests to consider the original and current snapshots as the same. The default tolerance percentage of snapshot testing is 0, meaning that there should be absolutely no difference in pixels in the original (reference) snapshot and the current snapshot.

Discussion

Imagine that you're using the same MyView class that we implemented previously (see Recipe 2.2), but that the red color that fills the screen can every now and then have a different alpha from pure red, and you don't want this change in the alpha of the red color to affect your snapshot tests.

Start by going into recording mode, by setting the recordMode property of your test case to true, and running your tests:

```
import XCTest
import FBSnapshotTestCase
@testable import SnapshotTesting

class MyViewSnapshotTest: FBSnapshotTestCase {

  override func setUp() {
    super.setUp()

    recordMode = true

  }

  func testMyView(){

    let rect = CGRect(x: 0, y: 0, width: 200, height: 200)
    let view = MyView(frame: rect)
    FBSnapshotVerifyView(view)

  }

}
```

Then get out of recording mode and use the tolerance property of the FBSnapshot VerifyView(_:) function to specify a rough estimate of the percentage of changes you expect to be occurring in your reference view before you fire a test failure:

```
import XCTest
import FBSnapshotTestCase
@testable import SnapshotTesting

class MyViewSnapshotTest: FBSnapshotTestCase {

  override func setUp() {
    super.setUp()

    recordMode = false

  }

  func testMyView(){
```

```
let rect = CGRect(x: 0, y: 0, width: 200, height: 200)
let view = MyView(frame: rect)

FBSnapshotVerifyView(view, tolerance: 0.2)

  }

}
```

Now, in `MyView`, go and change the alpha channel of your red circle background color to 0.9, instead of the default 1.0 alpha:

```
let circleColor = UIColor.red.withAlphaComponent(0.9).cgColor
```

Now if you build and run your tests with Cmd-Shift-U followed by Cmd-U, you will notice that your tests pass as expected. If you left the tolerance at the default of 0 your tests would fail, as expected, since you recorded the snapshot when the background color of the circle in the middle of `MyView` was pure red but ran the tests when the same color's alpha channel was changed from 1.0 to 0.9.

See Also

Recipes 2.1 and 2.2

2.4 Analyzing Snapshot Test Case Failures

Problem

You just got a test failure in one of your snapshot tests and you want to know what the problem is and why the test failed.

Solution

Follow these steps:

1. Open Finder to the root folder of your project.
2. Open the folder associated with your snapshot test case target. My main project is called *SnapshotTesting* and the test target is called *SnapshotTestingTests*, so I will open the *SnapshotTestingTests* folder.
3. You should now find a subfolder called *FailureDiffs*. Open that folder.
4. Open the folder associated with your test case. My test case is called *MyView SnapshotTest* and the folder associated with it is called *SnapshotTesting Tests.MyViewSnapshotTest*, which is the name of the test target followed by the name of the test case.
5. Under this folder, you should then be able to locate three images associated with every failure (see Figure 2-7): one image for the reference (original), the second

for the new (incorrect) image, and the last one depicting the difference between the two images.

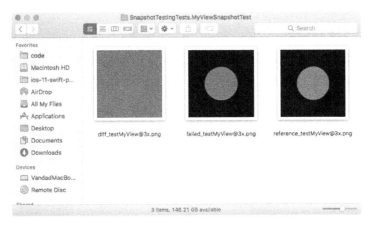

Figure 2-7. The three images that are saved on disk, associated with one test case that failed

Discussion

Snapshot tests are performed at the raw pixel level for your views. Using the *diff images*, you should be able to tell what the problem is and how the images are different.

The iOS Snapshot Test Case library that we are using can record images for various simulators. If you run your test cases in recording mode on multiple simulators, different reference images will be recorded for each simulator depending on that simulator's properties, such as pixel density and resolution (see Figure 2-7). Therefore, depending on where you received your failures, you might need to look through the *FailureDiffs* folder a bit more deeply, first to find the folder associated with your test case, and then to find the three images that are associated with that particular simulator. Every image saved under this folder is suffixed with the `scale` property of the screen on that simulator. For instance, if your test cases failed on an iPhone 7 Plus simulator, where the scale of the screen is 3x, your images will be suffixed with *@3x*.

If you search online, you can also find some Xcode plug-ins that allow you to see the snapshot differences right within Xcode. But their availability depends heavily on the Xcode version that you are running, so I will avoid recommending any particular plug-ins.

See Also

Recipe 2.5

2.5 Testing Table View Cell Snapshots

Problem

You want to perform snapshot tests to check whether particular cells have changed in a table view.

Solution

Follow these steps:

1. In your project's storyboard, ensure that you have assigned a storyboard identifier to the view controller that hosts your table view cells. We will use this identifier to load the cells using the table view controller, inside the snapshot test suite.
2. Ensure that every cell has its own reusable identifier that you can use to dequeue them from the test suite.
3. In your snapshot test suite, find an instance of your main app's bundle using the `Bundle(for:)` initializer of the `Bundle` class.
4. Use the `UIStoryboard(name:bundle:)` initializer of the `UIStoryboard` class to load your storyboard file into the test suite.
5. Use the `instantiateViewController(withIdentifier:)` method of the loaded storyboard to create an instance of your view controller inside the test suite, and pass your view controller's storyboard identifier to this call.
6. Instantiate your cells using the `tableView` property's `dequeueReusableCell(with Identifier:)` method in the table view controller, and provide your cell's identifier to this method.
7. Once you have the cell instance, you can get your cell's view using the `content View` property of the cell.
8. Pass the `contentView` property of your cell to the `FBSnapshotVerifyView(_:)` function, while your test suite is in recording mode (see Recipe 2.2), and then run your test suite.
9. Disable recording mode to go back to test mode, and then run your test suite to compare the current state of your cells with the original images.

Discussion

In this recipe, I've already designed, in my main project, a table view controller (see Figure 2-8), giving it a storyboard identifier of *TableViewController* so that we can refer to it easily from the test suite. The `TableViewController` is of type `UITableView Controller`, and its interface is prepared inside a storyboard file. Additionally, I've created two prototype cells inside the table view controller, and I've assigned the value of `pinkFloyd` to the first cell's identifier and the value of `symphonyX` to the second cell's identifier. We are going to use these names to dequeue these cells from our test target and take snapshots of them.

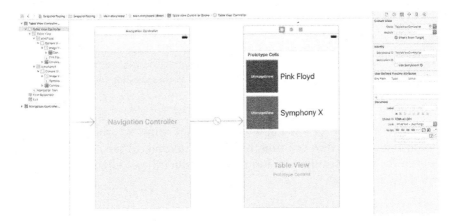

Figure 2-8. Table in a table view

I've also created a unit test case inside Xcode in my test target and named it Table ViewCellSnapshotTests. We will use this test case to test the two different cells that our table view controller can display. Then, in the setUp() function of our test case, we can get a reference to our table view controller so that the test functions inside this test case can easily refer to it:

```
import XCTest
import FBSnapshotTestCase
@testable import SnapshotTesting

class TableViewCellSnapshotTests: FBSnapshotTestCase {

  var tableViewController: TableViewController!

  override func setUp() {
    super.setUp()

    let appBundle = Bundle(for: TableViewController.self)

    guard let tableViewController =
      UIStoryboard(name: "Main", bundle: appBundle)
        .instantiateViewController(withIdentifier: "TableViewController")
        as? TableViewController else{

          XCTFail()
          return

    }

    self.tableViewController = tableViewController
```

```
recordMode = true
}
```

 The code sets the recordMode property of the test case to true, meaning that when you run this test case, the snapshots will be created. Once that is done, you should change the value of this property to false in order to actually run your snapshot tests against the original images.

Because the mechanism for loading both cells is the same, we can write a function that can load any table view cell from our TableViewController as long as we provide it with the cell's identifier. In addition to loading these cells, this function can perform the snapshot test:

```
func testCell(withIdentifier identifier: String){

  guard let cell = tableViewController
    .tableView.dequeueReusableCell(withIdentifier: identifier) else {

      XCTFail()
      return

  }

  let view = cell.contentView

  FBSnapshotVerifyView(view)

}
```

Last but not least, we will call our testCell(withIdentifier:) function from two different test functions, to capture a snapshot from the cells' content views and compare them with the originals:

```
func testPinkFloydCell() {

  testCell(withIdentifier: "pinkFloyd")

}

func testSymphonyXCell(){

  testCell(withIdentifier: "symphonyX")

}
```

See Also

Recipes 2.1 and 2.4

CHAPTER 3

SiriKit

Siri has been an integral part of iOS since Apple bought this technology and integrated it with the iPhone in 2011. However, Siri has been a closed technology up to now, and developers like you and me were not able to provide our own extensions.

iOS 11 has changed this situation. Now you can add your own extensions to Siri and allow users to interact with your apps and the services inside your apps through Siri.

Imagine that you have a financial app that allows users to send up to $20 to family and friends using their telephone numbers. The user can say, for instance, "Send 15 dollars to Max." Then your app looks in the user's address book to determine whether there is a contact called "Max" listed. If there is, you allow the financial transaction to go through. There are a few steps that you have to take in order to make your app Siri compatible, and we will have a look at those first.

3.1 Setting Up Your Project for Siri

Problem

You want to enable interactions with Siri in your app.

Solution

Follow these steps, the details of which can be found in this recipe's Discussion:

1. Create your app, if you don't already have one.
2. Enable Siri capabilities in your target's preferences in Xcode.
3. Add an Intents extension to your app as a new target.
4. Define your intents in the extension's *Info.plist* file.

5. In your app's *Info.plist* file, define the `NSSiriUsageDescription` key, along with a message explaining why you are intending to use Siri in your application. This message will be shown to the user when you attempt to ask for permission to integrate into Siri.

6. Import the `Intents` framework into your app.

7. Call the `requestSiriAuthorization(_:)` class method of the `INPreferences` class and ask the user for authorization to use Siri.

8. If the status is `authorized`, then you might need to wait a few minutes before Siri indexes your app's intents and understands that your app is going to need to interact with Siri.

Discussion

Let's consider the example of the user who interacts with Siri by saying something like, "Send 15 dollars to Max." Siri understands a few things from this message:

1. "Send" is the verb. From "dollars," Siri understands that this is a financial intent.
2. From the phrase "15 dollars," Siri understands that the quantity of this command is 15.
3. From "Max," Siri realizes that "Max" is the recipient of this financial transaction.

So now Siri knows what to do, but by default she doesn't know how to do it. How does she send the money? Siri therefore goes through the various apps and their exposed intents to find out which ones allow financial transactions and then negotiates the rest with the found app, if any.

An intent says what your app can do with the help of Siri. Every intent is represented by a class in the `Intents` framework. Some examples of these classes include:

`INBookRestaurantReservationIntent`
   To reserve a place at a restaurant.

`INCancelWorkoutIntent`
   To cancel an ongoing workout session.

`INSendPaymentIntent`
   To send a payment to someone.

We are going to look at `INSendPaymentIntent` in detail in this chapter. This recipe's Solution outlined how you can integrate your app with Siri, but now let's look at the steps in more detail:

1. Create your app if you haven't already created one. For the purposes of this example, I created a single view app, as shown in Figure 3-1.

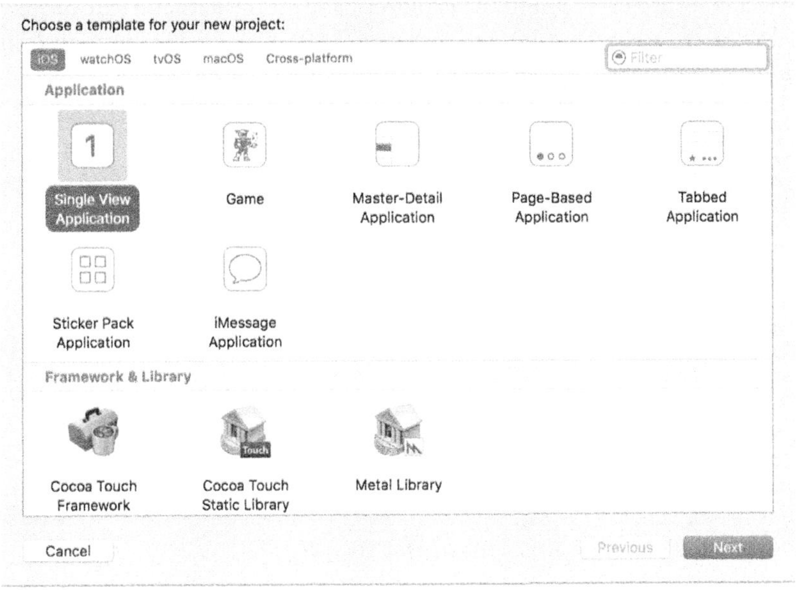

Figure 3-1. Create your app first

2. Give your app a product name (Figure 3-2), click Next, and save your project to disk.

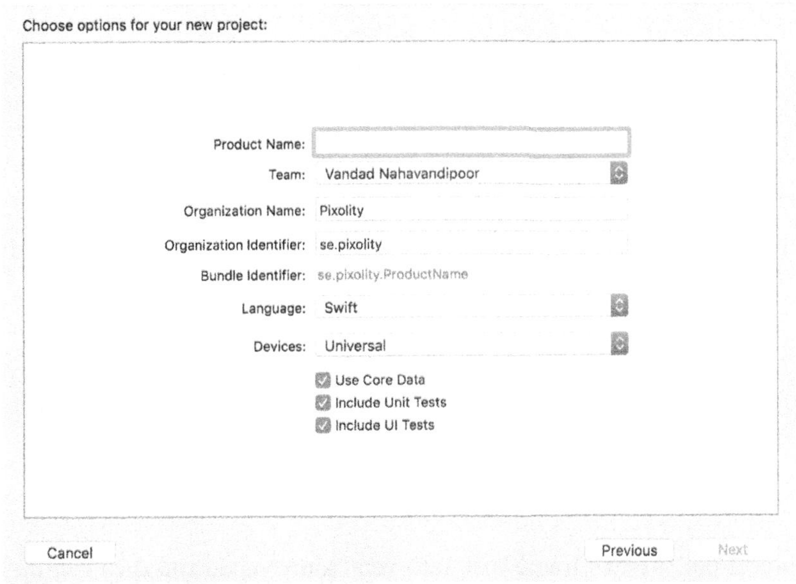

Figure 3-2. Give your app a name

3. Select your project's icon in the explorer pane on the lefthand side of Xcode, then select your target from the list that says TARGETS. Under the Capabilities section on top, enable Siri (Figure 3-3).

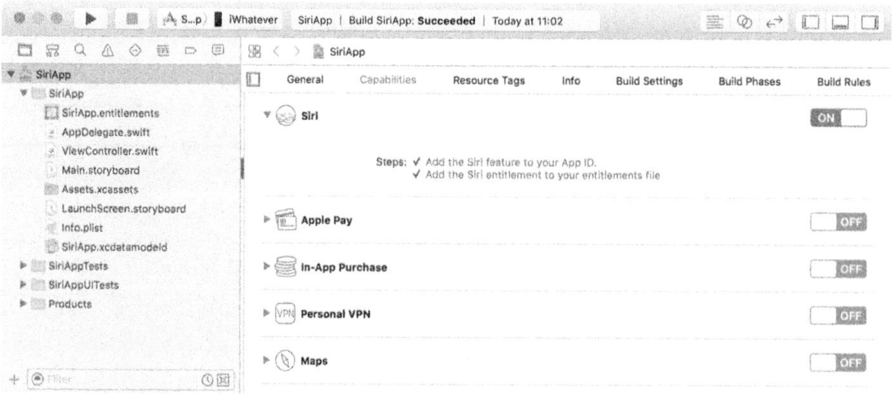

Figure 3-3. Enable the Siri capability for your app

4. Open the *Info.plist* file of your app. Create a new key-value pair in it, setting the key to NSSiriUsageDescription. For the value, enter a brief text message that tells the user why you are attempting to integrate your app with Siri (Figure 3-4).

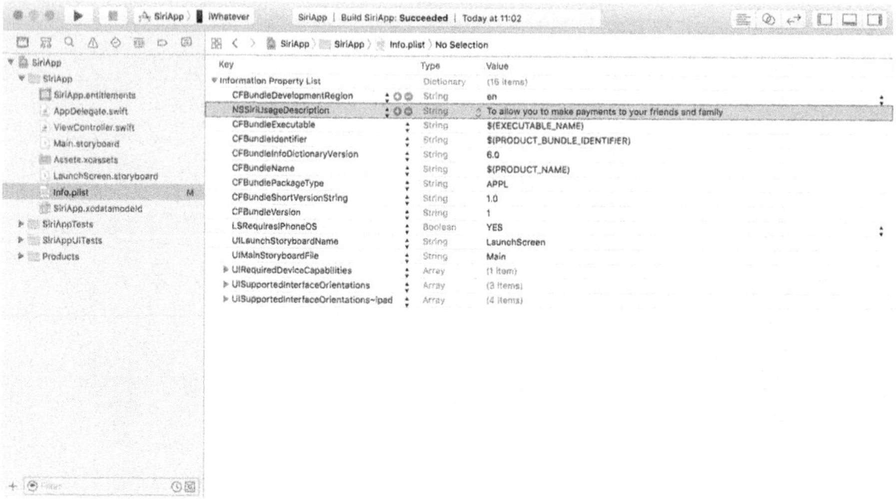

Figure 3-4. Tell the user why you are integrating with Siri

5. Import the Intents framework into your source code and then call the reques tSiriAuthorization(_:) class method of the INPreferences class to request access to Siri:

```
typealias SiriAccessCompletionHandler = (Bool) -> Void
func requestSiriAccess(
  completionHandler: @escaping SiriAccessCompletionHandler){

  INPreferences.requestSiriAuthorization {status in
    switch status{
    case .authorized:
      completionHandler(true)
    default:
      completionHandler(false)
    }
  }

}
```

6. Go to the Files menu and select New and then Target. On the screen that appears, under the Application Extension section, choose Intents Extension (Figure 3-5) and click Next.

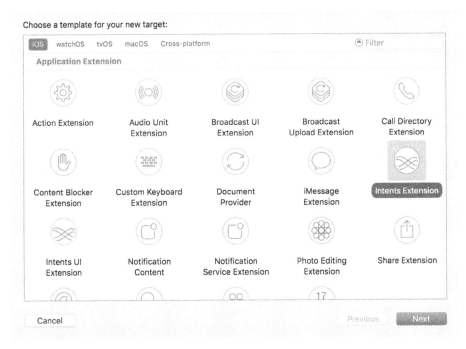

Figure 3-5. Create an Intents extension for Siri

7. Give the Intents extension a name (Figure 3-6), then press Finish to save and add it to the project. An Intents extension is your delegate through to Siri's capabilities, and this extension is your window to your users, through Siri!

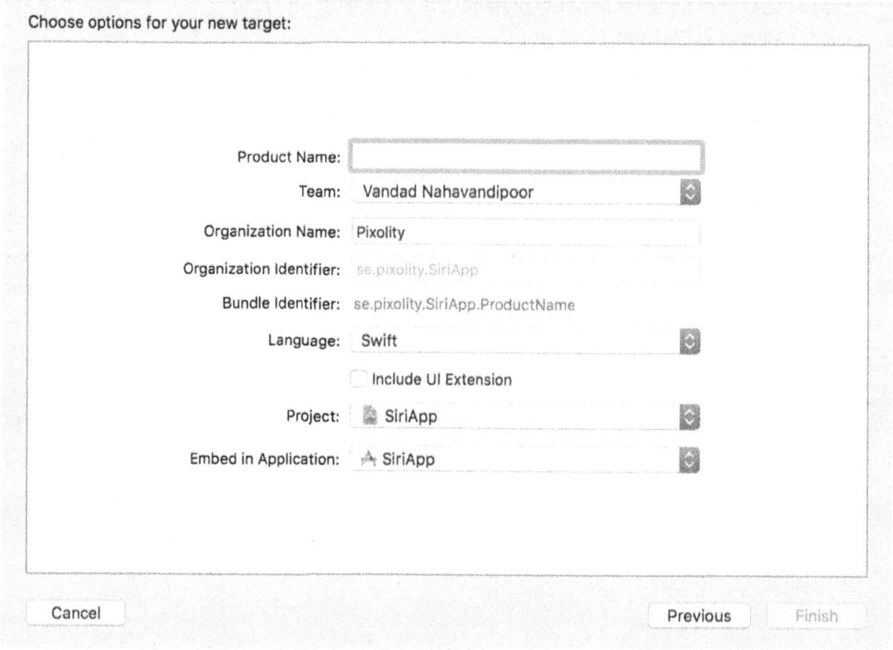

Choose options for your new target:

Product Name:	
Team:	Vandad Nahavandipoor
Organization Name:	Pixolity
Organization Identifier:	se.pixolity.SiriApp
Bundle Identifier:	se.pixolity.SiriApp.ProductName
Language:	Swift
	☐ Include UI Extension
Project:	🅰 SiriApp
Embed in Application:	🅰 SiriApp

Cancel   Previous   Finish

Figure 3-6. Give your Intents extension a name

8. In your newly created Intents extension's *Info.plist* file, go to the NSExtension key, expand it down to NSExtensionAttributes, and further expand that down to IntentsSupported and IntentsRestrictedWhileLocked. Under these two arrays of strings, you can list the names of the classes (such as INSendPaymentIntent) that your extension supports. Intents listed under the IntentsSupported key will be supported by your app. Intents listed under IntentsRestrictedWhileLocked will require the user's device to be locked before those intents can be resolved. You can use this latter functionality to create more secure intents, such as when you want the user to be able to send money to a friend or a family member.

The INSendPaymentIntent that we want to use requires the device to be locked for the sake of security, so you have to list it under IntentsSupported to indicate that your app supports this intent and under IntentsRestrictedWhileLocked to tell iOS that this intent requires the user's device to be locked before the user can use it.

If you forget to place your intent under IntentsSupported, it will not be recognized at all by iOS. And even worse, if your Intents Supported is empty, you won't even be able to compile and run your app on an iOS device.

The following section from an *Info.plist* file shows the Intents target that we have just set up:

```
<plist version="1.0">
  <dict>
    <key>NSExtension</key>
    <dict>
      <key>NSExtensionAttributes</key>
      <dict>
        <key>IntentsRestrictedWhileLocked</key>
        <array>
          <string>INSendPaymentIntent</string>
        </array>
        <key>IntentsSupported</key>
        <array/>
      </dict>
      <key>NSExtensionPointIdentifier</key>
      <string>com.apple.intents-service</string>
      <key>NSExtensionPrincipalClass</key>
      <string>$(PRODUCT_MODULE_NAME).IntentHandler</string>
    </dict>
  </dict>
</plist>
```

You can now run your app on a device. It will take a while before Siri can recognize that your app supports Siri intents, so give it a few minutes before asking Siri any questions that can be handled with INSendPaymentIntent.

3.2 Defining an Intent Handler

Problem

You want to handle a specific Siri intent, and you want to be able to handle all its related delegate messages to and from Siri.

Solution

Follow these steps, assuming that you have created your Intents extension target as discussed in Recipe 3.1:

1. Create a new Cocoa Touch class under your Intents extension target (Figure 3-7).

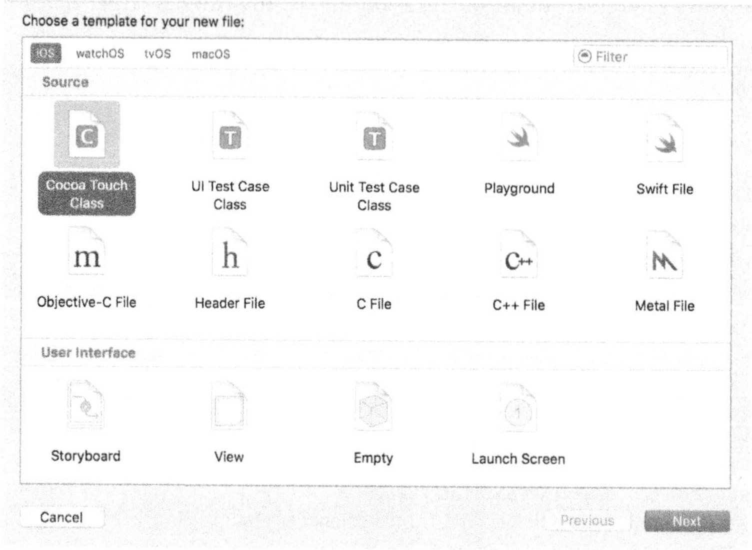

Figure 3-7. Create a new handler class for the intent

2. In the Subclass field, enter the class name of the intent that you wish to handle, such as INSendPaymentIntent. Then enter the name of the class that you wish to create in your own project, such as SendPaymentHandler (Figure 3-8). Proceed to the next screen to add it to your Intents extension target and save the file on disk.

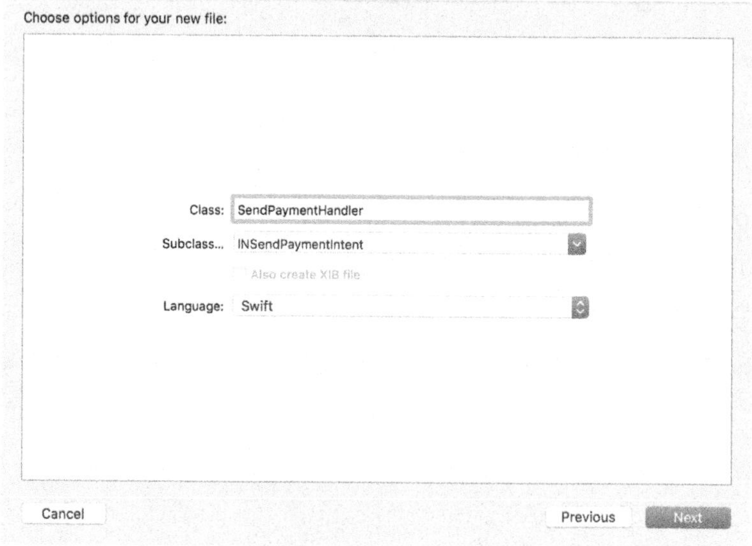

Figure 3-8. Give your intent class a name

3. The newly created file will be opened for you. Xcode will complain that this file isn't compilable, because Xcode doesn't import the Intents framework by default, so help Xcode by importing it:

```
import UIKit
import Intents

class SendPaymentHandler: INSendPaymentIntent {

}
```

4. Every intent handler has to conform to a protocol named *X*Handling, where *X* is the name of the intent class. For instance, if your intent handler is called INSendPaymentIntent, your intent handler class must conform to the INSendPaymentIntentHandling protocol:

```
import UIKit
import Intents

class SendPaymentHandler: INSendPaymentIntent, INSendPaymentIntentHandling {

    func confirm(intent: INSendPaymentIntent,
              completion: @escaping (INSendPaymentIntentResponse) -> Void) {

    }

    func handle(intent: INSendPaymentIntent,
              completion: @escaping (INSendPaymentIntentResponse) -> Void) {


    }

    //optional
    func resolvePayee(for intent: INSendPaymentIntent,
                    with completion: @escaping (INPersonResolutionResult)
                    -> Void) {

    }

    //optional
    func resolveCurrencyAmount(
      for intent: INSendPaymentIntent,
      with completion: @escaping (INCurrencyAmountResolutionResult) -> Void) {

    }

    func resolveNote(for intent: INSendPaymentIntent,
                    with completion: @escaping (INStringResolutionResult)
                    -> Void) {
```

```
    }

  }
```

5. Open the *IntentHandler.swift* file that was created for you when you created your
   Intents extension target. In the `handle(for:)` method of `INExtension`, return an
   instance of your newly created `SendPaymentHandler` class whenever an intent of
   type `INSendPaymentIntent` is about to be resolved:

```
import Intents

class IntentHandler: INExtension{

  override func handler(for intent: INIntent) -> Any {

    if intent is INSendPaymentIntent{
      return SendPaymentHandler()
    } else {
      return self
    }

  }

}
```

Discussion

If you have followed all the steps in this recipe's Solution, you can now choose the
Intents extension target that Xcode created for you when you created the target in
Recipe 3.1 and then press the Run button in Xcode. A dialog will appear asking you
to choose the app to which you want to attach your intent. In this dialog, choose Siri
(Figure 3-9) and then press the Run button.

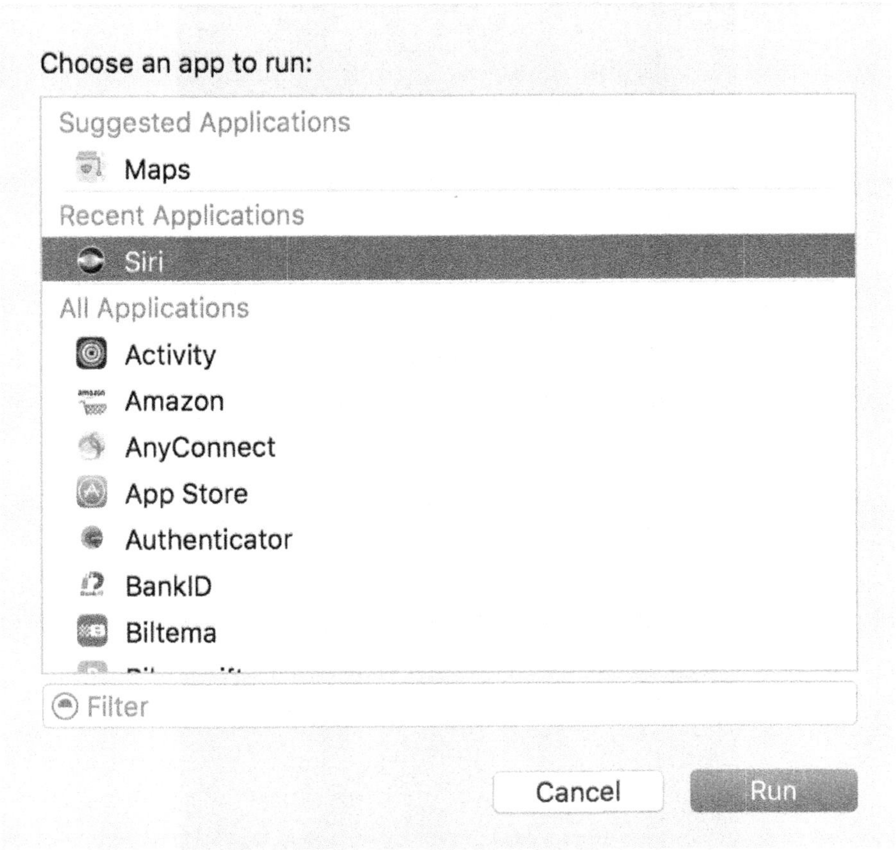

Choose an app to run:

Suggested Applications

🗺 Maps

Recent Applications

⬤ Siri

All Applications

◎ Activity

🛒 Amazon

🔵 AnyConnect

🅰 App Store

🟢 Authenticator

🏦 BankID

🅱 Biltema

◉ Filter

Cancel   Run

Figure 3-9. You have to attach your Intents extension to Siri to be able to test it

This will run Siri with your extension attached to it. Once Siri is up and running, say "Send 15 dollars to Anthony." This will cause Siri to ask you to confirm that you want to make this payment using the app that we have been working on (Figure 3-10).

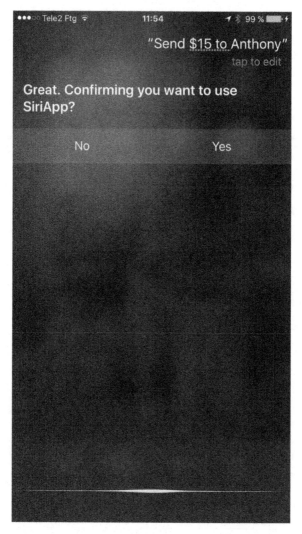

Figure 3-10. Siri is asking us if we want the payment to be handled by our app

If this is the first time you are giving this permission, Siri will ask to access your app's data with a dialog similar to Figure 3-11.

Figure 3-11. Siri needs access to your app's data before it can integrate with the app for the first time

Press the Siri Settings button that is provided to you and allow access (Figure 3-12).

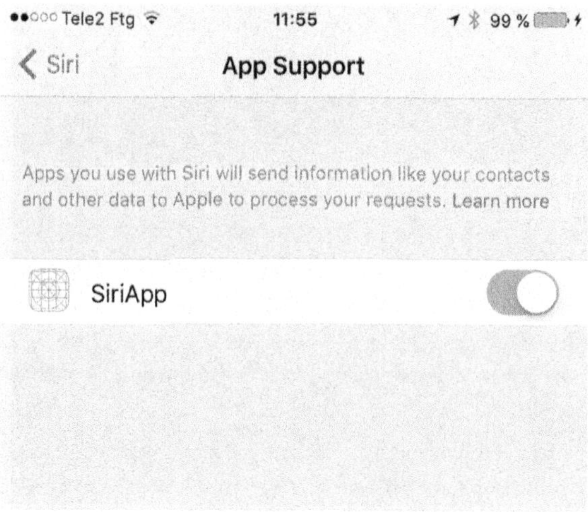

Figure 3-12. Allow Siri to access the app and integrate itself into it

Now if you go back to Siri and repeat this request, your extension will be run. However, it will time out after a while, because we didn't really implement any of the
required callbacks in our shiny new `SendPaymentHandler` class. You will learn how to
do that in the upcoming recipes.

See Also

Recipe 3.1

3.3 Resolving Ambiguity in an Intent

Problem

Your intent delegate finds multiple entities that match what Siri asked you to operate
on. For example, multiple people might match the name to which the user wants to
send a payment, multiple activities might match the one the user asked to be paused,
and so on.

> This recipe builds on what we discussed in Recipe 3.2, so it is
> essential that you read and run that recipe first before proceeding
> with this one.

Solution

Use the ambiguity APIs that are provided in every *X*Handling protocol, where *X* is the intent that you are working with. If you are working with sending payments from within your intents, you have to create a subclass of INSendPaymentIntent and then implement the delegate methods in INSendPaymentIntentHandling. One of these methods is resolvePayee(for:with:), which gives you the payee who Siri believes to be the user specified along with a completion handler that you can call. The completion handler contains a value of type INPersonResolutionResult that specifies whether:

- The given payee resolves unambiguously to a payee that your app recognizes. This is a success.
- The given payee doesn't resolve to any payees that your app can recognize. This is a failure.
- The given payee resolves to more than one recognized payee in your app. This is an ambiguity.

Discussion

Let's examine a case where the user says, "Send 15 dollars to Anthony" but has two contacts named Anthony:

- Anthony Foo
- Anthony Bar

People that the user can pay should be of type INPerson, so let's define these two people in our app by creating a function that can create an instance of this class, accepting a first name, last name, and other pertinent information, including the telephone number (which is necessary for payment processing purposes):

```
import UIKit
import Intents

class SendPaymentHandler: INSendPaymentIntent, INSendPaymentIntentHandling {

    private func person(givenName: String,
                        lastName: String,
                        imageName: String,
                        telephone: String) -> INPerson{

        let personHandle = INPersonHandle(value: telephone, type: .phoneNumber)
        var nameComponents = PersonNameComponents()
        nameComponents.givenName = givenName
        nameComponents.familyName = lastName
        let displayName = "\(givenName) (\(lastName))"
        let image = INImage(named: imageName)
```

```
      return INPerson(personHandle: personHandle,
                  nameComponents: nameComponents,
                  displayName: displayName,
                  image: image,
                  contactIdentifier: nil, customIdentifier: nil)

}

  ...
```

We can then proceed to create these two person instances and designate one of them as the default person to whom all payments are made:

```
private var anthonyFoo: INPerson{
  return person(givenName: "Anthony",
              lastName: "Foo",
              imageName: "Alert",
              telephone: "111-222-333")
}

private var anthonyBar: INPerson{
  return person(givenName: "Anthony",
              lastName: "Bar",
              imageName: "Burning",
              telephone: "444-555-666")
}

var persons: [INPerson]{
  return [anthonyFoo, anthonyBar]
}

var defaultPerson: INPerson{
  return anthonyFoo
}
```

Then we need to start implementing the resolvePayee(for:with:) function of our payment delegate. In here, we first look at the payee that Siri has interpreted as the intended recipient of the payment, and then attempt to find this payee in the list of people that our app supports sending money to. If we find such a person, we proceed. If we find more than one person with the given name, we ask Siri to resolve the problem. Siri does this by running a procedure called a *disambiguation*. Siri shows the user a dialog containing all the possible payees, prompts the user to choose the intended recipient of the payment, and then calls a completion handler to carry out the operation.

Finally, if we don't find any person with the given name, we provide the default person that we defined just a few seconds ago and ask the user to confirm whether she wants to send the payment to this user:

```
func resolvePayee(
  for intent: INSendPaymentIntent,
```

```
with completion: @escaping (INPersonResolutionResult) -> Void) {

guard let payee = intent.payee else {

  let result = INPersonResolutionResult
    .confirmationRequired(with: defaultPerson)

  completion(result)

  return
}

//do we have a person with the given display name already?
if let foundPerson =
  persons.filter({$0.displayName == payee.displayName}).first{
  //we found a person, we can confirm that this person exists and can
  //be used
  let result = INPersonResolutionResult.success(with: foundPerson)
  completion(result)
  return
}

var foundPersons = [INPerson]()
for person in persons{
  if person.nameComponents?.givenName?.lowercased() ==
    payee.nameComponents?.givenName?.lowercased(){
    foundPersons.append(person)
  }
}

let result: INPersonResolutionResult
switch foundPersons.count{
case 0:
  //we found nobody that matches the required user
  result = .confirmationRequired(with: defaultPerson)
case 1:
  //we did find the user
  result = INPersonResolutionResult.success(with: foundPersons[0])
default:
  //we found more than 1 user
  result = INPersonResolutionResult.disambiguation(with: foundPersons)
}

  completion(result)

}
```

When we have more than one match, we trigger Siri's disambiguation, passing as an argument the list of matches we created.

When sending payments we have to also code the `resolveCurrencyAmount` (`for:with:`) function of `INSendPaymentIntentHandling`. In there we will be given the amount of money that the person is trying to send and the currency in which she is sending it. Then we can provide a resolution of type INCurrency AmountResolutionResult, where we can either:

- Confirm that the amount and the currency are supported.
- Say that the amount and/or currency has multiple matches and requires a disambiguation.
- Ask the user to confirm whether a change that we made to the given amount or currency is acceptable. This option is helpful in cases where the user specifies a currency that is not supported by our app or requests sending an amount above the maximum allowed. For example, if the user asks to send a friend $500 (which is above our app's $20 limit), the app would change the amount to $20 and ask the user to confirm that this is acceptable.

So, let's define the list of currencies that we support:

```
enum SupportedCurrencies : String{
  case USD
  case SEK
  case GBP

  static func allValues() -> [String]{
    let allValues: [SupportedCurrencies] = [.USD, .SEK, .GBP]
    return allValues.map{$0.rawValue}
  }

  static var defaultCurrency = SupportedCurrencies.USD

}
```

And then define our minimum and maximum payment values:

```
func resolveCurrencyAmount(
  for intent: INSendPaymentIntent,
  with completion: @escaping (INCurrencyAmountResolutionResult) -> Void) {

  let minimumPayment = 5.0
  let maximumPayment = 20.0
  let defaultCurrencyAmount = INCurrencyAmount(amount: 15,
                                               currencyCode: "USD")

  ...
```

When the user makes a request to send money, we can then check whether she has specified a valid currency value and amount. If not, we will provide our default currency and amount and ask the user to confirm them:

```
guard let givenCurrency = intent.currencyAmount,
  let currencyCode = givenCurrency.currencyCode,
  let currencyAmount = givenCurrency.amount else {
  let result = INCurrencyAmountResolutionResult
```

```
    .confirmationRequired(with: defaultCurrencyAmount)
  completion(result)
  return
}
```

We then look for the given currency code in the array of our supported currencies:

```
let currencyAmountDoubleValue = currencyAmount.doubleValue

// do we support this currency code?
let foundCurrencies = SupportedCurrencies.allValues()
  .filter{$0 == currencyCode}
let foundCurrencyCount = foundCurrencies.count
```

Depending on whether we could find this currency code, we decide how to call the completion handler:

```
let result: INCurrencyAmountResolutionResult

switch foundCurrencyCount{

case 0:
  result = INCurrencyAmountResolutionResult
    .confirmationRequired(with: defaultCurrencyAmount)

case 1 where currencyAmountDoubleValue >= minimumPayment &&
  currencyAmountDoubleValue <= maximumPayment:
  result = .success(with: givenCurrency)

case 1:
  // the amount is not acceptable, ask for confirmation
  let amount: NSDecimalNumber = 20
  let newAmount = INCurrencyAmount(amount: amount,
                                   currencyCode: currencyCode)
  result = .confirmationRequired(with: newAmount)

default:
  // the currency code gave more than one result

  var amounts = [INCurrencyAmount]()
  for foundCurrency in foundCurrencies{
    let amount = INCurrencyAmount(amount: currencyAmount,
                                  currencyCode: foundCurrency)
    amounts.append(amount)
  }

  result = .disambiguation(with: amounts)
}

completion(result)
```

We also have to handle the resolveNote(for:with) method of INSendPayment IntentHandling. This lets the user who is making the payment attach a note of type

String to be sent alongside the payment to the recipient. Here we also have the chance to either accept that note or resolve any ambiguity in it. In this example, we simply override any given note with a constant string for the sake of simplicity, but you get the idea!

```
func resolveNote(
  for intent: INSendPaymentIntent,
  with completion: @escaping (INStringResolutionResult) -> Void) {


    completion(.success(with: "This is your payment"))

}
```

So now if the user asks Siri to "Send 15 dollars to Anthony," she will first see the dialog shown in Figure 3-13, asking for confirmation of whether she would like to use SiriApp.

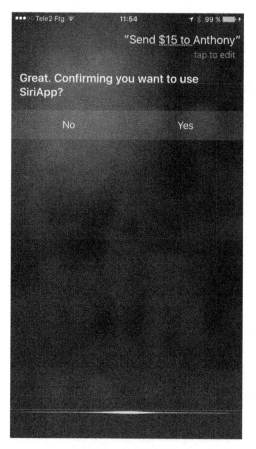

Figure 3-13. Siri confirming which app should be used to make the payment

After the user confirms that she would like to use SiriApp, Siri will ask the user to clarify the intended recipient, since there are two instances of Anthony in our app (Figure 3-14).

Figure 3-14. Resolving ambiguity in the recipient of the payment

Then we will resolve the payment amount. Because $15 is in our acceptable range, Siri will proceed to call our delegate's `confirm(sendPayment:completion:)` method, which we have not yet implemented.

See Also

Recipe 3.1

3.4 Reporting Progress for Resolving an Intent

Problem

You need some time to handle a Siri intent and you want to be able to report progress to the user.

 This recipe builds on what you learned in Recipe 3.3, so I strongly suggest reading that recipe before continuing further.

Solution

Implement the `confirm(_:completion:)` method of your *X*Handling protocol, where *X* is the name of the intent you are handling, such as `INSendPaymentIntentHandling`.

Discussion

In this recipe, we will implement confirmation in `INSendPaymentIntentHandling`. The `confirm(intent:completion:)` method requires you to call the given completion handler with a parameter of type `INSendPaymentIntentResponse`. The initializer for this response is:

```
init(code: INSendPaymentIntentResponseCode, userActivity: NSUserActivity?)
```

The response code of `INSendPaymentIntentResponseCode` is the most important thing to note here, because this is the response code that you can change and send back every now and then, as you progress through the payment, to the user. Some of the values in `INSendPaymentIntentResponseCode` are:

`ready`
> We are ready to begin making the payment. No other transfers are in progress right now.

`inProgress`
> We are confirming that the payment can in fact be made.

`success`
> We successfully made the payment.

`failure`
> We could not confirm that making the payment was possible.

Keep in mind that we will not do the actual work of processing the payment in this method. Instead, we will determine whether the payment is possible—for instance, by checking that the user has sufficient funds in her bank account. Once this is confirmed, we will have to do the actual work of processing the payment (you will see how this is done in Recipe 3.5).

Let's have a look at an example. In our `confirm(intent:completion:)` method, the `completion` parameter accepts a block object that has one parameter of type `INSend PaymentIntentResponse`, which we need to call when we confirm whether the payment can be made. The `INSendPaymentIntentResponse` class instance can be instantiated with a parameter of type `INSendPaymentIntentResponseCode`, so in our method we can create a local function that can easily report these codes directly to the completion handler without us having to create an instance of `INSendPayment IntentResponse` every time:

```
func confirm(intent: INSendPaymentIntent,
             completion: @escaping (INSendPaymentIntentResponse) -> Void) {

  func report(code: INSendPaymentIntentResponseCode){
    completion(INSendPaymentIntentResponse(code: code, userActivity: nil))
  }

  ...
```

When we begin to confirm whether the payment is possible, we report the code `.ready` so that Siri knows we have begun. Then we confirm that the given payment information is bundled within the intent—otherwise, we report `.failure`:

```
report(code: .ready)

guard let amount = intent.currencyAmount?.amount?.doubleValue else {
  report(code: .failure)
  return
}
```

Right after that, we confirm whether the payment value is within the allowed range. If it's less than the minimum we report `.failurePaymentsAmountBelowMinimum`, and if it's more than the maximum we report `.failurePaymentsAmountAboveMaximum`:

```
let minimumPayment = 5.0
let maximumPayment = 20.0

if amount < minimumPayment{
  report(code: .failurePaymentsAmountBelowMinimum)
  return
}

if amount > maximumPayment{
  report(code: .failurePaymentsAmountAboveMaximum)
  return
}
```

After we have confirmed the amount, we can signal that we have started the work of checking the user's bank account for sufficient funds (and any other checks that we want to do) by reporting the `.inProgress` code. Once all the checks are completed, we report either `.failure` or `.success`:

```
// do the actual work here
report(code: .inProgress)

// when done, signal that you have either successfully finished
// or failed
report(code: .success) // or .failure
```

See Also

Recipes 3.1 and 3.2

3.5 Handling an Intent

Problem

You have resolved all ambiguities regarding a Siri intent that you are handling and have also confirmed that the intent can in fact go through successfully. Now you have to actually see the process through and handle the intent.

Solution

Implement the `handle(_:completion:)` method of your *X*Handling protocol, where *X* is the name of the intent you are handling, such as INSendPaymentIntentHandling.

Discussion

In the case of INSendPaymentIntentHandling, the method that you need to program is called `handle(intent:completion:)` and the completion block requires you to send a parameter of type INSendPaymentIntentResponse, which we already discussed in Recipe 3.4.

To ensure that Siri can show the user a consistent flow of progress updates while the intent is being handled by your extension, Apple recommends that the methods `handle(intent:completion:)` and `confirm(intent:completion:)` report almost identical, if not exactly identical, INSendPaymentIntentResponseCode codes, so that Siri can show the user a consistent flow of progress updates while the intent is being handled by your extension. For instance, if during the confirmation stage you go through the codes of `.ready`, `.inProgress`, and then `.success` or `.failure`, you should do the same in the handling stage. The only difference is that when you handle the payment, you won't have to look again at the conditions, such as the amount of money being transferred, that you have already checked during the confirmation stage. So, your handling stage will hopefully be less complicated.

Let's now have a look at an example based on what we learned in Recipe 3.4. We define have a local function that can report our codes to the completion handler:

```
func handle(intent: INSendPaymentIntent,
            completion: @escaping (INSendPaymentIntentResponse) -> Void) {

  func report(code: INSendPaymentIntentResponseCode){
    completion(INSendPaymentIntentResponse(code: code, userActivity: nil))
  }

  ...
```

Then we extract the amount that has to be transferred and ensure that it is present:

```
report(code: .ready)

guard let amount = intent.currencyAmount?.amount?.doubleValue else {
  report(code: .failure)
  return
}
```

Last but not least, we make the payment and then report either `.success` or `.failure` to the user:

```
// here you don't have to check the amount again, as we have done that
// already in confirm(sendPayment:completion:)

// send the payment and then report success or failure
report(code: .success)
```

See Also

Recipe 3.4

CHAPTER 4

Measurements and Units

We've all been there! You need to convert one unit to another, and you begin your journey, most of the time, by Googling what the conversion should be. You can now use some built-in structures to represent and convert your units.

The following classes and structures appear throughout this chapter:

Unit
> The base class for all the units that are in the SDK itself. This class defines a symbol for the unit, such as m for meters.

Dimension
> The class that inherits from Unit and defines the converter to be used between various units.

UnitLength, UnitMass, *and the like*
> Basic units that inherit from Dimension. Each unit offers alternative ways of representing a particular measure, such as length or mass. Each unit also standardizes the various symbols for its measure, such as m for meters, km for kilometers, and smi for Scandinavian miles (with each Scandinavian mile being equal to 10 kilometers).

Measurement
> The base structure for defining a value with a unit. Every measurement has a value of type Double and a unit of type Unit.

4.1 Converting Between and Working with Length Units

Problem

You want to be able to represent values with the unit of length, such as kilometers and miles, and would like to be able to perform some basic tasks on them, such as converting one unit to another, or adding and subtracting values represented in different units.

Solution

Follow these steps:

1. Represent your values first by constructing instances of Measurement with your given value. Use one of the units defined in UnitLength as the unit for your measurement, such as UnitLength.meters.
2. After you have your Measurement instances, you can use the various operators such as + and - between them as long as they are from the same base unit.
3. You can also use the converted(to:) function of your Measurement structure instances to convert your values to another unit type of the same base unit. For instance, converting meters to miles is fine, as they are both from the UnitLength base unit, but converting kilometers to hours is not going to work because hours are represented by the UnitDuration unit.

Discussion

Your values are representable by instances of the Measurement structure with a given unit. Let's create two values, one for 5 meters and the other for 1 kilometer:

```
let meters = Measurement(value: 5, unit: UnitLength.meters) // 5.0 m
let kilometers = Measurement(value: 1, unit: UnitLength.kilometers) // 1.0 km
```

You can then check out the return value of type(of:) on these values to see what data type they have:

```
type(of: meters) // Measurement<UnitLength>
type(of: kilometers) // Measurement<UnitLength>
```

Their data type is Measurement, which itself is generic, and its generic parameter is set to UnitLength since both values are lengths.

You can then simply add these values together if you want:

```
let result = meters + kilometers // 1005.0 m
type(of: result) // Measurement<UnitLength>
```

This + operator is defined in the Foundation framework as follows:

```
public func +<UnitType : Dimension>(lhs: Measurement<UnitType>,
          rhs: Measurement<UnitType>) -> Measurement<UnitType>
```

Eventually, you can convert the result into various other units of length, such as miles:

```
let finalKilometers = result.converted(to: .kilometers) // 1.005 km
let finalMeters = result.converted(to: .meters) // 1005.0 m
let finalMiles = result.converted(to: .miles) // 0.6224 mi
let finalScandinavianMiles = result.converted(to: .scandinavianMiles)
                                                  // 0.1005 smi
```

If you wish to present these values to the user, which are of type `Measurement<Unit>`, read the `value` and the `unit.symbol` properties from them. The `value` will be of type `Double` and the `unit.symbol` of type `String`. This gives you the information you need to display values on UI components, such as a `UILabel` instance.

See Also

Recipe 4.2

4.2 Working with and Switching Between Angle Units

Problem

You want to use, convert, represent, and display angles in your applications without having to convert them manually.

Solution

Just like length units (see Recipe 4.1), values that represent an angle can also be encapsulated inside an instance of the `Measurement` structure. The unit is `UnitAngle`.

Discussion

Let's have a look at how you can represent 100 gradians in your application:

```
let gradians = Measurement(value: 100, unit: UnitAngle.gradians) // 100.0 grad
```

You can then convert this value to degrees using the `convert(to:)` function of the `Measurement` structure:

```
gradians.converted(to: UnitAngle.degrees) // 90 degrees
```

And if you read the return value of `type(of:)` on this value, you will get the value of `Measurement<UnitAngle>`:

```
type(of: gradians) // Measurement<UnitAngle>
```

Similarly, you can represent degrees with the `Measurement` structure:

```
let degrees = Measurement(value: 180, unit: UnitAngle.degrees) // 180.0
```

And just like the + operator we saw used before with `Measurement` types, you also have a - operator that is defined like so:

```
public func -<UnitType : Dimension>(lhs: Measurement<UnitType>,
rhs: Measurement<UnitType>) -> Measurement<UnitType>
```

You can use this operator between any two instances of the `Measurement` structure as long as their base units are the same:

```
let total = gradians - degrees // -90 degrees
```

Once you have your angle measurements, you can convert them to each other:

```
let finalGradians = total.converted(to: .gradians) // -100 grad
let finalDegrees = total.converted(to: UnitAngle.degrees) // -90 degrees
```

Additionally, you can show this value to your users with the `value: Double` and `unit.symbol: String` properties of your `Measurement` instance:

```
let string = "\(finalDegrees.value) \(finalDegrees.unit.symbol)"
                          // "-90 degrees"
```

See Also

Recipe 4.1

4.3 Representing and Converting Between Durations of Time

Problem

You want to represent units of time with their values and the type of unit they represent, such as hours or seconds, but you don't want to fuss with counting in bunches of 60 to calculate conversions between units.

Solution

To solve this problem, instantiate the `Measurement` structure with your time values and use the `UnitDuration` for your base unit. You can then use +, -, and other basic operators between your units without worrying about what unit they are represented with, as long as they come from the `UnitDuration` base unit.

Discussion

Let's have a look at an example of how we can convert hours, minutes, and seconds to one another, but let's spice it up a little bit. It's clear that we can use `Measurement` to represent all three values with `UnitDuration`, but we can instead extend `Double` so that any number can then be turned into an hour, minute, or second value represented by `Measurement`:

```
extension Double{
  var hours: Measurement<UnitDuration>{
    return Measurement(value: self, unit: UnitDuration.hours)
  }
  var minutes: Measurement<UnitDuration>{
    return Measurement(value: self, unit: UnitDuration.minutes)
  }
  var seconds: Measurement<UnitDuration>{
    return Measurement(value: self, unit: UnitDuration.seconds)
  }
}
```

Now that this is done, we can put together a few values using these properties:

```
let trainJourneyDuration = (1.25).hours
trainJourneyDuration.converted(to: .minutes) // 75.0 min

let planeJourneyDuration = (320.0).minutes
planeJourneyDuration.converted(to: .hours) // 5.333 hr

let boatJourneyDuration = (1500.0).seconds
boatJourneyDuration.converted(to: .minutes) // 25.0 min
```

These values each represent a sub-journey of a bigger journey from one destination to another and they are in minutes, hours, and seconds. We can put them all together inside an array and calculate their total value in minutes, using each `Measurement` instance's `convert(to:)` method:

```
let journeys = [
  trainJourneyDuration,
  planeJourneyDuration,
]

let finalJourneyDurationInMinutes = journeys.reduce(0.0){
  return $0 + $1.converted(to: UnitDuration.minutes).value
}

finalJourneyDurationInMinutes // 395
```

Representing time with `Measurement` makes it much easier to work with existing classes such as `Timer`. For instance, if you want a timer that runs for *n* seconds, all you have to do is create a `Measurement` instance of type `UnitDuration.seconds` and then, once the measurement's `value` property is less than or equal to 0, you can invalidate the timer:

```
import UIKit
import PlaygroundSupport

PlaygroundPage.current.needsIndefiniteExecution = true

extension Double{
  var seconds: Measurement<UnitDuration>{
```

```
      return Measurement(value: self, unit: UnitDuration.seconds)
  }
}

var remainingTime = Measurement(value: 10, unit: UnitDuration.seconds)
Timer.scheduledTimer(withTimeInterval: 1.0, repeats: true) {timer in
  let minutesRemaining = remainingTime.converted(to: UnitDuration.minutes)
  print("\(minutesRemaining.value) minutes remaining before the timer stops")
  remainingTime = remainingTime - (1.0).seconds
  if remainingTime.value <= 0.0{
    timer.invalidate()
  }
}
```

 The `PlaygroundSupport` framework is used alongside the `Play` ground `Page.current.needsIndefiniteExecution:` `Bool` property, which you can set to `true` if you need an infinite loop in your playground so that your playground doesn't just start at one point and end at another. In contrast with the default behavior of playgrounds, starting at the top and ending after the execution of the last line of code in the playground, yours becomes a fully fledged application that lives until you ask it to stop.

See Also

Recipes 4.1 and 4.4

4.4 Using and Working with Frequency Units

Problem

You want to use and convert between frequency units, such as megahertz and gigahertz.

Solution

Represent your values with the `Measurement` structure and use `UnitFrequency` as the base unit. The `UnitFrequency` class has various class variables such as:

- terahertz
- gigahertz
- megahertz
- kilohertz

Discussion

If you build computers in your spare time (as I used to do more frequently, before I had three children!), you'll see keywords such as megahertz and gigahertz all over the place. It's a great idea to represent all these values with some structure in Swift, and with `Measurement` now you can do that by choosing `UnitFrequency` as your base unit.

Here is an example of representing two CPU clock speeds in Swift, using gigahertz and then megahertz:

```
var myCpuClock = Measurement(value: 3.5, unit: UnitFrequency.gigahertz)
var yourCpuClock = Measurement(value: 3400, unit: UnitFrequency.megahertz)
```

You can then use the built-in > and < operators to see which values are bigger or smaller:

```
if myCpuClock > yourCpuClock{
  "My CPU is faster than yours."
} else if yourCpuClock > myCpuClock{
  "Your CPU is faster than mine. Good for you!"
} else {
  "It seems our CPU clocks are the same!"
}
```

These two operators are defined for you already in the Foundation framework so that you don't have to write them yourself:

```
public func ><UnitType : Dimension>(lhs: Measurement<UnitType>,
    rhs: Measurement<UnitType>) -> Bool

public func <<UnitType : Dimension>(lhs: Measurement<UnitType>,
    rhs: Measurement<UnitType>) -> Bool
```

Now that you have two CPUs whose clock speeds are represented in various forms of the frequency unit, you can put them inside an array and iterate through this array to get their clock speeds shown in gigahertz:

```
let baseUnit = UnitFrequency.gigahertz
[myCpuClock, yourCpuClock].enumerated().forEach{offset, cpuClock in
  let converted = cpuClock.converted(to: baseUnit)
  print("CPU #\(offset + 1) is \(converted.value) \(converted.unit.symbol)")
}
```

And the output will be as shown here:

```
CPU #1 is 3.5 GHz
CPU #2 is 3.4 GHz
```

See Also

Recipe 4.1

4.5 Working with and Using Power Units

Problem

You want to be able to convert between and use power units, but you don't want to lift a finger and do any of the work manually yourself.

Solution

Simply use `Measurement` to represent your power units with the unit equal to `Unit Power` and then use the `convert(to:)` function of the `Measurement` structure to convert your values to other power units, some of which are listed here:

- `terawatts`
- `gigawatts`
- `megawatts`
- `kilowatts`
- `watts`
- `horsepower`

Discussion

Let's check out an example. Let's say that you are riding a bicycle and moving forward by putting 160 watts of energy into the pedals. Now, a super-duper cyclist that has won three Tour de France tournaments has a pedaling power of 0.40 horsepower. Are you putting more power into the pedals than this super cyclist, or the other way around? How can you find the answer without having to convert one of these values to the other or both values to another base unit?

Well, the answer is quite easy. Simply represent these values with `Measurement`:

```
let myCyclingPower = Measurement(value: 160, unit: UnitPower.watts)
let superCyclistPower = Measurement(value: 0.40, unit: UnitPower.horsepower)
```

And then use the > and < operators that are already defined for you to find out which value is larger:

```
if myCyclingPower > superCyclistPower{
  "Wow, I am really strong."
} else if myCyclingPower < superCyclistPower{
  "The super cyclist is of course stronger than I am."
} else {
```

```
    "It seems I am as strong as the super cyclist!"
}
```

But how does iOS do this, and how does it know how to compare these values? The answer is simple: base units. If you Command-click `UnitPower` in Xcode, you will see some code like this:

```
@available(iOS 10.0, *)
public class UnitPower : Dimension, NSSecureCoding {

    /*
    Base unit - watts
    */
```

There you can see that the base unit is watts. iOS converts all your power units to watts and then compares their `value` properties to find which one is higher.

See Also

Recipes 4.6 and 4.7

4.6 Representing and Comparing Temperature Units

Problem

You want to convert between and work with temperature units, such as Celsius and Fahrenheit, without having to do any manual work.

Solution

To avoid having to convert different temperature units, encapsulate your temperature values inside an instance of the `Measurement` structure with the `UnitTemperature` unit type. Then you can use the `convert(to:)` method of the `Measurement` structure to convert different types to each other and also use the existing greater-than, less-than, and other operators to manipulate or compare these measurements.

Discussion

Let's have a look at an example. Say that we have three temperatures of types Celsius, Fahrenheit, and Kelvin and our goal is to convert them all to Celsius and then sort them in ascending order. Let's first represent our temperatures:

```
let cakeTemperature = Measurement(value: 180, unit: UnitTemperature.celsius)
let potatoesTemperature = Measurement(value: 200, unit:
                        UnitTemperature.fahrenheit)
let beefTemperature = Measurement(value: 459, unit: UnitTemperature.kelvin)
```

Next we can sort them by their Celsius values in an ascending order:

```
let sorted = [cakeTemperature, potatoesTemperature, beefTemperature]
  .sorted { (first, second) -> Bool in
    return first.converted(to: .celsius) < second.converted(to: .celsius)
}
```

When we have a sorted array, we can convert all the values to Celsius to get our final
sorted array of Celsius temperatures:

```
let allCelsiusTemperatures = sorted.map{
  $0.converted(to: .celsius)
}

allCelsiusTemperatures // 93.33, 180, 185.8
```

See Also

Recipe 4.5

4.7 Working with and Converting Volume Units

Problem

You need to work with values represented as volumes such as liters and pints, but you
don't want to manually do the work of comparing and converting them.

Solution

Encapsulate your values inside instances of the Measurement structure with the unit
type UnitVolume.

Discussion

Imagine that you are baking a cake and three of the ingredients that you need are represented in different units, namely liters, deciliters, and pints:

```
let milk = Measurement(value: 2, unit: UnitVolume.liters)
let cream = Measurement(value: 3, unit: UnitVolume.deciliters)
let water = Measurement(value: 1, unit: UnitVolume.pints)
```

You can add all these values together with the + operator and convert the total to various other volumes, such as cups:

```
let total = milk + cream + water
let totalDeciliters = total.converted(to: .teaspoons)
let totalLiters = total.converted(to: .tablespoons)
let totalPints = total.converted(to: .cups)
```

You can also go through all the values and print their details, such as their raw values
and the symbols that represent their units:

```
func showInfo(for measurement: Measurement<UnitVolume>){
  let value = measurement.value
  let symbol = measurement.unit.symbol
  print("\(value) \(symbol)")
}
```

```
[totalDeciliters, totalLiters, totalPints].forEach{showInfo(for: $0)}
```

The output printed to the console will be similar to this:

```
562.633599246894 tsp
187.544025752698 tbsp
11.5549 cup
```

See Also

Recipe 4.2

CHAPTER 5

Core Data

Every application needs to store information, whether during the course of a single session or permanently. To aid in the difficult task of managing and searching stored data, Apple has developed a whole framework called Core Data, which you might already be familiar with. In iOS 11 SDK, Core Data, especially in Swift, has been changed a little bit, so in this chapter we will have a look at these changes as well as some basics of accessing Core Data.

Before we go further, ensure that you have added the necessary Core Data code to your application. When you create your project file, make sure to tell Xcode to import Core Data into your application. You do this when you enter your product's name in Xcode's new project dialog, as shown in Figure 5-1. Core Data is one of the three features you can choose at the bottom of the dialog.

Choose options for your new project:

Product Name:	
Team:	Vandad Nahavandipoor
Organization Name:	Pixolity
Organization Identifier:	se.pixolity
Bundle Identifier:	se.pixolity.ProductName
Language:	Swift
Devices:	Universal

☑ Use Core Data
☑ Include Unit Tests
☑ Include UI Tests

Cancel   Previous   Next

Figure 5-1. At the bottom of this dialog, you can ask Xcode to add Core Data to your project

5.1 Designing Your Database Scheme

Problem

You want to begin storing data in Core Data.

Solution

The idea behind Core Data is that your data is organized and stored in the database through what are known as *schemes*. Schemes tell Core Data how your data is structured, and can be designed through a visual editor that's part of Xcode.

 Ensure that you have added Core Data to your project by following the instructions given in this chapter's introduction.

Discussion

When you create a project with Core Data enabled, you should be see a file with the *.xcdatamodel* extension in your project. If you cannot find this file, press Cmd-Shift-O in Xcode and then type in **xcdatamodel**. Once you find the file, press the Enter key on your keyboard to open it (Figure 5-2).

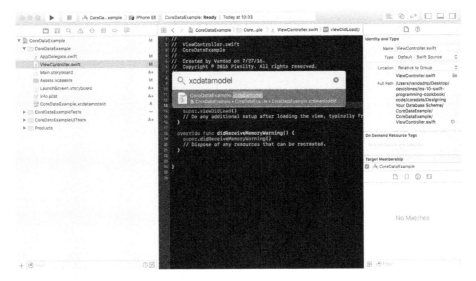

Figure 5-2. Locating the Core Data model file

Figure 5-2 shows the visual editor for your Core Data scheme file, where you can create entities. An *entity* is similar to a table in a database, where you can define the columns and their data types. Let's create a Car entity that has a maker and a model name of type String:

1. In the visual editor of your scheme, press the Add Entity button at the bottom of the screen. This will create a new entity for you called Entity. From the Data Model inspector on the righthand side of Xcode, change this name from Entity to Car (Figure 5-3). The Data Model inspector allows you to change many aspects of your entities and their columns.

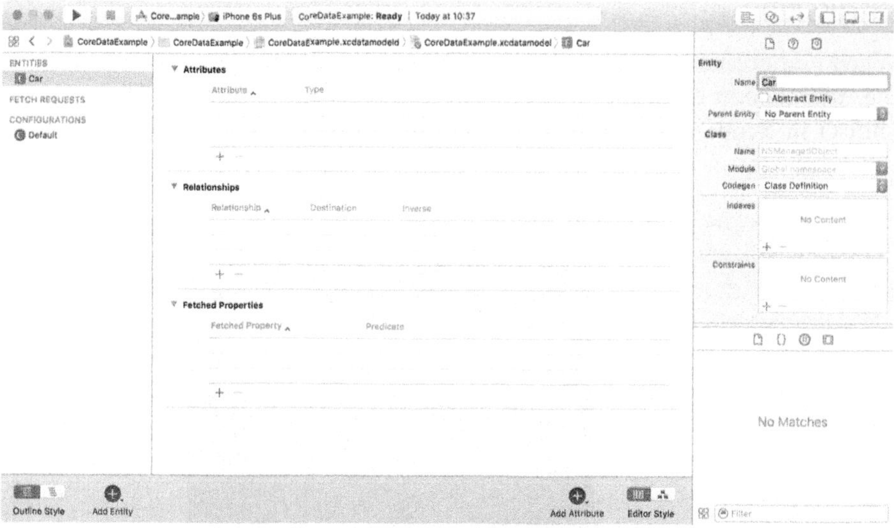

Figure 5-3. Setting the name of your entity on the right side of the screen

2. Under the Attributes section of the editor (at the top), press the little + button to create a new attribute. Name this new attribute maker, and change its type to String. Also, in the Data Model inspector on the right side, uncheck the Optional box so that the maker of the car becomes a mandatory attribute (Figure 5-4).

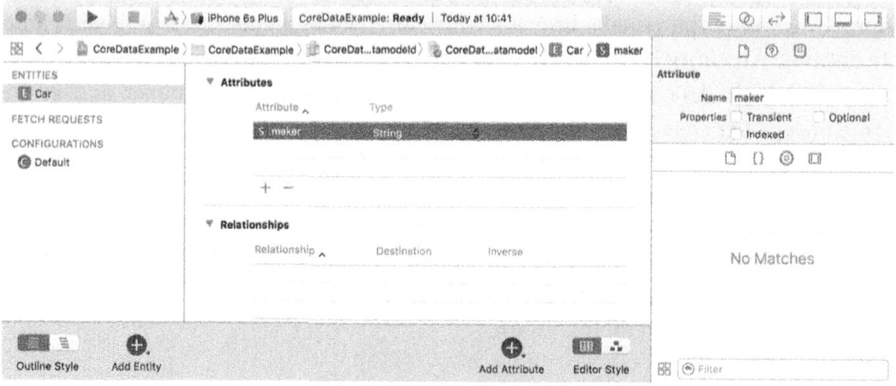

Figure 5-4. The car has a new mandatory attribute called maker of type String

3. Do the same thing that you did with the maker attribute and create another mandatory attribute of type String, called model (Figure 5-5).

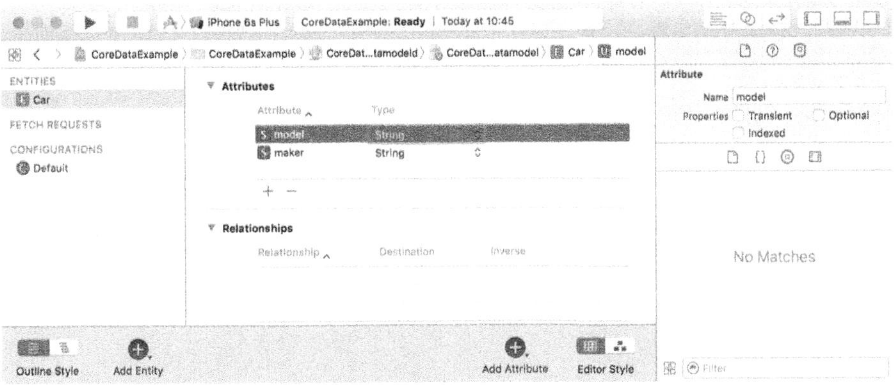

Figure 5-5. Now the car has a maker and a model

4. Create another entity now. Call it `Person`, and add two new mandatory attributes of type `String` called `firstName` and `lastName` (Figure 5-6).

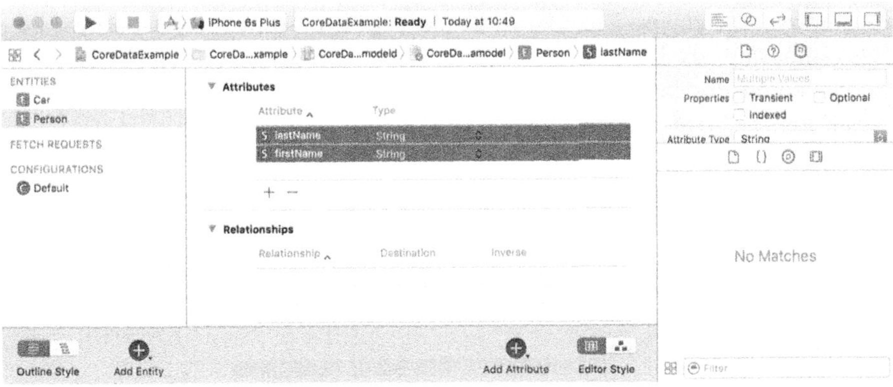

Figure 5-6. The Person entity has two mandatory fields

5. In real life, a person can have multiple cars, although a car generally has one owner. This ownership status can be defined as a relationship between the two entities. Start by opening the `Car` entity. Under the Relationships section of the editor, press the + button and name the new relationship `owner`, with the destination of `Person` (Figure 5-7). Make the relationship mandatory by unchecking the Optional checkbox in the data model editor. Leave the Inverse section empty for now.

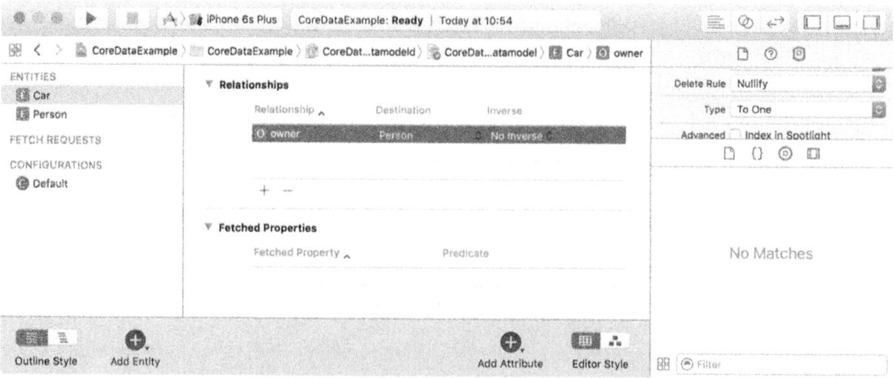

Figure 5-7. The Car entity now has an owner!

6. Open the `Person` entity and create a new optional relationship there. Name it `cars` and set the destination as the `Car` entity. Also set the Inverse field to the `owner` field of the `Car` entity. Then, in the data model editor, under the Relationship section, choose "To Many" in the Type drop-down to set the type of this relationship (see Figure 5-8). Because this relationship is optional, a person does not necessarily have to have cars. Because the relationship is "To Many," every person *can* have more than one car. On the other hand, because a car's `owner` relationship is mandatory, each car always has to have an owner, and only one owner at a time.

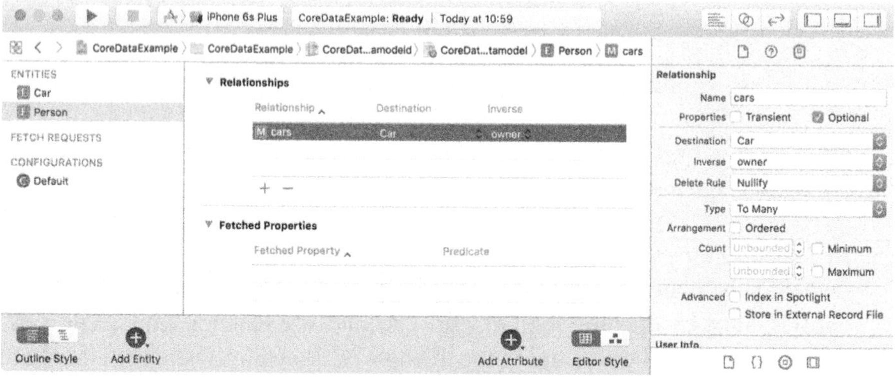

Figure 5-8. Every person can have more than one car

7. Last but not least, for the `Car` and `Person` entities, go to the Data Model inspector and enter **Car** and **Person**, respectively, into the Name text field under the Class section. Core Data creates a class in your project's automatically generated code to represent each entity in your scheme, assigning the class the name you pro-

vide. Each class also has one property for each attribute in the entity. For instance, the Car class has a maker property and a model property, each set to the value you store for it in the database.

After designing your entities and their relationships and attributes, you can go to your Swift code and import the Core Data module if it's not already imported. Then you can start instantiating your entities, as I'll explain in the next recipe.

5.2 Writing Data to the Database

Problem

You have created your model objects and would now like to insert instances of those models into your database for later retrieval.

This recipe is based on the data scheme that we designed in Recipe 5.1.

Solution

Follow these steps:

1. Your app delegate has your Core Data stack, so if you are in another class and would like to save your objects from there, you need to get a reference to your app delegate's context using the persistentContainer.viewContext: NSManagedObjectContext property like so:

```
var context: NSManagedObjectContext?{
  return (UIApplication.shared().delegate as? AppDelegate)?
    .persistentContainer.viewContext
}
```

2. You can insert an object into your database using the (context:) initializer that is coded for you automatically by Xcode. Pass a managed object context to this initializer to create your object on that context. Let's create an instance of our Person object now and set the person's firstName and lastName mandatory properties. If you attempt to save your data into the database without setting a value for all the object's mandatory properties, your app will crash by default:

```
let person = Person(context: context)
person.firstName = "Foo"
person.lastName = "Bar"
```

3. Now let's extend our Car class so that we can configure an instance of it with a simple method instead of having to set all the properties one by one:

```
extension Car{
  func configured(maker _maker: String,
                  model _model: String,
                  owner _owner: Person) -> Self {
    maker = _maker
    model = _model
    owner = _owner
    return self
  }
}
```

4. Then we can create two cars for the current person:

```
person.cars = NSSet(array: [
  Car(context: context).configured(maker: "VW",
                                   model: "Sharan",
                                   owner: person),
  Car(context: context).configured(maker: "VW",
                                   model: "Tiguan",
                                   owner: person)
])
```

5. Once you are done with that, you can save your data into the database by calling your app delegate's saveContext() function.

Discussion

By default, the saveContext() function crashes your application if something goes wrong. I prefer not to do that and instead to make this function throw an exception that I can catch later. So let's change this function's definition:

```
func saveContext() throws{
  let context = persistentContainer.viewContext
  if context.hasChanges {
    try context.save()
  }
}
```

Then, every time you call this function to save your data, ensure that you catch the possible exceptions that might occur:

```
do{
  try saveContext()
} catch {
  // something bad happened, handle this situation appropriately
}
```

5.3 Reading Data from the Database

Problem

You have saved some data to your Core Data database and would like to read it back.

 This recipe's database scheme is based on what was described in Recipe 5.1.

Solution

Follow these steps:

1. Call the fetchRequest() class method of your managed object (such as the Car object) to get an object of type NSFetchRequest<*T*>, where *T* is your class name (such as Car).
2. Once the fetch request is returned to you, configure it using some of the properties described here:

   fetchLimit: Int
   : The maximum number of instances of the current class to fetch as the result of the search.

   relationshipKeyPathsForPrefetching: [String]?
   : An array of strings that denote the relationships of the current object whose results must also be fetched. For instance, our Person object has an optional one-to-many cars relationship; if you want to find what cars this person owns (if any), as well as the identity of the person, insert the name of the cars relationship into this array.

   propertiesToFetch: [AnyObject]?
   : An array of the attribute names of the managed object whose values you want to prefetch. For instance, the firstName and the lastName properties of the Person object can be passed to this array to ensure that their values are prefetched for you.

3. Once your fetch request is ready, execute it on your managed object context using its fetch(_:) function.

Discussion

1. Let's have a look at an example. First ensure that you have completed the steps described in Recipe 5.2. Now you should be able to read the data you wrote to your database. Imagine that you want to read the instances of the `Person` entity, represented by a class of the same name. Let's put the code that writes these instances to the database into a function so that we can easily call it from another place:

```
func writeData() throws{

    let context = persistentContainer.viewContext

    let person = Person(context: context)
    person.firstName = "Foo"
    person.lastName = "Bar"

    person.cars = NSSet(array: [
      Car(context: context).configured(maker: "VW",
                                       model: "Sharan",
                                       owner: person),
      Car(context: context).configured(maker: "VW",
                                        model: "Tiguan",
                                        owner: person)

    ])

    try saveContext()

}
```

2. And then start by writing a function that can read only one `Person` object back from the database if one exists:

```
func readData() throws -> Person{
  // we are going to code this function now
}
```

3. In this function, assuming it is being written in your app delegate's class where you have access to your managed object context, construct a fetch request on your `Person` object like so:

```
let context = persistentContainer.viewContext
let personFetchRequest: NSFetchRequest<Person> = Person.fetchRequest()
```

4. Tell Core Data that you want to prefetch the `cars` relationship of the `Person` entity and that you want to fetch only one instance of the `Person` object:

```
personFetchRequest.fetchLimit = 1
personFetchRequest.relationshipKeyPathsForPrefetching = ["cars"]
```

5. Then call the `fetch(_:)` function of your managed object context to retrieve the results:

```
let persons = try context.fetch(personFetchRequest)
```

6. We are also going to check that we fetched only one `Person` instance from the database. Otherwise, we will throw a new exception, since our function is marked with `throws`:

```
guard let person = persons.first,
    persons.count == personFetchRequest.fetchLimit else {
    throw ReadDataExceptions.moreThanOnePersonCameBack
}
```

 `ReadDataExceptions` is an enumeration that we have defined ourselves like so:

```
enum ReadDataExceptions : Error{
    case moreThanOnePersonCameBack
}
```

7. Once you are done, return this new `person` object:

```
return person
```

Now that we have both the `writeData()` and `readData()` functions ready, we can call them in one place as shown here:

```
func writeData() throws{

  let context = persistentContainer.viewContext

  let person = Person(context: context)
  person.firstName = "Foo"
  person.lastName = "Bar"

  person.cars = NSSet(array: [
    Car(context: context).configured(maker: "VW",
                                     model: "Sharan",
                                     owner: person),
    Car(context: context).configured(maker: "VW",
                                     model: "Tiguan",
                                     owner: person)
  ])

  try saveContext()

}
```

And the results will be printed to the console like so:

```
Successfully read the person
Optional("Foo")
Optional("Bar")
Car #1
Optional("VW")
Optional("Tiguan")
Car #2
Optional("VW")
Optional("Sharan")
```

See Also

Recipes 5.1 and 5.2

5.4 Searching for Data in the Database

Problem

You want to search in your database for various entities or attributes and relationships.

Solution

Follow these steps:

1. Call the `fetchRequest()` function of your entity to create a fetch request.
2. Instantiate the `Predicate` class and create your search format.
3. Set this predicate as the `predicate` property of your fetch request.
4. Execute your fetch request using the `fetch(_:)` function of your managed object context.

Discussion

The `Predicate` class's `format` initializer parameter is very important. It defines your search and what you want to find in the database. Without overwhelming you with too much information, I will introduce the various searches that you can perform on your database by providing you with different examples.

 I assume that you have already gone through the earlier recipes in this chapter, especially Recipe 5.3, which covers how to read your data back from the database.

As the first example, let's write a function that can find any `Person` instance in the database with a given first and last name:

```
func personsWith(firstName fName: String,
                 lastName lName: String) throws -> [Person]?{

  let context = persistentContainer.viewContext
  let request: NSFetchRequest<Person> = Person.fetchRequest()

  request.predicate = NSPredicate(format: "firstName == %@ && lastName == %@",
                                  argumentArray: [fName, lName])

  return try context.fetch(request)

}
```

Here we are constructing a `Predicate` instance using its (`format:argumentArray:`) initializer. The format is a `String` and the argument array is of type `[AnyObject]?`. The format of the predicate is quite interesting, though, if you have a closer look. The `==` operator is being used to compare strings and `%@` is used as a placeholder for the given first and last name, which are placed in the arguments array. In addition, `&&` is used to ensure both the first and last name conditions have been satisfied by this search.

For our next example, let's write a function that can find all instances of the `Person` object in the database whose first name starts with a specific character:

```
func personsWith(firstNameFirstCharacter char: Character) throws -> [Person]?{

  let context = persistentContainer.viewContext
  let request: NSFetchRequest<Person> = Person.fetchRequest()

  request.predicate = NSPredicate(format: "firstName LIKE[c] %@",
                                  argumentArray: ["\(char)*"])

  return try context.fetch(request)

}
```

There are a few things to explain about this predicate:

The `LIKE` *syntax*
: This is a pattern matching syntax. If you want to look for any string whose first character is M followed by anything else, you can use `LIKE` with the value of `M*`.

The `[c]` *syntax*
: This tells Core Data to search case-insensitively in the database.

```
"\(char)*"
```
This takes the given character and makes it a pattern by appending an asterisk to its end.

In the next example, we want to find all instances of the `Person` object who have at least one car from a specific maker:

```
func personsWith(atLeastOneCarWithMaker maker: String) throws -> [Person]?{

let context = persistentContainer.viewContext
let request: NSFetchRequest<Person> = Person.fetchRequest()
request.relationshipKeyPathsForPrefetching = ["cars"]

request.predicate = NSPredicate(format: "ANY cars.maker ==[c] %@",
                                argumentArray: [maker])

  return try context.fetch(request)

}
```

These are the interesting statements in this predicate:

ANY

This is an aggregate operation that operates on collections. Other operations exist as well, such as `ALL`, `NONE`, and `IN`, whose names indicate what they do. In the case of `ANY`, it indicates that we are looking for a person who has at least one car with a given maker (`maker: String`).

cars.maker

This is a key path operation that allows us to perform our search on the `Person` entity but dig into its `cars` relationship and read the `maker` attribute's value.

==[c]

This makes sure the maker of the car is a given value, searched case-insensitively.

The preceding examples should give you a feel for the rich interface Core Data offers for search, and should help you find your way through the documentation for other options.

See Also

Recipe 5.1

5.5 Performing Background Tasks with Core Data

Problem

You want to perform some heavy operations on your Core Data stack, such as saving thousands of records at one go, and you don't want to slow down the UI thread by doing this.

Solution

Follow these steps:

1. First, get a reference to your app's persistent container, which should be of type `NSPersistentContainer`.
2. Call the `newBackgroundContext()` function on your container to get a new background context where you can do your background Core Data work. This should be of type `NSManagedObjectContext`.
3. Set the `automaticallyMergesChangesFromParent` property of your new context to `true`, so that the new objects from the view context will be automatically brought into yours. This lets you get the latest objects if any changes are made to the view context.
4. Call the `perform(_:)` function on your new background context and do your background work in the block that you pass to this function.
5. Once you are done, call the `save()` function on your background context.

 I'm basing this recipe's code on what you learned in Recipe 5.4.

Discussion

Background tasks are very important in Core Data programming. Without a doubt, they are one of those weapons that you must have in your arsenal before going wild with Core Data.

Let's write a function that allows us to save many `Person` instances in our database and, when done, call a completion handler on the main thread so the thread can pick up work on the new data. Here is the function's definition:

```
func writeManyPersonObjectsToDatabase(completion: @escaping () -> Void) throws{

  // we are going to code this function now
```

```
}
```

We are then going to create a new background context and make sure it merges changes automatically from the view context:

```
let context = persistentContainer.newBackgroundContext()
context.automaticallyMergesChangesFromParent = true
```

After this, we will write our `Person` instances into this new background context and then save it. Once that is done, we call the completion handler:

```
context.perform {
  let howMany = 999
  for index in 1...howMany{
    let person = Person(context: context)
    person.firstName = "First name \(index)"
    person.lastName = "First name \(index)"
  }
  do{
    try context.save()
    DispatchQueue.main.async{completion()}
  } catch {
    // catch the errors here
  }

}
```

To confirm that these objects were successfully saved to the coordinator and that they are present on the view context as well, we will write a function that can count the total number of `Person` object instances in the database, with the following definition:

```
func countOfPersonObjectsWritten() throws -> Int{

  // we will code this function now

}
```

In this function, we will create a new fetch request of type `NSFetchRequest<Person>`. But since we are interested in counting only the `Person` instances, we will not fetch the instances themselves, but instead set the `resultType: NSFetchRequestResult Type` property of the fetch request to `.countResultType`:

```
let request: NSFetchRequest<Person> = Person.fetchRequest()
request.resultType = .countResultType
let context = persistentContainer.viewContext
```

Because we set the `resultType: NSFetchRequestResultType` property of the fetch request to `.countResultType`, the result of the `execute(_:)` function of our context will be of type `NSAsynchronousFetchResult<NSNumber>`. One of the properties of `NSA synchronousFetchResult<NSNumber>` is `finalResult: [ResultType]?`. We'll read the first item in this optional array and ensure that it is an instance of Int. This Int instance will be the count of the items that were found in the database:

```
guard let result = (try context.execute(request)
  as? NSAsynchronousFetchResult<NSNumber>)?
  .finalResult?
  .first as? Int else {return 0}
```

```
return result
```

We can then put all of this together, write all our objects to the database, and get the count of those objects back and print it to the console:

```
do{
  try writeManyPersonObjectsToDatabase(completion: {[weak self] in
    guard let strongSelf = self else {return}
    do{
      let count = try strongSelf.countOfPersonObjectsWritten()
      print(count)
    } catch {
      print("Could not count the objects in the database")
    }

  })
} catch {
  print("Could not write the data")
}
```

See Also

Recipe 5.1

CHAPTER 6

Swift and Cocoa Touch

In this chapter we will have a look at what's new in Swift 4 and Cocoa Touch, such as the addition of built-in JSON parsing mechanisms. You'll see how you can utilize these new features to make your code even more robust and easier to read.

6.1 Extending Typed Arrays

Problem

You have some homogeneous arrays (containing objects of the same type) and you want to add a property or a function to arrays of that particular type, without affecting other arrays.

Solution

Create an extension on `Array` that applies only when the `Element` of that array is equal to your specific type. For instance, if you want to add a property to all arrays that contain `Int` instances, and you want the return value of this property to be the largest integer in the array, you can extend an array of integers as follows:

```
extension Array where Element == Int{

  var largestInteger: Element?{
    return sorted().last
  }

}
```

Now you can use this property on arrays of integers, as shown here:

```
let numbers = [10, 20, 1, 4, 9]
print(numbers.largestInteger ?? 0)
```

Discussion

Swift now has the ability to extend collections of specific element types. For instance, imagine that you have the following structure:

```
struct Person{
  let name: String
  let age: Int
}
```

You can then create an array of `Person` as shown here:

```
let persons = [
  Person(name: "Foo", age: 22),
  Person(name: "Bar", age: 30),
  Person(name: "Baz", age: 19)
]
```

If you wanted to find the youngest `Person` instance this array traditionally, you would create a loop like this:

```
var youngestPerson = persons[0]

for person in persons{
  if person.age < youngestPerson.age{
    youngestPerson = person
  }
}

print("Youngest person = \(youngestPerson)")
```

You can make this code shorter by doing it in a functional way, of course:

```
if let youngestPerson = persons.sorted(by: {$0.age < $1.age}).first{
  print("Youngest person = \(youngestPerson)")
}
```

This looks good! But if you have to do this sorting and finding a few times inside your code in different places, you encounter the problem of duplicated code. To avoid that, you can extend an array of `Person` instances with a property called youngest of type `Person` as shown here:

```
extension Array where Element == Person{
  var youngest: Element?{
    return sorted(by: {$0.age < $1.age}).first
  }
}
```

And you can call that property as shown here:

```
if let youngestPerson = persons.youngest{
  print("Youngest person = \(youngestPerson)")
}
```

6.2 Taking Advantage of Open Collection Ranges

Problem

You regularly work with collections, such as arrays and dictionaries, and are tired of having to always specify a start or an end index to your ranges.

Solution

Use open ranges, as shown here:

Fully open-ended range
> This has the syntax *X...* where *X* is an integer indicating the first index of the collection to include in the range. The compiler infers the end of the range automatically, based on the collection this range is applied on.

Fully open-starting range
> This has the syntax *...X* where *X* is an integer indicating the last index of the collection to include in the range. The compiler starts at the beginning of the collection, going up to and including index *X*.

Half open-starting range
> This has the syntax *..<X* where *X* is an integer indicating the index that *follows* the end of the collection. The compiler starts at the beginning of the collection, stopping just before index *X*.

Arrays, as always, are counted with the index of 0 on the first element.

Discussion

Let's have a look at the open-ended range, where the ending of the range is not specified. Imagine that you have an array of strings as shown here:

```
let names = ["foo", "bar", "baz"]
```

You want to retrieve all items in this array except for the first item. One way of doing this is to use the array's dropFirst() function:

```
let allNamesExceptForFirstName = names.dropFirst()
//allNamesExceptForFirstName = ["bar", "baz"]
```

Another, perhaps more explicit way of reaching your goal is to create an open-ended range that skips the first item and directly goes to the second item, reading everything after that until the end of the array:

```
let exceptForFirstName = names[1...]
//exceptForFirstName = ["bar", "baz"]
```

The other syntaxes denote open-starting ranges, where the start of the range is not specified and is inferred to be the first item in the collection. You can use open-ended and open-starting ranges to do pattern matching as well. Imagine that you are given a constant called age and you have to decide whether this person is allowed to drive a vehicle, assuming that the legal age of obtaining a license is 16:

```
func decideIfAppropriateAgeForDriving(_ age: Int){

  switch age{
  case ..<0:
    print("Unborn child?!")
  case 16...:
    print("Allowed to drive")
  default:
    print("Not allowed to drive")
  }

}
```

In this function we use an open-starting range to define a pattern for our pattern matching where the given age cannot be any negative number, in which case we just print out "Unborn child?!" Then we use the open-ended range where anyone starting at the age of 16, up to the maximum range of Int, will cause the program to say "Allowed to drive" (not accounting for the edge cases where the age is ridiculously large!). Then we use the default case of the switch statement to mark everything else as an invalid age to drive, such as the age of 14. We can use our function as shown here:

```
//open-starting range
decideIfAppropriateAgeForDriving(-10) //prints "Unborn child?!"

//default case
decideIfAppropriateAgeForDriving(0) //prints "Not allowed to drive"
decideIfAppropriateAgeForDriving(14) //prints "Not allowed to drive"
decideIfAppropriateAgeForDriving(10) //prints "Not allowed to drive"

//open-ended range
decideIfAppropriateAgeForDriving(16) //prints "Allowed to drive"
decideIfAppropriateAgeForDriving(52) //prints "Allowed to drive"
```

6.3 Organizing Private Functions and Properties with Extensions

Problem

You use extensions to organize your code and you want a sophisticated mix of private and public functions to restrict access to functions and properties in your classes and structures.

Solution

You already know that you can keep properties and functions in one file from being available to code in other files by marking the properties and functions with the `private` keyword. By placing them inside extensions, you can open up some access to them.

Discussion

There are a few rules that you need to know when you use `private` and `public` access controls in Swift:

- Private properties and functions can be reached from public properties and functions as long as both the private and the public properties and functions are defined in the same Swift file, and are inside extensions. This last bit is very important. That is to say, private properties and functions of a struct or class are *not* visible to other structures and classes that are defined in the same Swift file, or even other Swift files for that matter.
- Private properties and functions can be reached from other private properties and functions as long as both are defined in the same Swift file, and are inside extensions.
- Public properties and functions can be reached from both public and private properties and functions regardless of which files they are defined in.

Imagine that you have a file in your project called *Person.swift* and you define a Person structure inside it as shown here:

```
import Foundation

struct Person{
  let name: String
  let age: Int
}
```

Now switch to another Swift file inside your project and create an extension to the Person structure. By labeling it `private`, you make sure it is visible only inside this new Swift file. This extension's job is to extract the first name of the person from the name property:

```
private extension Person{
  //private var can access public "name" property
  private var firstName: String?{
    return name.components(separatedBy: " ").first
  }
}
```

Notice how this new private variable called `firstName` can access the public `name` property of the person even though they are implemented in different Swift files.

That's because you didn't include the `private` keyword when you defined `Person`, so that structure is by default `internal`.

You can also extend the `Person` structure with another file-private extension to expose the last name of the person, again making it `private`:

```
private extension Person{
  //private var can access public "name" property
  private var lastName: String?{
    let components = name.components(separatedBy: " ")
    guard components.count >= 2 else {return nil}
    return components.last
  }
}
```

In the same Swift file where you've implemented the `firstName` and `lastName` private properties, define another extension on `Person` where you can validate the `firstName` property:

```
private extension Person{
  //private var can access private "firstName" property
  //as long as both are defined in the same file
  private var hasValidFirstName: Bool{
    return (firstName ?? "").characters.count >= 2
  }
}
```

Notice how this private property has access to the `firstName` private property because they are implemented in the same file. This works only in extensions though, which means if you have another class that is defined inside the same Swift file as one of these `private` extensions to the `Person` structure, it won't be able to access the `private` properties of `Person`. Only extensions can do this.

Now implement another private property inside a file-private extension to `Person`, just like you did for the `hasValidFirstName` property, but this time validate the last name:

```
private extension Person{
  //private var can access private "lastName" property
  //since both are defined in the same file
  private var hasValidLastName: Bool{
    return (lastName ?? "").characters.count >= 3
  }
}
```

To put this all to use, you can define a `public` property on your `Person` structure inside a public extension in the same Swift file where you defined your `private` variables in `private` extensions on the `Person` structure. This new computed property will check whether the name of the person (first name and last name) is valid:

```
extension Person{
  //public var can access private "hasValidFirstName" and
  //"hasValidLastName" properties since it is defined in the same file
  var hasValidName: Bool{
    return hasValidFirstName && hasValidLastName
  }
}
```

This demonstrates that a public property defined inside an extension to `Person` has access to the private properties `hasValidFirstName` and `hasValidLastName` of `Person` since they are all defined in the same Swift file. Now you can call the `hasValidName` property from any file in your project, as shown here:

```
let fooBar = Person(name: "Foo Bar", age: 22)
print("Foo bar valid name? = \(fooBar.hasValidName)")
```

See Also

Recipes 6.7 and 6.8

6.4 Defining Key Paths in Swift

Problem

When a function returns an object, which may be the caller is interested in one or more properties of the object, sometimes hidden deep in the object hierarchy. You want to return not the entire object, but a shortcut that points to a nested property of special interest.

Solution

Use key paths in Swift, of type `KeyPath`, by writing your object structure relationship prefixed with a backslash character (\).

Discussion

Imagine that you have a `Car` structure and a `Person` structure that has a `car: Car` property, as shown here:

```
struct Car{
  let name: String
}

struct Person{

  let name: String
  let age: Int
  let car: Car
```

```
}
```

We'll go ahead and define a few instances of the Person and Car structures:

```
let foo = Person(name: "Foo", age: 22, car: Car(name: "VW up!"))
let bar = Person(name: "Bar", age: 25, car: Car(name: "VW Tiguan"))
let baz = Person(name: "Baz", age: 30, car: Car(name: "VW Sharan"))
```

Now imagine that you want to define a constant that points to any Person instance's car property and then goes further into the name property of the car. You can do that by writing the relationship exactly as it is, Person.car.name, but prefixing it with a backslash, as shown here:

```
let carNameKeyPath = \Person.car.name
```

The constant of carNameKeyPath is of type KeyPath<Person, String>, where the first qualifier (Person) is the root or starting point of the relationship, and the second (String) is the data type of the field being retrieved. The name property of Car is String, so the data that this key path will return is of type String.

Every object has a subscript called [keyPath:] that takes in a KeyPath instance and returns the data associated with that KeyPath object:

```
let carNames = [foo, bar, baz].map{$0[keyPath: carNameKeyPath]}
carNames // ["VW up!", "VW Tiguan", "VW Sharan"]
```

Key path objects are of type KeyPath, and this type is a class that has its own functions and properties. One of the functions provided by this type is called append ing(path:). It allows you to append another KeyPath object to the end of the current KeyPath to form a longer KeyPath. Imagine the same object hierarchy as before, where the Person instance owns a car of type Car and each Car instance has a name property. Now we can define two separate key paths as shown here:

```
let personCarKeyPath = \Person.car
let nameOfCarKeyPath = \Car.name
```

The first key path points to the car property of the Person structure and the second one points to the name property of the Car structure. You can join these two key paths to create a KeyPath property that points to the name property of the car property of the Person structure:

```
let fullKeyPath = personCarKeyPath.appending(path: nameOfCarKeyPath)
```

And you can continue using this new key path like you did with the other ones:

```
let carNames = [foo, bar, baz].map{$0[keyPath: fullKeyPath]}
carNames // ["VW up!", "VW Tiguan", "VW Sharan"]
```

See Also

Recipe 6.1

6.5 Parsing from and to JSON with Swift

Problem

You want to be able to convert your custom data types to JSON and also be able to convert JSON data into your custom types.

Solution

Follow these steps:

1. Make your custom types conform to the `Codable` protocol.
2. Instantiate `JSONEncoder` and use its `encode(_:)` function to convert your `Codable`-conforming custom types into an instance of `Data`. This is how you convert your custom data types into JSON.
3. Use the `decode(_:from:)` function of an instance of `JSONDecoder` to convert JSON-formatted strings into a given custom data type.

Discussion

Let's imagine that we have the same `Person` and `Car` structures as before (see Recipe 6.4), but this time we will make them conform to the `Codable` protocol:

```
struct Car: Codable{
  let name: String
}

struct Person: Codable{

  let name: String
  let age: Int
  let car: Car

}
```

As you can see, the effort is practically zero to get your types ready to be encoded and decoded into and from JSON. All you have to do is ensure they conform to the `Codable` protocol. Now we are going to make an instance of the `Person` structure so that we can convert it to JSON:

```
let foo = Person(name: "Foo", age: 22, car: Car(name: "VW up!"))
```

We are going to convert this instance to JSON and then back from JSON into another instance of Person. Then we'll compare the new instance with the instance named foo created just now to see whether they are the same and confirm that JSON serialization and deserialization work as expected. The following functions ensure that our Person and Car structures are equatable:

```
func == (lhs: Car, rhs: Car) -> Bool{
  return lhs.name == rhs.name
}

func == (lhs: Person, rhs: Person) -> Bool{
  return
    lhs.name == rhs.name &&
      lhs.age == rhs.age &&
      lhs.car == rhs.car
}
```

We now dive in and convert the foo instance to JSON data and then back again into an instance of Person, and then compare the two instances to ensure everything went as expected:

```
if let data = try? JSONEncoder().encode(foo){
  if let newFoo = try? JSONDecoder().decode(Person.self, from: data){
    if newFoo == foo{
      print("They are the same")
    } else {
      print("They are not the same")
    }
  }
}
```

See Also

Recipe 6.6

6.6 Handling Corner Cases in JSON Parsing with Swift

Problem

You have a JSON file that you want to parse but are facing one of the following issues:

- The keys in the JSON don't turn into good constant names in Swift. For instance, the key person_age, which contains an underscore, doesn't read very well in Swift; you could say that it's not very *Swifty*!
- You want to insert data into your Swift model for key-value pairs that might be missing from your JSON. In other words, the data is required in your application but it might not be sent by your server, and you need to create the data with a default value.

- While encoding your Swift model into JSON, you want to insert extra logic for sophisticated operations, such as transforming a value that is not JSON encodable into one that is.

Solution

Here are the solutions to the problems listed in the Problem section:

For JSON keys that aren't "Swifty" constant or variable names:
1. Define the resulting Swift object for your model, making it conform to the `Decodable` protocol, `Encodable` protocol, or `Codable` protocol (which is both decodable and encodable).

2. Define a private `enum` in your model named `CodingKeys`. The `enum` object, in addition to being private, must be of type `String` and must conform to the `CodingKey` protocol.

3. In the object, define a case whose name is the Swift variable or constant name you want produced and whose corresponding value is the JSON key that turns into that name.

To insert defaults for missing data:
1. Make sure that your Swift object model conforms to `Decodable`, and implement the `init(from decoder: Decoder)` throws initializer from `Decodable`.

2. In this initializer, use the `container(keyedBy:)` function of the decoder parameter to get a container of type `KeyedDecodingContainer`.

3. Use this container to read the values inside the JSON object. If you cannot find the value you are looking for, use the function to assign a default value to your constant or variable.

To add extra logic to an encoding from Swift to JSON:
1. Ensure that your model object in Swift conforms to the `Encodable` protocol, or `Codable` if you want to do both encoding and decoding, and implement the protocol's `func encode(to encoder: Encoder)` throws function.

2. Inside this function, run the `encoder` parameter's `container(keyedBy:)` function. Then encode constants and variables from the model. You can make changes to each constant or variable, such as implementing error checking or providing a default value.

In the Discussion section we will examine these solutions in more detail.

Discussion

Let's have a look at an example of the first problem. Imagine you have the following JSON:

```
let personJson = """
  {
    "first_name" : "Foo",
    "last_name" : "Bar",
    "age" : 29
  }
  """
```

You'll notice how the `first_name` and `last_name` keys in this JSON don't make good constant names in Swift. What we want is `firstName` and `lastName`. So how can we define a JSON object in Swift that represents this JSON but with proper Swifty constant names? We will use the `private` enum called `CodingKeys`, as explained in the Solution section:

```
struct Person: Codable{
  let firstName: String
  let lastName: String
  let age: Int

  private enum CodingKeys: String, CodingKey{
    case firstName = "first_name"
    case lastName = "last_name"
    case age
  }

}
```

Now for the second problem, where your Swift constants are mandatory but the responding keys in JSON might or might not be present. You will need to implement the `init(from decoder: Decoder)` throws function and place your specific logic there. Suppose you added an `address` field to your Swift model object:

```
struct Person: Codable{
  let firstName: String
  let lastName: String
  let age: Int
  let address: String

  private enum CodingKeys: String, CodingKey{
    case firstName = "first_name"
    case lastName = "last_name"
    case age
    case address
  }

}
```

If you provided the same JSON as before and tried to decode it into an instance of Person with the newly added address field, JSONDecoder would throw an error because this field is missing from the JSON and is not defined as optional in the model. To solve this problem, implement the init(from decoder: Decoder) throws function from Decodable and place logic there that fills in the default value for the address field:

```swift
struct Person: Codable{
  let firstName: String
  let lastName: String
  let age: Int
  let address: String

  private enum CodingKeys: String, CodingKey{
    case firstName = "first_name"
    case lastName = "last_name"
    case age
    case address
  }

  init(from decoder: Decoder) throws{
    let container = try decoder.container(keyedBy: CodingKeys.self)
    firstName = try container.decode(String.self, forKey: .firstName)
    lastName = try container.decode(String.self, forKey: .lastName)
    age = try container.decode(Int.self, forKey: .age)

    address =
      (try container.decodeIfPresent(String.self, forKey: .address))
      ?? "Unknown Address"

  }

}
```

To address the last problem, placing some extra logic into the encoding process between a Swift model object and its JSON representation, implement the func encode(to encoder: Encoder) throws function from Encodable. For instance, go back to the Person structure with firstName, lastName, and age fields. Suppose that, when encoding an instance of Person into JSON, you would like to change the age of the person to the maximum of 130 if it exceeds that value:

```swift
struct Person: Codable{
  let firstName: String
  let lastName: String
  let age: Int

  func encode(to encoder: Encoder) throws{
    var container = encoder.container(keyedBy: CodingKeys.self)
    try container.encode(firstName, forKey: .firstName)
    try container.encode(lastName, forKey: .lastName)
```

```
    try container.encode(min(age, 130), forKey: .age)
  }

}
```

Now go ahead and create an instance of Person and intentionally set the age property to 140. Then encode this Person instance to Data and read the Data back again into an instance of Person, to see whether the desired change was made:

```
let person = Person(firstName: "Foo", lastName: "Bar", age: 140)

guard let personJsonData = try? JSONEncoder().encode(person) else {return}

guard let samePerson = try? JSONDecoder().decode(
  Person.self, from: personJsonData) else {return}

print(person)
print(samePerson)
```

If everything worked as expected in the JSON encoding, the age saved to the JSON data should be 130, not 140. Let's have a look:

```
Person #1(firstName: "Foo", lastName: "Bar", age: 140)
Person #1(firstName: "Foo", lastName: "Bar", age: 130)
```

See Also

Recipe 6.5

6.7 Partitioning Arrays into Segments

Problem

You have an array of homogenous objects that you want to separate according to some criterion of your choice.

Solution

Follow these steps:

1. Create your array.
2. Instantiate a Dictionary using its init(grouping:by:) initializer.
3. For the grouping parameter, pass your array.
4. For the by parameter, pass a closure that takes in one item of your array at a time, and returns a Hashable object.

Discussion

If you specify the property of X in the by parameter of the dictionary initializer, all the objects inside your array with the same value for the X parameter will form a new array and will be placed inside the returning dictionary. The array will be the value of a key equal to X.

This can be very difficult to digest, or even explain, for that matter, so I think it is best shown by an example. Imagine that you have the following array:

```
let names = [
  "Joey",
  "Andrew",
  "Suzanne",
  "Jonathan",
  "Sara",
  "Adriana",
]
```

You want to group all names that start with the same letter into their own array, so Joey and Jonathan will be in an array of their own, Andrew and Adriana in their own, and Suzanne and Sara in their own. The process in this recipe will place these arrays inside a dictionary where the keys are these first letters (that is to say, J, A, and S) and the values to these keys are the arrays of names whose first letter is J, A, and S:

```
let dict = Dictionary(grouping: names) {(items: String) -> Character in
  return items.first ?? "?"
}
```

The `first` method extracts the first letter of each name. The final question mark in quotation marks indicates that any name whose first letter cannot be extracted should be placed into a default dictionary whose key is the question mark. We don't expect to have any problems extracting the first letter, but include this default to prevent any errors.

If you try to read the value of the `dict` constant, you will see the following:

```
["J": ["Joey", "Jonathan"],
 "A": ["Andrew", "Adriana"],
 "S": ["Suzanne", "Sara"]]
```

You can take advantage of this feature in Swift to group array items that are somehow related to each other. *How* they are connected is something for you to decide. As another example, you can place all the names inside the names array into groups that are separated by their length:

```
let dict = Dictionary(grouping: names) {(items: String) -> Int in
  return items.characters.count
}
```

And if you print out the value of `dict` now you will see the following results:

```
[6: ["Andrew"],
 7: ["Suzanne", "Adriana"],
 4: ["Joey", "Sara"],
 8: ["Jonathan"]]
```

The way this initializer works is by going through the initial array one item at a time, calling the by closure for every item and returning a `Hashable` value, such as the length of the string. All the array objects for which the same `Hashable` object is returned inside the by parameter will be placed inside the same array, which will then be placed inside the dictionary. The key will be the exact `Hashable` returned from your by parameter.

See Also

Recipe 6.9

6.8 Setting Constraints on Extensions

Problem

You want to extend a data type while constraining your extension by certain criteria, as allowed by the data type. For example, suppose that you have a data type that represents a JSON object:

```
struct JsonObject<Key: Hashable, Value>{
  let key: Key
  let value: Value
}
```

And you want to extend this data type whenever the `Value` generic parameter is of type `String`.

Solution

Use the `where` clause in your extension as shown here:

```
extension JsonObject where Value == String{

  //your code

}
```

Discussion

In the code in the Solution section of this recipe, we are writing an extension that applies to the data type `JsonObject` as long as the `Value` generic type of this structure is a `String`. This is a direct comparison of the data types. However, you may sometimes need to check whether a specific generic type of a structure or class conforms to a certain protocol. In that case, instead of using the `==` syntax in the extension's definition, you'd have to use the `:` syntax as shown here:

```
extension JsonObject where Value: ExpressibleByStringLiteral{

  //your code

}
```

Let's take another example that is a little bit more advanced. Suppose that you want to write a protocol that defines the basics of an object that is initializable with a JSON object. JSON objects are collections, either arrays or dictionaries. If they are arrays, they have to contain other objects, each of which is a dictionary, and each dictionary in a JSON object has to have keys of type `String` with values commonly of type `String`, `Int`, `Array`, or `Double`. Here is a typical definition of such a protocol:

```
protocol JsonRepresentable{
  associatedtype JsonType: Collection
  var json: JsonType {get}
  init(json: JsonType)
}
```

Suppose that you want to implement a `Person` structure that can get initialized by a JSON dictionary. The initializer must look inside this dictionary for `name` and `age` keys and assign default values to them if they cannot be found. Here is the implementation:

```
struct Person: JsonRepresentable{

  typealias JsonType = [String : Any]

  let name: String
  let age: Int
  let json: JsonType

  init(json: JsonType) {
    name = json["name"] as? String ?? "Foo Bar"
    age = json["age"] as? Int ?? 18
    self.json = json
  }

}
```

Notice how the `JsonRepresentable` protocol has an associated type called `JsonType` that is constrained to be of type `Collection`? This means that this protocol requires you to define, in your types that implement this protocol, a `typealias` that defines what type of JSON object you are dealing with, and that type must be a `Collection` (array or dictionary).

Now that you have these types in place, you can start writing extensions even on the base protocol, JsonInitializable. Suppose that for every JsonInitializable that has a JsonObject of type Dictionary with keys of type String and values of type Any, you want to add a new property to this type called hasAge. That property will look inside the JSON object for a key called age. If it finds the key with a value of type Int, it returns true, and otherwise it returns false:

```
extension JsonRepresentable where JsonType == Dictionary<String, Any>{
  var hasAge: Bool{
    if let _ = json["age"] as? Int{
      return true
    } else {
      return false
    }
  }
}
```

We are using the == syntax in our where constraint on the JsonRepresentable protocol to limit the scope of this extension to situations where the JSON representable object is a Dictionary whose keys are String objects and whose values are any type. Now that we have this extension, we can proceed to use it for appropriate types that conform to these criteria:

```
let json = ["name" : "Foo Bar", "age": 22] as [String : Any]
let foo = Person(json: json)
if foo.hasAge{
  //do something here
}
```

See Also

Recipe 6.12

6.9 Defining Object Requirements Through Protocols

Problem

You want to create a reusable piece of code using protocol extensions and you require the data type that implements your protocol to conform to a certain interface.

Solution

In the definition of your protocol, define your contract and conformance obligations. In the implementation of your protocol, implement the reusable code through an extension.

Discussion

Suppose that you want all instances of URL and String to all of a sudden have the ability to fetch their own data, should they contain a valid URL. Let's have a look at a typical fetch function's definition. We can start by defining an enumeration that describes either success or failure, but not both:

```
enum Either<V, E: Error>{
  case value(V)
  case error(E)
}
```

Then we can define a few typical errors that might happen during a fetch operation:

```
enum FetchError: Error{
  case nilUrl
  case connectionError(Error)
  case emptyData
}
```

Now that we have defined some possible errors, we can start writing the implementation of the fetch function:

```
func fetch(url: URL?,
           completion: @escaping (Either<Data, FetchError>) -> Void){

  guard let url = url else {
    completion(.error(.nilUrl))
    return
  }

  //code the function here

}
```

A URL instance can be constructed from a String instance, and it would be lovely if every instance of URL and String could all of a sudden have a fetch(...) function. That is the power of protocols that expect to receive data from you but in turn give you some functionality. Suppose that we wrote a protocol called Fetchable that is able to fetch any URL. What is the data that is expected from conforming types of Fetchable? A URL, of course. If we could return a URL to this protocol, we could get a fetch(...) function in return.

This would be the default *declaration* (as opposed to *implementation*) of our Fetch able protocol:

```
protocol Fetchable{
  var fetchUrl: URL? {get}
}
```

The required, read-only `fetchUrl` variable inside `Fetchable` asks any conforming type for an optional URL from which to download the data. The URL data type is optional because the conforming type cannot guarantee that it can return a URL. It's the job of `Fetchable` to make sure `fetchUrl` is nonnil. In our case, if it is nil, the protocol will throw a `FetchError.nilUrl` error.

After declaring our `Fetchable` protocol, it's time to implement the default `fetch(...)` function as part of an extension on this protocol:

```
extension Fetchable{

  func fetch(completion: @escaping (Either<Data, FetchError>) -> Void){

    guard let url = fetchUrl else {
      completion(.error(.nilUrl))
      return
    }

    //code the function here

  }

}
```

After the protocol is ready, we can conform both `String` and `URL` directly to it:

```
extension String: Fetchable{
  var fetchUrl: URL?{
    return URL(string: self)
  }
}

extension URL: Fetchable{
  var fetchUrl: URL?{
    return self
  }
}
```

Through this code, both `URL` and `String` all of a sudden get a `fetch(completion:)` function. Here is `String` with the aforementioned function:

```
"https://apple.com".fetch {either in
  switch either{
  case .error(let err):
    print(err)
  case .value(let data):
    print(data)
  }
}
```

And here is `URL` with the same function:

```
URL(string: "https://apple.com")?.fetch{either in
  switch either{
  case .error(let err):
    print(err)
  case .value(let data):
    print(data)
  }
}
```

See Also

Recipe 6.8

6.10 Creating New Data Types by Combination

Problem

You want to combine existing data types into a new one.

Solution

Data types can be combined using the ampersand (&) in several circumstances:

- To create a new data type in a `typealias` statement
- To apply a protocol to the combined data types, using `associatedtype`
- On the fly, inline, such as to find out whether an object conforms to a set of protocols and object types

Discussion

Imagine that you have two protocols:

```
protocol Foo{}
protocol Bar{}
```

Here is an example of the third, on-the-fly use of & mentioned in the Solution section. Swift provides the `is` syntax to check the data type of an object. As the following example shows, you can use & in this statement. The example tests objects of type `Any` to see whether they conform to both `Foo` and `Bar` protocols:

```
func isFooBar(_ obj: Any){
  if obj is Foo & Bar{
    print("Foo & Bar") // The code will finish here
  } else {
    print("Not Foo & Bar") // This line will not be executed
  }
}
```

Now you can pass any object to this function to test for conformance to the Foo and Bar protocols:

```
let someObject = "Foo Bar"
isFooBar(someObject)
```

What we did was define a new data type that conforms to both the Foo and Bar protocols.

In protocols, to enforce conformance to two or more types at once, we use the associatedtype syntax. Imagine that we've defined three protocols that define which properties a typical vehicle has—wheels, gears, and an engine:

```
protocol HasWheels{
  var wheelCount: Int {get}
}

protocol HasGears{
  var gearCount: Int {get}
}

protocol HasEngine{
  var hoursePower: Int {get}
}
```

Any data type that wants to have a vehicle has to define a data type that conforms to the three aforementioned properties of a vehicle. Here we define a protocol to enforce that rule:

```
protocol HasVehicle{
  associatedtype Vehicle = HasWheels & HasGears & HasEngine
  var vehicle: Vehicle {get}
}
```

Then we can define a Volvo V90 vehicle structure that conforms to the HasWheels, HasGears, and HasEngine protocols. We won't conform to the HasVehicle protocol here, because a car cannot *have* a vehicle, but in fact *is* a vehicle. The Volvo defines a variable it needs to conform to each of the three protocols from which it inherits:

```
struct Volvo: HasWheels, HasGears, HasEngine{
  let wheelCount: Int
  let gearCount: Int
  let hoursePower: Int

  static var v90: Volvo{
    return Volvo(wheelCount: 4, gearCount: 6, hoursePower: 185)
  }

}
```

Take note of the `v90` static computed property of the `Volvo` structure, which defines a Volvo V90 vehicle.

Now we can define a `Person` structure that conforms to the `HasVehicle` protocol. As her vehicle, she can have the Volvo V90:

```
struct Person: HasVehicle{
  typealias Vehicle = Volvo
  let vehicle: Vehicle
}

let fooBar = Person(vehicle: .v90)
print(fooBar)
```

See Also

Recipe 6.11

6.11 Adding Logic Through Protocols

Problem

You want to inherit *logic* from a protocol, and not just method and variable names.

Solution

In your protocol, add an extension where you write the code to be shared by those who implement the protocol. For instance, in the following `HasFullName` protocol, an extension called `HasFullName` defines a variable using some simple coding:

```
protocol HasFullName{
  var firstName: String {get}
  var lastName: String {get}
}

extension HasFullName{
  var fullName: String{
    return "\(firstName) \(lastName)"
  }
}
```

The extension can calculate the full name of any type, as long as that type has `first Name` and `lastName` properties. Now you can define a structure called `Person` that conforms to this protocol:

```
struct Person: HasFullName{
  let firstName: String
  let lastName: String
}
```

And then you can read the `fullName` property of the `Person` structure, even though `Person` doesn't define the property. You have inherited `fullName` from the `HasFull Name` protocol, but as programming logic rather than a static definition:

```
let fooBar = Person(firstName: "Foo", lastName: "Bar")
print(fooBar.fullName) // "Foo Bar"
```

Discussion

Extensions can do much more than provide a new property, as the previous example did. Let's have a look at another example. Imagine that you want to be able to download content specified through a URL object. Let's begin by defining our protocol:

```
protocol Fetchable{
  var fetchableUrl: URL? {get}
}
```

This protocol checks the conforming type's `fetchableUrl` property for a URL from which the protocol will try to download data. If a conforming type doesn't have a `fetchableUrl` property, we will not attempt to download its contents. Now let's extend our `Fetchable` type to define a `fetch(...)` function that downloads the content:

```
extension Fetchable{
  typealias FetchCompletion = (Either<Data, FetchError>) -> Void
  func fetch(completion: @escaping FetchCompletion){
    //provide your implementation here
  }
}
```

We have to be prepared for errors whenever dealing with downloads, so we allow the result to be either data or an error. We do this using an `enum` called `Either` that we are going to define now. Additionally, the completion handler raises errors of type `Fetch Error` that we also need to define:

```
enum Either<V, E>{
  case value(V)
  case error(E)
}

enum FetchError: Error{
  case noUrlGiven
  case connectionError
}
```

This makes it possible for us to extend existing data types so they can run the code in the Fetchable extension and automatically retrieve a web page from a URL. Error handling is built in as well, and happens consistently across different objects. A data type that conforms to the Fetchable protocol inherits the fetch(completion:) function, as shown here:

```
extension URL: Fetchable{
  var fetchableUrl: URL?{
    return self
  }
}

extension String: Fetchable{
  var fetchableUrl: URL?{
    return URL(string: self)
  }
}
```

And all of a sudden these types get the aforementioned function. Here is the URL that uses this function:

```
URL(string: "https://www.apple.com")?.fetch{either in
  switch either{
  case .value(let data):
    print(data)
  case .error(let error):
    print(error)
  }
}
```

And here is a string that uses the same function to fetch the data that might be associated with the URL that the String holds:

```
"https://www.apple.com".fetch {either in
  switch either{
  case .value(let data):
    print(data)
  case .error(let error):
    print(error)
  }
}
```

See Also

Recipe 6.9

6.12 Defining Constraints on Protocols

Problem

You want to write an extension on a protocol, but have it apply only if a certain condition is met.

Solution

Use protocol extensions with the `where` clause followed by an `associatedtype` check on the extension.

Discussion

Imagine that you define a base protocol for any vehicle and then you define two separate protocols for heavy and light vehicles:

```
protocol Vehicle{
  var wheelCount: Int {get}
}

protocol HeavyVehicle: Vehicle{
  func tankWithDiesel(liters: Int)
}

protocol LightVehicle: Vehicle{
  func tankWithPetrol(liters: Int)
}
```

The light vehicle type requires conforming types to implement a function called `tankWithPetrol(liters:)` and the heavy vehicle type requires conforming types to implement a function called `tankWithDiesel(liters:)`.

Then you can go ahead and define a protocol that defines any data type that can own a vehicle. Any data type that conforms to this protocol will have to define a property called `vehicle` of type `Vehicle`:

```
protocol OwnsVehicle{
  associatedtype VehicleType: Vehicle
  var vehicle: VehicleType {get}
}
```

Imagine that you now want to extend the `OwnsVehicle` protocol with a function called `fillVehicleTankWithDiesel()` for diesel cars. Because this function can handle only diesel and not petrol, it should be available only to data types whose `associatedtype` of `VehicleType` is `HeavyVehicle`. You can do that using the `where` clause on your `extension`:

```
extension OwnsVehicle where VehicleType: HeavyVehicle{
  func fillVehicleTankWithDiesel(){
    //we don't have to implement this now!
  }
}
```

Next, go ahead and define one light and one heavy vehicle:

```
struct VolvoV90: LightVehicle{
  let wheelCount = 4
  func tankWithPetrol(liters: Int) {
    //we don't have to implement this now!
  }
}

struct Van: HeavyVehicle{
  let wheelCount = 4
  func tankWithDiesel(liters: Int) {
    //we don't have to implement this now!
  }
}
```

Then define two person types, one that owns a light vehicle and the other that owns a heavy vehicle, both conforming to the OwnsVehicle protocol:

```
struct PersonWithLightVehicle: OwnsVehicle{
  typealias VehicleType = VolvoV90
  let vehicle = VolvoV90()
}

struct PersonWithHeavyVehicle: OwnsVehicle{
  typealias VehicleType = Van
  let vehicle = Van()
}
```

The VehicleType of vehicles owned by PersonWithLightVehicle is VolvoV90, which itself is of type LightVehicle. Therefore, these people don't have access to the fillVehicleTankWithDiesel() function from our OwnsVehicle constrained extension:

```
let foo = PersonWithLightVehicle()
//foo doesn't have the fillVehicleTankWithDiesel() function
```

However, if you create an instance of PersonWithHeavyVehicle that conforms to OwnsVehicle, it will own a VehicleType equal to Van, which conforms to Heavy Vehicle. So, that person will have access to the fillVehicleTankWithDiesel() function:

```
let bar = PersonWithHeavyVehicle()
bar.fillVehicleTankWithDiesel()
```

See Also

Recipe 6.11

6.13 Handling Errors in Swift

Problem

You want to know how to throw and handle exceptions in Swift.

 The terms *error* and *exception* are used interchangeably throughout this book. When an error occurs in our apps, we usually *catch* it, as you will soon see, and handle it in a way that is pleasant and understandable to the user.

Solution

To throw an exception, use the `throw` syntax. To catch exceptions, use the `do`, `try`, `catch` syntax.

Discussion

Let's say that we want to create a method that takes in a first name and last name as two arguments and returns a full name. The first name and the last name have to each be at least one character long for this method to work. If one or both have 0 lengths, we are going to want to throw an exception.

The first thing that we have to do is define our errors, of type `Error`:

```
enum Errors : Error{
  case emptyFirstName
  case emptyLastName
}
```

And then we are going to define our method to take in a first and last name and join them together with a space in between:

```
func fullNameFromFirstName(_ firstName: String,
  lastName: String) throws -> String{

  if firstName.characters.count == 0{
    throw Errors.emptyFirstName
  }

  if lastName.characters.count == 0{
    throw Errors.emptyLastName
  }
```

```
  return firstName + " " + lastName
```

```
}
```

The interesting part is really how to call this method. We use the do statement like so:

```
do{
  let fullName = try fullNameFromFirstName("Foo", lastName: "Bar")
  print(fullName)
} catch {
  print("An error occurred")
}
```

The catch clause of the do statement allows us to trap errors in a fine-grained manner. Let's say that you want to trap errors in the Errors enum differently from instances of NSException. Separate your catch clauses like this:

```
  do{
    let fullName = try fullNameFromFirstName("Foo", lastName: "Bar")
    print(fullName)
  }
  catch let err as Errors{
    // handle this specific type of error here
    print(err)
  }
  catch let ex as NSException{
    // handle exceptions here
    print(ex)
  }
  catch {
    // otherwise, do this
  }
```

See Also

Recipe 6.6

6.14 Specifying Preconditions for Methods

Problem

You want to make sure a set of conditions are met before continuing with the flow of your method.

Solution

Use the guard syntax.

Discussion

The guard syntax allows you to:

- Specify a set of conditions for your methods.
- Bind variables to optionals and use those variables in the rest of your method's body.

Let's have a look at a method that takes an optional piece of data as the NSData type and turns it into a String only if the string has some characters in it and is not empty:

```
func stringFromData(_ data: Data?) -> String?{

  guard let data = data,
    let str = NSString(data: data, encoding: String.Encoding.utf8.rawValue)
    , data.count > 0 else{
    return nil
  }

  return String(str)

}
```

We are going to use it like so:

```
if let _ = stringFromData(nil){
  print("Got the string")
} else {
  print("No string came back")
}
```

We pass nil to this method for now and trigger the failure block ("No string came back"). What if we passed valid data? And to have more fun with this, let's create our NSData instance this time with a guard. Because the NSString constructor we are about to use returns an optional value, we put a guard statement before it to ensure that the value that goes into the data variable is in fact a value, and not nil:

```
guard let data = NSString(string: "Foo")
  .data(using: String.Encoding.utf8.rawValue), data.count > 0 else{
    return
}

if let str = stringFromData(data){
  print("Got the string \(str)")
} else {
  print("No string came back")
}
```

So, we can mix a guard and conditions in the same statement. How about multiple let statements inside a guard? Can we do that? You betcha:

```
func example3(firstName: String?, lastName: String?, age: UInt8?){

  guard let firstName = firstName, let lastName = lastName , let _ = age
    , firstName.characters.count > 0 && lastName.characters.count > 0 else{
      return
  }

  print(firstName, " ", lastName)

}
```

6.15 Ensuring the Execution of Code Blocks Before Exiting Methods

Problem

You have various conditions in your method that can cause the method to exit early. But you want to ensure that certain code blocks, such as cleanup code, always get executed before that happens.

Solution

Use the defer syntax.

Discussion

Anything that you put inside a defer block inside a method is guaranteed to get executed before your method returns to the caller. However, this block of code will get executed *after* the return call in your method. The code is also called when your method throws an exception.

Let's say that we want to define a method that takes in a string and renders it inside a new image context with a given size. Now if the string is empty, we want to throw an exception. However, before we do that, we want to make sure that we have ended our image context. Let's define our error first:

```
enum Errors : Error{
  case emptyString
  }
```

Then we move on to our actual method that uses the defer syntax:

```
func imageForString(_ str: String, size: CGSize) throws -> UIImage{

  defer{
    UIGraphicsEndImageContext()
  }
```

```
UIGraphicsBeginImageContextWithOptions(size, true, 0)

if str.characters.count == 0{
  throw Errors.emptyString
}

// draw the string here...

return UIGraphicsGetImageFromCurrentImageContext()!

}
```

I don't want to put print() statements everywhere in the code because it makes the code really ugly. So to see whether this really works, I suggest typing this code into Xcode—or even better, grab the source code for this book's examples from GitHub, where I have already placed breakpoints in the defer and the return statements so that you can see that they are working properly.

We can, of course, then call this method like so:

```
func imageForString(_ str: String, size: CGSize) throws -> UIImage{

  defer{
    UIGraphicsEndImageContext()
  }

  UIGraphicsBeginImageContextWithOptions(size, true, 0)

  if str.characters.count == 0{
    throw Errors.emptyString
  }

  // draw the string here...

  return UIGraphicsGetImageFromCurrentImageContext()!

}
```

6.16 Checking for API Availability

Problem

You want to check whether a specific API is available on the host device running your code.

Solution

Use the #available syntax.

Discussion

We've all been waiting for this for a very long time. The days of having to call the respondsToSelector: method are over (hopefully). Now we can just use #available to make sure a specific iOS version is available before making a call to a method.

Let's say that we want to write a method that can read an array of bytes from an NSDataobject. NSData offers a handy getBytes: method to do this, but Apple decided to deprecate it in iOS 8.1 and replace it with getBytes:length:, an improved version that minimizes the risk of buffer overflows. So, assuming that one of our deployment targets is iOS 8 or older, we want to ensure that we call this new method if we are on iOS 8.1 or higher and the older method if we are on iOS 8.0 or older:

```
enum Errors : Error{
  case emptyData
}


func bytesFromData(_ data: Data) throws -> [UInt8]{

  if (data.count == 0){
    throw Errors.emptyData
  }

  var buffer = [UInt8](repeating: 0, count: data.count)

  if #available(iOS 8.1, *){
    (data as NSData).getBytes(&buffer, length: data.count)
  } else {
    (data as NSData).getBytes(&buffer)
  }

  return buffer

}
```

And then we go ahead and call this method:

```
guard let data = "Foo".data(using: String.Encoding.utf8) else {
  return
}

do{
  let bytes = try bytesFromData(data)
  print("Data = \(bytes)")
} catch {
  print("Failed to get bytes")
}
```

6.17 Creating Your Own Set Types

Problem

You want to create a type in Swift that can allow all operators that normal sets allow, such as the `contain` function.

Solution

Conform to the `OptionSet` protocol. As a bonus, you can also conform to the `Custom DebugStringConvertible` protocol, as shown in this recipe, in order to set custom debug descriptions that the `print()` function can use during debugging of your sets.

Discussion

Let's say that you have a structure that keeps track of iPhone models. You want to be able to create a set of this structure's values so that you can say that you have an iPhone 6, iPhone 6+, and iPhone 5s (fancy you!). Here is the way you would do that:

```swift
struct IphoneModels : OptionSet, CustomDebugStringConvertible{

  let rawValue: Int
  init(rawValue: Int){
    self.rawValue = rawValue
  }

  static let Six = IphoneModels(rawValue: 0)
  static let SixPlus = IphoneModels(rawValue: 1)
  static let Five = IphoneModels(rawValue: 2)
  static let FiveS = IphoneModels(rawValue: 3)

  var debugDescription: String{
    switch self{
    case IphoneModels.Six:
      return "iPhone 6"
    case IphoneModels.SixPlus:
      return "iPhone 6+"
    case IphoneModels.Five:
      return "iPhone 5"
    case IphoneModels.FiveS:
      return "iPhone 5s"
    default:
      return "Unknown iPhone"
    }
  }


}
```

And then you can use it like so:

```
func example1(){

  let myIphones: [IphoneModels] = [.Six, .SixPlus]

  if myIphones.contains(.FiveS){
    print("You own an iPhone 5s")
  } else {
    print("You don't seem to have an iPhone 5s but you have these:")
    for i in myIphones{
      print(i)
    }
  }

}
```

Note how you could create a set of you new type and then use the `contains` function on it just as you would on a normal set. Use your imagination—this is some really cool stuff.

See Also

Recipe 6.18

6.18 Conditionally Extending a Type

Problem

You want to be able to extend existing data types that pass a certain test.

Solution

Use protocol extensions. Swift allows protocol extensions to contain code.

Discussion

Let's say that you want to add a method on any array in Swift where the items are integers. In your extension, you want to provide a method called `canFind()` that can find a specific item in the array and return yes if it could be found—I know that we can do this with other system methods, but I am offering this simple example to demonstrate how protocol extensions work:

```
extension Sequence where Iterator.Element == Int{
  public func canFind(_ value: Iterator.Element) -> Bool{
    return contains(value)
  }
}
```

Then you can go ahead and use this method like so:

```
func example1(){

  if [1, 3, 5, 7].canFind(5){
    print("Found it")
  } else {
    print("Could not find it")
  }

}
```

As another example, let's imagine that you want to extend all array types in Swift (Sequence) that have items that are either doubles or floating points. It doesn't matter which method you add to this extension. We'll add an empty method for now:

```
extension Sequence where Iterator.Element : FloatingPoint{
  // write your code here
  func doSomething(){
    // TODO: code this
  }
}
```

And you can, of course, use it like so:

```
func example2(){

  [1.1, 2.2, 3.3].doSomething()

}
```

However, if you try to call this method on an array that contains non–floating point data, you will get a compilation error.

Let me show you another example. Let's say that you want to extend all arrays that contain only strings, and you want to add a method to this array that can find the longest string. This is how you would do that:

```
extension Sequence where Iterator.Element == String{
  var longestString: String{
    var result = ""
    for value in self{
      if value.characters.count > result.characters.count{
        result = value
      }
    }
    return result
  }
}
```

Calling it is as simple as:

```
func example3(){

    print(["Foo", "Bar", "Vandad"].longestString

}
```

See Also

Recipe 6.17

6.19 Optimizing Your Swift Code

Problem

You want to adopt some simple practices that can make your Swift code run much faster than before.

Solution

Use the following techniques:

1. Enable whole module optimization on your code.
2. Use value types (such as structs) instead of reference types where possible.
3. Consider using `final` for classes, methods, and variables that aren't going to be overridden.
4. Use the `CFAbsoluteTimeGetCurrent()` function to profile your app inside your code.
5. Always use Instruments to profile your code and find bottlenecks.

Discussion

Let's have a look at an example. Let's say that we have a `Person` class like so:

```
class Person{
  let name: String
  let age: Int
  init(name: String, age: Int){
    self.name = name
    self.age = age
  }
}
```

Now we will write a method that will generate 100,000 instances of this class, place them inside a mutable array, and then enumerate the array. We will time this operation using the `CFAbsoluteTimeGetCurrent()` function. We'll then be able to tell how many milliseconds this took:

```
func example1(){

  var x = CFAbsoluteTimeGetCurrent()

  var array = [Person]()

  for _ in 0..<100000{
    array.append(Person(name: "Foo", age: 30))
  }

  // go through the items as well
  for n in 0..<array.count{
    let _ = array[n]
  }

  x = (CFAbsoluteTimeGetCurrent() - x) * 1000.0

  print("Took \(x) milliseconds")

}
```

When I ran this code, it took 41.28 milliseconds to complete; it will probably be different on your computer. Now let's create a struct similar to the class we created before but without an initializer, because we get that for free. Then do the same that we did before and time it:

```
struct PersonStruct{
  let name: String
  let age: Int
}

func example2(){

  var x = CFAbsoluteTimeGetCurrent()

  var array = [PersonStruct]()

  for _ in 0..<100000{
    array.append(PersonStruct(name: "Foo", age: 30))
  }

  // go through the items as well
  for n in 0..<array.count{
    let _ = array[n]
  }

  x = (CFAbsoluteTimeGetCurrent() - x) * 1000.0

  print("Took \(x) milliseconds")
```

```
}
```

 Don't suffix your struct names with "Struct" like I did. This is for demo purposes only, to differentiate between the class and the struct.

When I ran this code, it took only 35.53 milliseconds. A simple optimization brought some good savings. Also notice that in the release version these times will be massively improved, because your binary will have no debug information. I have tested the same code without the debugging, and the times were around 4 milliseconds. Also note that I am testing these on the simulator, not on a real device. The profiling will definitely report different times on a device, but the ratio *should* be about the same.

You will also need to determine which parts of your code are final and mark them with the `final` keyword. This will tell the compiler that you are not intending to override those properties, classes, or methods and will help Swift optimize the dispatch process. For instance, let's say we have this class hierarchy:

```
class Animal{
  func move(){
    if "Foo".characters.count > 0{
      // some code
    }
  }
}

class Dog : Animal{

}
```

And we create instances of the `Dog` class and then call the `move()` function on them:

```
func example3(){
  var x = CFAbsoluteTimeGetCurrent()
  var array = [Dog]()
  for n in 0..<100000{
    array.append(Dog())
    array[n].move()
  }
  x = (CFAbsoluteTimeGetCurrent() - x) * 1000.0
  print("Took \(x) milliseconds")
}
```

When we run this, the runtime will first have to detect whether the `move()` function is on the superclass or the subclass and then call the appropriate class based on this decision. This checking takes time. However, if you know that the move() function won't be overridden in the subclasses, you can mark it as final:

```
class AnimalOptimized{
  final func move(){
    if "Foo".characters.count > 0{
      // some code
    }
  }
}

class DogOptimized : AnimalOptimized{

}

func example4(){
  var x = CFAbsoluteTimeGetCurrent()
  var array = [DogOptimized]()
  for n in 0..<100000{
    array.append(DogOptimized())
    array[n].move()
  }
  x = (CFAbsoluteTimeGetCurrent() - x) * 1000.0
  print("Took \(x) milliseconds")
}
```

When I ran these on the simulator, I got 90.26 milliseconds for the nonoptimized version and 88.95 milliseconds for the optimized version. Not that bad.

I also recommend turning on whole module optimization for your release code. Go to your Build Settings and under the optimization for your release builds (App Store scheme), simply choose "Fast" with Whole Module Optimization, and you are good to go.

6.20 Building Equality Functionality into Your Own Types

Problem

You have your own structs and classes and you want to build equality-checking functionality into them.

Solution

Build your equality functionality into the protocols to which your types conform. This is the way to go!

Discussion

Let me give you an example. Let's say that we have a protocol called Named:

```
protocol Named{
  var name: String {get}
}
```

We can build the equality functionality into this protocol. We can check the `name` property and if the name is the same on both sides, then we are equal:

```
func ==(lhs : Named, rhs: Named) -> Bool{
  return lhs.name == rhs.name
}
```

Now let's define two types, a car and a motorcycle, and make them conform to this protocol:

```
struct Car{}
struct Motorcycle{}

extension Car : Named{
  var name: String{
    return "Car"
  }
}

extension Motorcycle : Named{
  var name: String{
    return "Motorcycle"
  }
}
```

That's it, really. You can see that I didn't have to build the equality functionality into Car and Motorcycle separately. I built it into the protocol to which both types conform. And then we can use it like so:

```
func example1(){

  let v1: Named = Car()
  let v2: Named = Motorcycle()

  if v1 == v2{
    print("They are equal")
  } else {
    print("They are not equal")
  }

}
```

This example will say that the two constants are not equal because one is a car and the other is a motorcycle, but what if we compared two cars?

```
func example2(){

  let v1: Named = Car()
  let v2: Named = Car()
```

```
if v1 == v2{
  print("They are equal")
} else {
  print("They are not equal")
}

}
```

Bingo. Now they are equal. So instead of building the equality functionality into your types, build them into the protocols that your types conform to and you are good to go.

6.21 Grouping switch Statement Cases Together

Problem

You want to design your cases in a `switch` statement so that some of them fall through to the others.

Solution

Use the `fallthrough` syntax. Here is an example:

```
let age = 30

switch age{
case 1...10:
  fallthrough
case 20...30:
  print("Either 1 to 10 or 20 to 30")
default:
  print(age)
}
```

 This is just an example. There are better ways of writing this code than to use `fallthrough`. You can indeed batch these two cases together into one `case` statement.

Discussion

In Swift, if you want one `case` statement to fall through to the next, you have to explicitly state the `fallthrough` command. This is more for the programmers to look at than the compiler, because in many languages the compiler is able to fall through to the next `case` statement if you just leave out the `break` statement. However, this is a bit tricky because the developer might have just forgotten to place the `break` state-

---

ment at the end of the case and all of a sudden her app will start behaving really strangely. Swift now makes you request fall-through behavior explicitly, which is safer.

6.22 Looping Conditionally Through a Collection

Problem

You want to go through the objects inside a collection conditionally and state your conditions right inside the loop's statement.

Solution

Use the new for x in y where syntax, specifying a where clause right in your for loop. For instance, here we will go through all the keys and values inside a dictionary and only get the values that are integers:

```
let dic = [
  "name" : "Foo",
  "lastName" : "Bar",
  "age" : 30,
  "sex" : 1,
] as [String : Any]

for (k, v) in dic where v is Int{
  print("The key \(k) contains an integer value of \(v)")
}
```

Discussion

In older versions of Swift, you'd have to create your conditions *before* you got to the loop statement—or even worse, if that wasn't possible and your conditions depended on the items inside the array, you'd have to write the conditions *inside* the loop. Well, no more.

Here is another example. Let's say that you want to find all the numbers that are divisible by 8, inside the range of 0 to 1,000, inclusive. You can do that as follows:

```
let nums = 0..<1000
let divisibleBy8 = {$0 % 8 == 0}
for n in nums where divisibleBy8(n){
  print("\(n) is divisible by 8")
}
```

And of course, you can have multiple conditions for a single loop:

```
let dic = [
  "name" : "Foo",
  "lastName" : "Bar",
```

```
  "age" : 30,
  "sex" : 1,
] as [String : Any]

for (k, v) in dic where v is Int && v as! Int > 10{
  print("The key \(k) contains the value of \(v) that is larger than 10")
}
```

6.23 Bundling and Reading Data in Your Apps

Problem

You want to bundle device-specific data into your app. At runtime, you want to easily load the relevant device's data and use it without having to manually distinguish between devices.

Solution

Follow these steps:

1. In your asset catalog, tap the + button and create a new data set (see Figure 6-1). Data sets contain our raw device-specific data.

Figure 6-1. Data sets contain our raw device-specific data

2. In the Attributes inspector of your data set, specify for which devices you want to provide data (see Figure 6-2).

Data Set

Name	rtf

Device
- ☐ Universal
- ☑ iPhone
- ☑ iPad
- ☐ Mac
- ☐ Apple Watch

Memory
- ☐ 1 GB
- ☐ 2 GB

Graphics
- ☐ Metal 1v2
- ☐ Metal 2v2

Figure 6-2. I have chosen to provide data for the iPad and iPhone in this example

3. Drag and drop your actual raw data file into place in IB.
4. In your asset list, rename your asset to something that you wish to refer to it by later (see Figure 6-3).

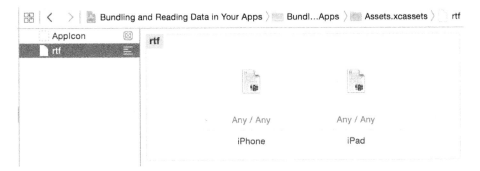

Figure 6-3. I have placed two RTF files into this data asset: one for iPhone and another for iPad

In the iPhone RTF I've written "iPhone Says Hello," and the iPad one says "iPad Says Hello"; the words iPhone and iPad are bold (attributed texts). I am then going to load these as attributed strings and show them on the user interface (see Figure 6-5).

5. In your code, load the asset with the `NSDataAsset` class's initializer.
6. Once that's done, use the `data` property of your asset to access the data.

Discussion

Place a label on your UI and hook it up to your code under the name `lbl` (see Figure 6-4).

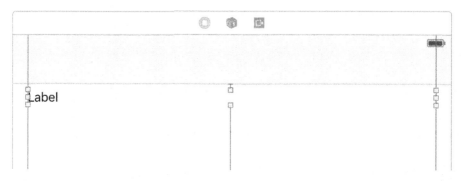

Figure 6-4. Place a label on your user interface and add all the constraints to it (Xcode can do this for you); hook it up to your code as well

Then create an intermediate property that can set your label's text for you:

```swift
import UIKit

class ViewController: UIViewController {

  @IBOutlet var lbl: UILabel!

  var status = ""{
    didSet{lbl.text = status}
  }

  ...
```

When the view is loaded, attempt to load the custom data set:

```swift
    guard let asset = NSDataAsset(name: "rtf") else {
      status = "Could not find the data"
      return
    }
```

The name of the data asset is specified in the asset catalog (see Figure 6-3).

Because data assets can be of any type (raw data, game levels, etc.), when loading an attributed string we need to specify what type of data we are loading in. We do that using an *options* dictionary that we pass to NSAttributedString's constructor. The important key in this dictionary is documentType, whose value in this case should be NSAttributedString.DocumentType.rtf. We can also specify the encoding of our data with the characterEncoding key:

```
let options = [
  .documentType : NSAttributedString.DocumentType.rtf,
  .characterEncoding : String.Encoding.utf8
] as [NSAttributedString.DocumentReadingOptionKey : Any]
```

Last but not least, load the data into the string and show it (see Figure 6-5):

```
do{
  let str = try NSAttributedString(data: asset.data, options: options,
    documentAttributes: nil)
  lbl.attributedText = str
} catch let err{
  status = "Error = \(err)"
}
```

Carrier 🛜   9:01 AM   ▬

iPhone Says Hello

Figure 6-5. This is how my string looked when I saved it in RTF format—it is now loaded into the user interface of my app

CHAPTER 7

Xcode 9 and Interface Builder

In this chapter, we are going to have a look at some of the updates to Xcode and Interface Builder. We will start with Xcode and some of the really exciting features that have been added to it since the previous version.

7.1 Changing Variable Names in the Current Scope

Problem

You want to quickly change the name of a variable in the local scope, for instance, inside the current function that you are in.

Solution

Follow these steps:

1. In the function where you have defined your variable or constant, move the keyboard cursor over to the variable or constant name. Where in the name doesn't matter.
2. Simultaneously press the Cmd-Ctrl-E keys on your keyboard.
3. The Xcode editor will then highlight the selected variable name in the entire scope of your function. If this variable or constant is defined outside the current function or scope, all instances where it is being used will now be highlighted.
4. Start altering the variable or constant name by typing a new name or just editing the existing one.
5. Once you are done, press the Enter key on your keyboard to finish the editing process.

Discussion

If you selected a variable name that is defined in the current function, changes that you make will not affect a variable of the same name that is outside this function's scope. You can see the scope where editing takes place in Figure 7-1. Here I am editing the name of a locally defined constant inside a function called `example()`. Another constant with the same name is defined globally outside this function's scope, but Xcode is intelligent enough to know that my intention is to change the name of the locally defined constant, and not the constant with the same name defined outside the scope of the current function.

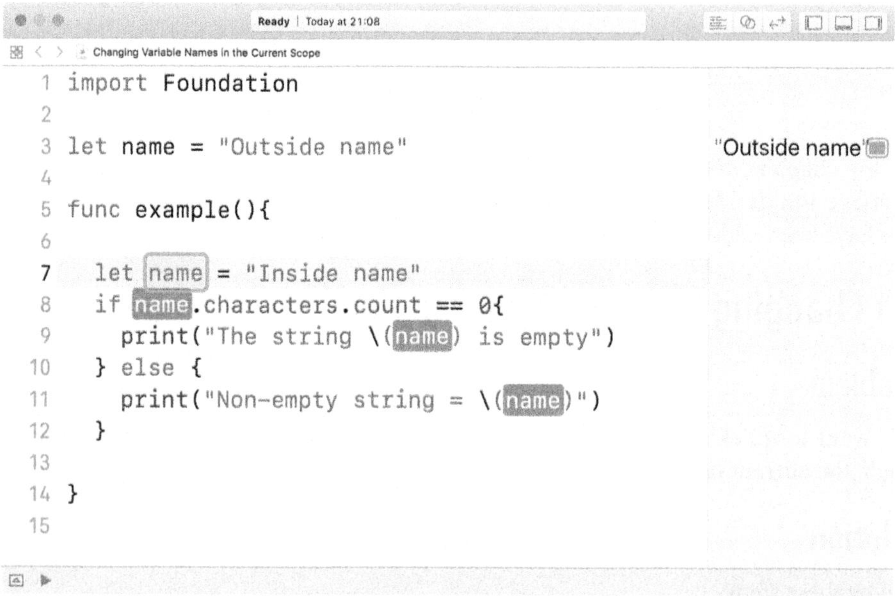

```
1  import Foundation
2
3  let name = "Outside name"                          "Outside name"
4
5  func example(){
6
7      let name = "Inside name"
8      if name.characters.count == 0{
9        print("The string \(name) is empty")
10     } else {
11       print("Non-empty string = \(name)")
12     }
13
14  }
15
```

Figure 7-1. Pressing Cmd-Ctrl-E affects only the constant in the local scope

If the variable or constant you choose is defined outside the current scope, Xcode will change the name of the constant or variable everywhere inside your code where you use it. In Figure 7-2, I have moved the keyboard cursor to the `example2()` function, where it refers to the global constant `name` in a `print()` statement. Now, when I press the Cmd-Ctrl-E keys on the keyboard, Xcode highlights every instance of this constant's name in the code and allows me to change this name by simply typing a new name or editing the existing one. The local constant Figure 7-1 is not affected.

It doesn't matter which instance of the constant or variable you move your keyboard cursor to in order to edit the name in a particular scope.

```
                        Ready | Today at 21:11

      Changing Variable Names in the Current Scope
1  import Foundation
2
3  let name = "Outside name"                          "Outside name'
4
5  func example1(){
6    if name.characters.count == 0{
7      print("The string \(name) is empty")
8    } else {
9      print("Non-empty string = \(name)")
10   }
11 }
12
13 func example2(){
14   print(name)
15 }
16
```

Figure 7-2. Pressing Cmd-Ctrl-E affects only the constant in the global scope

7.2 Utilizing Regular Expressions in Your Xcode Searches

Problem

You want to search your code using patterns (regular expressions).

Solution

Follow these steps:

1. Press the Cmd-Shift-F keys on your keyboard.
2. In the search field, press the Ctrl-Alt-Cmd-P keys in order to bring up the pattern matching dialog (see Figure 7-3).
3. Use the regular expressions provided in the form of predefined patterns and a combination of your own search terms to create the complete search text.
4. Once you are done, press the Enter key to perform your search.

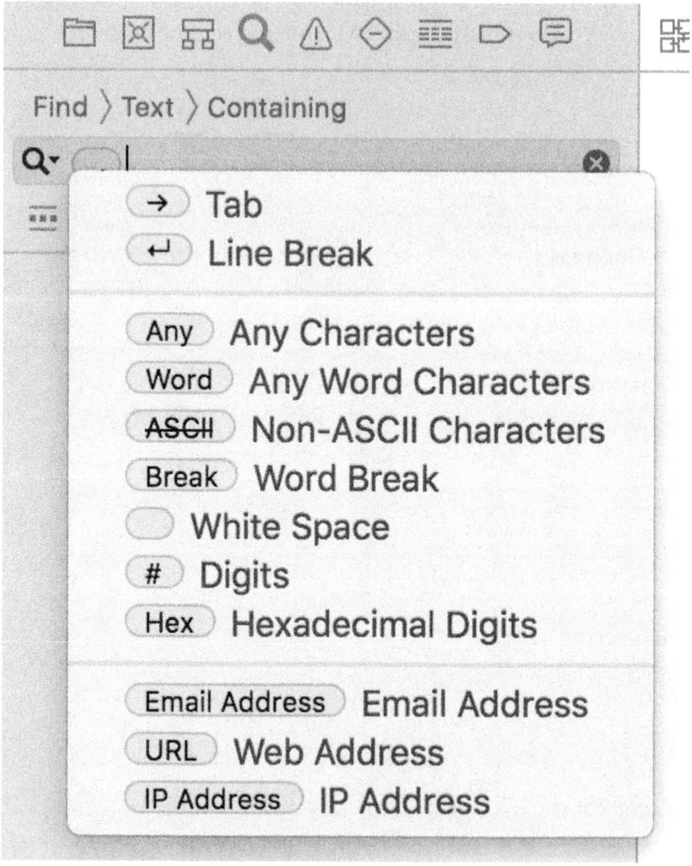

Figure 7-3. Opening the pattern matching dialog in Xcode's search field

Discussion

Here is an explanation of the different options available in the patterns dialog:

Tab
    A tab character. This option is used often if you are using tabs instead of spaces in your code for indentation.

Line Break
    A character that separates two lines of code or text from each other. In macOS this character is usually placed in documents when the user presses the Enter key on her keyboard.

Any Word Characters

Characters that normally make up a word. This does not include digits, white-space, most punctuation, etc.

White Space

A space, a tab, line break, and such.

Digits

Simple numerals, such as 1, 2, 3....

The value of a pattern or regular expression is that sometimes you might need to look for text that is too complicated to represent as plain characters. For instance, suppose you want to find any of the following instances of text in your application, with the focus being on the words *core* and *data*:

- Core Data
- CoreData
- Core performance in data
- Core data example

If you wanted to specify this search term in English, you would just look for any text that starts with the word "core" and ends with the word "data," allowing any other characters in between. To specify this search pattern, follow these steps:

1. Press Cmd-Shift-F to go to Xcode's global search.
2. In the search field, type in the word "core."
3. Then press the Ctrl-Alt-Cmd-P keys on your keyboard to open the available patterns (see Figure 7-3).
4. Choose the Any Characters item from the list.
5. Immediately after that, in the search field, type the word "data."
6. Press the Enter key on your keyboard to begin the search.

Here is another example. Imagine that you want to look for any method calls on `UIApplication.shared`. Note that you don't want to find any code that uses or changes a *property* on `UIApplication.shared`, but you want to find method calls. In that case, you can do the following:

1. Press Cmd-Shift-F in Xcode to open Xcode's global search.
2. Type "UIApplication.shared." in the search field, making sure to end the text with a dot as shown here.
3. Press Ctrl-Alt-Cmd-P to open the dialog for available patterns.
4. Select the Any Word Characters option to indicate that after *UIApplication.shared.* the user is allowed to write any word, without spaces, because those are the criteria for a function name. Spaces are not allowed in function names.

5. Then type in an opening parenthesis, because that's how a function call is invoked in Swift.
6. Press Ctrl-Alt-Cmd-P again. From the menu, choose Any Characters to denote that the user can type anything after the opening parenthesis.
7. Type in a closing parenthesis now to denote that the function call ends here.
8. Press the Enter key on your keyboard to perform the search. Sample results are shown in Figure 7-4.

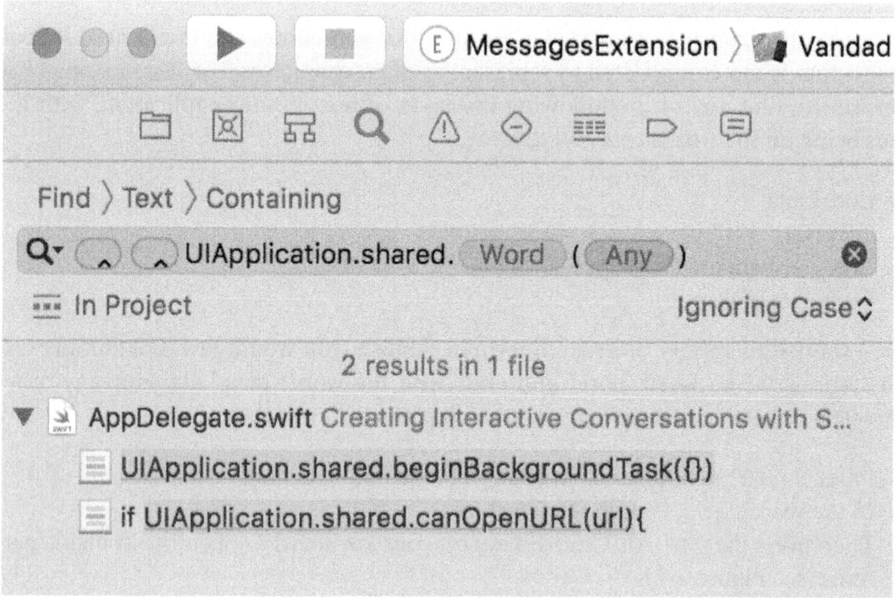

Figure 7-4. Finding all method calls to the UIApplication class in a project

 If your method call has a trailing closure argument, it can be short-handed by skipping the parentheses in Swift. That's an edge case that we are not covering in this example, but you can certainly specify a search pattern to find those method calls as well.

7.3 Debugging Apps on an iOS Device Wirelessly

Problem

You want to get rid of the cables that connect your iOS devices to your Mac while debugging your iOS apps, and instead wirelessly debug your applications on your various iOS devices.

Solution

Follow these steps:

1. For one last time, connect your device to your computer with a USB cable.
2. Open up Xcode if it's not already open.
3. From the Window menu, choose Devices and Simulators or simply press the Cmd-Shift-2 keys on your keyboard.
4. From the lefthand-side panel, select your connected device.
5. On the righthand side, ensure that the "Connect via network" option is selected (see Figure 7-5).
6. Once that is done, unplug your device from your computer.

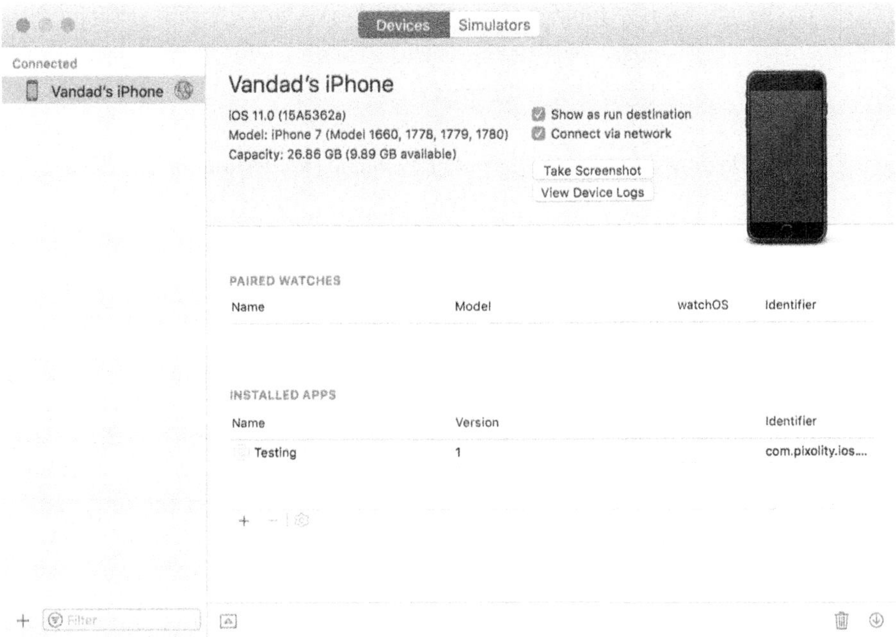

Figure 7-5. Enabling wireless debugging on an iOS device

Now in Xcode, you should be able to see your device in the list of available devices that can run your app (see Figure 7-6), with a little icon next to it indicating that wireless debugging is enabled on this particular device.

Device

✓ ■ Vandad's iPhone 🌐

Build Only Device

🔨 Generic iOS Device

iOS Simulators

📱 Vandad iPhone 7

📱 iPhone 7

Add Additional Simulators...
Download Simulators...

Figure 7-6. The iOS device appears in the list of available run destinations in Xcode

Discussion

Once you have enabled wireless debugging on an iOS device, as long as your local macOS instance is on the same network as that iOS device, you should be able to see the device in your list of debug destinations in Xcode.

Prior to Xcode 9, we developers had to always leave our devices connected to our Macintosh computers in order to be able to debug our applications on them. And since there are a limited number of USB ports on a Mac, we could connect only a few devices. There are, of course, USB hubs that you can purchase on the internet that allow you to expand a single USB 3.0 port to four to eight USB 2.0 ports, but that only clutters your desk with USB hubs and cables.

With the introduction of Xcode 9, you can hypothetically connect an unlimited number of iOS devices through the wireless network to your Macintosh, as long as your macOS and the iOS device are on the same network. This makes it a lot easier to share test devices. A team of iOS developers can maintain a pool of iOS devices that they share among themselves and debug their apps on, without having to move the devices around and constantly unplug them and plug them in again.

7.4 Making Sure UI Methods Run on the Main Thread

Problem

Your application sometimes crashes unexpectedly in production and you are not sure why. Alternatively, you get mysterious crashes every now and then with inscrutable crash logs, and don't know how to debug the problem.

Solution

Follow these steps:

1. Open your project in Xcode.
2. Hold down the Alt key on your keyboard and then click the Play button in Xcode.
3. In the lefthand panel, ensure that the Run section is selected (see Figure 7-7).
4. In the righthand panel, ensure that Diagnostics is selected at the top.
5. In the Runtime API Checking section, ensure that the Main Thread Checker is enabled.
6. Run your application and then go through different sections in your app where you believe the mysterious crashes might be occurring.

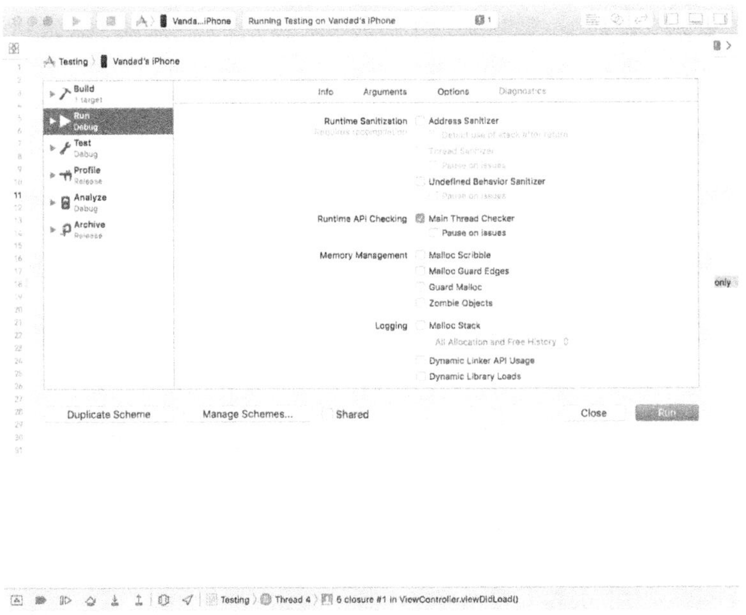

Figure 7-7. Enable the Main Thread Checker option for the project

If Xcode finds any UI method calls running on threads that are *not* the main thread, it will highlight those for you (see Figure 7-8).

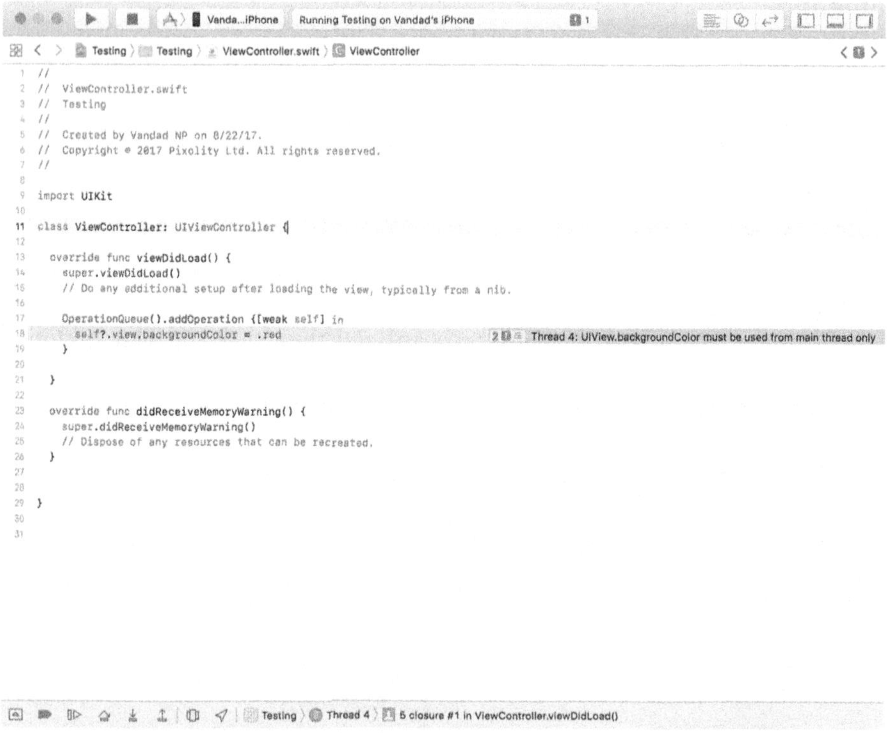

Figure 7-8. A UIKit method is running on a non-UI thread, and Xcode's Main Thread Checker has been able to detect and highlight the issue

Discussion

Only rarely can a UI method be called on a non-UI thread, and those exceptions are almost always documented explicitly by Apple. Otherwise, it is safe to assume that all UI-related methods must be called on the main (UI) thread. However, sometimes programmers make assumptions about which thread they are on, and end up calling a UI method and on a non-UI thread. This ends in one of the following circumstances:

- The code won't work, but it won't crash the app.
- The code will immediately crash the app.
- The code works, but the app ends up behaving unexpectedly.
- The code works and doesn't crash, but works only after a very long pause.

In all these circumstances, your application won't behave as expected and you will want to immediately fix those issues. Programmers who have used *Fabric.io* and *Crashlytics* know that Crashlytics can detect whether a crash is caused by a UI method running on a non-UI thread and can report those crashes to you and highlight those methods on its website. However, if you are not using *Fabric.io*, or if you simply want to avoid your application crashing or acting unexpectedly, the Main Thread Checker is a really good alternative. In fact, it is in many ways better than tools such as *Fabric.io*, because with the Main Thread Checker you can find these issues and correct them before your app is even in production. With *Fabric.io*, programmers usually wait until the app is in production and suffers from a high number of crashes before they fix the problem.

As a matter of fact, the Main Thread Checker is enabled by default for all projects created by the latest version of Xcode. If you have an old project, opening it with the new Xcode won't suffice; you will need to follow the instructions provided in this recipe to enable the Main Thread Checker.

Right below where you enabled the Main Thread Checker (see Figure 7-7), you should also see the "Pause on issues" option, which is not selected by default. If you enable this option, whenever a UI method is called on a non-UI thread not only will Xcode highlight it for you in the source code editor, but it will also break the debugger at that particular point so that you can issue debugging commands such as bt for backtrace.

7.5 Creating a GitHub Repository for Your Project in Xcode

Problem

You want to create a GitHub repository for your project right inside Xcode.

Solution

Follow these steps:

1. While in Xcode, press Cmd-2 in order to open the source control navigator.
2. From the Source Control menu, choose the Create Git Repositories... menu item.
3. In the dialog that appears, press the Create button. Xcode will now create a local Git repository for your project.

I am assuming that your project has neither a local nor a remote Git repository already associated with it.

4. Now that you are back in Xcode, press the Cmd-2 keys on your keyboard to bring up the source control navigator panel.

5. At the bottom-left corner of this panel, press the little gear button that will bring up a menu.

6. In this menu (see Figure 7-9), choose the item that begins with "Create," shows the name of your project, and ends with "Remote on GitHub...."

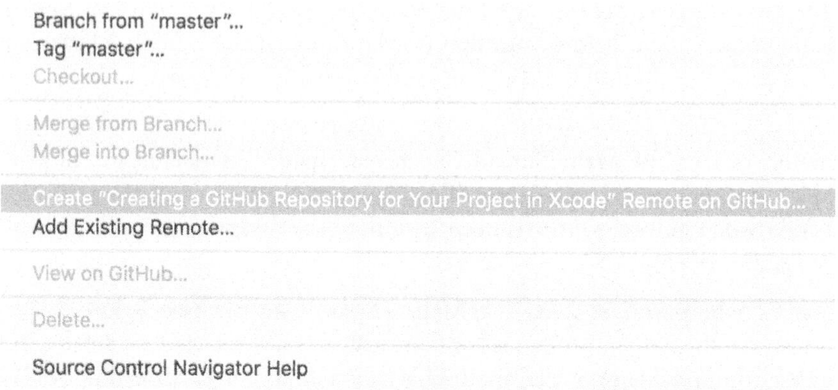

Branch from "master"...
Tag "master"...
Checkout...

Merge from Branch...
Merge into Branch...

Create "Creating a GitHub Repository for Your Project in Xcode" Remote on GitHub...
Add Existing Remote...

View on GitHub...

Delete...

Source Control Navigator Help

Figure 7-9. Creating a new remote for a project on GitHub

7. In the new dialog that appears (see Figure 7-10), either choose a previously logged-into GitHub account or log in to an account.

Figure 7-10. Enter the relevant information for your project and then press the Create button to create the new remote repository

8. Fill out the rest of the fields, such as Description. Once you are done, press the Create button to create your repository on GitHub.

Discussion

Xcode has built-in functionality for working with Git, and that's nothing new. However, in the new version of Xcode you can now interact with GitHub, which is one of the—if not *the*—most well-known Git remote servers.

Once you have created a remote for your project in GitHub, every git push command will send your code to the remote, which will then be in GitHub.

You can control all aspects of your Git commands through the Source Control menu in Xcode. That includes commands such as push, pull, commit, and clone. This might not be your preferred way of working. Some developers would rather work with Terminal instead of Xcode, so that they can have control over all commands and the parameters they pass to them. But Xcode is a very easy alternative that shouldn't simply be dismissed.

See Also

Recipe 7.6

7.6 Synchronizing Your Code with GitHub Inside Xcode

Problem

You want to ensure not only that you have the latest code that is on origin (GitHub in this case) but also that your coworkers have *your* latest code.

 In this recipe I am assuming that you have a good basic knowledge of how Git works. I won't go into details about Git or its commands; this recipe will try to teach you how to apply your Git knowledge to Xcode's built-in ability to work with Git and GitHub.

Solution

In order to ensure that you have the latest code that is placed on origin, you will need to issue a pull command. Follow these steps:

1. From the Source Control menu, choose the Pull menu item.
2. In the dialog that appears, choose the correct remote. The path is *origin/XXX*, where *XXX* is the name of the branch that you want to pull.

3. Once you are done, press the Pull button in this dialog.

Xcode will tell you whether your local repository is up to date, and will launch a pull request to update the repository if it is not.

In order to ensure that your local changes are pushed to the remote server—that is to say, that your changes are also sent to GitHub—follow these steps:

1. In the Source Control menu, click the Commit menu item.
2. In the dialog that appears (see Figure 7-11), choose the changes that you want to commit and then enter a message in the giant text box at the bottom of the screen. This message is known as the commit message and will be visible inside your Git repository's history for all other developers to see if your push succeeds. By "all other developers" I mean those with whom you have chosen to share your project. If you have created a free repository on GitHub, the entire world has access to your code, because free repositories on GitHub are public by default. To create private repositories on GitHub, you have to pay for them.

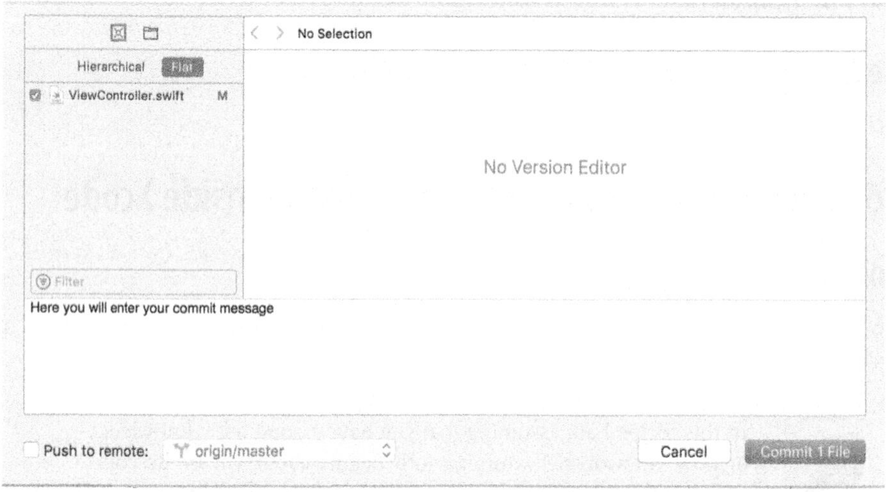

Figure 7-11. Choose the file to be committed and enter a commit message

3. Once you are done entering your commit message, press the Commit button.
4. Now, from the Source Control menu, choose the Push menu item.
5. In the dialog that appears (see Figure 7-12), choose the correct origin (usually *origin/XXX*, where *XXX* is your branch name) and then press the Push button.

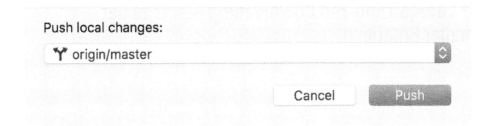

Figure 7-12. Choose the remote to push your code to

If everything goes fine, the dialog disappears automatically. But it is possible that before you made and pushed your commits, some changes occurred on the remote server, such as another developer pushing her changes to the remote. In that case, you will get to know about the synchronization problem later and you will need to do a Git pull before being able to push.

Discussion

GitHub is a very well-known host for Git repositories, and some programmers don't even know the difference between Git and GitHub—so let's make sure you understand the distinction. Xcode can work with any Git host. As long as it supports Git over SSH, Xcode can work with it. There are other Git hosts besides GitHub, but we don't have the time or the space to talk about all the different hosts, since new hosts are created frequently.

As for issuing the commands that interact with a Git host, some programmers choose to use Terminal, some choose to use SourceTree, and some choose to use Xcode. Xcode has a really easy way of working with Git repositories, but once you choose to use Xcode to synchronize your code with a remote, you will need to ensure that your coworkers also have your latest changes. As a rule of thumb, most observers recommend sending all your code changes to a remote before you leave your desk and go home. This ensures that no code is lost if you cannot make it to work the next day, and that your code is safely hosted in case your computer encounters a physical disaster overnight.

See Also

Recipe 7.5

7.7 Categorizing and Downloading Assets to Get Smaller Binaries

Problem

You have many assets in your app for various circumstances, and want to save storage space and network usage on each user's device by shipping the app without the optional assets. Instead, you want to dynamically download them and use them whenever needed.

Solution

Use Xcode to tag your assets and then use the `NSBundleResourceRequest` class to download them.

Discussion

For this recipe, I will create three packs of assets, each with three images in them. One pack may run for x3 screen scales, another for iPhone 6, and the last for iPhone 6+, for instance. I am taking very tiny clips of screenshots of my desktop to create these images—nothing special. The first pack will be called "level1," the second "level2," and the third "level3."

 Use the GitHub repo of this book for a quick download of these resources. Also, for the sake of simplicity, I am assuming that you are going to run this only on x3 scale screens such as iPhone 6+.

Place all nine images (three packs of three images) inside your *Assets.xcassets* file and name them as shown in Figure 7-13. Then select all the images in your first asset pack and open the Attributes inspector. In the On Demand Resource Tags section of the inspector, enter **level1**. Do the same thing for the other levels—but of course bump the number up for each pack.

Figure 7-13. Name your assets as shown

Now, in your UI, place three buttons and three image views, hook the buttons' actions to the code, and hook the image view references to the code:

```
@IBOutlet var img1: UIImageView!
@IBOutlet var img2: UIImageView!
@IBOutlet var img3: UIImageView!

var imageViews: [UIImageView]{
  return [self.img1, self.img2, self.img3]
}
```

To find out whether the resource pack that you need has already been downloaded, call the conditionallyBeginAccessingResourcesWithCompletionHandler() function on your resource request. Don't blame me! I didn't name this function. This will return a Boolean of true or false to tell you whether you have access to the resource. If you don't have access, you can simply download the resources with a call to the beginAccessingResourcesWithCompletionHandler() function. This will return an error if one happens, or nil if everything goes well:

```
var currentResourcePack: NSBundleResourceRequest?

func displayImagesForResourceTag(_ tag: String){
  OperationQueue.main.addOperation{
    for n in 0..<self.imageViews.count{
      self.imageViews[n].image = UIImage(named: tag + "-\(n+1)")
    }
  }
}

func useLevel(_ lvl: UInt32){
```

```
    let imageViews = [img1, img2, img3]

    for img in imageViews{
      img?.image = nil
    }

    let tag = "level\(lvl)"

    if let req = currentResourcePack{
      req.endAccessingResources()
    }

    currentResourcePack = NSBundleResourceRequest(tags: [tag])

    guard let req = currentResourcePack else {
      return
    }

    req.conditionallyBeginAccessingResources{available in
      if available{
        self.displayImagesForResourceTag(tag)
      } else {
        req.beginAccessingResources{error in
          guard error == nil else{
            // TODO: you can handle the error here
            return
          }
          self.displayImagesForResourceTag(tag)
        }
      }
    }

  }

}

@IBAction func useLevel3(_ sender: AnyObject) {
  useLevel(3)
}

@IBAction func useLevel2(_ sender: AnyObject) {
  useLevel(2)
}

@IBAction func useLevel1(_ sender: AnyObject) {
  useLevel(1)
}
```

 We keep a reference to the request that we send for our asset pack so that the next time our buttons are tapped, we don't have to check their availability again, but release the previously downloaded resources using the endAccessingResources() function.

Run the code now in your simulator. When Xcode opens, go to the Debug Navigator (press the Cmd-6 keys) and then click the Disk section. You will see results similar to those shown in Figure 7-14.

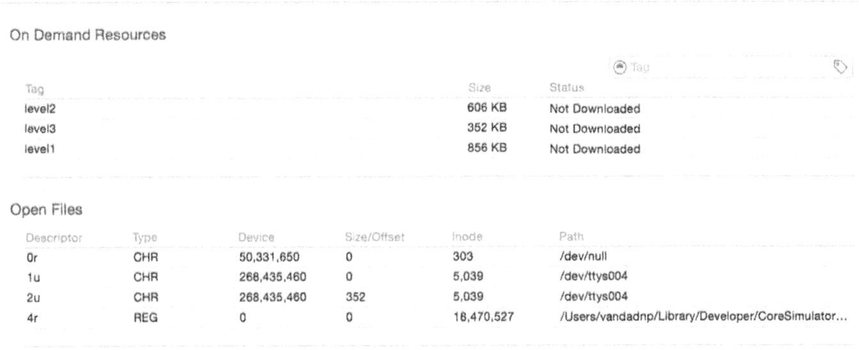

Figure 7-14. Xcode displaying On Demand Resources and the status of whether or not they are downloaded locally

Note how none of the asset packs are in use. Now in your UI, click the first button to get the first asset pack and watch how the first asset pack's status changes to "In Use." Once you switch from that pack to another, the previously chosen pack will be set to "Downloaded" and be ready to be purged.

See Also

Recipe 7.8

7.8 Exporting Device-Specific Binaries

Problem

You want to extract your app's binary for a specific device architecture to determine how big your binary will be on that device when the user downloads your app.

Solution

Follow these steps:

1. Archive your app in Xcode.
2. In the Archives screen, click the Export button.
3. Choose the "Save for Ad Hoc Deployment" option in the new screen and click Next.

4. In the new window, choose "Export for specific device" and then choose your device from the list.

5. Once you are done, click the Next button and save your file to disk.

Discussion

Bitcode is Apple's way of specifying how the binary that you submit to the App Store will be downloaded on target devices. For instance, if you have an asset catalog with some images for iPad and iPhone and a second set of images for iPhone 6 and 6+ specifically, iPhone 5 users should not get the second set of assets. This is the default functionality in Xcode, so you don't have to do anything special to enable it. If you are working on an old project, you can enable bitcode from Build Settings in Xcode.

If you are writing an app that has a lot of device-specific images and assets, I suggest that you use this method before submitting your app to the store to ensure that the required images and assets are indeed included in your final build. Remember, if bitcode is enabled in your project, Apple will detect the host device that is downloading your app from the store and will serve the right binary to that device. It's not necessary to separate your binaries when submitting to Apple—simply submit a big, fat, juicy binary and Apple will take care of the rest.

See Also

Recipe 7.7

7.9 Linking Separate Storyboards Together

Problem

You have a messy storyboard, and you would like to place some view controllers in their own storyboard and still be able to cross-reference them in your other storyboards.

Solution

Use IB's new "Refactor to Storyboard" feature under the Editor menu.

Discussion

I remember working on a project where we had a really messy storyboard and we had to separate the view controllers. What we ended up doing was putting the controllers on separate storyboards manually, after which we had to write code to link our buttons and other actions to the view controllers, instantiate them manually, and then show them. Well, none of that anymore. Apple has taken care of that for us!

As an exercise, create a single view controller project in Xcode and then open your main storyboard. Then open the Editor menu, and navigate to Embed In → Navigation Controller. Now your view controller has a navigation controller. Place a button on your view controller and then place another view controller on your storyboard. Select the button on the first view controller, hold down the Control key on your keyboard, and drag the line over to the second view controller. Then choose the "show" option in the menu that appears (Figure 7-15). This will ensure that when the user taps your button, the system will push the second view controller onto the screen.

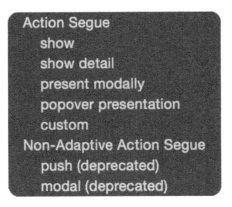

Figure 7-15. Adding a show segue to ensure that tapping our button will show the second view controller

Now select your second view controller and then, from the Editor menu, choose the "Refactor to Storyboard" item. In the dialog, enter *Second.storyboard* as the filename and save. That's really it. Now run your app and see the results if you want.

If you prefer to do some of this stuff manually instead of embedding things like this, you can always drag the new item called Storyboard Reference from the Object Library onto your storyboard and set up the name of the storyboard manually. Xcode will give you a drop-down box so that you don't have to write the name of the storyboard all by yourself. You will also be able to specify an identifier for your storyboard. This identifier will be useful when you are working with the segue (of course, you have to set up the ID for your view controller in advance).

7.10 Adding Multiple Buttons to the Navigation Bar

Problem

You want to add multiple instances of `UIBarButtonItem` to your navigation bar.

Solution

In Xcode, you can now add multiple bar button items to your navigation bar. Simply open the Object Library and search for "bar button." Once you find the buttons, drag and drop them onto your navigation bar and then simply reference them in your code if you have to. For instance, Figure 7-16 shows two bar buttons on the righthand side of the navigation bar. In previous versions of Xcode, we could add only one button to each side. If we wanted more buttons, we had to write code to add them.

Figure 7-16. Two buttons on the same side of the navigation bar

Discussion

Prior to the latest Xcode, you could not place multiple bar button items next to each other on your navigation bar. Well, now you can. You can also access these buttons just as you would expect, by creating a reference to them in your code. And you can always find them using the barButtonItems property of your navigation bar.

7.11 Showing the Header View of Your Swift Classes

Problem

You want to get an overview of what your Swift class's interface looks like.

Solution

Use Xcode's new Generated Interface assistant editor functionality. Open your Swift file first and then, in Xcode, use Show Assistant Editor, which you can find in the Help menu if you just type that name. After you open the assistant, you will get a split screen of your current view. In the second editor pane that opened, choose Generated Interface at the top instead of Counterparts (which is the default selection). You'll see your code as shown in Figure 7-17.

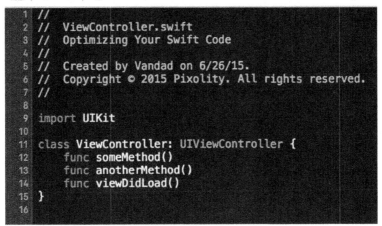

Figure 7-17. Code shown in Xcode's assistant editor

Discussion

The Generated Interface functionality of the assistant editor is quite handy if you want to get an overview of how clean your code is. It probably won't be day-to-day functionality that you use all the time, but I cannot be sure—maybe you will love it so much that you will dedicate a whole new monitor just to displaying your generated interface all the time. By the way, there is a shortcut to the assistant editor in Xcode: Cmd-Alt-Enter. To get rid of the editor, press Cmd-Enter.

7.12 Designing Interactive Interface Objects in Playgrounds

Problem

You want to design a view the way you want, but don't want to compile your app every time you make a change.

Solution

Use storyboards while designing your UI, and after you are done, put your code inside an actual class. In IB, you can detach a view so that it is always visible in your playground while you are working on it, and any changes you make will immediately be shown.

Discussion

Create a single view app and add a new playground to your project, as shown in Figure 7-18.

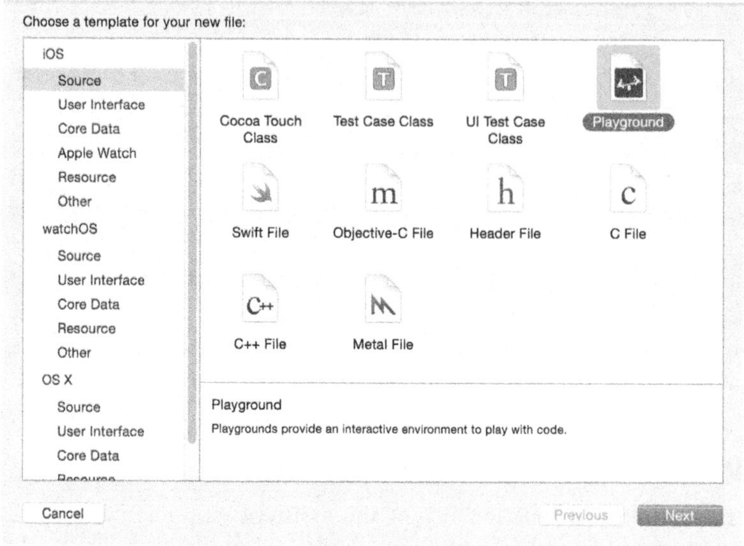

Figure 7-18. Add a new playground to your project

Write code similar to this to create your view:

```
import UIKit

var view = UIView(frame: CGRect(x: 0, y: 0, width: 300, height: 300))
view.backgroundColor = UIColor.green

view.layer.borderColor = UIColor.blue.cgColor
view.layer.borderWidth = 10
view.layer.cornerRadius = 20

view
```

Now on the righthand side of the last line of code that you wrote, you should see a + button. Click that (see Figure 7-19).

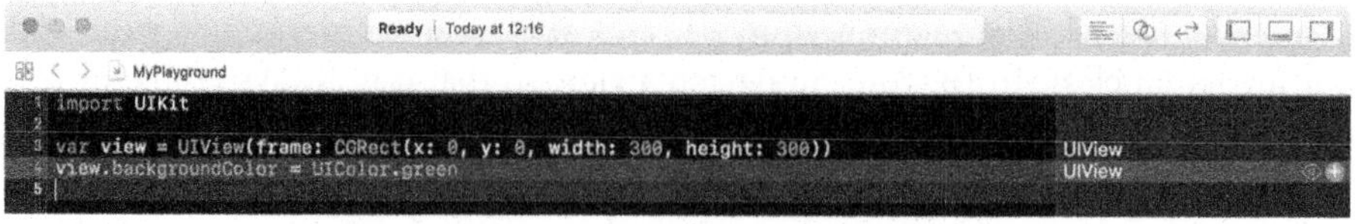

Figure 7-19. Click the little + button to get your view right onto your playground

By clicking that button, you will get a live preview of your view inside your playground. Now you can continue changing your view's properties and, once you are done, add a new preview of your view, so that you can compare the previous and the new states (see Figure 7-20). The first view shown has only the properties you had assigned to it up to the point that the view was drawn. The second view has more properties, such as the border width and color, even though it is the same view instance in memory—because it is drawn at a different time inside IB, it shows different results. This helps you compare how your views look before and after modifications.

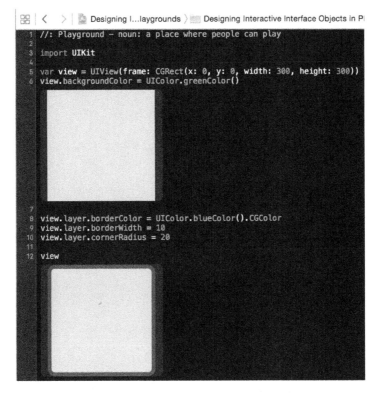

Figure 7-20. Two versions of a view

See Also

Recipe 7.10

CHAPTER 8

The User Interface

UIKit is the main framework for working with various UI components on iOS. You can use other frameworks, such as OpenGL, to build your own UI the way you want without being constrained by UIKit, but almost all developers use UIKit at some stage in their applications to bring intuitive user interfaces to their apps. One of the main reasons for this is that UIKit by default takes advantage of all the latest technologies in iOS and is kept up to date. For instance, many years back when Apple started producing Retina displays for iOS devices, all apps that were using UIKit could take advantage of the much sharper resolution afforded by Retina displays without requiring an update to their UIKit components. Applications that were using other technologies for rendering text had to update their apps to conform with Retina displays.

In this chapter, we will have a look at some of the most interesting features of UIKit and playgrounds.

8.1 Animating Details with Peek and Pop

Problem

You want to provide your users the ability to see details of content that you have placed on the screen, through the use of 3D Touch on their iOS devices.

Solution

Follow these steps:

1. Ask your view controller's `traitCollection.forceTouchCapability` property whether 3D Touch capabilities are available on the host device by comparing its value to `available`.

2. If 3D Touch is available, call the `registerForPreviewing(with:sourceView:)` method of your view controller to register your view controller's view for 3D Touch.

3. Make your view controller conform to the `UIViewControllerPreviewingDele gate` protocol.

4. Implement the `previewingContext(_:viewControllerForLocation:)` method of the aforementioned protocol in your view controller and in it, return the view controller which the iOS device will use to display the *peek* state of its animation.

5. Once your peek animation is finished, you can show the *pop* state of the animation by configuring a view controller that we will talk about shortly.

Discussion

3D Touch is a technology that adds another dimension (hence the name) to the tapping mechanism that you find in every iOS device. Traditionally, a user could perform the following actions on an iOS device's screen using her fingers:

- Tap
- Long tap
- Swipe
- Double tap

With the availability of 3D Touch on a device, a new vector that registers the strength of a touch on the screen is added to the formula, allowing the user to keep her finger on the screen and apply more pressure until an action (application specified) is performed. 3D Touch simply allows the iOS device to have access to how hard the user is pressing her finger on the screen, and this opens the door for a whole new set of applications.

There are two ways to take advantage of 3D Touch:

- Using storyboards and segue objects
- Custom peek and pop delegation

Let's have a quick look at the storyboard and segues method of dealing with 3D Touch. Follow these steps in order to implement peek and pop (3D Touch) functionality in your application using storyboards:

 The point of this exercise is to have a look at how 3D Touch works. In the process of doing so, I'm going to run you through setting up your project so that it can be integrated with 3D Touch.

1. Create a single view application in Xcode.
2. Open your *Main.storyboard* file in Interface Builder by simply clicking it.
3. Place a `UIButton` instance on your view controller.
4. From the object library, drag and drop a new instance of `UIViewController` onto your scene and then place an image view that covers the whole view controller.
5. Drag and drop a favorite image of yours onto your Xcode project and then assign that image to your image view.
6. Select your button on the first view controller, then press and hold down the Control key on your keyboard and drop the indicator onto the new view controller that contains the image view. Then release your mouse button (see Figure 8-1).
7. A pop-up will appear asking you which action you want this button to perform in relation to the image view controller. From the menu, choose Show.
8. Select your first view controller and then, from the Editor menu, choose Embed In followed by Navigation Controller.

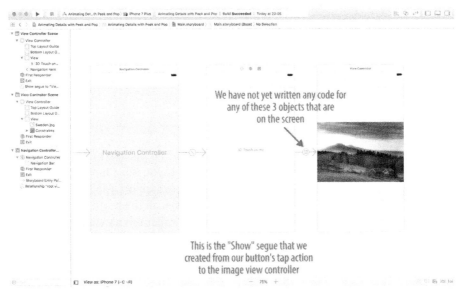

Figure 8-1. Creating the basic structure of an application that can take advantage of 3D Touch in Interface Builder

9. Select the segue object that you created between your view controller and the image view controller. Then, from the Attributes inspector in Interface Builder, in the Peek & Pop section, select the Preview & Commit Segues checkbox (see Figure 8-2). A few new options will now appear on your list. Don't touch them

for now as you won't be needing them in order to see the basic functionality of 3D Touch.

Figure 8-2. Creating a peek & pop animation between the root and the image view controllers with the help of Interface Builder

If you have a trackpad that supports 3D Touch, feel free to run your application now on an iOS simulator and see the results for yourself. If you don't have such a trackpad, you need to run your app on an iOS device that does support 3D Touch, such as the latest iPhone. When you run the app, hold your finger on the button and gently press it more and more until you see the image view controller animate automatically onto the screen, while blurring the background view controller. The harder you press, the closer this image view gets to you until it "pops" and fully covers the screen. You will then have the option to go back to the previous screen using the standard back button on the navigation bar.

This demonstrates the built-in support for 3D Touch in Xcode. However, if you have more complicated UI scenarios that require custom actions to be performed when the user presses down on an item on your view controller, you need to dig deeper into the 3D Touch APIs. Let's have a look at an example by creating a table view controller application that shows some images on the screen. I am going to assume that you already know how to do that, since creating a table view controller with images is not the objective of this recipe. I will skim through the required setup steps and hope you can follow:

1. Create a single view application in Xcode.
2. Open your *Main.storyboard* file and delete the default view controller. Also delete the *ViewController.swift* file that is already in your project.
3. Create a new class in your application called `TableViewController` of type `UITableViewController`. Now you should have a file in your application called *TableViewController.swift*.
4. Go to your *Main.storyboard*. From the object library, drop a table view controller onto the screen and change its class name to `TableViewController` so that now it points to your own subclass of `UITableViewController`.
5. Ensure that in Interface Builder you choose your table view controller as the initial view controller of the scene from the Attributes inspector by checking the Is Initial View Controller checkbox.
6. Choose your table view controller and in the Document Outline panel, choose your table view (see Figure 8-3).

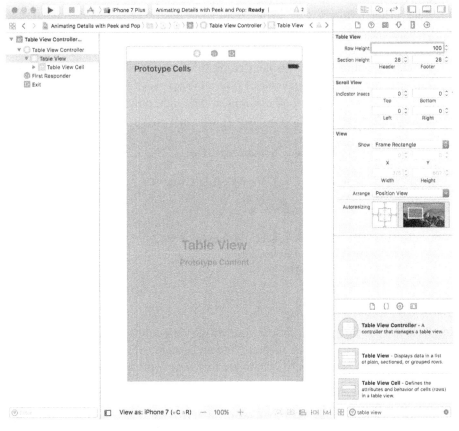

Figure 8-3. Choose a constant height for all your table view cells

7. Go to the Size Inspector panel and for row height, choose 100 instead of the default value that is already there. This ensures that all your table view cells are 100 points in height.

8. In the document outline, choose your table view. In the Attributes inspector, in the Content section, choose the value Static Cells instead of the default value of Dynamic Prototypes. This allows you to create cells right in Interface Builder.

9. Now go ahead and design a few cells with images and text in them. Ensure that your cells are of type Basic and that you use their Image property in Interface Builder to set their images. For the purpose of playing around, you can download some random images from the internet to display in the image views, and save them inside your project.

10. In the Document Outline panel, choose your table view controller. Then, from the Editor menu, choose Embed In followed by Navigation Controller.

11. In your Xcode project, create a new Cocoa Touch class of type `UIViewController` and call it `ImageViewController`.

12. Back in your storyboard, create a new view controller on your scene and associate its class name to `ImageViewController`.

13. Place an image view on this view controller, with scaling of type Aspect Fit, that covers the entire view controller. Hook this image view to your class under an outlet that is called `imageView` of type `UIImageView`. The code for your `Image ViewController` should look as simple as this right now:

```
import UIKit

class ImageViewController: UIViewController {

  @IBOutlet weak private var imageView: UIImageView!

  public var image: UIImage? = nil

  override func viewWillAppear(_ animated: Bool) {
    super.viewWillAppear(animated)
    imageView.image = image
  }

}
```

14. Back in your storyboard, choose your image view controller. Then, in the Identity Inspector panel, enter the value of **ImageViewController** in the Storyboard ID field. This will allow you to instantiate this view controller from your code using this identifier.

15. Now go to your *TableViewController.swift* file. When your view is loaded, register your table view for 3D Touch events if 3D Touch is enabled on the device, like so:

```
import UIKit

class TableViewController: UITableViewController,
UIViewControllerPreviewingDelegate {

    func previewingContext(_ previewingContext: UIViewControllerPreviewing,
                       commit viewControllerToCommit: UIViewController) {

    }

    func previewingContext(
      _ previewingContext: UIViewControllerPreviewing,
      viewControllerForLocation location: CGPoint) -> UIViewController? {
      return nil
    }

    override func viewDidLoad() {
      super.viewDidLoad()

      if traitCollection.forceTouchCapability == .available{
        registerForPreviewing(with: self, sourceView: tableView)
      }

    }

}
```

16. Now you need to implement the `previewingContext(_:viewControllerFor Location:)` function. In this function you get a point of type `CGPoint` where the user is holding her finger down on our target view (the table view). Using the table view's existing APIs, you can find which cell is under that point and then find the image for that cell. With this information, you can construct an instance of the `ImageViewController` and tell 3D Touch to show it to the user:

```
func previewingContext(
    _ previewingContext: UIViewControllerPreviewing,
    viewControllerForLocation location: CGPoint) -> UIViewController? {

    //construct a new image view controller
    guard let imageVc = UIStoryboard(name: "Main", bundle: nil)
      .instantiateViewController(withIdentifier: "ImageViewController")
      as? ImageViewController else {return nil}

    //get the image for the cell the user is 3D Touching
    guard let indexPath = tableView.indexPathForRow(at: location),
      let cell = tableView.cellForRow(at: indexPath),
      let image = cell.imageView?.image else {return nil}

    //tell iOS where to show the animation from
    previewingContext.sourceRect = tableView.rectForRow(at: indexPath)
```

```
//set the image and return the vc
imageVc.image = image
imageVc.preferredContentSize = CGSize(width: 200.0, height: 200.0)

return imageVc
}
```

17. Last but not least, you need to implement the previewingContext(_:commit:)
    function, where you to commit to your animation. In this method, you get a ref-
    erence to the view controller that you showed in the previewing context (the pre-
    vious step), and you can now decide whether you want to present it fully or not.
    You can even choose to display a whole new view controller. For the sake of sim-
    plicity, display the same view controller in full screen:

```
func previewingContext(_ previewingContext: UIViewControllerPreviewing,
                       commit viewControllerToCommit: UIViewController) {
    navigationController?.pushViewController(viewControllerToCommit,
                                            animated: false)
}
```

 You need an iOS device with 3D Touch to test this code on. You
can also test it on the iOS simulator as long as you have a trackpad
that supports 3D Touch.

See Also

Recipe 8.2

8.2 Providing Dynamic 3D Touch Menus on Home Screen

Problem

You want to provide customized menus on the home screen that serve as shortcuts
into different sections of your application. You also want to alter these shortcut items
over time as the user uses your app, based, for instance, on the user's preferences.
This recipe requires users to have 3D Touch on their devices.

Solution

Assign a new array of UIApplicationShortcutItem objects to the shortcutItems
property of your application instance. Every UIApplicationShortcutItem instance
can have a title and an image. When the user opens your application through one of

the shortcut items that you've defined, iOS calls the `application(_:performAction For:completionHandler:)` method of your app delegate. In this method, you get access to the instance of the `UIApplicationShortcutItem` object, and you can use information in that object to call functions or otherwise control the flow of the app.

Discussion

Let's have a look at an example where we assign an array of `UIApplicationShortcut Item` objects to the `shortcutItems` property of our app. In this example, I am not going to customize the menu; I'm simply going to show you that you can in fact change the value of this array to customize the menu of items that the user sees. One use for this customization would be to look at the user's behavior in your app over time and place the sections of your app that your user uses most often in the short-cuts menu.

Figure 8-4 shows what we will strive to create in our example.

Figure 8-4. Dynamically created shortcut menu items

Every object of type `UIApplicationShortcutItem` has two very important properties:

type: String
> An application-specified string that defines the type of action this item will take.

localizedTitle: String
> The title of the item, which can be localized if you have already localized your application. We won't do that in this recipe because localization is not what we are focusing on right now.

So, let's go and define our custom actions:

```
extension UIApplicationShortcutItem{
  static var books: UIApplicationShortcutItem{
    return UIApplicationShortcutItem(type: "book", localizedTitle: "Books")
  }
  static var magazines: UIApplicationShortcutItem{
    return UIApplicationShortcutItem(type: "mag", localizedTitle: "Magazines")
  }
  static var comics: UIApplicationShortcutItem{
    return UIApplicationShortcutItem(type: "com", localizedTitle: "Comics")
  }
}
```

We also need to override the conformance of `UIApplicationShortcutItem` to the `Equatable` protocol so that later we can intercept the shortcut item that the user has tapped on, and compare it to one of the shortcuts that we just defined. The default implementation of `Equatable` on `UIApplicationShortcutItem` comes from the `NSObject` class that converts the memory pointers. We want any two `UIApplicationShortcutItem` objects to be considered the same as long as their types and titles are the same, so we write:

```
func == (lhs: UIApplicationShortcutItem,
         rhs: UIApplicationShortcutItem) -> Bool{
  return lhs.hashValue == rhs.hashValue
}
```

Then in our app delegate, we assign our shortcut items to our app instance:

```
func application(_ application: UIApplication,
                 didFinishLaunchingWithOptions
  launchOptions: [UIApplicationLaunchOptionsKey: Any]?) -> Bool {

  application.shortcutItems = [.books, .magazines, .comics]

  return true
}
```

This way, when a shortcut item is tapped, we will get to know when the app delegate's `application(_:performActionFor:completionHandler:)` function is called. Here

---

we can use our `Equatable` implementation so we compare the incoming shortcut to our existing shortcuts and know which shortcut was chosen:

```
func application(_ application: UIApplication,
                 performActionFor shortcutItem: UIApplicationShortcutItem,
                 completionHandler: @escaping (Bool) -> Void) {

  if shortcutItem == .books{
    print("Books is selected")
    completionHandler(true)
  } else if shortcutItem == .magazines{
    print("Magazines is selected")
    completionHandler(true)
  } else if shortcutItem == .comics{
    print("Comics is selected")
    completionHandler(true)
  } else {
    //unhandled
    completionHandler(false)
  }

}
```

See Also

Recipe 8.1

8.3 Asking Your Users for App Store Reviews in Your App

Problem

You want to ask your users to place a review of your app on the App Store, without having to leave your app at all.

Solution

Utilize the `SKStoreReviewController` class.

Discussion

Prior to iOS 10.3, there was no way for developers to request reviews from their users, right in the apps, and post them to the App Store. This has caused a lot of headaches, and continues to do so, for developers whose frustrated users leave pointless or counterproductive one-word reviews in the App Store.

Now, using the `SKStoreReviewController` class, you can ask the user, wherever in your app that makes sense to your user's journey, to leave an honest review for your app right inside the app itself.

In order to achieve this, all you have to do is to call the `requestReview()` class function of the aforementioned class. In this example, I've placed a button on my user interface and linked that button to a function inside the app. In this function, I simply called the `requestReview()` class function of the `SKStoreReviewController` class as shown here:

```
@IBAction func leaveAReview(_ sender: Any) {
  SKStoreReviewController.requestReview()
}
```

There are internal limitations on how many times you can pester the user about leaving App Store reviews. These limitations might change from day to day, so it makes no sense to write about them here. It's important to note, however, that just because you call the `requestReview()` class function of the `SKStoreReviewController` class does not mean that the user will be asked to leave a review for your app immediately!

8.4 Providing Vibrational Feedback to Users

Problem

You want to make your user interface more lively by making the device vibrate when a user performs certain actions.

Solution

Use the Haptic engine that is built into some iOS devices, such as the iPhone 7, in order to generate various vibrational feedbacks that complement a user-initiated action inside your user interface.

Discussion

Apple has implemented a Haptic engine in some high-end iOS devices, and may possibly roll the same technology out in almost all iOS devices in the near future. The Haptic engine is a very small kinesthetic communications device, inside the iOS device's physical body, that is able to create small but real vibrational feedback to respond to a user-initiated action in an application.

For instance, when working with 3D Touch (see Recipe 8.1), by default, iOS uses the Haptic engine to generate some default vibrational feedbacks for you. For example, you can feel these effects when you hold your finger down on an image in the Messages application and keep pressing harder (3D Touch) until you get a nice "peek" effect, where iOS zooms into the build and displays the build in the center of the screen. Furthermore, you can continue to press harder on the screen in order to "pop" the image, displaying it on the full screen. These peek and pop effects have their own distinct haptic feedback, and in this recipe you will learn how to generate your own feedbacks with the built-in Haptic engine classes inside the iOS SDK.

There are three main categories of Haptic engine feedback:

Selection

This can be triggered when the user is choosing something from a list and decides to change the selection from one item to another, such as when choosing a birthdate from a wheel picker. For feedback of this type, use the UISelectionFeedbackGenera tor class.

Notification

This can be triggered when you want to produce a success, failure, or warning feed-back for an action, such as making a payment. Use the UINotificationFeedbackGen erator class to produce feedback of this type.

Impact

This can be triggered when you want to produce an effect that complements your UI, such as when the user drags down on an image to dismiss it. Use the UIImpactFeed backGenerator class to produce feedbacks of this type.

Using the UISelectionFeedbackGenerator class is very easy, so we can start with that. In order to create selection-changed feedback, all you have to do is to invoke this class's selectionChanged() function. For this example, we are going to develop a simple one-page application where a picker view at the bottom of the screen allows the user to pick her date of birth. As she rolls this picker view up and down to choose different values, we will call the selectionChanged() function on UISelectionFeed backGenerator (see Figure 8-5).

Carrier 🛜   10:34 PM

Feedback Generator

Run this example on a device with a
Haptic engine

1982
1983
1984

1985

1986
1987
1988

Figure 8-5. User interface of the birthday picker app

All we have to do now in order to implement this view controller is to conform to the
UIPickerViewDelegate and the UIPickerViewDataSource protocols in our view controller, and return an appropriate value to the picker view:

```
import UIKit

class ViewController: UIViewController,
UIPickerViewDelegate, UIPickerViewDataSource {

  lazy var selectionFeedbackGenerator: UISelectionFeedbackGenerator = {
```

```
    return UISelectionFeedbackGenerator()
}()

let years = Array(1935...2020)

func numberOfComponents(in pickerView: UIPickerView) -> Int {
  return 1
}

func pickerView(_ pickerView: UIPickerView,
                numberOfRowsInComponent component: Int) -> Int {
  return years.count

}

func pickerView(_ pickerView: UIPickerView,
                didSelectRow row: Int, inComponent component: Int) {
  selectionFeedbackGenerator.selectionChanged()
}

func pickerView(_ pickerView: UIPickerView, titleForRow row: Int,
                forComponent component: Int) -> String? {

  return "\(years[row])"
}

}
```

As you can see, using the UISelectionFeedbackGenerator class is straightforward, requiring only one function with no parameters.

For notifications, the UINotificationFeedbackGenerator class similarly provides one function, but this function takes one parameter of type UINotificationFeedback Type. The parameter's type is an enumeration that can have the value success, warn ing, or error. So, in order to generate a feedback for a payment that has successfully gone through, you can do as follows:

```
UINotificationFeedbackGenerator().notificationOccurred(.success)
```

Or if you want to indicate that the payment has gone through but is pending the banks' approval, you might want to generate a warning notification feedback:

```
UINotificationFeedbackGenerator().notificationOccurred(.warning)
```

Using the UIImpactFeedbackGenerator class is similar to using the UINotification FeedbackGenerator class, because it allows you to pick an impact style before you fire the haptic feedback. However, while the UINotificationFeedbackGenerator class allows you to choose the type of feedback when you want to fire it, with the UIImpact FeedbackGenerator class you need to initialize the class with the type of feedback you want to fire, and then fire it. That means that you need to initialize UIImpactFeed backGenerator instances for every impact style of type `UIImpactFeedbackStyle`. Here is an example that shows how you can issue a heavy-impact haptic feedback with `UIImpactFeedbackGenerator`:

```
UIImpactFeedbackGenerator(style: .heavy).impactOccurred()
```

Similarly, a medium-impact feedback can be issued as shown here:

```
UIImpactFeedbackGenerator(style: .medium).impactOccurred()
```

8.5 Supporting Drag and Drop in Your Apps

Problem

You want to let the user drag an item from one application to another on an iPad.

Solution

The most popular items that users drag and drop are images. Therefore, this recipe implements drag and drop for images, covering not only the mechanics of the operation but other useful tasks such as positioning the image and letting the user know through visual cues that it is being dragged.

Follow these steps:

1. Conform your view controller to the `UIDropInteractionDelegate` and `UIDragInteractionDelegate` protocols. These are responsible for controlling drag and drop, whether inside your app or between apps.
2. Set your view controller's view's `pasteConfiguration` to a valid instance of `UIPasteConfiguration`.
3. Instantiate `UIDropInteraction` and add the drop interaction to your view controller's view using its `addInteraction(_:)` function.
4. Similar to the previous step, instantiate `UIDragInteraction` and add the drag interaction to your view controller's view using its `addInteraction(_:)` function.
5. Implement the `UIDropInteractionDelegate` functions.
6. Similarly, implement the `UIDragInteractionDelegate` functions.

Discussion

Drag and drop is a useful feature implemented quite smoothly in iOS. On the iPhone, drag and drop works only inside the same app, not across applications. On the iPad, however, drag and drop works across applications, so that a user can drag an item such as an image from one application and drop it into another application. Multiple items can also be selected and moved. The application from which the item is coming must implement drag operations, and the application receiving the item must implement drop operations. Most apps that want to support drag and drop implement both sets of operations, which we will do in this recipe.

The drag-and-drop mechanism is embodied in `UIDropInteractionDelegate` and `UIDragInteractionDelegate` functions. You can implement one without the other if you want, so that for instance you can be the source of the drag and drop without allowing other apps to send you items. However, it's probably more intuitive for your users if your app allows them to drag items both into it and out of it.

Let's have a look at an example. When the user drags an image into our app, we'll create a new image view and place it on top of our view. The user can of course drag and drop the images around in our app as well. So, let's start by defining the necessary class and variables for our view controller. We'll create a single view application, making sure that the view controller conforms to the `UIDropInteractionDelegate` and `UIDragInteractionDelegate` protocols:

```
import UIKit

class ViewController: UIViewController,
UIDropInteractionDelegate, UIDragInteractionDelegate{

  var dropPoint = CGPoint.zero

  var imageViews = [UIImageView]()

  var images: [UIImage]{
    return imageViews.flatMap{$0.image}
  }

  //the rest of our implementation will follow soon...
```

The `dropPoint` variable will hold the `CGPoint` instance that we retrieve from the drop session when the user drops an image into our view. We will use this point to later create an image view where the user dropped the image, and place the image view inside the `imageViews` variable array.

We need to now accept dragging and dropping on our view. As mentioned in the Solution section, this is done through the `addInteraction(_:)` function of our view:

```
override func viewDidLoad() {
  super.viewDidLoad()

  view.pasteConfiguration = UIPasteConfiguration(forAccepting: UIImage.self)
  view.addInteraction(UIDropInteraction(delegate: self))
  view.addInteraction(UIDragInteraction(delegate: self))

}
```

The first method of `UIDragInteractionDelegate` that we are going to implement is `dropInteraction(_:canHandle:)`. This function will be called by the system before handing us the item the user wants to drop. We have to return a Boolean value that indicates whether we can handle the item that is being dropped onto our app. In order to check the item we're being asked to receive and make sure it's a data type we can handle here (an image), the function accepts an object of type `UIDropSession` as one of its parameters. We can query this session object using its `canLoad Objects(ofClass:)` function to see whether it contains objects of a specific type, such as `UIImage`, and then return this value back to the `dropInteraction(_:canHan dle:)` function:

```
func dropInteraction(_ interaction: UIDropInteraction,
                     canHandle session: UIDropSession) -> Bool {
  return session.canLoadObjects(ofClass: UIImage.self)
}
```

The next `UIDragInteractionDelegate` delegate function to implement is `dropInter action(_:sessionDidUpdate:)`. When the system calls this method, it expects us to return a value of type `UIDropProposal`. What we return from this function determines whether our application wants to:

- Make a copy of the dropped item.
- Move the item from its source into the destination.
- Indicate that dropping this particular item into our application is forbidden.
- Indicate that dropping items into our application is not allowed (cancelled).

 What is the difference between not allowing an item into our app and forbidding the content from being dropped? Imagine that your application has accepted so many images onto its canvas that it determines the user can't manage any more images. In that case, when the next image is being dropped into your app, you can say that dropping the image at this point in time is forbidden, even though it's an operation that is otherwise allowed. But if you cancel an operation, you effectively restrict drag-and-drop operations to those within your app, not from outside your app.

The common way to handle this choice is to check whether an item is coming from your own app, which is true when `session.localDragSession` is set. If it's set, you generally choose to move the item so you maintain a single copy. If the property is `nil`, you copy the item so that the app it came from doesn't lose its copy:

```
func dropInteraction(
  _ interaction: UIDropInteraction,
  sessionDidUpdate session: UIDropSession) -> UIDropProposal {

  let operation: UIDropOperation
  if session.localDragSession == nil{
    operation = .copy
```

```
  } else {
    operation = .move
  }

  return UIDropProposal(operation: operation)

}
```

The next function of the UIDropInteractionDelegate protocol that we have to implement is the dropInteraction(_:performDrop:) function. In this function, we effectively ask the source of the drag-and-drop session to provide us the content of what is being dropped into our app, because what the user is dragging around the screen before dropping it is a preview of the content, and not the entire content. As a parameter to this function, we get an object of type UIDropInteraction. It has a view property that is the view onto which the object is being dropped. As another parameter, we get an object of type UIDropSession. We can call its location(in:) function and pass our view to this function to get the location, of type CGPoint, where the user wants to drop the content. We also need to read the localDragSession property of our session object. As we have seen, this property is set to nil if the dragging is initiated from outside our application. If the drag-and-drop session is initiated inside our app, we don't have to load the image, because we already have that image. Otherwise, we have to ask the source application for the image's contents:

```
func dropInteraction(_ interaction: UIDropInteraction,
                     performDrop session: UIDropSession) {

  if let view = interaction.view{

    dropPoint = session.location(in: view)

    if session.localDragSession == nil{
      for item in session.items{
        extractImage(from: item.itemProvider, center: dropPoint)
      }
    }

  }

}
```

We are using the extractImage(from:center:) function in our implementation. This is a function that we are going to write shortly.

Next up, we need to implement the dropInteraction(_:previewForDropping:with Default:) function of the UIDropInteractionDelegate protocol. In this function, we need to return an object of type UITargetedDragPreview that tells the system how the preview of the dragged item will look as it gets dropped on the screen. The system by default creates a preview object of type UITargetedDragPreview and passes it to us through the defaultPreview parameter. We can take this default preview and just change its center point so that its center is precisely where the user dropped the item:

```
func dropInteraction(
  _ interaction: UIDropInteraction,
  previewForDropping item: UIDragItem,
  withDefault defaultPreview: UITargetedDragPreview)
  -> UITargetedDragPreview? {

  guard item.localObject != nil else {return nil}

  let target = UIDragPreviewTarget(container: view, center: dropPoint)
  return defaultPreview.retargetedPreview(with: target)

}
```

The next stop is the dropInteraction(_:item:willAnimateDropWith:) function of the UIDropInteractionDelegate protocol. In this function we can animate the drag-ged items. For this example, we choose first to fade the item to half its opacity and then, when the drop operation is completed, take the opacity value back to its normal value of 1. We do these animations with an object of type UIDragAnimating that is passed to us in this function through the animator parameter, using its addAnima tions(_:) and addCompletion(_:) functions:

```
func dropInteraction(
  _ interaction: UIDropInteraction,
  item: UIDragItem,
  willAnimateDropWith animator: UIDragAnimating) {

  animator.addAnimations {
    self.fade(items: [item], alpha: 0.5)
  }

  let center = dropPoint
  animator.addCompletion {_ in
    guard let index = item.localObject as? Int else {return}
    self.imageViews[index].center = center
    self.imageViews[index].alpha = 1.0
  }

}
```

In the dropInteraction(_:performDrop:) function that we have implemented already, we used a function called extractImage(from:center:), which I promised we would implement shortly. Let's do that now. In the from parameter of this function we passed an object of type NSItemProvider, and for the center parameter we passed a value of type CGPoint that was the dropping point of the object.

Using the NSItemProvider object we can load the session's associated object using the provider's loadObject(ofClass:completionHandler:), and for the ofClass parameter we can pass UIImage.self to indicate that we are interested in the image that the user is dragging and dropping on our app:

```
func extractImage(from itemProvider: NSItemProvider, center: CGPoint) {

  itemProvider.loadObject(ofClass: UIImage.self) {[weak self] object, _ in
    guard let `self` = self else {return}
    DispatchQueue.main.async {[weak self] in
      guard let `self` = self, let image = object as? UIImage else {return}
      let imageView = image.imageView
      imageView.center = center
      self.imageViews.append(imageView)
      self.view.addSubview(imageView)
    }
  }

}
```

In the previous code, when we extract the image from the item provider, we are calling the imageView property on the image to retrieve a new image view that contains the image. Let's implement this property on UIImage now:

```
extension CGSize{
  var rounded: CGSize{
    return CGSize(width: round(width), height: round(height))
  }
}

fileprivate extension UIImage{
  var imageView: UIImageView{
    let result = UIImageView(image: self)
    result.isUserInteractionEnabled = true
    result.contentMode = .scaleAspectFit

    let longestSide = max(size.width, size.height)
    let maxSize = CGFloat(300)

    //if the image's largest size is larger than 'maxSize', then we
    //shrink it down with a transformation
    if longestSide > maxSize {
      let scale = maxSize / longestSide
      let transform = CGAffineTransform(scaleX: scale, y: scale)
      result.frame.size = size.applying(transform).rounded
    }

    return result
```

```
    }
}
```

We also used a function called fade(items:alpha:) to animate our dropped items into the screen. Let's implement that function now:

```
func fade(items: [UIDragItem], alpha: CGFloat) {
  for item in items where item.localObject is Int {
    imageViews[item.localObject as! Int].alpha = alpha
  }
}
```

With all the preceding code, we have taken care of the drop-related functions inside the UIDropInteractionDelegate protocol. It's time to start implementing the drag-related functions inside the UIDragInteractionDelegate protocol.

The first function to implement is dragInteraction(_:itemsForBeginning:), which gets called whenever the user begins a drag operation on our view. This function expects a value of type [UIDragItem], an array of wrappers around the items that have to be dragged around the screen. Usually the array contains only one object, but if you have multiple objects at a specific drag point, such as stacked images, you might want to return them all to this function as an array so that they can be dragged around the screen simultaneously.

The session parameter of this function is of type UIDragSession. This session object has a function called location(in:) that you can call to get a CGPoint inside your view indicating where the user is initiating the drag. You can then find the image views that are at that point, extract the images from the image views, and place the images inside an object of type NSItemProvider. Once you have the NSItemProvider instance, you can create an instance of UIDragItem from it, as shown here:

```
func dragInteraction(
  _ interaction: UIDragInteraction,
  itemsForBeginning session: UIDragSession) -> [UIDragItem] {

  guard let interactionView = interaction.view else {return []}

  let point = session.location(in: interactionView)

  guard let hitTestView = view?.hitTest(point, with: nil) as? UIImageView,
    let index = imageViews.index(of: hitTestView) else {
    return []
  }

  let image = images[index]
  let itemProvider = NSItemProvider(object: image)
  let dragItem = UIDragItem(itemProvider: itemProvider)
  dragItem.localObject = index

  return [dragItem]
```

}

The next function in the `UIDragInteractionDelegate` protocol that we have to implement is `dragInteraction(_:previewForLifting:)`. This function gets called to let you customize the preview that iOS prepares when an object is being lifted into the "air" to later be dragged around the screen. This function has to return a value of type `UITargetedDragPreview`, which you can initialize with variety of values. In our app, we'll add in the most common value, a `UIView` instance, which we have because our image view of type `UIImageView` inherits from `UIView` (there are other choices: for instance, you could return a URL if the content to be dragged to the screen has to be loaded from a remote source by iOS):

```
func dragInteraction(
  _ interaction: UIDragInteraction,
  previewForLifting item: UIDragItem, session: UIDragSession)
  -> UITargetedDragPreview? {

  guard let index = item.localObject as? Int else {return nil}

  return UITargetedDragPreview(view: imageViews[index])

}
```

Up next is the `dragInteraction(_:willAnimateLiftWith:session:)` function. This function gets called when the item that is the target of the drag session is lifted off the screen to be dragged around. You can use this function to animate the source of the drag session. In our example, this function indicates visually to the user that the content is going to be copied instead of moved, by graying out the original object. If the item is actually moved, we remove it from the canvas altogether. We get an animator of type `UIDragAnimating` in this function's `animator` parameter and we can use this animator's `addCompletion(_:)` function to set an animation on the source object when the lift operation is finished:

```
func dragInteraction(
  _ interaction: UIDragInteraction,
  willAnimateLiftWith animator: UIDragAnimating,
  session: UIDragSession) {

  animator.addCompletion { position in
    if position == .end {
      self.fade(items: session.items, alpha: 0.5)
    }
  }

}
```

Similar to the `dragInteraction(_:willAnimateLiftWith:session:)` function, we also need to implement the `dragInteraction(_:item:willAnimateCancelWith:)`

function of the `UIDragInteractionDelegate` protocol. That function gets called when the drag session is cancelled. In this case, we can indicate to the user, by changing the alpha channel of the source object back to its default value of 1, that the source object is not being dragged around any longer:

```
func dragInteraction(
  _ interaction: UIDragInteraction,
  item: UIDragItem,
  willAnimateCancelWith animator: UIDragAnimating) {

  animator.addAnimations {
    self.fade(items: [item], alpha: 1)
  }

}
```

Just as we have to return the source object back to its alpha channel if the drag session is cancelled, we need to do the same thing if the drag session has successfully ended, meaning that the source object has been dropped to its destination. So we implement the `dragInteraction(_:session:willEndWith:)` function from the `UIDragInteractionDelegate` protocol, which gets called when the drag operation has successfully resulted in a drop operation:

```
func dragInteraction(
  _ interaction: UIDragInteraction,
  session: UIDragSession,
  willEndWith operation: UIDropOperation) {

  if operation == .copy {
    fade(items: session.items, alpha: 1)
  }

}
```

Last but not least, we need to implement the `paste(itemProviders:)` function, which gets called if the user pastes some images into our application using keyboard shortcuts (such as a Bluetooth external keyboard's Ctrl-V key combination). In this function, we get an array of `NSItemProvider` instances. We can just pass them to our `extractImage(from:center:)` function to paste them on the last drop point that the user had chosen. If the user had not previously pasted anything on the screen, we paste them at `CGPoint.zero`:

```
override func paste(itemProviders: [NSItemProvider]) {
  for item in itemProviders {
    extractImage(from: item, center: dropPoint)
  }
}
```

Quite a lot of code, but now it's over. That was all you had to implement to enable drag and drop in your app. Try it out on an iPad to get the full experience.

8.6 Scaling Fonts in Order to Support Dynamic Types

Problem

You want your application to reflect the user's preferred font sizes, taken from the Settings application on the iOS device.

Solution

Follow these steps:

1. Choose a default font and a default size for your label. (I will assume in this recipe that we are talking about a single label, but the technique can be applied to applications with any number of labels.)
2. Listen to the `UIContentSizeCategoryDidChange` notification that gets sent by the system when the user changes her settings with regard to font sizes in the Accessibility section in the Settings application.
3. When you get this notification, recalculate the size of the font for your label using `UIFontMetrics.default.scaledFont(for:compatibleWith:)` from the `UIFont Metrics` class. As the `for` parameter, pass your default font, and as the `compatibleWith` parameter, pass your view controller's `traitCollection` property.

Discussion

Users on an iOS device can navigate to the Settings application, then the General tab and the Accessibility tab, and from there choose Larger Text. In this section they can enable larger text sizes in iOS and adjust the font size to their liking (Figure 8-6).

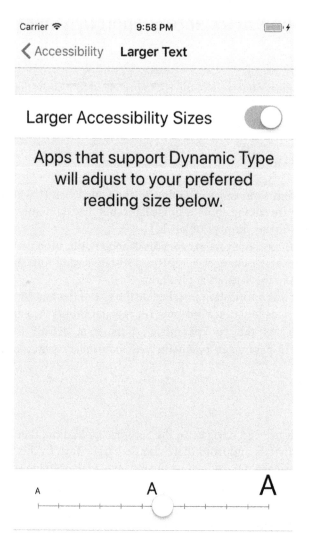

Figure 8-6. Users can adjust the font size for the system through this screen

Let's have a look at an example. For this example, I've gone online, looking for free TrueType fonts, and found a font called *Champignon*. You can either choose to do the same thing or use a system font. I have placed the new font in the application's *Info.plist* file as well so that it can be loaded by iOS when our app starts up:

```
<key>UIAppFonts</key>
<array>
  <string>Champignon.ttf</string>
  <string>champignonaltswash.ttf</string>
</array>
```

If you choose to load a custom font into your app, you will also need to find the name of the font by running this code in your app:

```
UIFont.familyNames.forEach{familyName in
  UIFont.fontNames(forFamilyName: familyName).forEach{fontName in
    print(fontName)
  }
}
```

So, let's have a look at our view controller. In this view controller, on the storyboard, I've placed a label that takes up the entire screen and is connected to an outlet in the view controller called label. Figure 8-7 shows the label on our view controller, with a custom font, connected to an outlet in our view controller so that we can later dynamically change its font when the user changes her font size preferences.

Figure 8-7. Preparing the view controller for a font change

We start by implementing a computed property on our view controller that returns our default font:

```
import UIKit

class ViewController: UIViewController {

  @IBOutlet weak var label: UILabel!

  var originalFont: UIFont{
    let defaultSize = CGFloat(40.0)
    return UIFont(name: "Champignon", size: defaultSize) ??
      UIFont.systemFont(ofSize: defaultSize)
  }

  //the rest of our code will be placed here...
```

Next we are going to write a function that uses the `scaledFont(for:compatible` `With:)` function of `UIFontMetrics.default` in order to scale our font according to the user's preferences:

```
func readjustLabelFontSize(){
  label.font = UIFontMetrics.default.scaledFont(
    for: originalFont, compatibleWith: traitCollection)

}
```

After our view controller is loaded, we will listen there to the `UIContentSize` `CategoryDidChange` notification. Once it gets sent, we will readjust the font of our label:

```
override func viewDidLoad() {
  super.viewDidLoad()

  readjustLabelFontSize()

  NotificationCenter.default.addObserver(
    self,
    selector: #selector(respondToSizeCategoryChangedNotification(_:)),
    name: .UIContentSizeCategoryDidChange,
    object: nil)

}

@objc func respondToSizeCategoryChangedNotification(
  _ notification: NSNotification){

  readjustLabelFontSize()

}
```

Suppose the user changes her font preferences to the largest size offered in the Settings application. Figure 8-8 shows that our app has responded by changing the font size for our label.

Hello World

Figure 8-8. View controller reflecting the larger font size

See Also

Recipe 8.7

8.7 Adjusting Labels While Supporting Dynamic Types

Problem

You have a view controller with labels, such as that shown in Figure 8-9. Both labels are long and can wrap. You want to ensure that you can support dynamic sizing while maintaining a good distance between the labels.

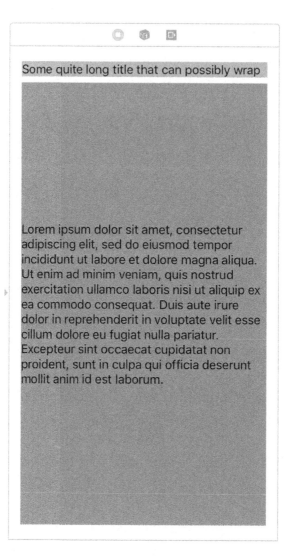

Figure 8-9. Two labels with distance between them: a title and a description

Solution

Follow these steps:

1. Ensure that your top label does not have a bottom constraint that locks it to a specific *y* position.

2. Ensure that your bottom label has a constraint that locks its first base line to the top label's last base line. This will ensure that, as the top label grows vertically, the bottom label readjusts its own top position.
3. Ensure that you don't have constant heights for your labels. This is to allow them to grow vertically in size as they support dynamic types.
4. Ensure that your labels have line counts of 0. As strange as this might seem, line counts of 1 allow labels to display an unlimited number of lines.
5. Place all your labels inside a scroll view, and ensure that the scroll view scrolls correctly as the labels grow in vertical size. In other words, the height of the content size of your scroll view has to be equal to the height of all your labels plus their top margins and the bottom margin of the last label.
6. As you learned earlier (see Recipe 8.6), in your app's code, listen for changes to the default font size by the user, and react accordingly.

Discussion

The goal in this recipe is to make sure that two pieces of text stay separated if they grow and wrap, responding to changes in font size requested by the user. We do this through some sleight-of-hand with base lines and constraints.

Let's have a look at an example. As you saw in Figure 8-9, we need to create our constraints for both the title and the description labels. The title label's constraints are:

- Trailing space to superview, with a constant value of 16.
- Leading space to superview, with a constant value of 16.
- Top space to superview, with a constant value of 20.
- Height that is greater than or equal to 21. The default size of a label in iOS is 21, so this constraint ensures that our label can contain *at least* one line of text and has the ability to grow larger, vertically, to contain an unlimited number of lines of text.

For the description label, we will create the following constraints:

- Trailing space to superview, with a constant value of 16.
- Leading space to superview, with a constant value of 16.
- Bottom space to superview equal to 20.

I have created this constraint with the knowledge that it will pin the label's bottom to the superview's bottom with a margin of 20 points. I've done this to make this recipe shorter and easier to understand without blending scroll view logic into it. As pointed out in the Solution section of this recipe, if you are working on a real application, you need to ensure that you have placed your labels inside a scroll view so that, should the user choose a very large default font size, your labels will still be able to display their entire contents, albeit by making the user scroll through them. If you don't use a scrolling view, the labels might not have enough space on the screen to display all their information at once.

- First base line equal to the title label's last base line. This constraint is super important and ensures that your top label's last base line pushes your bottom label's top base line down so that they still have the correct vertical spacing after an increase in font size.

Now let's look at our code. First we are going to have to connect our two labels to our code through outlets, so that we can control them programmatically:

```swift
import UIKit

class ViewController: UIViewController {

  @IBOutlet weak private var titleLabel: UILabel!
  @IBOutlet weak private var descriptionLabel: UILabel!

  //the rest of our code will be placed here...
```

Then, as we saw earlier in this chapter (see Recipe 8.6), we need a function that takes into account the user's preferences with regard to font sizes and then makes the necessary adjustments to our labels' fonts. In this example I've chosen to use the `title1` text style (of type `UIFontTextStyle`) for the top title label and the `body` text style for the bottom description label. This ensures that the top label by default appears larger (since it's a title) than the description label. To get font metrics of type `UIFontMetrics` by taking into account the text styles of `title` and `body`, we need to instantiate `UIFontMetrics` with the `UIFontMetrics(forTextStyle:)` initializer:

```
func readjustFonts(){

  let defaultTitleFont = UIFont.systemFont(ofSize: 20)

  titleLabel.font = UIFontMetrics(forTextStyle: .title1)
    .scaledFont(for: defaultTitleFont, compatibleWith: traitCollection)

  let defaultDescriptionFont = UIFont.systemFont(ofSize: 17)
  descriptionLabel.font = UIFontMetrics(forTextStyle: .body)
    .scaledFont(for: defaultDescriptionFont, compatibleWith: traitCollection)

}
```

When our view loads on the screen, we set the fonts according to the user's current settings, and then listen for the UIContentSizeCategoryDidChange notification as we saw before (see Recipe 8.6) to readjust the fonts whenever the user changes her font preferences in the Settings application:

```
override func viewDidLoad() {
  super.viewDidLoad()

  readjustFonts()

  NotificationCenter.default.addObserver(
    self,
    selector: #selector(respondToSizeCategoryChangedNotification(_:)),
    name: .UIContentSizeCategoryDidChange,
    object: nil)

}

@objc func respondToSizeCategoryChangedNotification(
  _ notification: NSNotification){

  readjustFonts()

}
```

After the user increases the font size, our labels look like Figure 8-10.

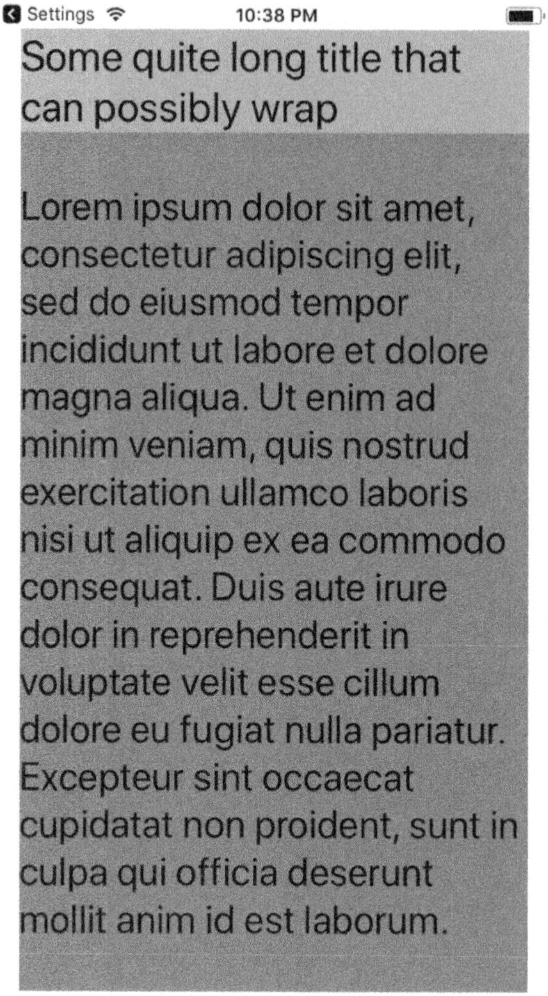
Settings
10:38 PM
Some quite long title that can possibly wrap
Lorem ipsum dolor sit amet, consectetur adipiscing elit, sed do eiusmod tempor incididunt ut labore et dolore magna aliqua. Ut enim ad minim veniam, quis nostrud exercitation ullamco laboris nisi ut aliquip ex ea commodo consequat. Duis aute irure dolor in reprehenderit in voluptate velit esse cillum dolore eu fugiat nulla pariatur. Excepteur sint occaecat cupidatat non proident, sunt in culpa qui officia deserunt mollit anim id est laborum.

Figure 8-10. Same labels as before, but with much larger font sizes

See Also

Recipe 8.6

8.8 Extracting Named Colors from Asset Catalogs

Problem

You want to create colors in your asset catalog and then refer to them by name in your code.

Solution

Follow these steps:

1. Open your asset catalog.
2. From the Editor menu at the top of the screen, choose Add Assets, then New Color Set.
3. Provide a name for your new color set. You will use this name later in code to load the color as an instance of UIColor.
4. From the Attributes inspector, choose the color of your choice for this particular color set and then choose whether it applies to all iOS devices, iPads only, iPhones only, or any other combination that matches your needs.
5. In your code, use the UIColor(named:) initializer for UIColor to load the color into your code.

 If your current device requests a color set with a name and that color set doesn't support the current device, the UIColor(named:) initializer will get the value of nil in return.

Discussion

All colors have RGB values that you can refer to in code, but a small set of standard colors have names such as Red or Taupe. If you create a custom color, it's convenient to assign a catchy name of your own. This recipe allows you to use such names in your code.

As an example, you can see in Figure 8-11 that I've created a color named *WaterBlue* and set its color using the Attributes inspector. I also ensured that it is a universal color, meaning that it can be loaded into any iOS device, because my application is a universal application.

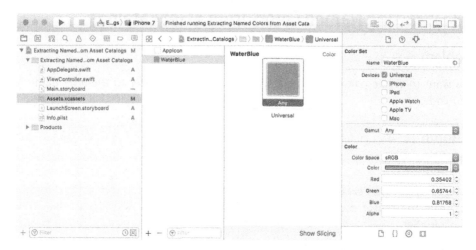

Figure 8-11. A color set that I've created, called WaterBlue

Inside my code, I can attempt to load the color and assign it, for instance, to the background of my view controller's view:

```
override func viewDidLoad() {
  super.viewDidLoad()

  view.backgroundColor = UIColor(named: "WaterBlue")

}
```

Aside from the `UIColor(named:)` initializer, you can also use the `UIColor(named:in:compatibleWith:)` initializer to load a named color set from another bundle.

8.9 Animating Views

Problem

You have an instance of `UIView` and you would like to apply various animations to it, such as changing its background color inside an animation block.

Solution

Use the `UIViewPropertyAnimator` class and specify the properties of your views that you would like to animate, including their new values. For instance, you can instantiate `UIViewPropertyAnimator` and set a delay and an animation length, and then change the background color of your view instances inside the animation block of your `UIViewPropertyAnimator` instance. You can then simply call the `startAnimation()` function on this instance to start the animation(s).

Discussion

Let's have a look at an example. Create a single view application in Xcode (see Figure 8-12). In your *Main.storyboard* file, place a `UIView` instance in the middle of the screen and then connect it to your view controller, under the name `animating View`. So now the top part of your view controller should look like this:

```
import UIKit

class ViewController: UIViewController {

  @IBOutlet var animatingView: UIView!

  ...
```

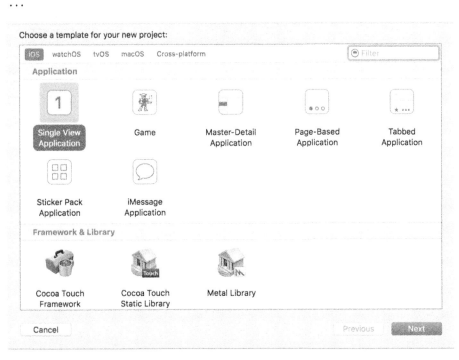

Figure 8-12. Create an application using this template

Our goal in this recipe is to change the background color of this new view to a random color every time the user taps on the view; in addition, we would like this color change to be animated. So, go to Interface Builder and in the Object Library, find Tap Gesture Recognizer (see Figure 8-13) and drag and drop it into your newly created view. Then connect the tap gesture recognizer's Sent Actions outlet to your view controller under a new method called `animatingViewTapped(_:)` (see Figure 8-13). The tap gesture recognizer placed on our view controller associates the gesture recognizer with that view.

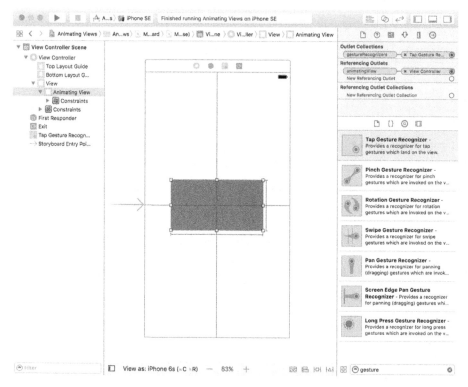

Figure 8-13. New view

In our view controller we will define an array of colors of type `UIColor`. Later we will pick a random one and assign it to this view whenever the user taps on it:

```
let colors: [UIColor] = [
 .red,
 .blue,
 .yellow,
 .orange,
 .green,
 .brown
]
```

Imagine picking a random color from this array of colors. What if that random color is the same color as the one currently assigned to the view? We need an algorithm that can pick a color that is *not* equal to the view's current color. So let's write that function:

```
func randomColor(notEqualTo currentColor: UIColor) -> UIColor{

  var foundColor = currentColor

  repeat{
    let index = Int(arc4random_uniform(UInt32(colors.count)))
    foundColor = colors[index]
  } while foundColor.isEqual(currentColor)

  return foundColor

}
```

In this function we use the `repeat...while` syntax in order to find a random value. We then compare it with the current color and if they are the same, repeat this process until we find a color that is not the same as the old one.

Last but not least, we need to program our `animatingViewTapped(_:)` function and use an instance of `UIViewPropertyAnimator` to animate the change of background color of our view. For that we can use the `init(duration:curve:animations:)` initializer of `UIViewPropertyAnimator`. `duration` is a value of type `TimeInterval`, which is the duration of the animation in seconds. `curve` is of type `UIViewAnimation Curve`, and that is where our animations will take place. This block has neither any parameters nor a return value. Once done, we call the `startAnimation()` method of our property animator:

```
@IBAction func animatingViewTapped(_ sender: AnyObject) {

  let animator = UIViewPropertyAnimator(duration: 1.0, curve: .easeIn){
    [weak animatingView, weak self] in

    guard
      let view = animatingView,
      let strongSelf = self,
      let viewBackgroundColor = view.backgroundColor
      else {return}

    view.backgroundColor = strongSelf.randomColor(
      notEqualTo: viewBackgroundColor)

  }

  animator.startAnimation()

}
```

Have a look at the code now in the simulator. When you see the view in the center of the screen, tap on it and watch how the background color changes!

8.10 Attaching Live Views to Playgrounds

Problem

You are working on a `UIView` instance (or one of its subclasses, such as `UITableView Cell`), are constantly making changes to it in order to get it right, and would like to see your changes continuously without having to recompile and rerun your app on the simulator.

Solution

Xcode now allows you to simulate screens the way the user sees them in special environments known as *playgrounds*. Follow these steps to add a live view to your playground:

1. Import the `PlaygroundSupport` framework into your playground with the `import` statement.
2. Set an instance of `UIView` or `UIViewController` to the `PlaygroundPage. current.liveView` property, which is of type `PlaygroundLiveViewable?`.
3. Press Cmd-Alt-Enter on your keyboard while in Xcode to show the assistant editor. After attaching a live view to your playground, you can see the view at all times as you make changes to it, in the assistant editor (Figure 8-14).

Figure 8-14. A live view displayed in the assistant editor

Discussion

Live views are great for seeing what you're doing while making rapid changes to a view or a view controller. The traditional way of monitoring the effects of such changes was to write the code first, then compile and run the application, which takes a lot more time than seeing your changes live in the playground.

The `liveView` property of the current playground is of type `PlaygroundLive Viewable?`, which itself is a protocol that is defined as shown here:

```
public protocol PlaygroundLiveViewable {

    /// A custom `PlaygroundLiveViewRepresentation` for this instance.
    ///
    /// The value of this property can but does not need to be the same every time;
    /// PlaygroundLiveViewables may choose to create a new view or view controller
    /// every time.
    /// - see also: `PlaygroundLiveViewRepresentation`
    public var playgroundLiveViewRepresentation:
        PlaygroundSupport.PlaygroundLiveViewRepresentation { get }
}
```

It expects conforming objects to implement a playgroundLiveViewRepresentation property of type PlaygroundSupport.PlaygroundLiveViewRepresentation. That's an enumeration defined in this way:

```
public enum PlaygroundLiveViewRepresentation {

  /// A view which will be displayed as the live view.
  ///
  /// - note: This view must be the root of a view hierarchy
  /// (i.e., it must not have a superview), and it must *not* be
  /// owned by a view controller.
  case view(UIView)

  /// A view controller whose view will be displayed as the live
  /// view.
  /// - note: This view controller must be the root of a view
  /// controller hierarchy (i.e., it has no parent view controller),
  /// and its view must *not* have a superview.
  case viewController(UIViewController)
}
```

In other words, every UIView or UIViewController instance can be placed inside the liveView property:

```
import UIKit
import PlaygroundSupport

extension Double{
  var toSize: CGSize{
    return .init(width: self, height: self)
  }
}

extension CGSize{
  var toRectWithZeroOrigin: CGRect{
    return CGRect(origin: .zero, size: self)
  }
}

let view = UIView(frame: 300.toSize.toRectWithZeroOrigin)
view.backgroundColor = .blue
PlaygroundPage.current.liveView = view
```

This means that custom objects that can be represented and drawn in a UIView instance, such as a Person structure, can conform to the PlaygroundLiveViewable protocol and then be assigned to the liveView property of your playground. This procedure allows you to modify the view representation of the object rapidly and see the changes immediately in the playground.

See Also

Recipe 7.12

8.11 Running Playgrounds as Interactive and Continuous Apps

Problem

You want your playground code to have a main loop to emulate a real iOS app that doesn't just run from start to finish, but rather lives for as long as the user presses the stop (or home) button. This will allow you to create interactive applications even in your playgrounds, when mixed with what you learned in Recipe 8.10.

Solution

Set the `needsIndefiniteExecution: Bool` property of your current playground to `true` when you need it to run indefinitely. Once you are done with your work, you can set this property back to `false` (its default value).

> You access this property by first importing the `PlaygroundSup port` framework. Then you can access this property through `Play groundPage.current.needsIndefiniteExecution`.

Discussion

Let's have a look at an example. Say that you are designing a view similar to the one in Recipe 8.10 and you are testing the addition of a new tap gesture recognizer. You want to make sure you get a callback when the user taps on the view. Follow these steps:

1. Make sure to ask for infinite execution time for your playground so that your app can run until you tap on the view, at which point your code can take action, such as to terminate execution:

   ```
   import UIKit
   import PlaygroundSupport

   PlaygroundPage.current.needsIndefiniteExecution = true
   ```

2. Subclass `UIView` and add your own tap gesture recognizer to it upon initialization. When the tap has come in, finish the execution of the playground with `Play groundPage.current.finishExecution()`:

```
class TappableView : UIView{

  @objc func handleTaps(_ sender: UITapGestureRecognizer){
    PlaygroundPage.current.finishExecution()
  }

  override init(frame: CGRect) {
    super.init(frame: frame)
    let recognizer = UITapGestureRecognizer(target: self, action:
      #selector(TappableView.handleTaps(_:)))
    addGestureRecognizer(recognizer)
  }

  required init?(coder aDecoder: NSCoder) {
    fatalError("init(coder:) has not been implemented")
  }

}
```

3. The rest is easy! Simply instantiate this view and set it as the `liveView` of your playground:

```
extension Double{
  var toSize: CGSize{
    return .init(width: self, height: self)
  }
}

extension CGSize{
  var toRectWithZeroOrigin: CGRect{
    return CGRect(origin: .zero, size: self)
  }
}

let view = TappableView(frame: 300.toSize.toRectWithZeroOrigin)
view.backgroundColor = .blue
PlaygroundPage.current.liveView = view
```

See Also

Recipes 7.12 and 8.10

8.12 Arranging Your Components Horizontally or Vertically

Problem

You have vertical or horizontal view hierarchies that you find cumbersome to manage with constraints.

Solution

Stacked views are the solution.

Discussion

Imagine that you want to create a view that looks like Figure 8-15.

Figure 8-15. Vertical and horizontal views

Prior to the latest Xcode version with support for stacked views, we had to set up massive amounts of constraints just to achieve a simple layout like Figure 8-15. Well, no more. Let's head to IB and drop an image view, three labels arranged vertically, and three arranged horizontally, like in the previous figure. Our image and labels look initially like Figure 8-16.

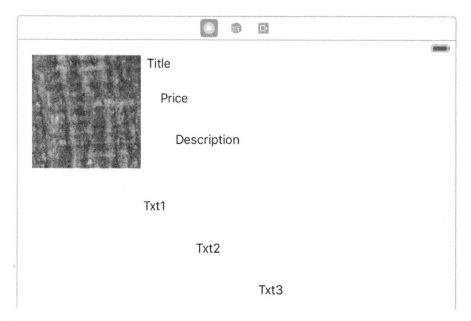

Figure 8-16. Stacked images

Grab the top three labels and press the little Stack button at the bottom of IB, shown in Figure 8-17.

Figure 8-17. The Stack button is the leftmost button

You will notice that your components are now aligned as you wanted them. Now select the top stack (your vertical components). Then, in the Attributes inspector, set the Spacing to 20. Then select your horizontal group and do the same. Bring your horizontal group up and align it to the bottom of the image view to end up with something like Figure 8-15.

See Also

Recipe 8.13

8.13 Customizing Stack Views for Different Screen Sizes

Problem

You want to customize the way your stack views appear on the screen, based on the screen size they are running on.

Solution

Use the size class customization features of Xcode, right in the Attributes inspector.

Discussion

You might have noticed tiny + buttons in various places inside IB. But what are they? Have you used them before? If not, you are missing out on a lot and I'm going to show you how to take advantage of them.

Size classes are encapsulated information about the dimensions of the current screen: possible values are "regular," "compact," and "any." These sizes have been defined to stop us from thinking in terms of pixels; you either have a regular size or a compact size.

Imagine your iPhone 6+ in portrait mode. The screen width is compact, and the screen height is regular. Once you go to landscape mode, your screen width is regular and your height is compact. Now imagine an iPad in portrait mode. Your screen width is regular and so is your height. Landscape, ditto.

Let's work on a project so that you can see more clearly how this works. I want you to achieve the effect shown in Figure 8-18 when running the app on an iPhone in portrait mode.

Figure 8-18. In portrait mode, our views have no spacing between them

And when you go to landscape, I want there to be 10-point spacing between the items, but only when the height of the screen is compact (Figure 8-19).

Figure 8-19. With compact screen height, we want spacing to be applied between our views

Get started by creating three colorful views on your main storyboard. I'll leave the colors to you to decide. Select all your views and then click the little Stack button (shown on the left Figure 8-17) in IB to group your views horizontally. Then place your stacked view at the top left of the view with proper top and left margin spacing (see Figure 8-20).

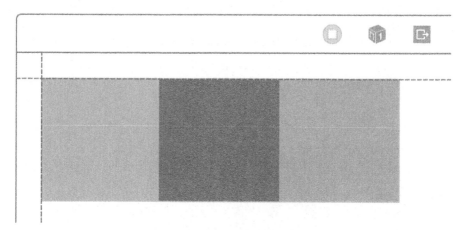

Figure 8-20. The IB guidelines appear when the view is at the top left of the super view

Once done, make sure your stacked view is the selected view and then click the Resolve Auto Layout Issues button (the rightmost button in Figure 8-17). Under Selected Views, choose "Reset to Suggested Constraints."

Now choose your stack view. In the Attributes inspector, under the Spacing section, find the little + button and click it. In the pop-up, choose Any Width, and then under that choose Compact Height. This will give you an additional text field to write the desired spacing value for any screen width while the height of the screen is compact. In this box, set the value to 10 (see Figure 8-21).

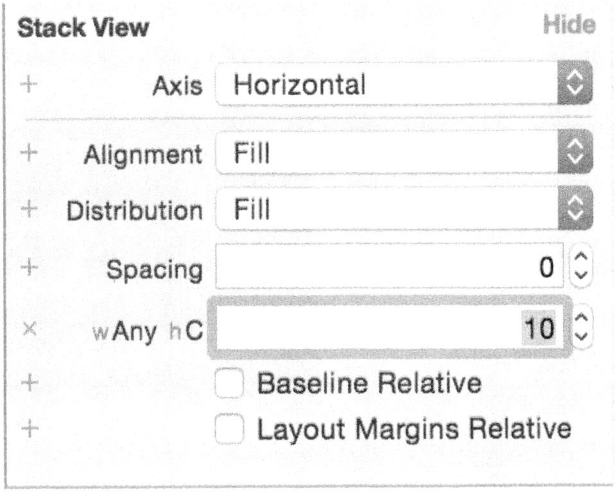

Figure 8-21. Set the value to 10 in the new text box

If you run your app on an iPhone 6+ and then switch to landscape, you *won't* see any spacing between the items—so what happened? The problem is that in landscape mode we are not increasing the width of our stack view. It doesn't currently have extra width to show the spaces between the views. To account for this, let's first add a normal width constraint to our stack view. You can do that by selecting the stack view in the list of views that you have, holding down the Control key on your keyboard, and dragging from the stack view to the stack view itself. From the pop-up that appears, choose Width (see Figure 8-22).

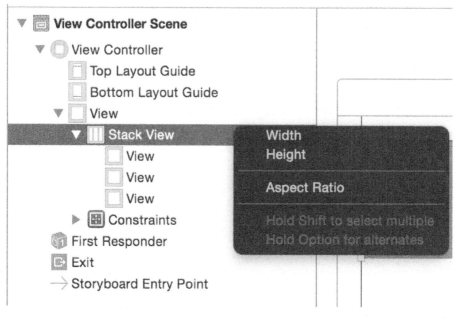

Figure 8-22. Choose the Width option in the pop-up to add a width constraint to the stack view

While your stack view is selected, go to the Size inspector and double-click the Width constraint that you just created. This will allow you to edit this constraint with size classes. How awesome is that? Next to the Constant text box, I can see the value of 300. You might see a different value based on the width of the views you placed in your stack view. My views were each 100 points wide, for a total of 300 points. I can also see a little + button next to the Constant box. Click that button and add a new constant for "Any Width and Compact Height." Set the value to $N+20$, where N is the value of your current constant. For me N is 300, so I'll enter the value of 320 in the new box (see Figure 8-23).

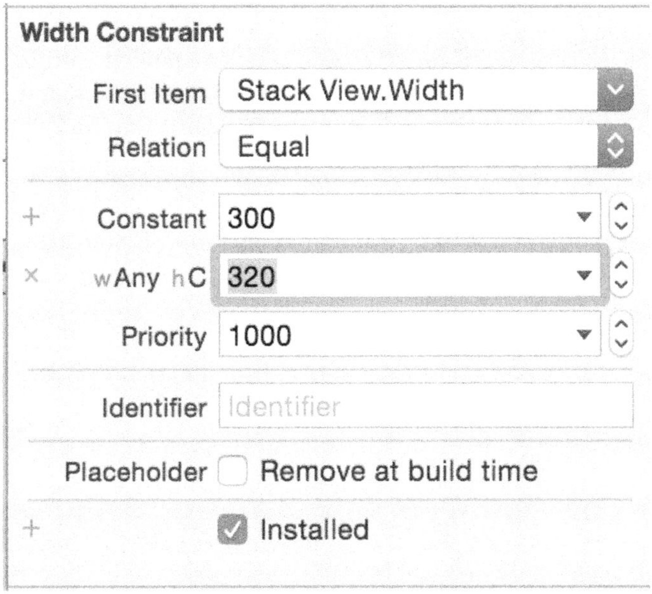

Figure 8-23. Add a new width constant class to the stack view

There is one more thing that you need to tell the stack view in order for it to stack your views correctly when its width changes. Select the stack view and, in the Attributes inspector, under the Distribution section, change the default value to Equal Spacing. Now run your app and enjoy the awesomeness that you just created. Rotate from portrait to landscape in any iPhone simulator (not iPad).

See Also

Recipes 8.12 and 8.16

8.14 Creating Anchored Constraints in Code

Problem

You want your code to use the same layout anchors that IB uses.

Solution

Use the new anchor properties on UIView (for example, leadingAnchor and trailingAnchor).

Discussion

Layout anchors are very useful for arranging your components on the screen. Let's say that you have two buttons on your view, arranged horizontally, and you want the second button to be placed 10 points to the right of the first button.

First create two buttons on your view using IB and then place them next to each other, horizontally. The horizontal space between them does not matter so much right now. Then select both of them and click the Resolve Auto Layout Issues button (the rightmost button in Figure 8-17). In the pop-up, under Selected Views, choose the Add Missing Constraints option (see Figure 8-24).

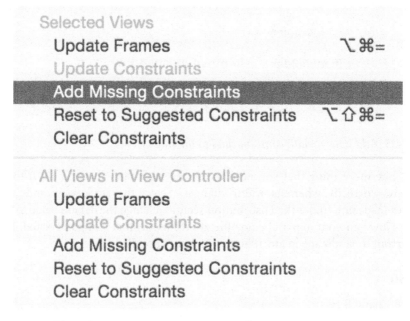

Figure 8-24. Adding the missing constraints to your buttons

Select the second button (on the right). In the Size Inspector panel, find the "Leading Space to" constraint, double-click it, and choose the "Remove at build time" option (see Figure 8-25). This will make sure that the leading constraint, which you are going to create in code, will be present in IB while you're checking things out, but that during the project run the constraint will be removed, giving you the ability to replace it.

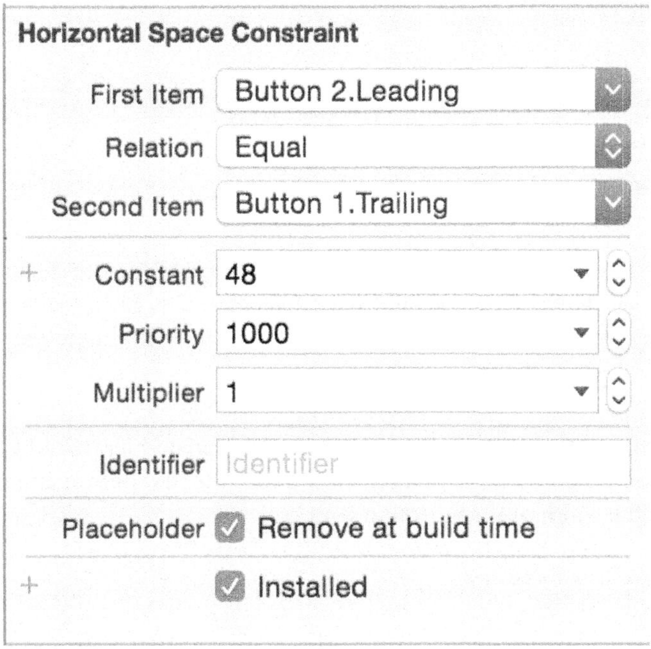

Horizontal Space Constraint

First Item	Button 2.Leading
Relation	Equal
Second Item	Button 1.Trailing
Constant	48
Priority	1000
Multiplier	1
Identifier	Identifier
Placeholder	☑ Remove at build time
	☑ Installed

Figure 8-25. Removing the leading constraint at build time will give you a window to replace it at runtime

Now link your buttons into your code with names such as btn1 and btn2. In the view DidLoad() method of your view controller, write the following code:

```
override func viewDidLoad() {
 super.viewDidLoad()

 btn2.leadingAnchor.constraint(equalTo: btn1.trailingAnchor,
   constant: 10).isActive = true

}
```

Now run your app and see how your second button is trailing your first button horizontally with a 10-point space between them. You can use the following anchors in your views:

- bottomAnchor
- centerXAnchor
- centerYAnchor
- firstBaselineAnchor
- heightAnchor
- lastBaselineAnchor

- `leadingAnchor`
- `leftAnchor`
- `rightAnchor`
- `topAnchor`
- `trailingAnchor`
- `widthAnchor`

 All of these anchors are direct or indirect subclasses of the `NSLay outAnchor` class. The horizontal anchors specifically are subclasses of the `NSLayoutXAxisAnchor` class and the vertical ones are subclasses of `NSLayoutYAxisAnchor`.

Now, just to play with some more anchors, create a view hierarchy like the one in Figure 8-26. You are going to place a red view under the first button and set the width of this view to the width of the button in your code.

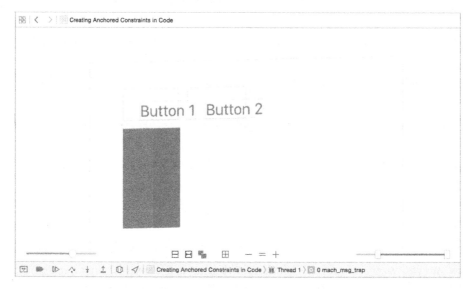

Figure 8-26. Two buttons and a view

In IB, drag and drop a view onto your main view and set the background color of it to red so that you can see it better. Drag and drop it so that it is aligned under the two buttons with proper left and top margins (see Figure 8-27).

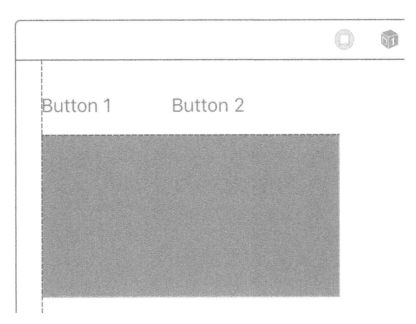

Figure 8-27. Align the red view like so

Anchor the views as follows:

1. Select the red view.
2. In IB, choose the Resolve Auto Layout Issues button.
3. Under the Selected View section in the pop-up, choose Add Missing Constraints.
4. Go to the Size inspector. For the red view, find the "Trailing Space to" constraint and delete it by selecting it and pressing the Delete button.
5. Select the red button in the view hierarchy, hold down the Control key on your keyboard, and drag and drop the button into itself.
6. A menu will appear. In the menu, choose Width to create a width constraint. Then find the new width constraint in the Size inspector, double-click it, and choose the "Remove at build time" option (see Figure 8-28).

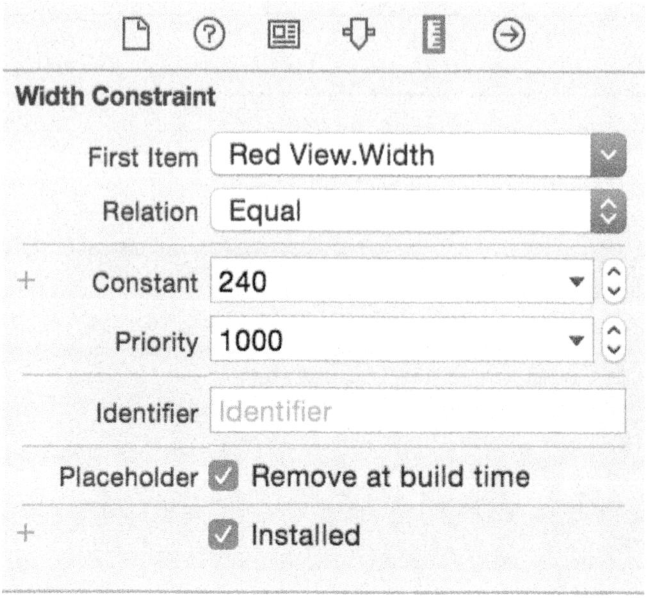

Figure 8-28. Remove the automatically built width constraint at build time so that you can replace it in code

Now create an outlet for this red view in your code (I've named mine v) and add the following code to your viewDidLoad() method:

```
v.widthAnchor.constraint(equalTo: btn2.widthAnchor,
  constant:0).isActive = true
```

8.15 Allowing Users to Enter Text in Response to Local and Remote Notifications

Problem

You want to allow your users to enter some text in response to local or push notifications that you display. And you would additionally like to be able to read this text in your app and take action on it.

Solution

Follow these steps:

1. Import the UserNotifications and Intents frameworks.

2. Get an instance of the user notification center using the `UNUserNotification Center` class and its `current()` class function.
3. Call the `requestAuthorization(options:completionHandler:)` method on your notification center and ensure that you are authorized to provide notifications to the user.
4. Create an instance of `UNTextInputNotificationAction` for your *enter text* action.
5. Create an instance of `UNNotificationAction` for your *cancel* action.
6. Create an instance of `UNNotificationCategory` to hold the category information for your notification.
7. Invoke the `setNotificationCategories(_:)` method of your notification center and pass your category in.
8. To schedule the notification, create an instance of `UNTimeIntervalNotification Trigger` in order to trigger the notification after a specific number of seconds. For instance, you may want to trigger a notifications 3 seconds after your app goes to the background.
9. Instantiate `UNMutableNotificationContent` and set this instance's body property to the text of your notification.
10. Set this instance's `categoryIdentifier` to the identifier of the category object of type `UNNotificationCategory` that you created earlier.
11. Create a notification request of type `UNNotificationRequest` with a unique identifier, your content object, and the trigger object.
12. Invoke the `add(request:completionHandler:)` function of your notification center to schedule the notification.

Discussion

Let's say that we want our app to register for local notifications and then ask the user for her name once the app has been sent to the background. The user enters her name and then we come to the foreground and take action on that name.

In the app delegate, we will start by ensuring our delegate conforms to the `UNUser NotificationCenterDelegate` protocol and getting a reference to the notification center:

```
import UIKit
import UserNotifications
import Intents

@UIApplicationMain
class AppDelegate: UIResponder, UIApplicationDelegate,
UNUserNotificationCenterDelegate {

  var window: UIWindow?
```

```
private var notificationCenter: UNUserNotificationCenter{
  return UNUserNotificationCenter.current()
}
```

```
//the rest of our code will follow here shortly...
```

Then we will write a function that first asks the user whether it's okay for us to schedule notifications, and then, if she agrees, invokes the setNotification Categories(_:) function of our notification center to register what types of notification categories we would like to provide to the user. Every category of type UNNotifi cationCategory has a few properties:

An identifier of type String

When you later want to create a request for a notification, you have will have to instantiate UNNotification Request, and that request will require a content object of type UNMutableNotificationContent. The content object has a property called categoryIdentifier that you will then have to link to this category through its identifier.

Actions, an array of type [UNNotificationAction]

You can pass instances of UNTextInputNotificationAction and UNNotifica tionAction to this array, because UNTextInputNotificationAction is a subclass of UNNotificationAction.

Options of type UNNotificationCategoryOptions

These can have values such as allowInCarPlay or customDismissAction.

So, let's create a function that can ask the user for permission to create local notifications. If the user agrees to that, we will also create a category object of type UNNotifi cationCategory and register the category with our notification center:

```
func registerForNotifications(){

  notificationCenter.delegate = self

  notificationCenter.requestAuthorization(options: [.alert]){[weak self]
    (succeeded, error) in

    guard let `self` = self else {return}

    if let error = error, succeeded == false{
      print("Failed, error = \(error)")
      return
    }

    let enterInfo = UNTextInputNotificationAction(identifier: "enter",
                                                  title: "Enter your name",
                                                  options: [.foreground])
```

```
let cancel = UNNotificationAction(identifier: "cancel",
                                  title: "Cancel",
                                  options: [])

let category = UNNotificationCategory(
  identifier: "texted",
  actions: [enterInfo, cancel],
  intentIdentifiers: [INSendMessageIntentIdentifier],
  hiddenPreviewsBodyPlaceholder: "Placeholder",
  options: [.hiddenPreviewsShowTitle])

self.notificationCenter.setNotificationCategories([category])

}
```

When our application has launched, we will immediately ask the user whether the authorization can schedule local notifications:

```
func application(
  _ application: UIApplication,
  didFinishLaunchingWithOptions
  launchOptions: [UIApplicationLaunchOptionsKey : Any]? = nil) -> Bool {

  registerForNotifications()

  return true
}
```

Now, when the user opens the application for the first time, she will see a system alert pop up (see Figure 8-29), asking her whether it's okay for our app to schedule local notifications.

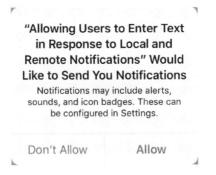

Figure 8-29. This system dialog is the result of us invoking the requestAuthorization(options:completionHandler:) function of our notification center of type UNUserNotificationCenter

We now need to write a function that schedules the notification. We will instantiate a trigger object of type UNTimeIntervalNotificationTrigger so that we can display our notification 3 seconds after our application has been sent to the background. Trigger objects of type UNNotificationTrigger are required for our notification request object (of type UNNotificationRequest), and the UNTimeIntervalNotificationTrigger class subclasses UNNotificationTrigger. The curious minds among you are probably asking what other trigger classes are out there. Here is a list:

UNPushNotificationTrigger
> Push notifications, as the name suggests.

UNCalendarNotificationTrigger
> Notifications that are bound to date objects, so that you can show a notification to the user at a specific time and date.

UNLocationNotificationTrigger
> Notifications bound to a region defined by CLRegion. For instance, a news application can use this type of notification to display local news.

Once we have our trigger object, we will also need to create a content object of type UNMutableNotificationContent, in which we can set the body of our notification message. We will also bind this content object to our category object, which we created earlier, using the content object's categoryIdentifier property:

```
func scheduleNotification(){

  let trigger = UNTimeIntervalNotificationTrigger(
    timeInterval: 3.0, repeats: false)

  let content = UNMutableNotificationContent()
  content.body = "Please enter your name now"
  content.categoryIdentifier = "texted"

  let request = UNNotificationRequest(
    identifier: UUID().uuidString, content: content, trigger: trigger)

  notificationCenter.add(request) {error in
    if let error = error {
      print("Could not schedule notification. Error = \(error)")
    } else {
      print("Successfully scheduled the notification")
    }
  }

}
```

As soon as the user sends our application to the background, we will invoke this function in order to schedule a notification. For this, we can use the applicationDid EnterBackground(_:) function of our app delegate:

```
func applicationDidEnterBackground(_ application: UIApplication) {
  scheduleNotification()
}
```

You can go ahead and run the application now. Once you allow the app (through the system dialog shown in Figure 8-29) to schedule local notifications, send the app to the background and wait 3 seconds. You should now see a notification appear on the screen asking for your name. Drag your finger down on this notification to reveal the actions that we associated with it (a button that allows you to enter your name, and a cancel button). Press the "Enter your name" button to see the text entry interface of the message (Figure 8-30).

Figure 8-30. The user can enter her name directly into this notification

But what happens when the user enters her name in the text field? This is why we set our app delegate as the `delegate` property of our notification center earlier. If you do that, you will be able to implement the `userNotificationCenter(_:didRe` ceive:withCompletionHandler:) function, which gets called when the user has provided a response to your notifications. The didReceive argument of this function is of type UNNotificationResponse, and in our example, since we scheduled a text notification action of type UNTextInputNotificationAction, we'll be looking for a response of type UNTextInputNotificationResponse. If that's the response object, we can read its userText property, which holds the text that the user has entered on the screen:

```
func userNotificationCenter(
  _ center: UNUserNotificationCenter,
  didReceive response: UNNotificationResponse,
  withCompletionHandler completionHandler: @escaping () -> Void) {

  guard let response = response as? UNTextInputNotificationResponse,
  response.actionIdentifier == "enter" else {
    completionHandler()
    return
  }

  print(response.userText)
  completionHandler()

}
```

8.16 Dealing with Stacked Views in Code

Problem

You want to programmatically manipulate the contents of stack views.

Solution

Use an instance of the UIStackView.

Discussion

For whatever reason, you might want to construct your stack views programmatically. I do not recommend this way of working with stack views because IB already can handle most of the situations where you would want to use stack views, and then some. But if you absolutely have to use stack views in your app, simply instantiate UIStackView and pass it your arranged views.

You can also then set the axis property to either vertical or horizontal. Remember to set the distribution property as well, of type UIStackViewDistribution. Some of the values of this type are fill, fillEqually, and equalSpacing. I also like to set the spacing property of the stack view manually so that I know how much space there is between my items.

Let's say that we want to create a stack view like Figure 8-31. The stack view is tucked to the right side of the screen and every time we press the button, a new label will be appended to the stack view.

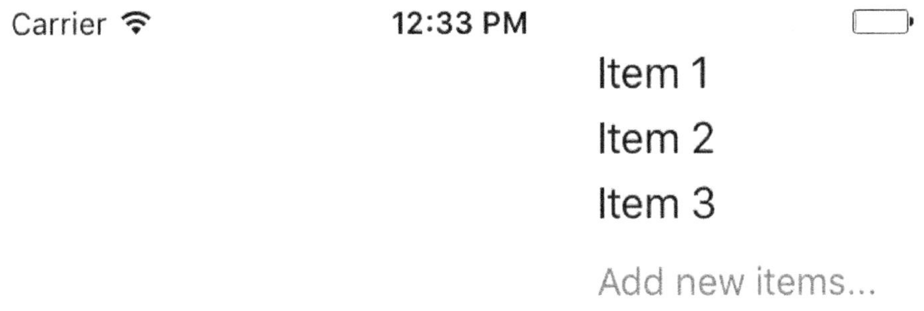

Carrier 🛜   12:33 PM   ▭▸

Item 1
Item 2
Item 3

Add new items...

Figure 8-31. This is the stack view that we want to create

First we define a stack view in our view controller:

```
var rightStack: UIStackView!
```

Then a few handy methods for creating labels and a button:

```
func lblWithIndex(_ idx: Int) -> UILabel{
  let label = UILabel()
  label.text = "Item \(idx)"
  label.sizeToFit()
  return label
}

func newButton() -> UIButton{
  let btn = UIButton(type: .system)
  btn.setTitle("Add new items...", for: UIControlState())
  btn.addTarget(self, action: #selector(addNewItem),
              for: .touchUpInside)
  return btn
}

@objc func addNewItem(){
  let n = rightStack.arrangedSubviews.count
  let v = lblWithIndex(n)
  rightStack.insertArrangedSubview(v, at: n - 1)
}
```

The addNewItem() function will be called when the button is pressed.

When our view is loaded on the screen, we will create the stack view and fill it with the three initial labels and the button. Then we will set up its axis, spacing, and distribution. Once done, we'll create its constraints:

```
override func viewDidLoad() {
  super.viewDidLoad()

  rightStack = UIStackView(arrangedSubviews:
    [lblWithIndex(1), lblWithIndex(2), lblWithIndex(3), newButton()])

  view.addSubview(rightStack)

  rightStack.translatesAutoresizingMaskIntoConstraints = false

  rightStack.axis = .vertical
  rightStack.distribution = .equalSpacing
  rightStack.spacing = 5

  rightStack.trailingAnchor.constraint(equalTo: view.trailingAnchor,
                                       constant: -20).isActive = true

  rightStack.topAnchor.constraint(
    equalTo: view.safeAreaLayoutGuide.topAnchor).isActive = true

}
```

See Also

Recipe 8.13

8.17 Showing Web Content in Safari View Controller

Problem

You want to take advantage of such awesome Safari functionalities as Reader mode in your own apps.

Solution

Use the SFSafariViewController class in the SafariServices framework. This view controller can easily be initialized with a URL and then displayed on the screen.

Discussion

Let's go ahead and build the UI. For this recipe, we are aiming for a UI like Figure 8-32.

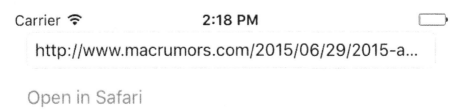

Figure 8-32. Create a UI that looks similar to this in your own storyboard

Place a text field and a button on your UI, then hook them up to your code. Once the button is tapped, the code that runs is:

```
@IBAction func openInSafari() {

  guard let text = textField.text, text.characters.count > 0,
    let url = URL(string: text)  else{
      //the URL is missing, you can further code this method if you want
      return
  }

  let configuration = SFSafariViewController.Configuration()
  configuration.entersReaderIfAvailable = true

  let controller = SFSafariViewController(
    url: url, configuration: configuration)

  controller.delegate = self
  present(controller, animated: true, completion: nil)

}
```

Now make your view controller conform to the SFSafariViewControllerDelegate protocol. Program the safariViewControllerDidFinish(_:) method to ensure that, when the user closes the Safari view controller, the view disappears:

```
func safariViewControllerDidFinish(_ controller: SFSafariViewController) {
  dismiss(animated: true, completion: nil)
}
```

Note that in the initializer of the Safari controller, I also specified that I would like to take advantage of Reader mode if it is available.

8.18 Laying Out Text-Based Content on Your Views

Problem

You would like to show text-based content to your users and want to lay it out on the screen in the optimal position.

Solution

Use the readableContentGuide property of UIView.

Discussion

The readableContentGuide property of UIView gives you the margins that you need to place your text content on the screen properly. On a typical iPhone 6 screen, this margin is around 20 points on both the left and the right. The top and bottom margins on the same device are usually set near 0. But don't take these numbers at face value—they might change, and you should never think about them as hardcoded values. That is why you should use the readableContentGuide property to place your components correctly on the screen.

There isn't really much more to it than that, so let's jump right into an example. In this code, I will create a label and stretch it horizontally and vertically to fill the readable section of my view. I will also make sure the top and left positioning of the label is according to the readable section's guides:

```
let label = UILabel()
label.translatesAutoresizingMaskIntoConstraints = false
label.backgroundColor = UIColor.green
label.text = "Hello, World"
label.sizeToFit()
view.addSubview(label)

label.leadingAnchor.constraint(
  equalTo: view.readableContentGuide.leadingAnchor).isActive = true

label.topAnchor.constraint(
  equalTo: view.readableContentGuide.topAnchor).isActive = true

label.trailingAnchor.constraint(
  equalTo: view.readableContentGuide.trailingAnchor).isActive = true

label.bottomAnchor.constraint(
  equalTo: view.readableContentGuide.bottomAnchor).isActive = true
```

8.19 Improving Touch Rates for Smoother UI Interactions

Problem

You want to be able to improve the interaction of the user with your app by decreasing the interval required between touch events.

Solution

Use the `coalescedTouchesForTouch(_:)` and `predictedTouchesForTouch(_:)` methods of the `UIEvent` class. The former method allows you to receive coalesced touches inside an event, while the latter allows you to receive predicted touch events based on iOS's internal algorithms.

Discussion

On selected devices such as the iPad Air 2, the display refresh rate is 60 Hz like on other iOS devices, but the touch scan rate is 120 Hz. This means that iOS on the iPad Air 2 scans the screen for updated touch events twice as fast as the display's refresh rate. These events obviously cannot be delivered to your app faster than the display refresh rate (60 times per second), so they are coalesced. At every touch event, you can ask for these coalesced touches and base your app's reactions on them.

In this recipe, imagine that we are just going to draw a line based on where the user's finger has been touching the screen. The user can move her finger over our view any way she wants, and we just draw a line on that path.

Create a single view app. In the same file as your view controller's Swift source file, define a new class of type `UIView` and name it `MyView`:

```
class MyView : UIView{

}
```

In your storyboard, set your view controller's view class to `MyView` (see Figure 8-33).

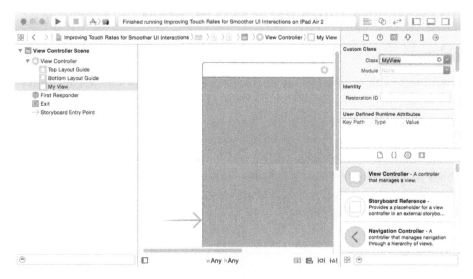

Figure 8-33. Your view is inside the view controller now

 Make sure that you are running this code on a device at least as advanced as an iPad Air 2. The iPhone 6 and 6+ do *not* have a 120 Hz touch scan rate.

Then, in your view, define an array of points and a method that can take a set of touches and an event object, read the coalesced touch points inside the event, and place them inside your array:

```
var points = [CGPoint]()

func drawForFirstTouchInSet(_ s: Set<UITouch>, event: UIEvent?){

  guard let touch = s.first, let event = event,
    let allTouches = event.coalescedTouches(for: touch),
    allTouches.count > 0 else{
      return
  }

  points += allTouches.map{$0.location(in: self)}

  setNeedsDisplay()

}
```

Now when the user starts touching your view, you start recording the touch points:

```
override func touchesBegan(_ touches: Set<UITouch>,
                           with event: UIEvent?) {

  points.removeAll()
  drawForFirstTouchInSet(touches, event: event)

}
```

Should you be told that the touch events sent to your app were sent by accident, and that the user really meant to touch another UI component on the screen, such as the notification center, you have to clear the display:

```
override func touchesCancelled(_ touches: Set<UITouch>,
                               with event: UIEvent?) {

  points.removeAll()
  setNeedsDisplay(bounds)

}
```

Every time the touch location moves, move with it and record the location:

```
override func touchesMoved(_ touches: Set<UITouch>,
                           with event: UIEvent?) {

  drawForFirstTouchInSet(touches, event: event)

}
```

Once the touches end, ask iOS for any predicted touch events that might have been calculated and draw them too:

```
override func touchesEnded(_ touches: Set<UITouch>,
                           with event: UIEvent?) {

  guard let touch = touches.first, let event = event,
    let predictedTouches = event.predictedTouches(for: touch),
    predictedTouches.count > 0 else{
      return
  }

  points += predictedTouches.map{$0.location(in: self)}
  setNeedsDisplay()

}
```

The drawing code is simple. It goes through all the points and draws lines between them:

```
override func draw(_ rect: CGRect) {

  let con = UIGraphicsGetCurrentContext()

  // set background color
```

```
con?.setFillColor(UIColor.black.cgColor)
con?.fill(rect)

con?.setFillColor(UIColor.red.cgColor)
con?.setStrokeColor(UIColor.red.cgColor)

for point in points{

  con?.move(to: point)

  if let last = points.last, point != last{
    let next = points[points.index(of: point)! + 1]
    con?.addLine(to: next)
  }

}

con?.strokePath()

}
```

Now run this on an iPad Air 2 and compare the smoothness of the lines that you draw with those on an iPhone 6 or 6+, for instance.

8.20 Supporting Right-to-Left Languages

Problem

You are internationalizing your app and, as part of this process, need to support languages that are written from right to left, such as Persian or Arabic.

Solution

Use a combination of the following tips:

- Use IB's view properties to arrange your items with proper semantic properties.
- Ensure that you create your constraints correctly, preferably using IB.
- Use the `userInterfaceLayoutDirectionForSemanticContentAttribute(_:)` class method of the `UIView` class to find the direction of the user interface based on the semantic attributes that are part of the `UISemanticContentAttribute` enum.
- If arranging your items in code, use the `semanticContentAttribute` property of your views to set their semantics correctly.

Discussion

Let's create an app that has a text view on top and four buttons arranged like the arrow keys on the keyboard: up, left, down, right. When each one of these buttons is pressed, we will display the corresponding word in the text field. The text field will be read-only, and when displaying right-to-left languages, it will of course show the text on the righthand side. Make sure that your UI looks (for now) something like Figure 8-34. There is one text field and four buttons.

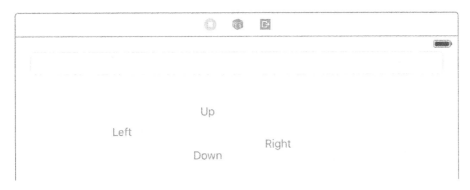

Figure 8-34. Initial layout

Now select the left, down, and right buttons on the UI (exclude the up button for now) and stack them up together. In the new stack that was created, set the spacing to 20 (see Figure 8-35). Set the horizontal stack view's spacing so that the buttons will be horizontally stacked with the proper distance from each other.

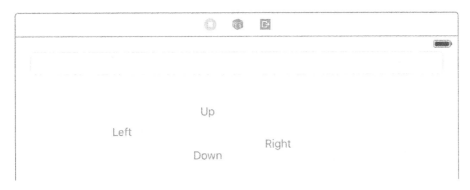

Figure 8-35. Horizontal spacing between buttons

Then select the newly created stack and the up button on IB and stack *those* up together. This will create a vertical stack view for you. Set the spacing for this new stack view to 10. Place the main stack view at the center of the screen. Use IB's Resolve Auto Layout Issues feature to add all missing constraints for all the components. Also make sure that you disable editing of the text field. Then hook up the text field to your code as an outlet and hook up the four buttons' touch events to your view controller as well. Now your UI should look like Figure 8-36 on IB.

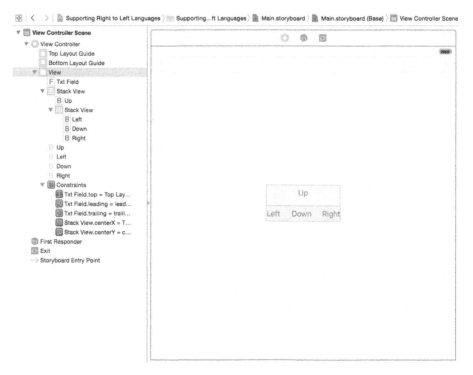

Figure 8-36. Your UI should look like this at the moment

Now choose the main stack view in your UI. In IB, in the Semantic section of the Attributes Inspector panel, choose Playback (see Figure 8-37). This will ensure that the views inside this stack view will *not* be mirrored right to left when the language changes to a right-to-left language.

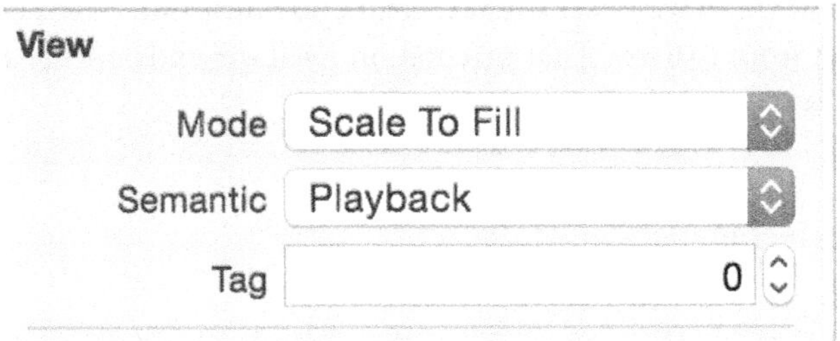

Figure 8-37. Choose the Playback view semantic

Now from Xcode, create a new strings file, name it *Localizable.strings*, and place your string keys in there:

```
"up" = "Up";
"down" = "Down";
"right" = "Right";
"left" = "Left";
```

Under your main project's info page in Xcode, choose Localizations and add Arabic as a localization. Then move over to your newly created *strings* file and enable the Arabic language on it (see Figure 8-38).

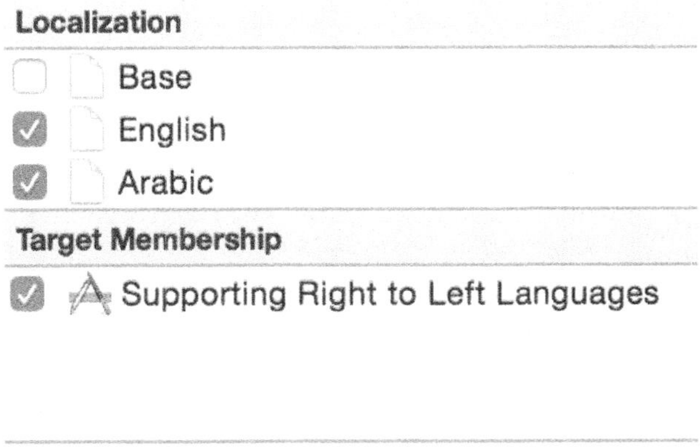

Figure 8-38. Localize the strings file so that you have both English and Arabic in the list

You will now have two strings files. Go into the Arabic one and localize the file:

```
"up" = "Up in Arabic";
"down" = "Down in Arabic";
"right" = "Right in Arabic";
"left" = "Left in Arabic";
```

In your code now, you have to set the text field's text direction based on the orientation that you get from UIView. That orientation itself depends on the semantics that you set on your text field before:

```swift
import UIKit

class ViewController: UIViewController {

  @IBOutlet var txtField: UITextField!

  @IBAction func up() {
    txtField.text = NSLocalizedString("up", comment: "")
  }

  @IBAction func left() {
    txtField.text = NSLocalizedString("left", comment: "")
  }

  @IBAction func down() {
    txtField.text = NSLocalizedString("down", comment: "")
  }

  @IBAction func right() {
    txtField.text = NSLocalizedString("right", comment: "")
  }

  override func viewDidAppear(_ animated: Bool) {

    let direction = UIView
      .userInterfaceLayoutDirection(
        for: txtField.semanticContentAttribute)

    switch direction{
    case .leftToRight:
      txtField.textAlignment = .left
    case .rightToLeft:
      txtField.textAlignment = .right
    }

  }

}
```

Now run the app on an English device and you will see English content in the text field aligned from left to right. Run it on an Arabic-localized device and you'll see the text aligned on the righthand side.

8.21 Associating Keyboard Shortcuts with View Controllers

Problem

You want to allow your application to respond to complex key combinations that a user can press on an external keyboard, to give the user more ways to interact with your app.

Solution

Construct an instance of the `UIKeyCommand` class and add it to your view controllers using the `addKeyCommand(_:)` method. You can remove key commands with the `removeKeyCommand(_:)` method.

Discussion

Keyboard shortcuts are very useful for users with external keyboards. In a word processing program, the user might expect to press Cmd-N to create a new document, whereas on an iOS device this may be achieved by the user pressing a button such as "New."

Let's say that we want to write a single view app that allows users with an external keyboard to press Cmd-Alt-Ctrl-N to see an alert controller. When our view is loaded, we will create the command and add it to our view controller:

```
override func viewDidLoad() {
  super.viewDidLoad()

  let command = UIKeyCommand(
    input: "N",
    modifierFlags: [.command, .alternate, .control],
    action: #selector(handleCommand(_:)))

  addKeyCommand(command)

}
```

When the command is issued, iOS will attempt to call the method that we have specified. In there, let's show the alert:

```
@objc func handleCommand(_ cmd: UIKeyCommand){

  let controller = UIAlertController(
    title: "Shortcut pressed",
    message: "You pressed the shortcut key",
    preferredStyle: .alert)
```

```
controller.addAction(
  UIAlertAction(title: "Ok!", style: .destructive, handler: nil))

present(controller, animated: true, completion: nil)
```

}

Open this in the simulator. From the Hardware menu, select Keyboard, and then select the Connect Hardware Keyboard menu item (see Figure 8-39). While the focus is on the simulator, press the aforementioned key combinations and see the results for yourself.

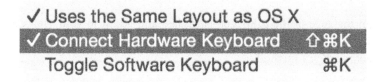

Figure 8-39. You can enable a hardware keyboard even in the simulator; this is necessary to test the output of this recipe

8.22 Recording the Screen and Sharing the Video

Problem

You want users to be able to record their screen while in your app and then edit and save the results. This is really important for games providing replay functionality to gamers.

Solution

Follow these steps:

1. Import `ReplayKit`.
2. After you have imported `ReplayKit`, get a recorder of type `RPScreenRecorder` using `RPScreenRecorder.sharedRecorder()`.
3. Call the `available` property of the recorder to see whether recording is available.
4. Set the `delegate` property of the recorder to your code and conform to the `RPScreenRecorderDelegate` protocol.
5. Call the `startRecordingWithMicrophoneEnabled(_:handler:)` method of the recorder.
6. Wait until your handler method is called and then check for errors.
7. If no error occurred, once you are done with recording, call the `stopRecording WithHandler(_:)` method on the same recorder object.

8. Wait for your handler to be called. In your handler, you'll get an instance of the `RPPreviewViewController` class.

9. Set the `previewControllerDelegate` property of the preview controller to your code and conform to the `RPPreviewViewControllerDelegate` protocol.

10. Preset your preview controller.

Discussion

The ability to record what's happening on the screen often comes in handy for users, particularly gamers who might want to share a particularly cool sequence of game play with their friends. To enable this, you first need to define your view controller:

```
import UIKit
import ReplayKit

class ViewController: UIViewController, RPScreenRecorderDelegate,
RPPreviewViewControllerDelegate {
  ...
```

Set up your UI as shown in Figure 8-40. The start and stop buttons are self-explanatory. The segmented control is there just so you can play with it while recording and then see the results after you've stopped the playback.

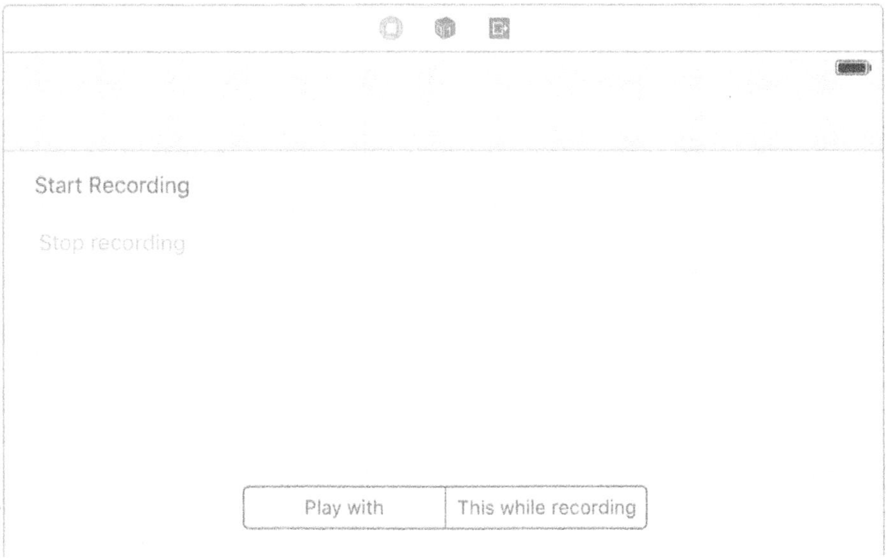

Figure 8-40. Initial layout

Hook up the buttons to your code:

```
@IBOutlet var startBtn: UIButton!
@IBOutlet var stopBtn: UIButton!
```

And define your delegate methods:

```
func previewControllerDidFinish(_ previewController: RPPreviewViewController) {
  print("Finished the preview")
  dismiss(animated: true, completion: nil)
  startBtn.isEnabled = true
  stopBtn.isEnabled = false
}


func previewController(_ previewController: RPPreviewViewController,
                       didFinishWithActivityTypes activityTypes: Set<String>) {
  print("Preview finished activities \(activityTypes)")
}


func screenRecorderDidChangeAvailability(_ screenRecorder: RPScreenRecorder) {
  print("Screen recording availability changed")
}


func screenRecorder(_ screenRecorder: RPScreenRecorder,
                    didStopRecordingWithError error: Error,
                    previewViewController: RPPreviewViewController?) {
  print("Screen recording finished")
}
```

The `previewControllerDidFinish(_:)` method is important, because it gets called
when the user is finished with the preview controller. Here you'll need to dismiss the
preview controller.

Then define the recorder object:

```
let recorder = RPScreenRecorder.shared()
```

When the record button is pressed, see whether recording is possible:

```
startBtn.isEnabled = true
stopBtn.isEnabled = false

guard recorder.isAvailable else{
  print("Cannot record the screen")
  return
}
```

If it is, start recording:

```
recorder.delegate = self

recorder.startRecording {[weak self]err in

  guard let strongSelf = self else {return}

  if let error = err as NSError?{
```

```
    if error.code == RPRecordingErrorCode.userDeclined.rawValue{
      print("User declined app recording")
    }
    else if error.code == RPRecordingErrorCode.insufficientStorage.rawValue{
      print("Not enough storage to start recording")
    }
    else {
      print("Error happened = \(err!)")
    }
    return
  } else {
    print("Successfully started recording")
    strongSelf.startBtn.isEnabled = false
    strongSelf.stopBtn.isEnabled = true
  }

}
```

 Here, we are checking the error codes for specific ReplayKit errors such as RPRecordingErrorCode.UserDeclined and RPRecordingEr rorCode.InsufficientStorage.

The first time you attempt to record the user's screen in any app, the user will be prompted to allow or disallow this with a dialog that looks similar to that shown in Figure 8-41.

Figure 8-41. Permission to record the screen is requested from the user

When the user is finished recording and presses the stop button, stop the recording and present the preview controller:

```
recorder.stopRecording{controller, err in

  guard let previewController = controller, err == nil else {
    self.startBtn.isEnabled = true
    self.stopBtn.isEnabled = false
    print("Failed to stop recording")
    return
  }

  previewController.previewControllerDelegate = self

  self.present(previewController, animated: true,
            completion: nil)
```

}

The preview controller looks like that shown in Figure 8-42.

Figure 8-42. The user can preview what was recorded on the screen earlier and can save and share the results

Throughout this whole process, your app doesn't get direct access to the recorded content. This protects the user's privacy.

CHAPTER 9

Document-Based Apps

An application can allow the user to browse and edit iCloud-backed documents using various objects and view controllers that are provided in the iOS SDK, such as `UIDocu mentBrowserViewController`. In the iOS SDK, you can find every class and technology that your app might require in order to create professional document-based applications for all kinds of documents.

iOS takes care of presenting and exporting a document's data to your application from iCloud. Another complex operation that iOS can take care of is syncing multiple simultaneous edit operations on the same file. What your application is responsible for is presenting the data to the user, allowing the user to edit that data (if possible), and then saving the data back to iOS, which in turn is responsible for saving that data back to iCloud.

9.1 Supporting File Browsing in Your App

Problem

You want to create a document-based application and would like to start by allowing the user to browse their existing documents.

Solution

Follow these steps:

1. Ensure your application's root view controller is of type `UIDocumentBrowserView Controller`.

2. Make sure that this root view controller is *not* embedded inside a navigation controller. The document browser has its own navigation controller and should not be wrapped inside an extra navigation controller.
3. In your app delegate, read your `window` property's `rootViewController`, now of type `UIDocumentBrowserViewController`, and set its `delegate` property to your app delegate.
4. Ensure that your app delegate conforms to the `UIDocumentBrowserViewControllerDelegate` protocol.
5. Open your *Info.plist* file in Xcode.
6. Right-click anywhere on this file and click the Show Raw Keys/Values menu opton.
7. Add a new key named `UISupportsDocumentBrowser`, of type `Boolean`, to the *Info.plist* file and assign the value of `YES` to it.

 All this action happens in your app delegate, because it is your app delegate that owns your `window` object, which in turn owns your root view controller. Therefore, the app delegate is a good place to start in order to begin creating a document-based application.

Discussion

Let's have a look at creating a root view controller in IB. First create a single view application in Xcode. Open your *Main.storyboard* file and select the view controller that has been created for you. From the Utilities panel, select the Identity inspector. Under Custom Class change the default class to `UIDocumentBrowserViewController`.

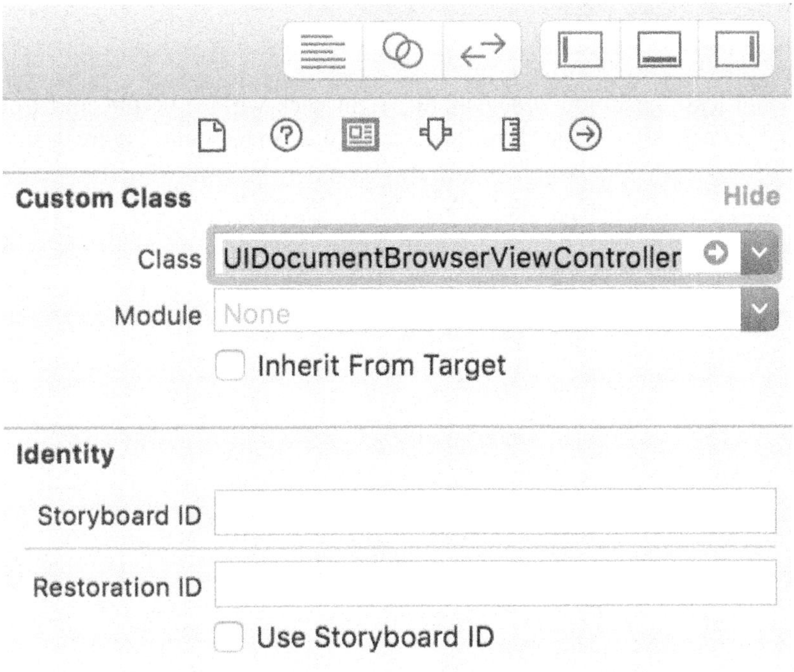

Figure 9-1. Set the root view controller's class to UIDocumentBrowserViewController

Now go to your app delegate's Swift file (usually called *AppDelegate.swift*) and ensure that your root view controller, of type `UIDocumentBrowserViewController`, has its delegate set to your app delegate, so that the view controller can react to various events that the document browser view controller sends it:

```swift
import UIKit

@UIApplicationMain
class AppDelegate: UIResponder, UIApplicationDelegate,
UIDocumentBrowserViewControllerDelegate {

  var window: UIWindow?

  func application(
    _ application: UIApplication,
    didFinishLaunchingWithOptions launchOptions:
    [UIApplicationLaunchOptionsKey: Any]?) -> Bool {

    (window?.rootViewController as? UIDocumentBrowserViewController)?
      .delegate = self

    return true
```

```
    }
}
```

Last but not least, click your *Info.plist* file, right-click within the file, and from the menu that appears, choose the Show Raw Keys/Values menu item (Figure 9-2).

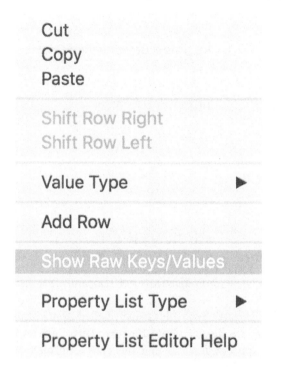

Figure 9-2. We are going to add a new key to our Info.plist file, using the key's raw name

Bring up the same menu, and click the Add Row menu item (also shown in Figure 9-2). For the name of the new key, choose UISupportsDocumentBrowser (see Figure 9-3); ensure that it is of type Boolean, and assign the value of YES to it. This lets iOS know that you want to partake of iCloud document browsing and creation.

Key	Type	Value
▼ Information Property List	Dictionary	(15 items)
Localization native development r... ◇	String	$(DEVELOPMENT_LANGUAGE)
UISupportsDocumentBrowser ◇ ⊕ ⊖	Boolean ◇	YES
Executable file ◇	String	$(EXECUTABLE_NAME)
Bundle identifier ◇	String	$(PRODUCT_BUNDLE_IDENTIFIER)
InfoDictionary version ◇	String	6.0
Bundle name ◇	String	$(PRODUCT_NAME)
Bundle OS Type code ◇	String	APPL
Bundle versions string, short ◇	String	1.0
Bundle version ◇	String	1
Application requires iPhone enviro... ◇	Boolean	YES
Launch screen interface file b... ◇ ⊕ ⊖	String	LaunchScreen
Main storyboard file base name ◇	String	Main
▶ Required device capabilities ◇	Array	(1 item)
▶ Supported interface orientations ◇	Array	(3 items)
▶ Supported interface orientations (i... ◇	Array	(4 items)

Figure 9-3. We've added the UISupportsDocumentBrowser key to our Info.plist file

See Also

Recipe 9.2

9.2 Associating File Types with Your App

Problem

You want your app to be able to open certain file types in document browsers (of type `UIDocumentBrowserViewController`).

In this recipe, and the rest of this chapter for that matter, we are going to focus on an image browser application and therefore work solely with image file types.

Solution

In the following steps, we will add support to let an app open JPEG and PNG images:

1. In your *Info.plist* file, add the `CFBundleDocumentTypes` key, of type `Array`. Xcode will automatically create an object of type `Dictionary` under this array for you.
2. Under this dictionary, for the `CFBundleTypeName` key, set the value of `Images`, which is of type `String`. The value of this key describes the type of files that your application allows the user to open.
3. Under the same dictionary, add the `LSHandlerRank` key, of type `String`, and set its value to `Default`. The value of the `LSHandlerRank` key determines how this particular file type should be handled. Provide one of the following values: `Owner`

(your application is the creator and owner of this type), `Default` (your app is a viewer and editor of this file type), `Alternate` (your app is a viewer of this file type), or `None` (your app is unable to open files of this type).

4. Under the same dictionary again, add a key named `LSItemContentTypes` of type `Array`. Under it, add two `String` values: `public.jpeg` and `public.png`.

5. Ensure that the instance of `UIDocumentBrowserViewController` is initialized in your app delegate, instead of through the storyboard. This change is necessary because you will now need to provide a list of supported data types to the document browser view controller, and you do this through its `UIDocumentBrowser VeiwController(forOpeningFilesWithContentTypes:)` initializer. For the supported data types, this recipe will use the `public.png` and `public.jpeg` choices you just entered in the previous step.

At this point, the `CFBundleDocumentTypes` key of your *Info.plist* file should look like this:

```
<key>CFBundleDocumentTypes</key>
<array>
  <dict>
    <key>CFBundleTypeName</key>
    <string>Images</string>
    <key>LSHandlerRank</key>
    <string>Default</string>
    <key>LSItemContentTypes</key>
    <array>
      <string>public.jpeg</string>
      <string>public.png</string>
    </array>
  </dict>
</array>
```

For a list of supported data types, see System-Declared Uniform Type Identifiers (*http://apple.co/2Ba3yrd*).

When a user browses for files to open, and icons to represent these files are available on the system, iOS displays them along with the filenames. By default, when the user browses for default file types such as PNG and JPEG, iOS has thumbnail images for them. If your application works with private and custom file types, such as file types owned by you or your company, you can add icons for them and iOS will display the icons. To do this, add the `CFBundleTypeIconFiles`, key of type `Array`, to the `CFBund leDocumentTypes` dictionary. Under this array, provide the filenames of icons that iOS can use to represent your custom file types.

Discussion

If you are doing some testing on the iOS simulator, it will have to contain some files of the types you support in your app. You are more likely to have some JPEG or PNG images in your iCloud Drive than in the Files app in the simulator. (The simulator has a Files app just as other iOS systems do.) So, here I will show how to download files from iCloud and import them into the simulator's Files app:

1. On the simulator, log in to iCloud Drive.
2. Open the Photos app on the simulator and click an image.
3. Tap the Share button in the Photos app.
4. From the bottom of the share sheet (Figure 9-4), tap the "Save to Files" button.

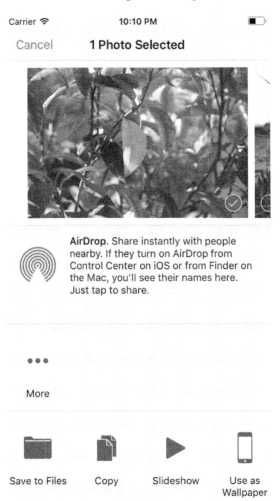

Figure 9-4. Saving an image from the Photos app on the simulator to the Files application

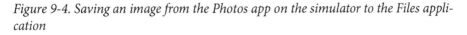

5. Now you will see a dialog asking where you want to save that file. Choose the *iCloud Drive* folder and then tap the Add button on the navigation bar (see Figure 9-5). This will save the selected photo in the root folder of iCloud Drive so that you can later easily import it into your app.

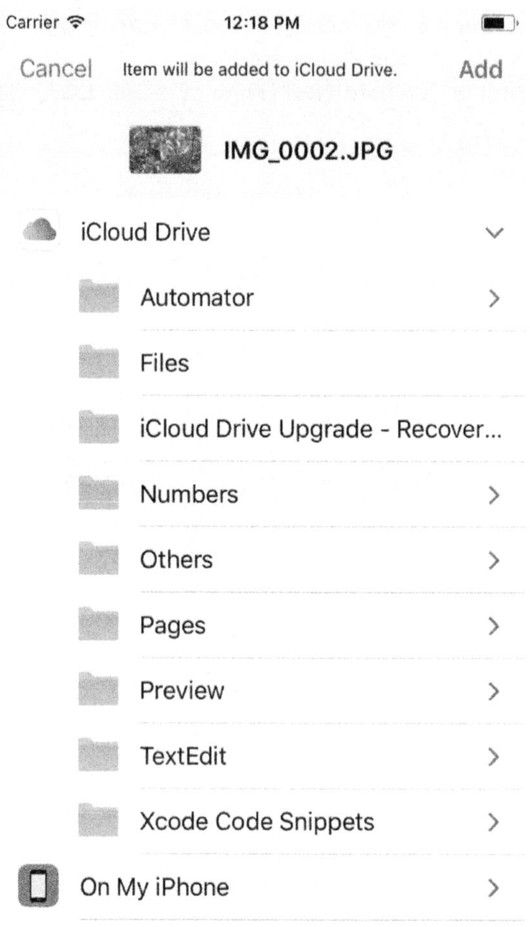

Carrier 📶   12:18 PM   🔋

Cancel   Item will be added to iCloud Drive.   Add

🖼️ **IMG_0002.JPG**

☁️ iCloud Drive   ⌄

📁 Automator   >

📁 Files

📁 iCloud Drive Upgrade - Recover...

📁 Numbers   >

📁 Others   >

📁 Pages   >

📁 Preview   >

📁 TextEdit   >

📁 Xcode Code Snippets   >

📱 On My iPhone   >

Figure 9-5. Saving an image from your photo library into your iCloud Drive

6. Do the same thing for a few more images (see Figure 9-6), so that you have about three or four images saved to the root folder of your iCloud Drive.

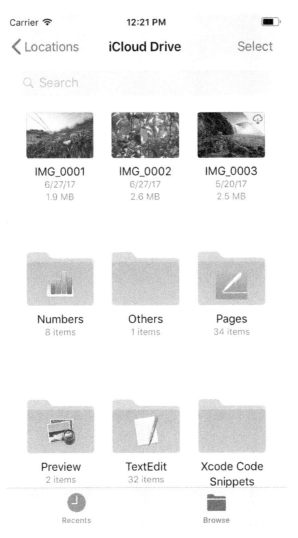

Figure 9-6. Save a selection of images from the Photos app into iCloud Drive

Next, initialize an instance of `UIDocumentBrowserViewController` in your app delegate, as described in the Solution section. You'll set the app delegate itself as the delegate of the document browser, so that later you can receive relevant delegate messages from it:

```
import UIKit

fileprivate extension Array where Element == String{
  static var fileTypes: [Element]{
    return [kUTTypePNG as Element]
```

```
    }
}

@UIApplicationMain
class AppDelegate: UIResponder, UIApplicationDelegate,
UIDocumentBrowserViewControllerDelegate {

  var window: UIWindow?

  func application(
    _ application: UIApplication,
    didFinishLaunchingWithOptions launchOptions:
    [UIApplicationLaunchOptionsKey: Any]?) -> Bool {

    let browser = UIDocumentBrowserViewController(
      forOpeningFilesWithContentTypes: .fileTypes)

    browser.delegate = self
    window?.rootViewController = browser

    return true

  }

}
```

In your *Info.plist* file, the hierarchy of the `CFBundleDocumentTypes` key should look similar to that shown in Figure 9-7. You can see there what the `CFBundleDocument Types` key and all its subkeys and values look like when viewing the *Info.plist* file of your app without raw keys. The `CFBundleDocumentTypes` key is shown as "Document types."

Key	Type	Value
▼ Information Property List	Dictionary	(15 items)
Localization native developm... ◇●⊖	String	$(DEVELOPMENT_LANGUAGE)
Supports Document Browser ◇	Boolean	YES
Document types ◇●⊖	Array ◇	(1 item)
▼ Item 0 (Images)	Dictionary	(3 items)
Document Type Name ◇	String	Images
Handler rank ◇	String	Default
▼ Document Content Type UTIs ◇	Array	(2 items)
Item 0	String	public.jpeg
Item 1	String	public.png

Figure 9-7. Document types supported by your app's Info.plist file

Now, if you run your app in the simulator, assuming that you have already logged in to iCloud, you will see that the document browser view controller immediately displays a view of your iCloud files and the rest of folders that are available on your drive.

See Also

Recipes 9.1 and 9.3

9.3 Creating New Documents

Problem

You want to allow your users to create new documents from the document browser.

Solution

When a document browser of type `UIDocumentBrowserViewController` is displayed to the user, while it has its `allowsDocumentCreation` property set to `true` (its default value), the user can tap the + button to request that application create a new document in the current folder (see Figure 9-8).

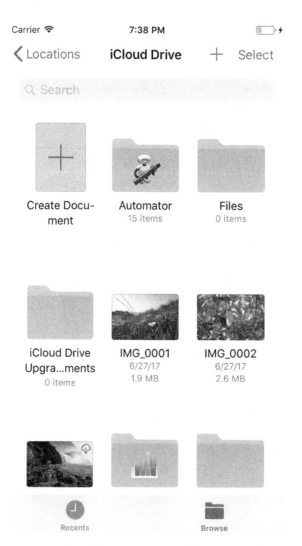

Figure 9-8. The user can tap the + button to request that your application create a new document

To enable this, follow these steps:

1. Create a new view controller that is responsible for creating a new document (with empty data) at a given URL inside your app's sandbox and for reporting back that URL to your app delegate.
2. Ensure that a view controller is prepared to present the empty document to the user, ready for manipulation.

3. In your app delegate that conforms to `UIDocumentBrowserViewController Delegate`, implement the `documentBrowser(_:didRequestDocumentCreation WithHandler:)` function.
4. In the aforementioned function, receive the URL where your view controller saved the new file, and pass it along to the `importHandler` argument.

Discussion

This process is quite straightforward after you've gone through it once, but it might sound quite complicated if you've just gotten started with document creation and document browsers. So I'll try to break it down a little bit.

When the user taps the + button in the document browser view controller, the controller calls its delegate's `documentBrowser(_:didRequestDocumentCreationWith Handler:)` function, asking that a new document be created at a temporary location and for that URL to be passed back to the document browser so that iOS can sync that URL to iCloud.

When you have prepared a view controller that can present an empty document to the user, you will also need to designate a URL, in the documents folder of your application, that will represent your file. In the beginning, depending on your file type, you can save an empty `Data` instance into that URL and then pass the URL to iOS in the aforementioned function.

 If you only designate a URL to your file but don't save its contents to disk and return the URL to iOS, you will receive an error in the console in Xcode telling you that iOS could not access the given URL. That message appears because iOS could not find any files saved at the given URL. So, if you are unsure what your file will contain in its empty state, simply create an instance of `Data` and call its `write(to:options:)` function to save the empty data to the URL.

Now let's have a look at an example. We will build this example based on the past recipes in this chapter, where we have successfully created a document browser as the root view controller of your app. We'll begin by creating a view controller that will be responsible for allowing our user to edit an image document. We will use this view controller to create a new document as well as allowing the user to edit an existing image that the user can pick from her iCloud library. So, create a new Swift file called *ImageEditorViewController.swift* of type `UIViewController`.

After that, create a storyboard file called *ImageEditorViewController.storyboard* and add a view controller to your scene. Change the class file of this view controller to `ImageEditorViewController` from the Identity inspector. Then, while your view controller is selected in the storyboard scene, go to the Editor menu, choose Embed In, and then choose Navigation Controller. This will wrap your view controller inside a navigation controller. Choose your navigation controller by clicking it. Then, in the Attributes Inspector panel, ensure that Is Initial View Controller is selected.

At this point, as Figure 9-9 shows, we have created our image editor view controller and wrapped it inside a navigation controller. We have ensured that we have backed our view controller with a class called `ImageEditorViewController` of type `UIView Controller` and that this class is associated with our view controller in the storyboard.

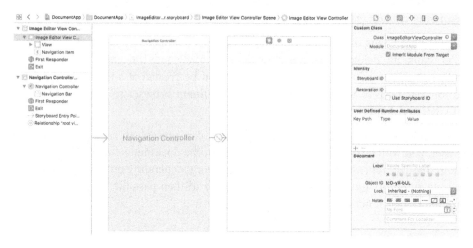

Figure 9-9. Creating an image editor view controller

We are going to allow the user to drag her finger around the screen, just for the sake of this example, on our image editor view controller, in order to draw any shapes that she wishes. We'll choose a color in the app, for the sake of simplicity in this example. Therefore, we will need our own view of type `UIView` associated with our image editor view controller. This view will also, periodically, capture its own state as an instance of `Data` that represents the drawn image as a PNG image, and will report it back to our view controller so that the view controller can save that data to disk.

So, go ahead and create a new Cocoa Touch class in Xcode and call it *ImageEditor-View.swift*. Ensure that the new class is of type `UIView`. We will add a very simple `delegate` property to this class so that our image editor view controller can conform to it later on and also ensure that we have an initializer that takes in a delegate:

```
import UIKit

protocol ImageEditorViewDelegate: class{
  //empty for now
}
```

```
class ImageEditorView: UIView {

  private var delegate: ImageEditorViewDelegate?

  init(delegate: ImageEditorViewDelegate) {
    super.init(frame: .zero)
    self.delegate = delegate
  }

  required init?(coder aDecoder: NSCoder) {
    super.init(coder: aDecoder)
  }

}
```

Now let's go over to our image editor view controller, which right now is empty. We'll ensure not only that it is a view controller, but also that it conforms to the ImageEditorViewDelegate protocol:

```
import UIKit

class ImageEditorViewController: UIViewController, ImageEditorViewDelegate {

  //rest of our code will be placed here...
```

If you remember from our description before, the app delegate is going to ask us, through the documentBrowser(_:didRequestDocumentCreationWithHandler:) function, to create a new document for the user, and we are going to make our image editor view controller responsible for this. We therefore need a new class function in our view controller that creates a new instance of our image editor view controller wrapped inside its navigation controller, loaded from the storyboard. We also need this view controller to create an empty document for the user and report that URL back to us. So let's write a function that can first return a URL to a new (nonexistent) file in the documents folder of our app:

```
private class var newFileUrl: URL?{

  let fileManager = FileManager()

  guard let documentsFolder = try? fileManager.url(
    for: .documentDirectory,
    in: .userDomainMask,
    appropriateFor: nil,
    create: true) else {
      return nil
  }

  let randomNumber = arc4random_uniform(10)
  let fileName = "Untitled \(randomNumber).png"
  let fileUrl = documentsFolder.appendingPathComponent(fileName)
```

```
guard !fileManager.fileExists(atPath: fileUrl.path) else{
  //the file exists already, we won't override it
  return nil
}

  return fileUrl

}
```

Our view controller is going to hold a reference to this file URL so that we can continually save the contents of our document into it, so let's create a constant for this URL:

```
private var fileUrl: URL!
```

After this, we need to write the class function that creates the document for us. We are going to get a new file URL from our `newFileUrl` computed class variable and then save an empty instance of `Data` into it. Once we have the URL, we load our view controller's storyboard, read the navigation controller alongside the image editor view controller from this storyboard, and return it, alongside our file URL, to the caller (our app delegate):

```
typealias NewDocumentHandler = (URL?, UIViewController?) -> Void
class func createNewDocumentViewController(
  withHandler handler: @escaping NewDocumentHandler){

  //get a file URL
  guard let fileUrl = newFileUrl else {
    handler(nil, nil)
    return
  }

  //we will create an empty file at the given path now
  do{
    try Data().write(to: fileUrl, options: .atomicWrite)
  } catch {
    handler(nil, nil)
    return
  }

  //load our view controller from the storyboard file
  guard let navController =
    UIStoryboard(
      name: "ImageEditorViewController",
      bundle: nil).instantiateInitialViewController()
      as? UINavigationController,
    let viewController = navController.viewControllers.first
      as? ImageEditorViewController else {
    handler(nil, nil)
    return
  }
```

```
//set the file URL and then call the handler
viewController.fileUrl = fileUrl

handler(fileUrl, navController)
}
```

Let's also display a Done button in our navigation bar when our view is loaded so that the user can press it and dismiss our view controller when she is done with the document. We do this by creating an instance of UIBarButtonItem and then adding it to the navigation bar through the setLeftBarButton(_:animated:) function of our view controller's navigationItem property. The only thing that this button will do is call our view controller's dismiss(animated:completion:) function:

```
override func viewDidLoad() {
  super.viewDidLoad()
  self.title = fileUrl.lastPathComponent

  let close = UIBarButtonItem(
    title: "Done", style: .done, target: self,
    action: #selector(ImageEditorViewController.done))
  navigationItem.setLeftBarButton(close, animated: false)

}

@objc func done(){
  dismiss(animated: true, completion: nil)
}
```

When the user creates a new document, we are going to present an instance of our ImageEditorView to her with a white background by default. Users might be confused about what we expect of them, so we are going to display a message to our users when they create a new document informing them of how they can start drawing shapes on the screen using their fingers. For this, we will create an instance of UIAlertController and present the alert controller just like we do any other view controller:

```
private func displayIntroMessage(){

  let alert = UIAlertController(
    title: nil,
    message: "Drag your finger across the screen to start drawing!",
    preferredStyle: .alert)

  alert.addAction(UIAlertAction(title: "OK", style: .default, handler: nil))
  present(alert, animated: true, completion: nil)
}

override func viewDidAppear(_ animated: Bool) {
  super.viewDidAppear(animated)
```

```
    displayIntroMessage()
}
```

By default, our view controller will get an instance of UIView as its view, but we want this to be an instance of ImageEditorView. So let's override our view controller's load View() function and instantiate our image editor view in there, using its ImageEditor View(delegate:) initializer:

```
override func loadView() {
  view = ImageEditorView(delegate: self)
  view.backgroundColor = .white
}
```

We are now done with our image editor view and view controller, so let's move to the app delegate and implement the documentBrowser(_:didRequestDocumentCreation WithHandler:) delegate function of the UIDocumentBrowserViewController Delegate protocol. The didRequestDocumentCreationWithHandler argument of this function is of type @escaping (URL?, UIDocumentBrowserViewController.Import Mode) -> Void, which means that it expects us to call it with an optional URL. It's optional because the function can set it to nil if something goes wrong (in creating the document, for instance). The function's other argument is an *import mode* of type UIDocumentBrowserViewController.ImportMode, which can be one of the following:

none
> Used if the URL could not be created.

copy
> Used when creating a new document, or if you are supporting drag-and-drop and you want to tell the originator of the drag-and-drop operation that you have successfully made a copy of the file.

move
> Used when an original document was provided to the app and the app, instead of making a copy of it, decides to move the original over into its sandbox. This is used in the of drags and drops from one app into another. In this case, the destination app requests the origin of the drag and drop to delete the file, flagging that the destination app has made a new copy of the file. The impact is to move the file from the source of the drag into the destination of the drop. This does not apply to our current example because we are not supporting drag and drop for the sake of simplicity.

So, in the documentBrowser(_:didRequestDocumentCreationWithHandler:) dele-gate function we will invoke our image editor view controller's createNewDocument ViewController(withHandler:) class function. Then, based on whether or not the URL could be created, we will call our function's import handler argument:

```
func documentBrowser(
  _ controller: UIDocumentBrowserViewController,
  didRequestDocumentCreationWithHandler importHandler:
  @escaping (URL?, UIDocumentBrowserViewController.ImportMode) -> Void) {

  ImageEditorViewController.createNewDocumentViewController {
    [weak self] url, viewController in

    guard let `self` = self else {
      importHandler(nil, .none)
      return
    }

    guard url != nil, let viewController = viewController else {
      importHandler(nil, .none)
      return
    }

    importHandler(url, .copy)
    self.present(viewController: viewController)


  }

}

private func present(viewController: UIViewController){
  window?.rootViewController?.present(viewController,
                                    animated: true, completion: nil)
}
```

You can now run our app in the simulator and see the results for yourself. Once the user taps the + button to create a new document, our app will present our image editor view controller that creates a new empty file for the user and displays an introductory alert (Figure 9-10).

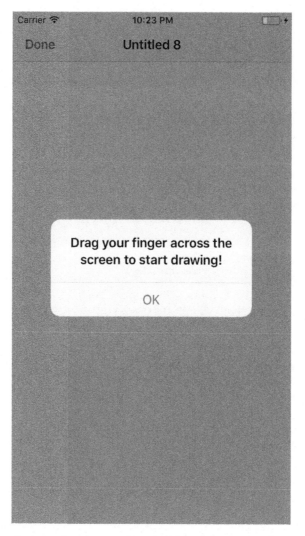

Figure 9-10. Introductory alert, letting the user know how she can draw shapes on the screen

Right now nothing else really works in our app; that's to say that the user cannot actually draw anything on the screen and we have no way to save anything to the disk. We will discuss these subjects in the rest of this chapter.

See Also

Recipes 9.1 and 9.4

9.4 Saving Your Documents

Problem

You want to allow your user to create and edit a document, and then save its content to iCloud.

Solution

Follow these steps:

1. Create a subclass of `UIDocument`.
2. In your subclass, override the `load(fromContents:ofType:)` function and load the given data as your document. This function is called when the data for the document is loaded and you need to associate that data with your document object.
3. In the same subclass, override the `contents(forType:)` function and return the data for your document. This function is called when the document is asked to save its contents.
4. In the `documentBrowser(_:didRequestDocumentCreationWithHandler:)` delegate function of your document picker, create a new filename (perhaps a random name), such as *untitled1.png*.
5. In the same function, use an instance of `NSMetadataQuery` to find out whether this file already exists in the user's iCloud Drive inside your application's container and handle the issue if the file already exists. You might want to display an alert to the user suggesting that they attempt to create the file again with a new name.
6. Assuming that the file does not exist, create a temporary URL for it (for instance, in your app bundle's documents folder).
7. Instantiate a subclass of `UIDocument` with this URL, then call its `save(to:for:)` function, and set its `for` argument to `.forCreating`. This will ensure that your document saves an empty state of itself (in our case, a `Data` instance that represents a white screen) at the given URL.

 You might want to save *some* data in the temporary folder, as otherwise your document browser will complain that it cannot reach the file while moving it to the cloud. My approach in this recipe is to create a new image context as large as the current screen bounds, fill it with a white color, and then extract that context's PNG data and save that data to the disk.

8. In your document browser's delegate (typically your app delegate), listen to the `documentBrowser(_:didImportDocumentAt:toDestinationURL:)` function, which gets called when the document browser has moved your temporary file to the cloud. The value of the `toDestinationURL` argument contains the new document URL in the cloud.

9. Use the value of the `toDestinationURL` argument to instantiate a subclass of `UIDocument`.

10. Use the `present(_:animated:completion:)` function to present a new editor view controller to your user, with the new document instance.

11. In your document browser's delegate, import the `documentBrowser(_:failed ToImportDocumentAt:)` function and ensure that you can handle the errors that might occur when moving your document to the cloud, perhaps by informing the user through an alert controller that something has gone wrong and giving her the option to create a new document.

12. Enable the iCloud capabilities in your Xcode project so that your application will have the right entitlements to create documents in the cloud.

 This recipe is based on what you learned in Recipe 9.3, and I highly recommend that you read that recipe before continuing with this one.

Discussion

Let's dive right into implementing our application. This recipe is based on an earlier recipe in this chapter, with some changes to the code. Instead of just mentioning the changes, I will make sure that you have the entirety of the code base explained in this recipe for the sake of clarity.

We will begin by going to our *Info.plist* to ensure that our application can handle PNG file types in the cloud and that iOS can associate our application with PNG files as a browser:

```
<key>CFBundleDocumentTypes</key>
<array>
  <dict>
    <key>CFBundleTypeName</key>
    <string>PNG Images</string>
    <key>LSHandlerRank</key>
    <string>Owner</string>
    <key>LSItemContentTypes</key>
    <array>
      <string>public.png</string>
    </array>
```

```
    </dict>
</array>
```

We should also create a class that can take in a filename, such as *untitled0.png*, and then find out whether this file exists in the iCloud container of our application. We will use this new class in our app delegate while creating a new file for the user. So, create a new Swift file in Xcode, called *DocumentFinder.swift*. This class will have to have two properties:

documentName, *of type* `String`

Holds the file (document) name that our app delegate wants to suggest to the user for creation.

completion, *of type* `(Bool) -> Void`

A completion handler that will be called with a `Bool` value of `true` or `false`, indicating whether or not the given filename already exists in our app's cloud container:

```swift
import Foundation

class DocumentFinder{

  //Bool = isFound
  typealias Completion = (Bool) -> Void

  private let documentName: String
  private let completion: Completion

  init(documentName name: String, completion handler: @escaping Completion){
    documentName = name
    completion = handler
  }

  //the rest of our code will be placed here shortly...
```

After we have stored the name of the file that we need to look for in our app's iCloud container, plus a completion handler, we need to construct our query of type `NSMetadataQuery`. We will set the `searchScopes` property of our query to `NSMetadataQueryUbiquitousDocumentsScope` so that the metadata query object can search in the documents folder in our app's iCloud container, where we store our files. We'll also set the query's `predicate` property to look for objects with an `NSMetadataItemFSNameKey` equal to the document name:

```swift
private lazy var query: NSMetadataQuery = {
  let query = NSMetadataQuery()
  query.searchScopes = [NSMetadataQueryUbiquitousDocumentsScope]

  query.predicate = NSPredicate(
    format: "%K ==[cd] '\(documentName)'",
    NSMetadataItemFSNameKey)
```

```
    return query
}()
```

We will also need a `start()` function on our document finder class. In this function, we will call the `start()` function of our query object of type `NSMetadataQuery`. We'll also listen to notifications of type `NSMetadataQueryDidFinishGathering`, which get sent when our query object has finished gathering data from the cloud:

```
@discardableResult func start() -> Bool{
  guard !query.isStarted else {return false}

  NotificationCenter.default.addObserver(
    self,
    selector: #selector(didFinishGathering(notification:)),
    name: .NSMetadataQueryDidFinishGathering,
    object: nil)

  return query.start()
}
```

When the `NSMetadataQueryDidFinishGathering` notification is posted, we are listening to it on the `didFinishGathering(notification:)` selector. In here, we will look at the `resultCount` property of our query object. If it's more than 0, it means that the query object found the filename in the cloud, meaning that a file of the name we chose already exists there. Once we know this, we can call our completion handler with the results:

```
@objc func didFinishGathering(notification: Notification){
  NotificationCenter.default.removeObserver(self)
  query.stop()
  completion(query.resultCount > 0)
}
```

After our implementation of the `DocumentFinder` class is done, we need to create a new Swift class of type `UIDocument`, named `ImageDocument`, that will be responsible for holding our image instances and their associated data. So, go ahead and create a new Cocoa Touch file in Xcode of type `UIDocument`, called *ImageDocument.swift*. The first thing that we will do in this file is define an == operator between `String?` and `CFString`. The reason for this is that when we override `UIDocument` functions such as `load(fromContents:ofType:)`, the ofType argument is of type `String?`. But it will be set to values such as `kUTTypePNG`, and `kUTTypePNG` is of type `CFString`. So we need way to tell whether the given type is the type that we accept, and unfortunately there are no default operators that can check for equality between `String?` and `CFString`. We do this as follows:

```
func == (lhs: String?, rhs: CFString) -> Bool{
  guard let lhs = lhs else {return false}
```

```
    return lhs == rhs as String
}
```

The only property that our `ImageDocument` class has is `imageData`, of type `Data?`, which gets set to the data for the image that is being worked on by the user. So let's define this property first:

```
class ImageDocument: UIDocument {

  var imageData: Data?

  //the rest of our code will be placed here shortly...
```

We should now override the `load(fromContents:ofType:)` function of `UIDocument`, ensuring there that the type of the document is `kUTTypePNG` and that the data is of type `Data`. If everything goes as expected, we will store the incoming data into our instance's `imageData` property:

```
override func load(
  fromContents contents: Any, ofType typeName: String?) throws {

  guard typeName == kUTTypePNG else {
    throw ImageDocumentErrors.invalidTypeName(typeName)
  }

  guard let data = contents as? Data else {
    throw ImageDocumentErrors.invalidContentType
  }

  imageData = data

}
```

As you can see, the `load(fromContents:ofType:)` function is marked as `throws`, meaning that it can throw exceptions if something is not as expected. We might throw exceptions of type `ImageDocumentErrors`, so let's define this enum as well:

```
enum ImageDocumentErrors: Error{
  case invalidTypeName(String?)
  case invalidContentType
}
```

Last but not least, we will have to override the `contents(forType:)` function of `UIDocument`. In this function, our responsibility is to return the image data in our `imageData` property, if it exists (meaning that it is not `nil`). On the other hand, if it is `nil`, we will return the data associated with a white image that covers the entire screen. This is very important! If you return `nil` from this function or, even worse, throw an exception while you don't have any data for your document, iOS won't be able to save your document to the cloud, so importing it from your app bundle into iCloud will fail:

```
override func contents(forType typeName: String) throws -> Any {

  guard typeName == kUTTypePNG else {
    throw ImageDocumentErrors.invalidTypeName(typeName)
  }

  let emptyImageData = self.dataForWhiteScreen
  return imageData ?? emptyImageData

}
```

You must have noticed that we are returning the value of the `imageData` property if it exists, and otherwise the return value of the `emptyImageData` computed property that we have to now program. In the `emptyImageData` property of type `Data`, all we have to do is create a new image context with the `UIGraphicsBeginImageContextWithOp tions(_:_:_:)` function as large as our `UIScreen`. Then we will get the current image context with the `UIGraphicsGetCurrentContext()` function and fill it with white color. Finally, we will use the `UIGraphicsGetImageFromCurrentImageContext()` function to get a `UIImage` instance out of our context, and turn that image into `Data` using the `UIImagePNGRepresentation()` function:

```
private var dataForWhiteScreen: Data{

  defer{
    UIGraphicsEndImageContext()
  }

  let size = UIScreen.main.bounds.size
  UIGraphicsBeginImageContextWithOptions(size, true, 0.0)
  guard let context = UIGraphicsGetCurrentContext() else {
    return Data()
  }
  UIColor.white.setFill()
  context.fill(CGRect(origin: .zero, size: size))
  guard let image = UIGraphicsGetImageFromCurrentImageContext() else {
    return Data()
  }
  return UIImagePNGRepresentation(image) ?? Data()
}
```

That was the entire implementation of our `ImageDocument` class. In Recipe 9.3 we implemented a very basic view of type `UIView`, called `ImageEditorView`, with an empty delegate definition. In this recipe, since we are going to allow the user to drag her fingers on the view in order to draw shapes, we need to implement this view class properly. Then, every time the user has lifted her finger off the screen, we will grab an image representation of our view and everything that is drawn on it, and report that image's data to our delegate. So let's define our delegate protocol to account for this behavior:

```
import UIKit

protocol ImageEditorViewDelegate: class{
  func imageEditorView(view: ImageEditorView, hasDataForImage data: Data)
}
```

We will capture the point where the user is dragging her finger and use that as the center of an ellipse with a certain radius, because we need an instance of CGRect to draw our ellipse later. It would be good for CGRect to be able to initialize itself with a center point and a radius, so let's extend CGRect to add that initializer to it:

```
fileprivate extension CGRect{
  init(center: CGPoint, radius: CGFloat){
    self = CGRect(origin: CGPoint(x: center.x - radius, y: center.y - radius),
                 size: CGSize(width: radius * 2, height: radius * 2))
  }
}
```

As the user moves her finger on the screen, we will have to save all the touch points in an array, and every time we redraw our view on the screen, we will draw those points as well. So we need a property that can hold an array of CGPoint instances, with every point representing a point on the screen the user has touched:

```
class ImageEditorView: UIView {

  private var weak delegate: ImageEditorViewDelegate?
  private var touchPoints = [CGPoint]()

  init(delegate: ImageEditorViewDelegate) {
    super.init(frame: .zero)
    self.delegate = delegate
  }

  required init?(coder aDecoder: NSCoder) {
    super.init(coder: aDecoder)
  }

  //the rest of our code will be written here shortly...
```

In the touchesBegan(_:with:) function of our view, we will extract the touch point, append it to the touchPoints array, and then ask the view to draw its contents by calling the view's setNeedsDisplay() function. We will do the exact same thing in the touchesMoved(_:with:) function:

```
func draw(touches: Set<UITouch>){
  guard let touchPoint = touches.first?.location(in: self) else {return}
  touchPoints.append(touchPoint)
  setNeedsDisplay()
}

override func touchesBegan(_ touches: Set<UITouch>, with event: UIEvent?) {
  super.touchesBegan(touches, with: event)
```

```
  draw(touches: touches)
}

override func touchesMoved(_ touches: Set<UITouch>, with event: UIEvent?) {
  super.touchesMoved(touches, with: event)
  draw(touches: touches)
}
```

So, let's implement the draw(_:) function of our view. In this function, after having filled the entire background of our view with its default color of white, we will read all the touch points in our touchPoints property of type [CGPoint], and for every point in this array, we will draw an ellipse on our view with a black color:

```
override func draw(_ rect: CGRect) {
  guard let context = UIGraphicsGetCurrentContext() else {return}

  //background color
  UIColor.white.setFill()
  context.fill(rect)

  touchPoints.forEach{point in
    UIColor.black.setFill()
    let ellipseRect = CGRect(center: point, radius: 10.0)
    context.fillEllipse(in: ellipseRect)
  }

}
```

When the touchesEnded(_:with:) function of our view gets called, we will take a dump of our view's context into an image of type PNG, extract the PNG's data into an instance of Data, and report it to our delegate:

```
var imageData: Data?{

  UIGraphicsBeginImageContext(bounds.size)

  defer{UIGraphicsEndImageContext()}

  guard drawHierarchy(in: bounds, afterScreenUpdates: true) else {return nil}

  guard let image = UIGraphicsGetImageFromCurrentImageContext()
    else {return nil}

  return UIImagePNGRepresentation(image)

}

override func touchesEnded(_ touches: Set<UITouch>, with event: UIEvent?) {
  super.touchesEnded(touches, with: event)
  guard let data = imageData else {return}
```

```
  delegate?.imageEditorView(view: self, hasDataForImage: data)
}
```

Now it's time to program our `ImageEditorViewController` class. We started the implementation of this class in Recipe 9.3, but in this recipe, we are going to almost completely rewrite the class to meet our requirements. The first thing that we are going to do in this view controller is create a reference to our image document of type `ImageDocument`. When the delegate function of our view gets called, we will set the data of our image document to the incoming data of the view and then call the `save(to:for:completionHandler:)` function of our `UIDocument` subclass with the `for` argument carrying the value of `forOverwriting`. This overwrites the entire document with the new data:

```
import UIKit

class ImageEditorViewController: UIViewController, ImageEditorViewDelegate {

  //will get set in our custom initializer
  private var fileUrl: URL!

  private var imageDocument: ImageDocument!

  func imageEditorView(view: ImageEditorView, hasDataForImage data: Data) {
    imageDocument.imageData = data

    imageDocument.save(
      to: imageDocument.fileURL,
      for: .forOverwriting) {succeeded in

        if succeeded{
          print("Successfully saved the data")
        } else {
          print("Failed to save the document")
        }

    }
  }

  //the rest of the code will be written here shortly...
```

Because our app delegate is going to be responsible for retrieving a URL for our document, our view controller has to be concerned only with getting initialized with a new document URL. So let's create a class function for our view controller where it can read the *ImageEditorViewController.storyboard* file (see Recipe 9.3) and return the navigation controller that holds an instance of the image editor view controller. When defining the function, we'll set each instance's `fileUrl` property to the incoming file URL:

```
class func newInstance(withFileUrl fileUrl: URL) -> UIViewController{
```

```
//load our view controller from the storyboard file
guard let navController =
  UIStoryboard(
    name: "ImageEditorViewController",
    bundle: nil).instantiateInitialViewController()
    as? UINavigationController,
  let viewController = navController.viewControllers.first
    as? ImageEditorViewController else {
      return UIViewController()
}

//set the file URL and then call the handler
viewController.fileUrl = fileUrl

return navController

}
```

When our view is loaded, we will set the title of our view controller to the name of the file that we are displaying on the screen. We will also place a Done button on the navigation bar that will call the close(completionHandler:) function of our UIDocument subclass. This will close the document, at which time we will dismiss our view controller:

```
override func viewDidLoad() {
  super.viewDidLoad()
  self.title = fileUrl.lastPathComponent

  let close = UIBarButtonItem(
    title: "Done", style: .done, target: self,
    action: #selector(ImageEditorViewController.done))
  navigationItem.setLeftBarButton(close, animated: false)

}

@objc func done(){
  imageDocument.close {[weak self] succeeded in
    guard let `self` = self else {return}

    if succeeded{
      print("Successfully closed the document")
    } else {
      print("Failed to close the document")
    }

    self.dismiss(animated: true, completion: nil)
  }

}
```

When the viewWillAppear(_:) function of our view controller is called, we will instantiate our document of type ImageDocument with its ImageDocument(fileUrl:)

---

initializer (inherited from `UIDocument`) and then call its `open(completionHandler:)` method. That method asks iOS to read the file's contents from the cloud and then get back to us through our completion handler. This completion handler contains only a Boolean value that indicates whether the opening of the document went well. If it didn't go as planned, we will display an alert to the user. We will store the instance of `ImageDocument` in our view controller's `imageDocument` property:

```
override func viewWillAppear(_ animated: Bool) {
  super.viewWillAppear(animated)

  imageDocument = ImageDocument(fileURL: fileUrl)

  imageDocument.open {[weak self] succeeded in
    guard let `self` = self else {return}
    guard succeeded else {
      self.displayFailedToOpenDocumentAlert()
      return
    }
  }

}

private func displayFailedToOpenDocumentAlert(){

  let alert = UIAlertController(
    title: nil,
    message: "Failed to open the document!",
    preferredStyle: .alert)

  alert.addAction(UIAlertAction(title: "OK", style: .default, handler: nil))
  present(alert, animated: true, completion: nil)

}
```

And as we saw in Recipe 9.3, we will display an introductory message to the user once our view controller appears on the screen, telling them how they can draw shapes with their fingers:

```
private func displayIntroMessage(){

  let alert = UIAlertController(
    title: nil,
    message: "Drag your finger across the screen to start drawing!",
    preferredStyle: .alert)

  alert.addAction(UIAlertAction(title: "OK", style: .default, handler: nil))
  present(alert, animated: true, completion: nil)
}

override func viewDidAppear(_ animated: Bool) {
  super.viewDidAppear(animated)
```

```
displayIntroMessage()
}
```

Last but not least, this view controller overrides the `loadView()` function so that we can replace the default `UIView` instance with our custom `UIView` of type `ImageEditor View`:

```
override func loadView() {
  view = ImageEditorView(delegate: self)
  view.backgroundColor = .white
}
```

That was everything that we needed to do to implement our image editor view controller, so let's focus our attention on our app delegate. That's an integral part of any app, but in our app it's even more important than usual because it takes care of the interactions with our document browser view controller and its delegate functions. Let's first create an instance of our document browser view controller:

```
import UIKit
import MobileCoreServices

fileprivate extension Array where Element == String{
  static var fileTypes: [Element]{
    return [kUTTypePNG as Element]
  }
}


@UIApplicationMain
class AppDelegate: UIResponder, UIApplicationDelegate,
UIDocumentBrowserViewControllerDelegate {

  var window: UIWindow?

  func application(
    _ application: UIApplication,
    didFinishLaunchingWithOptions launchOptions:
    [UIApplicationLaunchOptionsKey: Any]?) -> Bool {

    let browser = UIDocumentBrowserViewController(
      forOpeningFilesWithContentTypes: .fileTypes)

    browser.delegate = self
    window?.rootViewController = browser

    return true

  }

  //the rest of our implementation will be written here shortly...
```

This was the same implementation that we looked at in Recipe 9.3, so I won't explain it again. Let's now focus our attention on writing a function that uses our Document

Finder class to provide a suggestion for a filename that does not already exist in the app's documents folder. We'll write a function with a completion handler that returns a value of type URL? that is either a valid URL for a file that is inside our app bundle's documents folder or just nil if something goes wrong, such as an attempt to create a duplicate file:

```
private var documentFinder: DocumentFinder?
private func newFileUrl(completion: @escaping (URL?) -> Void){

  let fileManager = FileManager()

  //get the URL to the app's documents folder
  guard let documentsFolder = try?
    fileManager.url(for: .documentDirectory,
                    in: .userDomainMask,
                    appropriateFor: nil, create: true) else {
    completion(nil)
    return
  }

  //create a random filename
  let randomNumber = arc4random_uniform(100)
  let fileName = "untitled\(randomNumber).png"
  let fileUrl = documentsFolder.appendingPathComponent(fileName)

  //find out if the file exists already in the cloud or not
  documentFinder = DocumentFinder(
  documentName: fileName){[weak self] found in

    guard let `self` = self else {
      completion(nil)
      return
    }

    self.documentFinder = nil

    if found{
      completion(nil)
    } else {
      completion(fileUrl)
    }
  }

  documentFinder?.start()

}
```

Inside the documentBrowser(_:didRequestDocumentCreationWithHandler:) function of our app delegate we will call our new function, named newFileUrl(completion:), to get the URL where we need to save our file temporarily in our app delegate. If that URL is nil, we will display an alert informing the user that we could not

find an appropriate URL for the file. If the URL is not `nil`, we will instantiate our
ImageDocument with its `ImageDocument(fileUrl:)`, provide the suggested file URL
to it, and then call the `save(to:for:completionHandler:)` function on it with the
for argument equal to forCreating so that we create the file in the suggested location, ready for it to be imported to the cloud. Last but not least, we need to call the
`close(completionHandler:)` function of our document before it can be moved over
to the cloud:

```
func documentBrowser(
    _ controller: UIDocumentBrowserViewController,
    didRequestDocumentCreationWithHandler importHandler:
    @escaping (URL?, UIDocumentBrowserViewController.ImportMode) -> Void) {

    newFileUrl{[weak self] newFileUrl in

        guard let `self` = self else {return}

        //get a file URL
        guard let fileUrl = newFileUrl else {
            importHandler(nil, .none)
            controller.present(self.existingFileAlert,
                            animated: true, completion: nil)
            return
        }

        let document = ImageDocument(fileURL: fileUrl)
        document.save(to: fileUrl, for: .forCreating) {succeeded in
            guard succeeded else {
                importHandler(nil, .none)
                return
            }

            document.close{closed in
                importHandler(fileUrl, .move)
            }
        }

    }

}

private var existingFileAlert: UIAlertController{

    let message = """
I came up with a new name for this document but it
appears to already exist in your iCloud Drive.
Create a new document with a new name!
"""

    let controller = UIAlertController(
```

```
     title: "Existing Document",
     message: message, preferredStyle: .alert)

  let action = UIAlertAction(title: "OK", style: .default, handler: nil)
  controller.addAction(action)

  return controller
}
```

After we have created and then closed this document, iOS will move it over to the cloud and then get back to us, calling our app delegate's documentBrowser(_:did ImportDocumentAt:toDestinationURL:) delegate function, and pass us the new cloud URL for this file using the toDestinationURL parameter. We then take this URL and open our image editor view controller with the given cloud URL:

```
func documentBrowser(_ controller: UIDocumentBrowserViewController,
                     didImportDocumentAt sourceURL: URL,
                     toDestinationURL destinationURL: URL) {

  let imageEditorViewController =
    ImageEditorViewController.newInstance(withFileUrl: destinationURL)

  controller.present(
    imageEditorViewController, animated: true, completion: nil)

}
```

We also need to handle any errors that might occur while importing documents to the cloud. For the sake of simplicity, I've implemented the documentBrowser(_:fail edToImportDocumentAt:) function with a simple log in it, but feel free to implement this function in a way that works for your application:

```
func documentBrowser(_ controller: UIDocumentBrowserViewController,
                     failedToImportDocumentAt documentURL: URL, error: Error?) {
  print("Failed to import the document")
}
```

One last detail that we need to take care of is enabling iCloud entitlements. Click your project's icon in Xcode and choose your target. Then click the Capabilities tab. In the iCloud section, turn on the switch and ensure that iCloud Documents is turned on as shown in Figure 9-11.

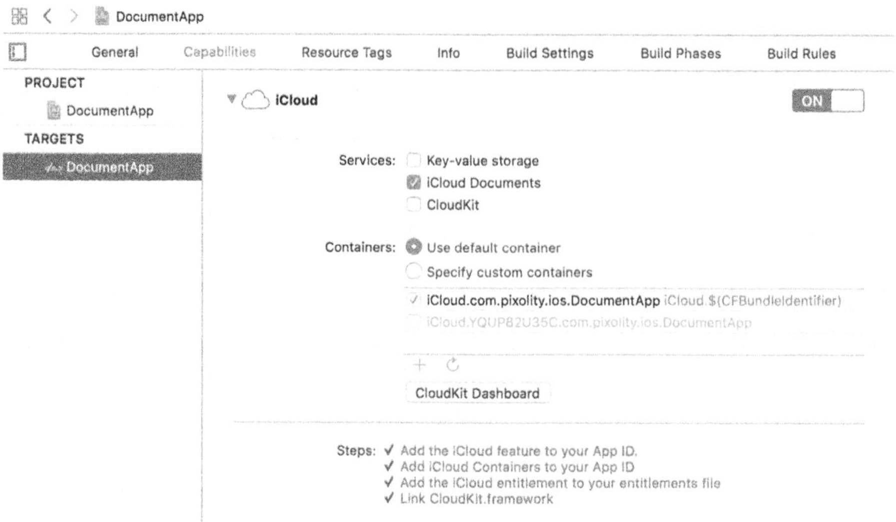

▣	General	Capabilities	Resource Tags	Info	Build Settings	Build Phases	Build Rules

PROJECT
📄 DocumentApp

TARGETS
📄 DocumentApp

▼ ☁ iCloud   `ON`

Services: ☐ Key-value storage
☑ iCloud Documents
☐ CloudKit

Containers: ⦿ Use default container
◯ Specify custom containers
✓ iCloud.com.pixolity.ios.DocumentApp iCloud.$(CFBundleIdentifier)
☐ iCloud.YQUPB2U35C.com.pixolity.ios.DocumentApp

\+ ↻

CloudKit Dashboard

Steps: ✓ Add the iCloud feature to your App ID.
✓ Add iCloud Containers to your App ID
✓ Add the iCloud entitlement to your entitlements file
✓ Link CloudKit.framework

Figure 9-11. Select iCloud Documents to enable iCloud entitlements and let your app create documents in the cloud

Run your app either in the simulator or on a device and watch the results. When the document browser shows up, go to the container folder for your application and press the + button, which will then create a new document that will immediately be moved to the cloud. You can then work with the document and press the Done button in order to save and close the document.

See Also

Recipes 9.1 and 9.3

9.5 Loading Existing Documents

Problem

You want to allow your application to open existing documents that are available through the document browser of type UIDocumentBrowserViewController.

Solution

Follow these steps:

1. Implement the documentBrowser(_:didPickDocumentURLs:) delegate function of your document browser (usually in the app delegate).

2. For every picked URL, create an instance of your custom `UIDocument` and present the document to the user.

 This recipe relies heavily on what you learned in Recipe 9.4. If you haven't read the aforementioned recipe, I highly recommend that you do that now, because the duplicated code will not be explained in this recipe.

Discussion

Let's take the exact same code that we wrote in Recipe 9.4 and jump to the app delegate's code. There, we are going to implement the `documentBrowser(_:didPick DocumentURLs:)` delegate function of the document browser and then present an instance of our `ImageEditorViewController` to the user, using its `ImageEditorView Controller(withFileUrl:)` initializer:

```
func documentBrowser(_ controller: UIDocumentBrowserViewController,
                didPickDocumentURLs documentURLs: [URL]) {

  guard let url = documentURLs.first else {return}

  let imageEditorViewController =
    ImageEditorViewController.newInstance(withFileUrl: url)

  controller.present(
    imageEditorViewController, animated: true, completion: nil)

}
```

We also need to ensure that when we call the `open(completionHandler:)` function on the document in our view controller, if everything goes as planned and the document is opened successfully, we read the `ImageDocument` instance's `imageData` property (see Recipe 9.4) and then provide that data to our view of type `ImageEditorView`. This will allow the image data to be drawn as the background image on the view. Then the user can carry on dragging her finger on the screen to draw shapes on top of the background image:

```
override func viewWillAppear(_ animated: Bool) {
  super.viewWillAppear(animated)

  imageDocument = ImageDocument(fileURL: fileUrl)

  imageDocument.open {[weak self] succeeded in
    guard let `self` = self else {return}
    guard succeeded else {
      self.displayFailedToOpenDocumentAlert()
      return
```

```
  }

  (self.view as? ImageEditorView)?.backgroundData =
    self.imageDocument.imageData

  }

}
```

We are reading the data from the document object and setting it as the background Data property of our view of type ImageEditorView. We haven't created that property yet, because we didn't need it in the previous recipe on which this one is based. So let's implement the property by going to the implementation of our ImageEditorView class and adding the property to it:

```
public var backgroundData: Data?{
  didSet{
    guard backgroundData != nil else {return}
    setNeedsDisplay()
  }
}
```

Setting this property to valid data will now cause our view to redraw. So, in the draw(_:) function of the view we will read the value of this property, try to create a valid instance of UIImage out of it, and then draw that image in the center of our view, *before* we draw the touch points that the user has dragged her finger on as she attempts to draw shapes on the screen:

```
override func draw(_ rect: CGRect) {
  guard let context = UIGraphicsGetCurrentContext() else {return}

  //background color
  UIColor.white.setFill()
  context.fill(rect)

  //then we draw the background if there is some
  if let backgroundData = backgroundData,
    let image = UIImage(data: backgroundData){

    let imageWidth = bounds.width
    let imageHeight = (image.size.height * imageWidth) / image.size.width
    let x = center.x - (imageWidth / 2.0)
    let y = center.y - (imageHeight / 2.0)
    let rect = CGRect(x: x, y: y, width: imageWidth, height: imageHeight)
    image.draw(in: rect)
  }

  //draw the touch points
  touchPoints.forEach{point in
    UIColor.black.setFill()
    let ellipseRect = CGRect(center: point, radius: 10.0)
```

```
      context.fillEllipse(in: ellipseRect)
  }

}
```

Now you can run the app. Find a PNG image in your iCloud library through the document browser and just open it with the app! The image will be opened, you will be able to draw shapes on it using your finger, and pressing the Done button in the navigation bar will save your changes back to the original file in the cloud.

See Also

Recipe 9.1

9.6 Customizing Your Document Browser

Problem

You want to adjust the look and feel of the document browser of type `UIDocument BrowserViewController` so that it matches your application's UI better.

Solution

Document browsers of type `UIDocumentBrowserViewController` have a few properties that you can use in order to adjust their look and feel. Here they are:

`browserUserInterfaceStyle: UIDocumentBrowserUserInterfaceStyle`
> This property defines the type of colors that the interface for the document browser chooses for its components. The value can be `white`, `light`, or `dark`.

`additionalLeadingNavigationBarButtonItems: [UIBarButtonItem]`
> An array of bar button items of type `UIBarButtonItem` that you can place on the lefthand side of the navigation item of the document browser, in addition to the existing system buttons.

`additionalTrailingNavigationBarButtonItems: [UIBarButtonItem]`
> An array of bar button items that you can place, in addition to the system buttons, to the righthand side of the navigation item of the document browser.

Discussion

Let's have a look at an example. Assuming that our application's main interface is quite dark, we are going to set the `browserUserInterfaceStyle` property of our document browser view controller to `dark`. We'll also add one bar button to the `additionalLeadingNavigationBarButtonItems` property and another to the `additionalTrailingNavigationBarButtonItems` property:

```swift
func application(
  _ application: UIApplication,
  didFinishLaunchingWithOptions launchOptions:
  [UIApplicationLaunchOptionsKey: Any]?) -> Bool {

  let browser = UIDocumentBrowserViewController(
    forOpeningFilesWithContentTypes: .fileTypes)

  browser.browserUserInterfaceStyle = .dark

  browser.additionalLeadingNavigationBarButtonItems = [
    UIBarButtonItem(title: "Left", style: .plain, target: self,
                    action: #selector(leftButtonPressed(_:)))
  ]

  browser.additionalTrailingNavigationBarButtonItems = [
    UIBarButtonItem(title: "Right", style: .plain, target: self,
                    action: #selector(rightButtonPressed(_:)))
  ]

  browser.delegate = self
  window?.rootViewController = browser

  return true

}

@objc func leftButtonPressed(_ sender: UIBarButtonItem){
  print("Left")
}

@objc func rightButtonPressed(_ sender: UIBarButtonItem){
  print("Right")
}
```

Let's run our application in the simulator and have a look at the new interface of the document browser (see Figure 9-12).

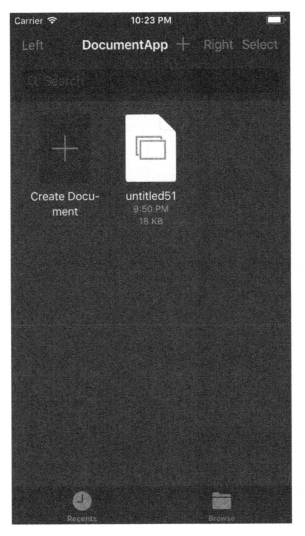

Figure 9-12. Our document browser now has a dark interface with additional buttons in the navigation bar

See Also

Recipes 9.1 and 9.5

Apple Watch

The latest version of watchOS gives us developers a lot more control and brings cool features to the users as well. Now that we can download files directly and get access to sensors directly on the watch, the users will benefit.

In this chapter, I am going to assume that you have a simple iOS application in Xcode already created and you want to add a watchOS 3 target to your app. So, go to Xcode and create a new target. In the new window, choose Watch OS on the lefthand side and select WatchKit App on the right (see Figure 10-1). Then click Next.

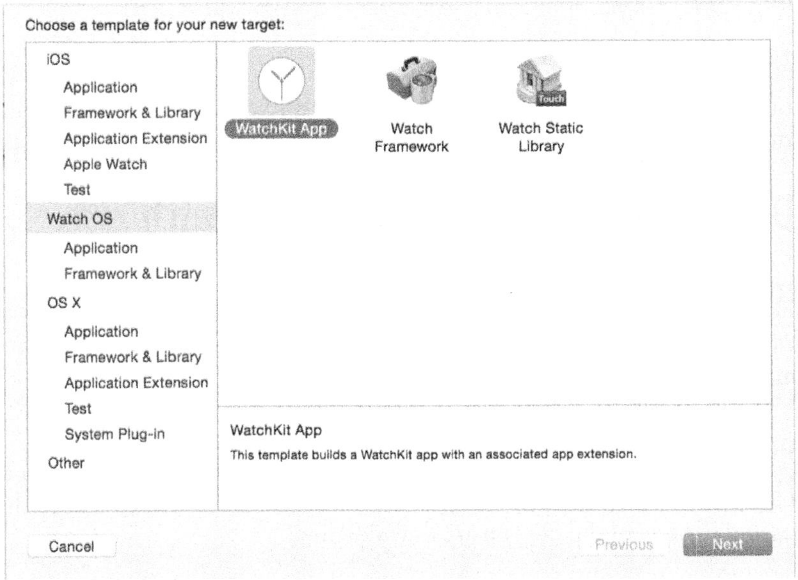

Figure 10-1. Adding a WatchKit App target to your main application

On the next screen, make sure that you have enabled complications (we'll talk about this later) and the glance scene (see Figure 10-2).

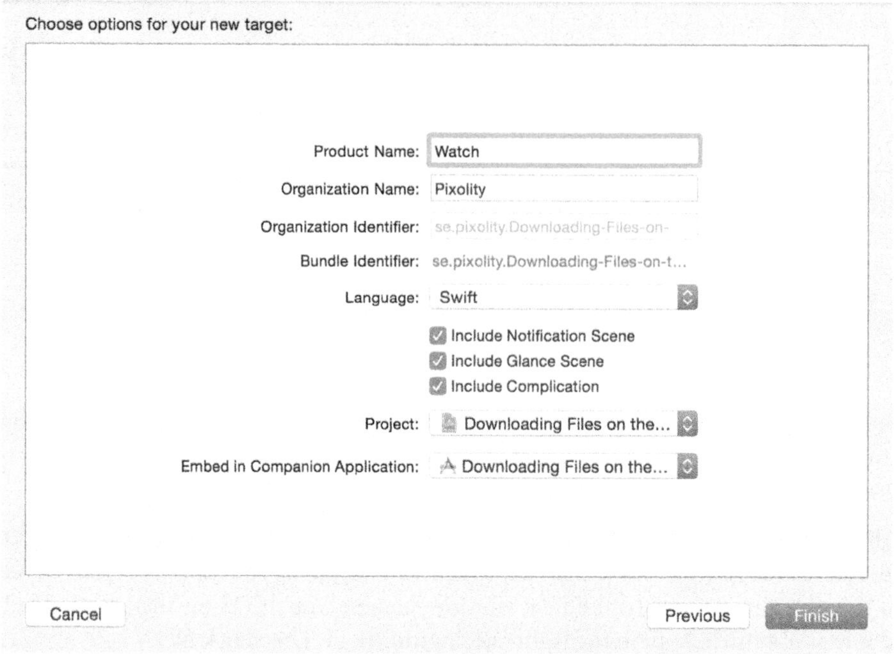

Choose options for your new target:

Product Name:	Watch
Organization Name:	Pixolity
Organization Identifier:	se.pixolity.Downloading-Files-on-
Bundle Identifier:	se.pixolity.Downloading-Files-on-t...
Language:	Swift
	☑ Include Notification Scene
	☑ Include Glance Scene
	☑ Include Complication
Project:	Downloading Files on the...
Embed in Companion Application:	Downloading Files on the...

Cancel   Previous   Finish

Figure 10-2. Add a complication and a glance scene to your watch app

After you have created your watch extension, you want to be able to run it on the simulator. To do this, simply choose your app from the targets in Xcode and click the Run button.

10.1 Downloading Files onto the Apple Watch

Problem

You want to be able to download files from your watch app directly without needing to communicate your intentions to the paired iOS device.

Solution

Use URLSession as you would on a phone, but with more consideration toward resources and the size of the file you are downloading.

Always consider whether or not you need the file immediately. If you need the file and the size is quite manageable, download it on the watch itself. If the file is big, try to download it on the companion app on the iOS device first and then send the file over to the watch, which itself takes some time.

Discussion

Let's create an interface similar to Figure 10-3 in our watch extension.

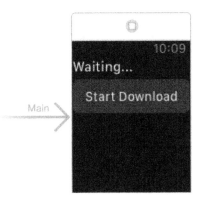

Figure 10-3. Place a label and a button on your interface

Make sure the label can contain at least four lines of text (see Figure 10-4).

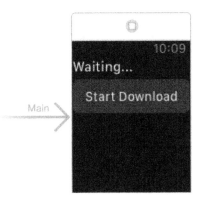

Figure 10-4. The Lines property must be set to at least 4

Hook up your button's action to a method in your code named download(). Also hook up your label to code under the name statusLbl:

```
import WatchKit
import Foundation

class InterfaceController: WKInterfaceController, URLSessionDelegate,
  URLSessionDownloadDelegate {

  @IBOutlet var statusLbl: WKInterfaceLabel!

  var status: String = ""{
    didSet{
      DispatchQueue.main.async{[unowned self] in
        self.statusLbl.setText(self.status)
      }
    }
  }

  ...
```

 URLSession delegate methods get called on private queues (not the main thread), so I've coded a property on our class called status. This is a string property that allows us to set the value of our label —always on the main thread—regardless of where this property gets set from, since UI work (including changing a label's text) can only be performed on the main thread.

The most important method of the URLSessionDownloadDelegate protocol that we are going to have to implement is the URLSession(_:downloadTask:didFinishDown loadingToURL:) method. It gets called when our file has been downloaded into a URL onto the disk, accessible to the watch. The file there is temporary; when this method returns, the file will be deleted by watchOS. In this method, you can do two things:

- Read the file directly from the given URL. If you do so, you have to do the reading on a separate thread so that you won't block URLSession's private queue.
- Move the file using FileManager to another location that is accessible to your extension and then read it later.

We are going to move this file to a location that will later be accessible to our app:

```
func urlSession(_ session: URLSession,
  downloadTask: URLSessionDownloadTask,
  didFinishDownloadingTo location: URL) {

  let fm = FileManager()

  let url = try! fm.url(
    for: .downloadsDirectory,
    in: .userDomainMask,
```

```
    appropriateFor: location, create: true)
    .appendingPathComponent("file.txt")

  do{
    try fm.removeItem(at: url)
    try fm.moveItem(at: location, to: url)
    self.status = "Download finished"
  } catch let err{
    self.status = "Error = \(err)"
  }

  session.invalidateAndCancel()

}
```

The task that we are going to start in order to download the file (you'll see that soon) will have an identifier. This identifier is quite important for controlling the task after we have started it.

You can see that we also have to call the invalidateAndCancel() method on our task so that we can reuse the same task identifier later. If you don't do this, the next time you tap the button to redownload the item you won't be able to.

We will then implement a few more useful methods from URLSessionDelegate and URLSessionDownloadDelegate just so we can show relevant status messages to the user as we are downloading the file:

```
func urlSession(
  _ session: URLSession,
  downloadTask: URLSessionDownloadTask, didWriteData bytesWritten: Int64,
  totalBytesWritten: Int64, totalBytesExpectedToWrite: Int64) {
  status = "Downloaded \(bytesWritten) bytes"
}

func urlSession(
  _ session: URLSession,
  downloadTask: URLSessionDownloadTask,
  didResumeAtOffset fileOffset: Int64, expectedTotalBytes: Int64) {
  status = "Resuming the download"
}

func urlSession(_ session: URLSession, task: URLSessionTask,
                didCompleteWithError error: Error?) {
  if let e = error{
    status = "Completed with error = \(e)"
  } else {
    status = "Finished"
  }
}

func urlSession(_ session: URLSession,
                didBecomeInvalidWithError error: Error?) {
```

```
  if let e = error{
    status = "Invalidated \(e)"
  } else {
    // no errors occurred, so that's all right
  }
}
```

When the user taps the download button, we first define our URL:

```
let url = URL(string: "http://localhost:8888/file.txt")!
```

 I am running MAMP and hosting my own file called *file.txt*. This URL won't get downloaded successfully on your machine if you are not hosting the exact same file with the same name on your local machine on the same port, so I suggest that you change this URL to something that makes more sense for your app.

Then we use the `backgroundSessionConfigurationWithIdentifier(_:)` class method of `URLSessionConfiguration` to create a background URL configuration that we can use with `URLSession`:

```
let id = "se.pixolity.app.backgroundtask"
let conf = URLSessionConfiguration
  .background(withIdentifier: id)
```

Once all of that is done, you can go ahead and create a download task and start it (see Figure 10-5):

```
let session = URLSession(configuration: conf, delegate: self,
      delegateQueue: OperationQueue())

let request = URLRequest(url: url)

session.downloadTask(with: request).resume()
```

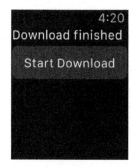

Figure 10-5. Our file is successfully downloaded

10.2 Noticing Changes in Pairing State Between the iOS and Watch Apps

Problem

You want to know, both on the watch and in your companion iOS app, whether there is connectivity between them and whether you can send messages between them. Specifically, you want to find out whether one device can receive a signal sent from the other.

Solution

To begin working through this problem, you first need to import the `WatchConnectivity` framework in both projects. Then, after you've imported the framework, you can use the `WCSession`'s delegate of type `WCSessionDelegate` to implement the `sessionWatchStateDidChange(_:)` method on the iOS side and the `sessionReachabilityDidChange(_:)` method on the watchOS side. These methods get called by `Watch Connectivity` whenever the state of the companion app is changed (whether that is on the iOS side or on the watchOS side).

Discussion

Both devices contain a flag called *reachability* that indicates whether the device can connect to the other. This is represented by a property on `WCSession` called `reachable`, of type `Bool`. On the iOS side, if you check this flag it tells you whether your companion *watch app* is reachable, and if you check it on the watchOS side, it tells you whether your companion *iOS app* is reachable.

The idea here is to use the `WCSession` object to listen for state changes. Before doing that, you need to find out whether the session is actually supported. You do that using the `isSupported()` class function of `WCSession`. Once you know that sessions are supported, you have to do the following on the iOS app side:

1. Obtain your session with `WCSession.default`.
2. Set the `delegate` property of your session.
3. Become the delegate of your session, of type `WCSessionDelegate`.
4. Implement the `sessionWatchStateDidChange(_:)` function of your session delegate and in there, check the `reachable` flag of the session.
5. Call the `activateSession()` method of your session.

Make sure that you do this in a function that can be called even if your app is launched in the background.

On the watch side, you'll follow the exact same steps you completed on the iOS side, but instead of implementing the sessionWatchStateDidChange(_:) method you'll implement the sessionReachabilityDidChange(_:) method.

 The sessionWatchStateDidChange(_:) delegate method is called on the iOS side when at least one of the properties of the session changes. These properties include paired, watchAppInstalled, complicationEnabled, and watchDirectoryURL, all of type Bool. In contrast, the sessionReachabilityDidChange(_:) method is called on the watch side only when the reachable flag of the companion iOS app is changed, as the name of the delegate method suggests.

So, on the iOS side, implement an extension on WCSession that can print all its relevant states, so that when the sessionWatchStateDidChange(_:) method is called you can print the session's information:

```
extension WCSession{
  public func printInfo(){

    //paired
    print("Paired: ", terminator: "")
    print(self.isPaired ? "Yes" : "No")

    //watch app installed
    print("Watch app installed: ", terminator: "")
    print(self.isWatchAppInstalled ? "Yes" : "No")

    //complication enabled
    print("Complication enabled: ", terminator: "")
    print(self.isComplicationEnabled ? "Yes" : "No")


    if let watchDirectoryURL = self.watchDirectoryURL{
      //watch directory
      print("Watch directory url", terminator: "")
      print(watchDirectoryURL)
    }

  }
}
```

Make your app delegate the delegate of the session as well:

```
@UIApplicationMain
class AppDelegate: UIResponder, UIApplicationDelegate, WCSessionDelegate {

  var window: UIWindow?
```

...

Now start listening for state and reachability changes:

```
func sessionReachabilityDidChange(_ session: WCSession) {
  print("Reachable: ",  terminator: "")
  print(session.isReachable ? "Yes" : "No")
}

func sessionWatchStateDidChange(_ session: WCSession) {
  print("Watch state is changed")
  session.printInfo()
}

func session(
  _ session: WCSession,
  activationDidCompleteWith activationState: WCSessionActivationState,
  error: Error?) {
  // empty for now
}

func sessionDidBecomeInactive(_ session: WCSession) {
  // empty for now
}

func sessionDidDeactivate(_ session: WCSession) {
  // empty for now
}
```

Last but not least, on the iOS side, set up the session and start listening to its events:

```
guard WCSession.isSupported() else {
  print("Session is not supported")
  return
}

let session = WCSession.default
session.delegate = self
session.activate()
```

Now on the watch side, in the ExtensionDelegate class, import WatchConnectivity and become the session delegate as well:

```
import WatchKit
import WatchConnectivity

class ExtensionDelegate: NSObject, WKExtensionDelegate, WCSessionDelegate {

  ...
```

And listen for reachability changes:

```
func session(
  _ session: WCSession,
  activationDidCompleteWith activationState: WCSessionActivationState,
  error: Error?) {
  // empty for now
}

func sessionReachabilityDidChange(_ session: WCSession) {
  print("Reachability changed. Reachable?", terminator: "")
  print(session.isReachable ? "Yes" : "No")
}
```

Then, in the applicationDidFinishLaunching() function of your extension delegate, set up the session:

```
guard WCSession.isSupported() else {
  print("Session is not supported")
  return
}

let session = WCSession.default
session.delegate = self
session.activate()
```

10.3 Transferring Small Pieces of Data to and from the Watch

Problem

You want to transfer some *plist*-serializable content between your apps (iOS and watchOS). This content can be anything—for instance, information about where a user is inside a game on an iOS device, or more random information that you can serialize into a *plist* (strings, integers, Booleans, dictionaries, and arrays). Information can be sent in either direction.

Solution

Follow these steps:

1. Use what you learned in Recipe 10.2 to find out whether both devices are reachable.
2. In the sending app, use the updateApplicationContext(_:) method of your session to send the content over to the other app.
3. In the receiving app, wait for the session(_:didReceiveApplicationContext:) delegate method of WCSessionDelegate, where you will be given access to the transmitted content.

It's important to note that the content that you transmit must be of type [`String` : `AnyObject`].

Discussion

Various types of content can be sent between iOS and watchOS. One is *plist*-serializable content, also called an *application context*. Let's say that the user is playing a game on watchOS and you want to send the game status to iOS. You can use the application context for this.

Let's begin by creating a sample application. Create a single view iOS app and add a watchOS target to it as well (see Figure 10-1). Design your main interface like Figure 10-6. We'll use the top label to show the download status. The buttons are self-explanatory. The bottom label will show the pairing status between our watchOS and iOS apps.

Ready...

Download

Send to watch

Reachability Status...

Figure 10-6. Labels and button for sample app

Hook up the top label to your view controller as `statusLbl`, the first button as `sendBtn`, the second button as `downloadBtn`, and the bottom label as `reachabilityStatusLbl`. Hook up the action of the download button to a method called `download()` and the send button to a method called `send()`.

Download and install MAMP (*https://www.mamp.info/en/*) (it's free) and host the following contents as a file called *people.json* in your local web server's root folder:

```
{
  "people" : [
    {
```

```
        "name" : "Foo",
        "age" : 30
      },
      {
        "name" : "Bar",
        "age" : 50
      }
    ]
}
```

Now the top part of your iOS app's view controller should look like this:

```
import UIKit
import WatchConnectivity

class ViewController: UIViewController, WCSessionDelegate,
  URLSessionDownloadDelegate {

  @IBOutlet var statusLbl: UILabel!
  @IBOutlet var sendBtn: UIButton!
  @IBOutlet var downloadBtn: UIButton!
  @IBOutlet var reachabilityStatusLbl: UILabel!

  ...
```

When you download that JSON file, it will become a dictionary of type [String : AnyObject], so define that as a variable in your view controller:

```
var people: [String : AnyObject]?{
  didSet{
    DispatchQueue.main.async{
      self.updateSendButton()
    }
  }
}

func updateSendButton(){
  sendBtn.isEnabled = isReachable && isDownloadFinished && people != nil
}
```

Setting the value of the people variable will call the updateSend Button() function, which in turn enables the send button only if all the following conditions are met:

- The watch app is reachable.

- The file is downloaded.

- The file was correctly parsed into the people variable.

Also define a variable that can write into your status label whenever the reachability flag is changed:

```
var isReachable = false{
  didSet{
    DispatchQueue.main.async{
      self.updateSendButton()
      if self.isReachable{
        self.reachabilityStatusLbl.text = "Watch is reachable"
      } else {
        self.reachabilityStatusLbl.text = "Watch is not reachable"
      }
    }
  }
}
```

You need two more properties—one that sets the status label and another that keeps track of when your file is downloaded successfully:

```
var isDownloadFinished = false{
  didSet{
    DispatchQueue.main.async{
      self.updateSendButton()
    }
  }
}

var status: String?{
  get{return self.statusLbl.text}
  set{
    DispatchQueue.main.async{
      self.statusLbl.text = newValue
    }
  }
}
```

 All three variables that defined here—people, isReachable, and isDownloadFinished—call the updateSendButton() function, so the send button will be disabled if any conditions are not met and enabled otherwise.

Now when the download button is pressed, start a download task:

```
@IBAction func download() {

    // if loading HTTP content, make sure you have disabled ATS
    // for that domain
    let url = URL(string: "http://localhost:8888/people.json")!
    let req = URLRequest(url: url)
    let id = "se.pixolity.app.backgroundtask"
```

```
let conf = URLSessionConfiguration
    .background(withIdentifier: id)

let sess = URLSession(configuration: conf, delegate: self,
                               delegateQueue: OperationQueue())

sess.downloadTask(with: req).resume()
}
```

After that, check if you got any errors while trying to download the file:

```
func urlSession(_ session: URLSession,
  task: URLSessionTask,
    didCompleteWithError error: Error?) {

  if error != nil{
    status = "Error happened"
    isDownloadFinished = false
  }

  session.finishTasksAndInvalidate()

}
```

Now implement the URLSession(_:downloadTask:didFinishDownloadingToURL:) method of URLSessionDownloadDelegate. Inside there, tell your view controller that you have downloaded the file by setting isDownloadFinished to true. Then construct a more permanent URL for the temporary URL to which your JSON file was downloaded by iOS:

```
func urlSession(_ session: URLSession,
  downloadTask: URLSessionDownloadTask,
    didFinishDownloadingTo location: URL){

  isDownloadFinished = true

  // got the data, parse as JSON
  let fm = FileManager()
  let url = try! fm.url(for: .downloadsDirectory,
                 in: .userDomainMask,
                 appropriateFor: location,
                 create: true).appendingPathComponent("file.json")

  ...
```

Then move the file over:

```
do {try fm.removeItem(at: url)} catch {}

do{
  try fm.moveItem(at: location, to: url)
} catch {
  status = "Could not save the file"
```

```
  return
}
```

After that, simply read the file as a JSON file with `JSONSerialization`:

```
// now read the file from URL
guard let data = try? Data(contentsOf: url) else{
  status = "Could not read the file"
  return
}

do{
  let json = try JSONSerialization.jsonObject(
    with: data,
    options: .allowFragments) as! [String : AnyObject]

  self.people = json
  status = "Successfully downloaded and parsed the file"
} catch{
  status = "Could not read the file as json"
}
```

Great—now go to your watch interface, place a label there, and hook it up to your code under the name `statusLabel` (see Figure 10-7).

In the interface controller file, place a variable that can set the status:

```
import WatchKit
import Foundation

class InterfaceController: WKInterfaceController {

  @IBOutlet var statusLabel: WKInterfaceLabel!

  var status = "Waiting"{
    didSet{
      statusLabel.setText(status)
    }
  }

}
```

Figure 10-7. Our watch interface has a simple label only

Go to your *ExtensionDelegate* file on the watch side and follow these steps:

1. Define a structure that can hold the instances of `Person` you will get in your application context.
2. Define a property called `status` that, when written to, will set the `status` property of the interface controller:

```
import WatchKit
import WatchConnectivity

struct Person{
  let name: String
  let age: Int
}

class ExtensionDelegate: NSObject, WKExtensionDelegate, WCSessionDelegate{

  var status = ""{
    didSet{
      DispatchQueue.main.async{
        guard let interface =
          WKExtension.shared().rootInterfaceController as?
          InterfaceController else{
            return
        }
        interface.status = self.status
      }
```

```
      }
    }

    ...
```

Now activate the session using what you learned in Recipe 10.2. The session will wait for the session(_:didReceiveApplicationContext:) method of the WCSessionDele gate protocol to come in. When that happens, just read the application context and convert it into Person instances:

```
func session(
  _ session: WCSession,
  activationDidCompleteWith activationState: WCSessionActivationState,
  error: Error?) {
  // empty for now
}

func session(
  _ session: WCSession,
  didReceiveApplicationContext applicationContext: [String : Any]) {

  guard let people = applicationContext["people"] as?
    Array<[String : AnyObject]>, people.count > 0 else{
      status = "Did not find the people array"
      return
  }

  var persons = [Person]()
  for p in people where p["name"] is String && p["age"] is Int{
    let person = Person(name: p["name"] as! String, age: p["age"] as! Int)
    persons.append(person)
  }

  status = "Received \(persons.count) people from the iOS app"

}
```

Now run both your watch app and your iOS app. At first glance, your watch app will look like Figure 10-8.

Figure 10-8. Your watch app is waiting for the context to come through from the iOS app

Your iOS app in its initial state will look like Figure 10-9.

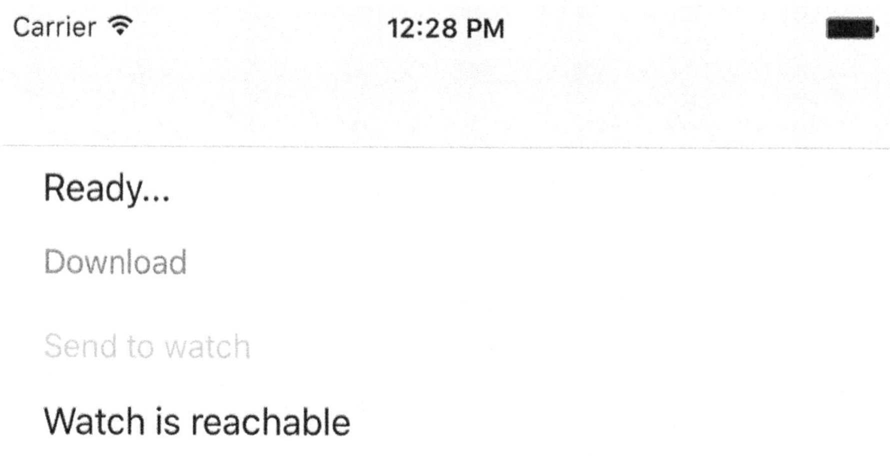

Carrier 📶   **12:28 PM**   🔋

Ready...

Download

Send to watch

Watch is reachable

Figure 10-9. Your iOS app has detected that its companion watch app is reachable

When you press the download button, your iOS app's interface will change to Figure 10-10.

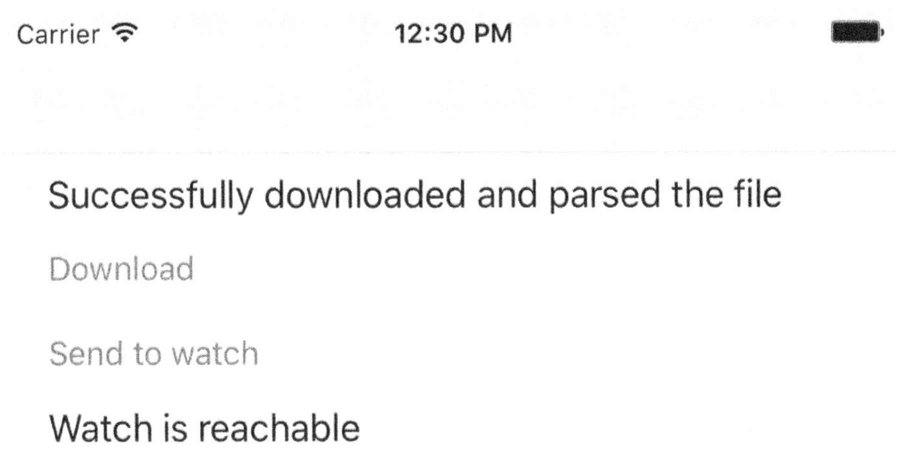

Carrier
12:30 PM
Successfully downloaded and parsed the file
Download
Send to watch
Watch is reachable

Figure 10-10. The iOS app is now ready to send the data over to the watch app

After you press the send button, the watch app's interface will change to something like Figure 10-11.

12:31
Received 2 people from the iOS app

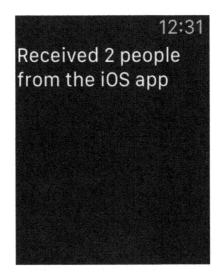

Figure 10-11. The watch app received the data

See Also

Recipes 10.1, 10.4, and 10.5

10.4 Transferring Dictionaries in Queues to and from the Watch

Problem

You want to send dictionaries of information to and from the watch in a queuing (FIFO) fashion.

Solution

Call the transferUserInfo(_:) method on your WCSession on the sending side. On the receiving side, implement the session(_:didReceiveUserInfo:) method of the WCSessionDelegate protocol.

A lot of the things that I'll refer to in this recipe have been discussed already in Recipe 10.3, so have a look at that if you feel a bit confused.

Discussion

Create a single view app in iOS and put your root view controller in a nav controller. Then add a watch target to your app (see this chapter's introduction for an explanation). Make sure that your root view controller in IB looks like Figure 10-12.

Status

Send user info

Figure 10-12. Place a label and a button on your UI

Hook up the label to a variable in your code named statusLbl and hook up the button to a variable named sendBtn. Hook up your button's action to a method in your code called send(). The top of your view controller should now look like this:

```
import UIKit
import WatchConnectivity
```

```
class ViewController: UIViewController, WCSessionDelegate {

  @IBOutlet var statusLbl: UILabel!
  @IBOutlet var sendBtn: UIButton!

  . . .
```

You also need a property that can set the status for you on your label. The property must be on the main thread, because `WCSession` methods (where you may want to set your status property) usually are *not* called on the main thread:

```
var status: String?{
  get{return self.statusLbl.text}
  set{
    DispatchQueue.main.async{
      self.statusLbl.text = newValue
    }
  }
}
```

When the user presses the send button, you will use the `WCSession.default.trans ferUserInfo(_:)` method to send a simple dictionary whose only key is `kCFBundleIdentifierKey` and a value that will be our *Info.plist*'s bundle identifier:

```
@IBAction func send() {

  guard let infoPlist = Bundle.main.infoDictionary else{
    status = "Could not get the Info.plist"
    return
  }

  let key = kCFBundleIdentifierKey as String

  let plist = [
    key : infoPlist[key] as! String
  ]

  let transfer = WCSession.default.transferUserInfo(plist)
  status = transfer.isTransferring ? "Sent" : "Could not send yet"

}

func updateUiForSession(_ session: WCSession){
  status = session.isReachable ? "Ready to send" : "Not reachable"
  sendBtn.isEnabled = session.isReachable
}

func session(
  _ session: WCSession,
  activationDidCompleteWith activationState: WCSessionActivationState,
  error: Error?) {
  // empty for now
```

```
}

func sessionDidBecomeInactive(_ session: WCSession) {
  // empty for now
}

func sessionDidDeactivate(_ session: WCSession) {
  // empty for now
}

func sessionReachabilityDidChange(_ session: WCSession) {
  updateUiForSession(session)
}
```

The `transferUserInfo(_:)` method returns an object of type `WCSessionUserInfo Transfer` that has properties such as `userInfo` and `transferring` and a method called `cancel()`. If necessary, you can always use the `cancel()` method of an instance of `WCSessionUserInfoTransfer` to cancel the transfer of this item if it is not already `transferring`. You can also find all the user info transfers that are ongoing by using the `outstandingUserInfoTransfers` property of your session object.

The app also contains code to disable the button if the watch app is not reachable, but I won't discuss that code here because we have already reviewed it in Recipes 10.2 and 10.3.

On the watch side, in `InterfaceController`, write the exact same code that you wrote in Recipe 10.3. In the `ExtensionDelegate` class the code will be a bit different, but its `status` property is exactly how you wrote it in Recipe 10.3.

When the `applicationDidFinishLaunching()` method of your delegate is called, you'll set up the session just as you did previously in Recipe 10.2. You will wait for the `session(_:didReceiveUserInfo:)` method of the `WCSessionDelegate` protocol to be called. There, you will simply read the bundle identifier from the user info and display it in your view controller:

```
func session(
  _ session: WCSession,
  activationDidCompleteWith activationState: WCSessionActivationState,
  error: Error?) {
  // empty for now
}

func session(_ session: WCSession,
             didReceiveUserInfo userInfo: [String : Any] = [:]) {

  guard let bundleVersion = userInfo[kCFBundleIdentifierKey as String]
    as? String else{
```

```
        status = "Could not read the bundle version"
        return
    }

    status = bundleVersion

}
```

If you run the iOS app, your UI should look like Figure 10-13.

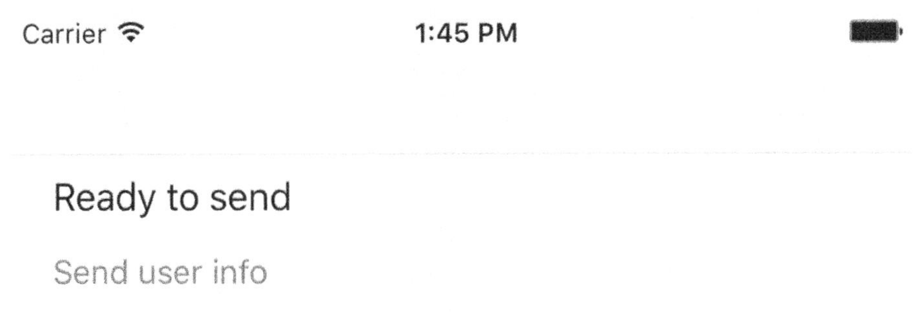

Carrier
1:45 PM
Ready to send
Send user info

Figure 10-13. The app has detected that the watch app is reachable so the button is enabled

And your watch app should look like Figure 10-14.

1:45
Waiting

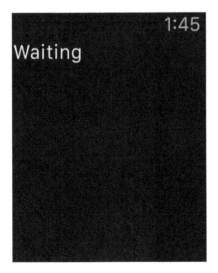

Figure 10-14. The watch app is waiting for incoming user info data

When you press the send button, the user interface will change to Figure 10-15.

Sent

Send user info

Figure 10-15. The data is sent to the watch

And the watch app will look like Figure 10-16.

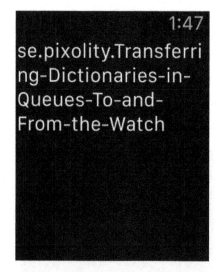

Figure 10-16. The watch app successfully received your user info

See Also

Recipe 10.3

10.5 Transferring Files to and from the Watch

Problem

You want to transfer a file between your iOS app and the watch app. The technique should work in both directions.

Solution

Follow these steps:

1. Use the `transferFile(_:metadata:)` method of your `WCSession` object on the sending device.
2. Then implement the `WCSessionDelegate` protocol on the sender and wait for the `session(_:didFinishFileTransfer:error:)` delegate method to be called. If the optional `error` parameter is `nil`, it indicates that the file was transferred successfully.
3. On the receiving side, become the delegate of `WCSession` and then wait for the `session(_:didReceiveFile:)` delegate method to be called.
4. The incoming file on the receiving side is of type `WCSessionFile` and has properties such as `fileURL` and `metadata`. The metadata is the same metadata of type `[String : AnyObject]` that the sender sent with the `transferFile(_:meta data:)` method.

Discussion

Let's have a look at a simple UI on the sending device (the iOS side in this example). It contains a label that shows the status and a button that sends the file. When the button is pressed, we create a file in the iOS app's *caches* folder and then send that file through to the watch app if it is reachable (see Recipe 10.2).

Make your UI on the iOS (sender) side look like Figure 10-17. The button will be disabled if the watch app is not reachable (see Recipe 10.2).

Figure 10-17. Status label and button on sender

Hook up your button's action code to a method in your view controller called `send()` and make sure your view controller conforms to `WCSessionDelegate`:

```
import UIKit
import WatchConnectivity
```

```
class ViewController: UIViewController, WCSessionDelegate {

  @IBOutlet var statusLbl: UILabel!
  @IBOutlet var sendBtn: UIButton!

  var status: String?{
    get{return self.statusLbl.text}
    set{
      DispatchQueue.main.async{
        self.statusLbl.text = newValue
      }
    }
  }

  func sessionDidBecomeInactive(_ session: WCSession) {
    // empty for now
  }

  func sessionDidDeactivate(_ session: WCSession) {
    // empty for now
  }

  func session(
    _ session: WCSession,
    activationDidCompleteWith activationState: WCSessionActivationState,
    error: Error?) {
    // empty for now
  }

  ...
```

We implemented and talked about the status property of our view controller in Recipe 10.3, so I won't explain it here.

Then, when the send button is pressed, construct a URL that will point to your file. It doesn't exist yet, but you will write it to disk soon:

```
let fileName = "file.txt"

let fm = FileManager()

let url = try! fm.url(for: .cachesDirectory,
                      in: .userDomainMask, appropriateFor: nil,
                      create: true).appendingPathComponent(fileName)
```

Now write some text to disk, reachable through the URL:

```
let text = "Foo Bar"
```

```
do{
  try text.write(to: url, atomically: true,
                 encoding: String.Encoding.utf8)
} catch {
  status = "Could not write the file"
  return
}
```

Once that is done, send the file over:

```
let metadata = ["fileName" : fileName]
WCSession.default.transferFile(url, metadata: metadata)
```

Also, when your session's reachability state changes, enable or disable your button:

```
func updateUiForSession(_ session: WCSession){
  status = session.isReachable ? "Ready to send" : "Not reachable"
  sendBtn.isEnabled = session.isReachable
}

func sessionReachabilityDidChange(_ session: WCSession) {
  updateUiForSession(session)
}
```

On the watch side, make your UI look like that shown in Figure 10-7. Then, in your ExtensionDelegate class, implement the exact same status property that you implemented in Recipe 10.3.

Now implement the session(_:didReceiveFile:) method of WCSessionDelegate. Start by double-checking that the metadata is as you expected it:

```
func session(_ session: WCSession, didReceive file: WCSessionFile) {

  guard let metadata = file.metadata, metadata["fileName"]
    is String else{
    status = "No metadata came through"
    return
  }

  ...
```

If it is, read the file and show it in the user interface:

```
do{
  let str = try String(NSString(contentsOf: file.fileURL,
    encoding: String.Encoding.utf8.rawValue))
  guard str.characters.count > 0 else{
    status = "No file came through"
    return
  }
  status = str
} catch {
  status = "Could not read the file"
}
```

```
    return
}
```

When you run the watch app, it will look like Figure 10-14. When you run the iOS app, it will look like Figure 10-18.

Carrier 🛜   3:28 PM   ▬

Ready to send

Send file

Figure 10-18. The file is ready to be sent from iOS to watchOS

When the file is sent, your user interface on iOS will look like Figure 10-19.

Carrier 🛜   3:29 PM   ▬

Successfully sent the file

Send file

Figure 10-19. iOS sent the file to watchOS

And the UI on your receiver (watchOS) will look like Figure 10-20.

Figure 10-20. watchOS successfully received the file, read its content, and is displaying it in the label

See Also

Recipes 10.3 and 10.4

10.6 Communicating Interactively Between iOS and watchOS

Problem

You want to interactively send messages from iOS to watchOS (or vice versa) and receive a reply immediately.

Solution

On the sender side, use the sendMessage(_:replyHandler:errorHandler:) method of WCSession. On the receiving side, implement the session(_:didReceive Message:replyHandler:) method to handle the incoming message if your sender expected a reply, or implement session(_:didReceiveMessage:) if no reply was expected from you. Messages and replies are of type [String : AnyObject].

Discussion

Let's implement a chat program where the iOS app and the watch app can send messages to each other. On the iOS app, we will allow the user to type text and then send it over to the watch. On the watch, since the user cannot type anything, we will have four predefined messages that the user can send. In order to decrease the amount of data the watch sends, we'll define these messages as Int and send the integers instead. The iOS app will read the integers and then print the correct message onto the screen. So let's first define these messages. Create a file called *PredefinedMessages* and write the following Swift code there:

```
import Foundation

enum PredefinedMessage : Int{
  case hello
  case thankYou
  case howAreYou
  case iHearYou
}
```

Add this file to both your watch extension and your iOS app so that they both can use it (see Figure 10-21).

Figure 10-21. Include the messages file in the iOS app and the watch extension

Now move to your main iOS app's storyboard and design a UI that looks like Figure 10-22. There are two labels that say "..." at the moment. They will be populated dynamically in our code.

Realtime Communication   Send

Type something here...

 Watch Status: ...

 Watch Said: ...

Figure 10-22. Initial iOS app UI

Hook up your UI to your code as follows:

1. Hook up your send button to an outlet called `sendBtn`. Hook up its action method to a function called `send(_:)` in your view controller.
2. Hook up the text field to your code under the name `textField`.
3. Hook up the label that says "..." in front of "Watch Status:" to an outlet called `watchStatusLbl`.
4. Hook up the label that says "..." in front of "Watch Said:" to an outlet called `watchReplyLbl`.

So now the top part of your view controller on the iOS side should look like this:

```
import UIKit
import WatchConnectivity
import SharedCode

class ViewController: UIViewController, WCSessionDelegate {

  @IBOutlet var sendBtn: UIBarButtonItem!
  @IBOutlet var textField: UITextField!
  @IBOutlet var watchStatusLbl: UILabel!
  @IBOutlet var watchReplyLbl: UILabel!

  ...
```

As we have done before, we need two variables that can populate the text inside the `watchStatusLbl` and `watchReplyLbl` labels, always on the main thread:

```
var watchStatus: String{
  get{return self.watchStatusLbl.text ?? ""}
  set{onMainThread{self.watchStatusLbl.text = newValue}}
}

var watchReply: String{
  get{return self.watchReplyLbl.text ?? ""}
  set{onMainThread{self.watchReplyLbl.text = newValue}}
}
```

The definition of `onMainThread` is very simple. It's a custom function I've written in a library to make life easier:

```
import Foundation

public func onMainThread(_ f: @escaping () -> Void){
  DispatchQueue.main.async(execute: f)
}
```

When the send button is pressed, we first have to make sure that the user has entered some text into the text field:

```
@IBAction func send(_ sender: AnyObject) {
```

```
guard let txt = textField.text, txt.characters.count > 0 else{
  textField.placeholder = "Enter some text here first"
  return
}

...
```

Then we will use the sendMessage(_:replyHandler:errorHandler:) method of our
session to send the text over:

```
WCSession.default.sendMessage(["msg" : txt],
  replyHandler: {dict in

    guard dict["msg"] is String &&
      dict["msg"] as! String == "delivered" else{
      self.watchReply = "Could not deliver the message"
      return
    }

    self.watchReply = dict["msg"] as! String

}){err in
  self.watchReply = "An error happened in sending the message"
}
```

Later, when we implement the watch side, we will also be sending messages from the
watch over to the iOS app. Those messages will be inside a dictionary whose only key
is msg and the value of this key will be an integer. The integers are already defined in
the PredefinedMessage enum that we saw earlier. So in our iOS app, we will wait for
messages from the watch app, translate the integer we get to its string counterpart,
and show it on our iOS UI. Remember, we send integers (instead of strings) from the
watch to make the transfer snappier. So let's implement the session(_:didReceive
Message:) delegate method in our iOS app:

```
func session(
  _ session: WCSession,
  activationDidCompleteWith activationState: WCSessionActivationState,
  error: Error?) {
  // empty for now
}

func sessionDidBecomeInactive(_ session: WCSession) {
  // empty for now
}

func sessionDidDeactivate(_ session: WCSession) {
  // empty for now
}

func session(_ session: WCSession,
            didReceiveMessage message: [String : Any],
```

```
                replyHandler: @escaping ([String : Any]) -> Void) {

    guard let msg = message["msg"] as? Int,
      let value = PredefinedMessage(rawValue: msg) else{
        watchReply = "Received invalid message"
      return
    }

    switch value{
    case .hello:
      watchReply = "Hello"
    case .howAreYou:
      watchReply = "How are you?"
    case .iHearYou:
      watchReply = "I hear you"
    case .thankYou:
      watchReply = "Thank you"
    }

}
```

Let's use what we learned in Recipe 10.2 to enable or disable our send button when the watch's reachability changes:

```
func updateUiForSession(_ session: WCSession){
  watchStatus = session.isReachable ? "Reachable" : "Not reachable"
  sendBtn.isEnabled = session.isReachable
}

func sessionReachabilityDidChange(_ session: WCSession) {
  updateUiForSession(session)
}
```

On the watch side, design your UI like Figure 10-23. Although users cannot type on the watch, they can press a predefined message in order to send it (remember PredefinedMessage?). That little line between "Waiting..." and "Send a reply" is a separator.

Figure 10-23. Strings that a user can send from a watch

Hook up your watch UI to your code by following these steps:

1. Hook up the "Waiting..." label to an outlet named `iosAppReplyLbl`. We will show the text that our iOS app has sent to us in this label.
2. Place all the buttons at the bottom of the page inside a group and hook that group up to an outlet called `repliesGroup`. We will hide this whole group if the iOS app is not reachable to our watch app.
3. Hook the action of the "Hello" button to a method in your code called `send Hello()`.
4. Hook the action of the "Thank you" button to a method in your code called `send ThankYou()`.
5. Hook the action of the "How are you?" button to a method in your code called `sendHowAreYou()`.
6. Hook the action of the "I hear you" button to a method in your code called `sendI HearYou()`.

In our `InterfaceController` on the watch side, we need a generic method that takes in an `Int` (our predefined message) and sends it over to the iOS side with the `send Message(_:replyHandler:errorHandler:)` method of the session:

```
import WatchKit
import Foundation
import WatchConnectivity

class InterfaceController: WKInterfaceController {

  @IBOutlet var iosAppReplyLbl: WKInterfaceLabel!
  @IBOutlet var repliesGroup: WKInterfaceGroup!

  func send(_ int: Int){

    WCSession.default.sendMessage(["msg" : int],
      replyHandler: nil, errorHandler: nil)

  }

  ...
```

And whenever any of the buttons is pressed, we call the `send(_:)` method with the right predefined message:

```
@IBAction func sendHello() {
  send(PredefinedMessage.hello.hashValue)
}

@IBAction func sendThankYou() {
  send(PredefinedMessage.thankYou.hashValue)
}

@IBAction func sendHowAreYou() {
  send(PredefinedMessage.howAreYou.hashValue)
}

@IBAction func sendIHearYou() {
  send(PredefinedMessage.iHearYou.hashValue)
}
```

In the `ExtensionDelegate` class on the watch side, we want to hide all the reply buttons if the iOS app is not reachable. To do that, write a property called `isReachable` of type `Bool`. Whenever this property is set, the code sets the `hidden` property of our replies group:

```
import WatchKit
import WatchConnectivity


class ExtensionDelegate: NSObject, WKExtensionDelegate, WCSessionDelegate{
```

```
var isReachable = false{
  willSet{
    self.rootController?.repliesGroup.setHidden(!newValue)
  }
}

var rootController: InterfaceController?{
  get{
    guard let interface =
      WKExtension.shared().rootInterfaceController as?
      InterfaceController else{
        return nil
    }
    return interface
  }
}

func session(
  _ session: WCSession,
  activationDidCompleteWith activationState: WCSessionActivationState,
  error: Error?) {
  // empty for now
}

...
```

You also are going to need a `String` property that will be your iOS app's reply. Whenever you get a reply from the iOS app, place it inside this property. As soon as this property is set, the watch extension will write this text on the UI:

```
var iosAppReply = ""{
  didSet{
    DispatchQueue.main.async{
      self.rootController?.iosAppReplyLbl.setText(self.iosAppReply)
    }
  }
}
```

Now let's wait for messages from the iOS app and display those messages on our UI:

```
func session(_ session: WCSession,
  didReceiveMessage message: [String : Any],
    replyHandler: @escaping ([String : Any]) -> Void) {

  guard message["msg"] is String else{
    replyHandler(["msg" : "failed"])
    return
  }

  iosAppReply = message["msg"] as! String
  replyHandler(["msg" : "delivered"])

}
```

Also, when our iOS app's reachability changes, we want to update our UI and disable the reply buttons:

```
func sessionReachabilityDidChange(_ session: WCSession) {
  isReachable = session.isReachable
}

func applicationDidFinishLaunching() {

  guard WCSession.isSupported() else{
    iosAppReply = "Sessions are not supported"
    return
  }

  let session = WCSession.default
  session.delegate = self
  session.activate()
  isReachable = session.isReachable

}
```

Running our app on the watch first, we will see an interface similar to Figure 10-24. The user can scroll to see the rest of the buttons.

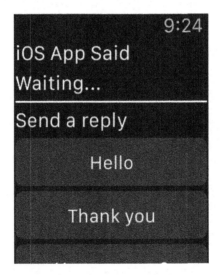

Figure 10-24. Available messages on watch

And when we run our app on iOS while the watch app is reachable, the UI will look like Figure 10-25.

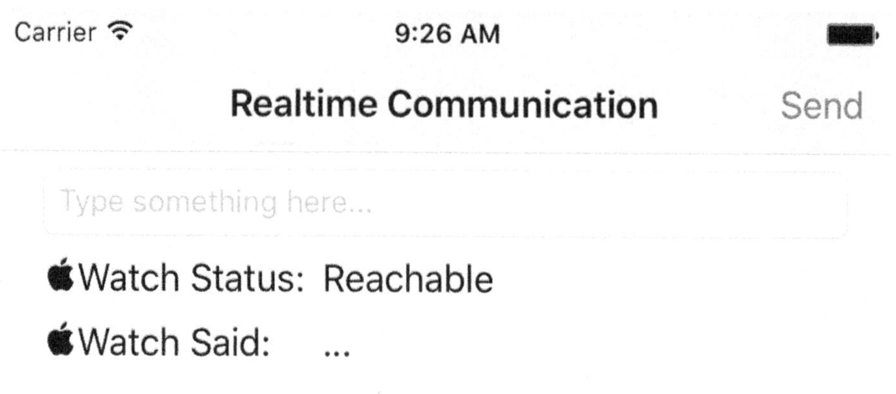

Carrier
9:26 AM
Realtime Communication
Send
Type something here...
Watch Status: Reachable
Watch Said: ...

Figure 10-25. The send button on our app is enabled and we can send messages

Type "Hello from iOS" in the iOS UI and press the send button. The watch app will receive the message (see Figure 10-26).

9:28
iOS App Said
Hello from iOS
Send a reply
Hello
Thank you

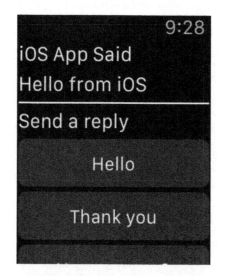

Figure 10-26. The watch app received the message sent from the iOS app

Now press the "How are you?" button on the watch UI and see the results in the iOS app (Figure 10-27).

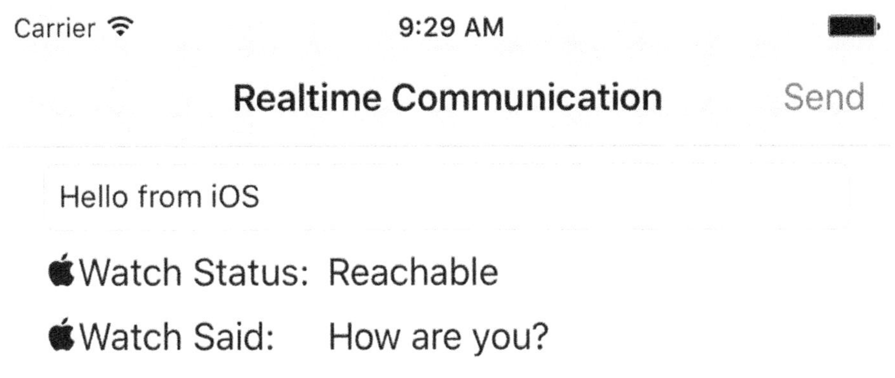

Carrier 📶   9:29 AM

Realtime Communication   Send

Hello from iOS

 Watch Status: Reachable

 Watch Said: How are you?

Figure 10-27. The iOS app received the message from the watch app

See Also

Recipe 10.2

10.7 Setting Up the Apple Watch for Custom Complications

Problem

You want to create a bare-bones watch project with support for complications and you would like to see a complication on the screen.

Solution

Follow these steps:

1. Add a watch target to your project (see Figure 10-1). Make sure that it includes complications upon setting it up (see Figure 10-2).
2. In Xcode, in your targets, select your watch extension. Under the General tab, ensure that the Modular Small family of complications is the only one that is enabled. Disable all the others (see Figure 10-28).
3. Write your complication code in your `ComplicationController` class. We'll discuss this code soon.
4. Run your app on the watch simulator.
5. Once your app is opened in the simulator, press Cmd-Shift-H to go to the clock face.

6. Press Cmd-Shift-2 to simulate Deep Press on the watch simulator and then tap and hold on the watch face (see Figure 10-29).

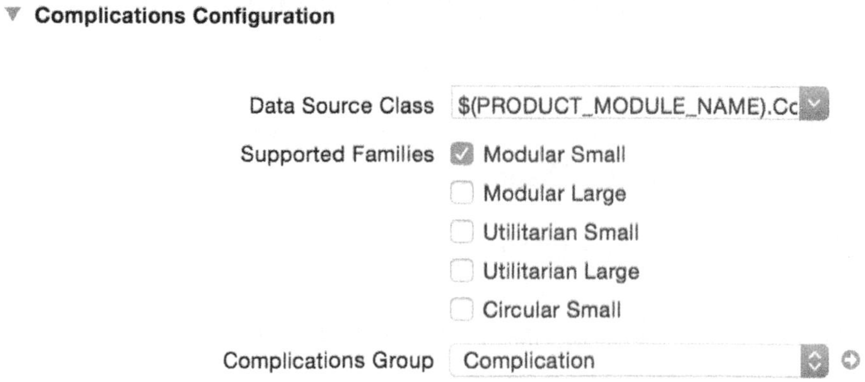

▼ **Complications Configuration**

Data Source Class $(PRODUCT_MODULE_NAME).Cc ⌄

Supported Families ☑ Modular Small
☐ Modular Large
☐ Utilitarian Small
☐ Utilitarian Large
☐ Circular Small

Complications Group Complication ⬍ ○

Figure 10-28. We are going to support only modular small complications

Figure 10-29. Deep Press to customize the watch face

7. Press Cmd-Shift-1 to simulate Shallow Press and then scroll to the modular watch face (see Figure 10-30).

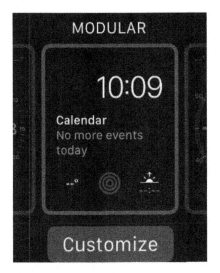

Figure 10-30. Select the modular watch face

8. Press the Customize button (see Figure 10-31).

Figure 10-31. Now you can customize your modular watch face

9. Scroll to the next page to the right, and then tap the small modular complication at the bottom left of the screen until it becomes selected (see Figure 10-32). You will replace this with your own complication.

Figure 10-32. Select the small modular complication at the bottom left

10. Now use the up and down arrow keys on your keyboard (or, if on the device, use the digital crown) to select your complication (see Figure 10-33). What you see on the screen is the preview template that you have provided to the system. We will implement this template soon, but in the figure I have already done that, hence the number 22.

Figure 10-33. Your own small modular complication is shown

11. Press Cmd-Shift-2 to simulate Deep Press and then tap the screen (see Figure 10-34).

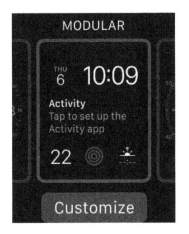

Figure 10-34. You have now configured your complication on the selected watch face

12. Press Cmd-Shift-H to go to the clock app on the screen (see Figure 10-35). Notice that your complication shows no data. That is because what was displayed on the screen while you were configuring your watch face was just a preview template. What the clock app displays is real data, and you are not providing any of it.

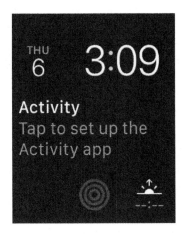

Figure 10-35. Your complication is on the bottom left but is empty

Discussion

Complications are pieces of information that apps can display on a watch face. They are divided into a few main categories:

Modular small

A very small amount of space with minimal text and/or a very small image (see Figure 10-36; the date at the top left is a modular small complication).

Modular large

An image, title, and up to two lines of text (see Figure 10-36; the calendar event in the center of the screen is a modular large complication).

Utilitarian small

A small image with optional text (see Figure 10-36; the activity icon at the bottom center is of this type).

Utilitarian large

A date/text mixed with an image, rendered on one line. This is similar to modular large but on just one line.

Circular small

A circular image with optional text (see Figure 10-36; the sunrise/sunset complication at the bottom right is an example of a circular small complication).

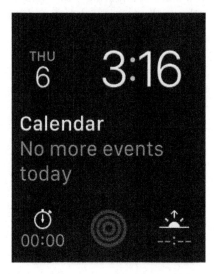

Figure 10-36. Everything except the time is a complication

Assuming that you have already created a watch target with a complication attached to it, go into your `ComplicationController` class and find the `getPlaceholder TemplateForComplication(_:withHandler:)` method. This method gets called by iOS when your complication is being added to a watch face. This gives you the chance to provide a placeholder for what the user will see while adjusting her watch face. It won't usually be real data.

After this method is called, you will need to create a complication template of type CLKComplicationTemplate (or one of its many subclasses) and return that into the replyHandler block that you are given. For now, implement the template like this:

```
func getPlaceholderTemplate(
  for complication: CLKComplication,
  withHandler handler: @escaping (CLKComplicationTemplate?) -> Void) {

  let temp = CLKComplicationTemplateModularSmallSimpleText()
  temp.textProvider = CLKSimpleTextProvider(text: "22")
  handler(temp)

}
```

I am not going to discuss the details of this code right now. You'll learn them in other recipes in this chapter.

One more thing that you have to know is that once you have provided watchOS with your placeholder template, you won't be asked to do it again unless the user uninstalls your watchOS app and installs it again from her iPhone (see Figure 10-37).

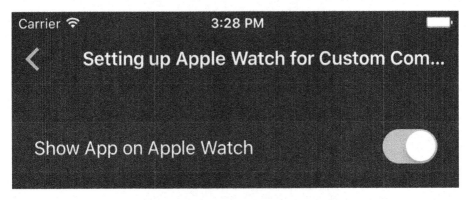

Figure 10-37. If the user uninstalls and reinstalls your app, it can provide a new placeholder template

If you would like to test out different templates while you are working on the get PlaceholderTemplateForComplication(_:withHandler:) method, you can simply reset the watch simulator and then run your app again. This will retrigger the getPla `ceholderTemplateForComplication(_:withHandler:)` method on your complication controller.

See Also

Recipe 10.8

10.8 Constructing Small Complications with Text and Images

Problem

You want to construct a small modular complication and provide the user with past, present, and future data.

Solution

In this example, a small modular complication (Figure 10-38, bottom left) shows the current hour with a ring swallowing it. The ring is divided into 24 sections and increments for every 1 hour in the day. At the end of the day, the ring will be completely filled and the number inside the ring will show 24.

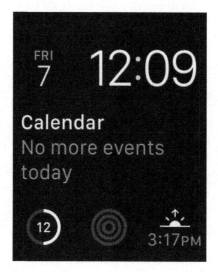

Figure 10-38. Small modular complication (bottom left) showing the current hour surrounded by a ring

To implement this, follow these steps:

---

1. Create your main iOS project with a watch target and make sure your watch target has a complication.
2. In your complication, implement the `getSupportedTimeTravelDirectionsFor Complication(_:withHandler:)` method of the `CLKComplicationDataSource` protocol. In this method, return your supported time travel directions (more on this later). The directions are of type `CLKComplicationTimeTravelDirections`.
3. Implement the `getTimelineStartDateForComplication(_:withHandler:)` method inside your complication class and call the given handler with a `Date` object that indicates the start date of your available data.
4. Implement the `getTimelineEndDateForComplication(_:withHandler:)` method of your complication and call the handler with the last date for which your data is valid.
5. Implement the `getTimelineEntriesForComplication(_:beforeDate:limit: withHandler:)` method of your complication, create an array of type `CLKCompli cationTimelineEntry`, and send that array into the given handler object. These will be the timeline entries before the given date that you would want to return to the watch (more on this later).
6. Implement the `getTimelineEntriesForComplication(_:afterDate:limit: withHandler:)` method of your complication and return all the events that your complication supports after the given date.
7. Implement the `getNextRequestedUpdateDateWithHandler(_:)` method of your complication and let watchOS know when it has to ask you next for more content.

Discussion

When providing complications, you are expected to provide data to watchOS as the time changes. In our example, for every hour in the day, we want to change our complication. So each day we'll return 24 events to the runtime.

With the digital crown on the watch, the user can scroll up and down while on the watch face to engage in a feature called "time travel." This allows the user to change the time known to the watch just so she can see how various components on the screen change with the new time. For instance, if you provide a complication to the user that shows all football match results of the day, the user can then go back in time a few hours to see the results of a match she has just missed. Similarly, in the context of a complication that shows the next fast train time to the city where the user lives, she can scroll forward, with the digital crown on the watch face, to see the future times that the train leaves from the current station.

The time is an absolute value on any watch, so let's say that you want to provide the time of the next football match in your complication. Let's say it's 14:00 right now and the football match starts at 15:00. If you give 15:00 as the start of that event to your complication, watchOS will show the football match (or the data that you provide for that match to your user through your complication) to the user at 15:00, not before. That is a bit useless, if you ask me. You want to provide that information to the user *before* the match starts so she knows what to look forward to, and when. So, keep that in mind when providing a starting date for your events.

watchOS complications conform to the `CLKComplicationDataSource` protocol. They get a lot of delegate messages from this protocol calling methods that you have to implement even if you don't want to return any data. For instance, in the `getNext RequestedUpdateDateWithHandler(_:)` method, you get a handler as a parameter that you must call with a `Date` object, specifying when you want to be asked for more data next time. If you don't want to be asked for any more data, you still have to call this handler object, but with a `nil` date. You'll find out soon that most of these handlers ask for optional values, so you can call them with `nil` if you want to.

While working with complications, you can tell watchOS which directions of time travel you support, or if you support time travel at all. If you don't support it, your complication returns only data for the current time, and if the user scrolls the watch face with the digital crown your complication won't update its information. I don't suggest you opt out of time travel unless your complication really cannot provide relevant data to the user. Certainly, if your complication shows match results, it cannot show results for matches that have not happened. But even then, you can still support forward and backward time travel. If the user chooses forward time travel, just hide the scores, show a question mark, or do something similar.

As you work with complications, it's important to construct a data model to return to the watch. What you usually return to the watch for your complication is either of type `CLKComplicationTemplate` or of type `CLKComplicationTimelineEntry`. The template defines how your data is viewed on the screen. The timeline entry only binds your template (your visible data) to a date of type `Date` that dictates to the watch when it has to show your data. It's as simple as that. In the case of small modular complications, you can provide the following templates to the watch:

`CLKComplicationTemplateModularSmallSimpleText`
    Has just text.

`CLKComplicationTemplateModularSmallSimpleImage`
    Has just an image.

`CLKComplicationTemplateModularSmallRingText`
    Has text inside a ring that you can fill from 0 to 100%.

`CLKComplicationTemplateModularSmallRingImage`
    Has an image inside a ring that you can fill.

`CLKComplicationTemplateModularSmallStackText`
Has two lines of code, the second of which can be highlighted.

`CLKComplicationTemplateModularSmallStackImage`
Has an image and text, with the text able to be highlighted.

`CLKComplicationTemplateModularSmallColumnsText`
Has a 2×2 text display where you can provide four pieces of textual data. The second column can be highlighted and have its text alignment adjusted.

As you saw earlier, in Figure 10-32, this example bases our small modular template on `CLKComplicationTemplateModularSmallRingText`. So, we provide only text (the current hour) and a value between 0 and 1 that will tell watchOS how much of the ring around our number it has to fill (0...100%).

Let's now begin defining our data for this example. For every hour, we want our template to show the current hour. Just before midnight, we provide another 24 new complication data points for that day to the watch. So let's define a data structure that can contain a date, the hour value, and the fraction (between 0 and 1) to set for our complication. Start off by creating a file called *DataProvider.swift* and write all this code in that:

```
protocol WithDate{
  var hour: Int {get}
  var date: Date {get}
  var fraction: Float {get}
}
```

Now we can define our actual structure that conforms to this protocol:

```
struct Data : WithDate{
  let hour: Int
  let date: Date
  let fraction: Float
  var hourAsStr: String{
    return "\(hour)"
  }
}
```

Later, when we work on our complication, we will be asked to provide inside the `getCurrentTimelineEntryForComplication(_:withHandler:)` method of `CLKComplicationDataSource` a template to show to the user for the current time. We are also going to create an array of 24 `Data` structures. So it would be great if we could always, inside this array, easily find the `Data` object for the current date:

```
extension Date{
  func hour() -> Int{
    let cal = Calendar.current
    let unitsArray: [Calendar.Component] = [.hour]
    let units = Set(unitsArray)
```

```
    return cal.dateComponents(units, from: self).hour!
  }
}

extension Collection where Iterator.Element : WithDate {

  func dataForNow() -> Iterator.Element?{
    let thisHour = Date().hour()
    for d in self{
      if d.hour == thisHour{
        return d
      }
    }
    return nil
  }

}
```

The dataForNow() function goes through any collection that has objects that conform to the WithDate protocol that we specified earlier, and finds the object whose current hour is the same as that returned for the current moment by Date().

Let's now create our array of 24 Data objects. We do this by iterating from 1 to 24, creating Date objects using DateComponents and Calendar. Then, using those objects, we construct instances of the Data structure that we just wrote:

```
struct DataProvider{

  func allDataForToday() -> [Data]{

    var all = [Data]()

    let now = Date()
    let cal = Calendar.current

    let unitsArray: [Calendar.Component] = [.month, .day]
    let units = Set(unitsArray)

    var comps = cal.dateComponents(units, from: now)
    comps.minute = 0
    comps.second = 0

    for i in 1...24{
      comps.hour = i
      let date = cal.date(from: comps)!
      let fraction = Float(comps.hour!) / 24.0
      let data = Data(hour: comps.hour!, date: date, fraction: fraction)
      all.append(data)
    }
```

```
    return all

  }

}
```

That was our entire data model. Now let's move on to the complication class of our watch app. In the getNextRequestedUpdateDateWithHandler(_:) method of the CLKComplicationDataSource protocol to which our complication conforms, we are going to be asked when watchOS should next call our complication and ask for new data. Because we are going to provide data for the whole day, *today*, we would want to be asked for new data for tomorrow. So we need to ask to be updated a few seconds before the start of the next day. For that, we need a Date object that tells watchOS when the next day is. So let's extend Date:

```
extension Date{

  static func endOfToday() -> Date{
    let cal = Calendar.current

    let unitsArray: [Calendar.Component] = [.year, .month, .day]
    let units = Set(unitsArray)

    var comps = cal.dateComponents(units, from: Date())
    comps.hour = 23
    comps.minute = 59
    comps.second = 59
    return cal.date(from: comps)!
  }

}
```

Moving to our complication, let's define our data provider first:

```
class ComplicationController: NSObject, CLKComplicationDataSource {

  let dataProvider = DataProvider()

  ...
```

We know that our data provider can give us an array of Data objects, so we need a way of turning those objects into our templates so they that can be displayed on the screen:

```
func templateForData(_ data: Data) -> CLKComplicationTemplate{
  let template = CLKComplicationTemplateModularSmallRingText()
  template.textProvider = CLKSimpleTextProvider(text: data.hourAsStr)
  template.fillFraction = data.fraction
  template.ringStyle = .closed
  return template
}
```

Our template of type `CLKComplicationTemplateModularSmallRingText` has a few important properties:

`textProvider` *of type* `CLKTextProvider`
> Tells watchOS how our text has to appear. We never instantiate `CLKTextProvider` directly, though. We use one of its subclasses, such as the `CLKSimpleTextPro vider` class. There are other text providers that we will talk about later.

`fillFraction` *of type* `Float`
> A number between 0.0 and 1.0 that tells watchOS how much of the ring around our template it has to fill.

`ringStyle` *of type* `CLKComplicationRingStyle`
> The style of the ring we want around our text. It can be `Open` or `Closed`.

Later we are also going to be asked for timeline entries of type `CLKComplicationTime lineEntry` for the data that we provide to watchOS. So, for every `Data` object, we need to be able to create a timeline entry:

```
func timelineEntryForData(_ data: Data) -> CLKComplicationTimelineEntry{
  let template = templateForData(data)
  return CLKComplicationTimelineEntry(date: data.date as Date,
    complicationTemplate: template)
}
```

In the example shown here, we support forward and backward time travel (of type `CLKComplicationTimeTravelDirections`), so let's tell watchOS that:

```
func getSupportedTimeTravelDirections(
  for complication: CLKComplication,
  withHandler handler: @escaping (CLKComplicationTimeTravelDirections) -> Void) {
    handler([.forward, .backward])
}
```

> If you don't want to support time travel, call the `handler` argument with the value of `CLKComplicationTimeTravelDirections.None`.

At this point, the next thing we have to do is implement the `getTimelineStartDate ForComplication(_:withHandler:)` method of `CLKComplicationDataSource`. This method gets called on our delegate whenever watchOS wants to find out the beginning of the date/time range of our time travel. For our example, since we want to provide 24 templates, one for each hour in the day, we tell watchOS the date of the first template:

```
func getTimelineStartDate(for complication: CLKComplication,
  withHandler handler: @escaping (Date?) -> Void) {
```

```
    handler(dataProvider.allDataForToday().first!.date as Date)
}
```

Similarly, for the `getTimelineEndDateForComplication(_:withHandler:)` method, we provide the date of the last event:

```
func getTimelineEndDate(for complication: CLKComplication,
  withHandler handler: @escaping (Date?) -> Void) {
  handler(dataProvider.allDataForToday().last!.date)
}
```

Complications can be displayed on the watch's lock screen. Some complications might contain sensitive data, so they might want to opt out of appearing on the lock screen. For this, we have to implement the `getPrivacyBehaviorForComplication(_:with Handler:)` method as well. We call the handler with an object of type `CLKComplica tionPrivacyBehavior`, such as `ShowOnLockScreen` or `HideOnLockScreen`. Because we don't have any sensitive data, we show our complication on the lock screen:

```
func getPrivacyBehavior(for complication: CLKComplication,
  withHandler handler: @escaping (CLKComplicationPrivacyBehavior) -> Void) {
  handler(.showOnLockScreen)
}
```

Now to the stuff that I like. The `getCurrentTimelineEntryForComplication(_:with Handler:)` method will get called on our delegate whenever the runtime needs to get the complication timeline (the template plus the date to display) for the complication to display on. Do you remember the `dataForNow()`method that we wrote a while ago as an extension on `Collection`? Well, we are going to use that now:

```
func getCurrentTimelineEntry(for complication: CLKComplication,
  withHandler handler: @escaping ((CLKComplicationTimelineEntry?) -> Void)) {

    if let data = dataProvider.allDataForToday().dataForNow(){
      handler(timelineEntryForData(data))
    } else {
      handler(nil)
    }

}
```

 Always implement the handlers that the class gives you. If they accept optional values and you don't have any data to pass, just pass `nil`.

Now we have to implement the `getTimelineEntriesForComplication(_:before Date:limit:beforeDate:)` method of our complication delegate. This method gets called whenever watchOS needs timeline entries for data before a certain date, with a maximum of *limit* entries. So let's say that you have 1,000 templates to return but the limit is 100. Do not return more than 100 in that case. In our example, I will go through all the data items that we have, filter them by their dates, find the ones coming before the given date (the `beforeDate` parameter), and create a timeline entry for all of those with the `timelineEntryForData(_:)` method that we wrote:

```
func getTimelineEntries(for complication: CLKComplication,
    before date: Date, limit: Int,
    withHandler handler: @escaping (([CLKComplicationTimelineEntry]?) -> Void)) {

    let entries = dataProvider.allDataForToday().filter{
      date.compare($0.date as Date) == .orderedDescending
    }.map{
      self.timelineEntryForData($0)
    }

    handler(entries)
}
```

Similarly, we have to implement the `getTimelineEntriesForComplication(_:after Date:limit:withHandler:)` method to return the timeline entries *after* a certain date (the `afterDate` parameter):

```
func getTimelineEntries(for complication: CLKComplication,
    after date: Date, limit: Int,
    withHandler handler: @escaping (([CLKComplicationTimelineEntry]?) -> Void)) {

    let entries = dataProvider.allDataForToday().filter{
      date.compare($0.date as Date) == .orderedAscending
    }.map{
      self.timelineEntryForData($0)
    }

    handler(entries)

}
```

The `getNextRequestedUpdateDateWithHandler(_:)` method is the next method we need to implement. This method gets called to ask us when we would like to be asked for more data later. For our app we specify the next day, because we have already provided all the data for today:

```
func getNextRequestedUpdateDate(handler: @escaping (Date?) -> Void) {
    handler(Date.endOfToday());
}
```

Last but not least, we have to implement the `getPlaceholderTemplateForComplica tion(_:withHandler:)` method that we talked about before. This is where we provide our placeholder template:

```
func getPlaceholderTemplate(for complication: CLKComplication,
  withHandler handler: @escaping (CLKComplicationTemplate?) -> Void) {
    if let data = dataProvider.allDataForToday().dataForNow(){
      handler(templateForData(data))
    } else {
      handler(nil)
    }
}
```

Now when I run the app on my watch, if the time is 10:24 and the hour is 10, our complication will show 10 and fill the circle around it to show how much of the day has passed by 10:00 (see Figure 10-39).

Figure 10-39. Our complication on the bottom left is showing the hour and how much of the day has passed

And if I engage time travel and move forward to 18:23 (6:23 on a 12-hour clock), our complication updates itself as well, showing 18 as the hour (see Figure 10-40).

Figure 10-40. The user moves the time to the future and our complication updates itself as well

See Also

Recipes 10.7 and 10.9

10.9 Displaying Time Offsets in Complications

Problem

The data that you want to present has to be shown as an offset to a specific time. For instance, you want to show the remaining minutes until the next train the user can take to get home.

Solution

Use the `CLKRelativeDateTextProvider` to provide your information inside a template. In this example, we are going to use `CLKComplicationTemplateModularLargeStandardBody`, which is a large modular template.

Discussion

In this recipe, we'll create a watch app that shows the next available train that the user can take to get home. Trains can have different properties:

- Date and time of departure

- Train operator
- Type of train (high speed, commuter, etc.)
- Service name (as shown on the timetable)

In our example, I want the complication to look like Figure 10-41. The complication shows the next train (a Coastal service) and how many minutes away that train's departure is.

MON
10
11:57
Next train
25 MIN
Coastal
--°
3:20PM

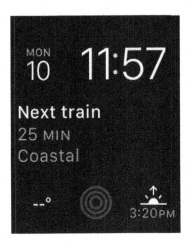

Figure 10-41. Our complication shows that the next train leaves in 25 minutes

When you create your watchOS project, enable only the Modular Large complication family in the target settings (see Figure 10-42).

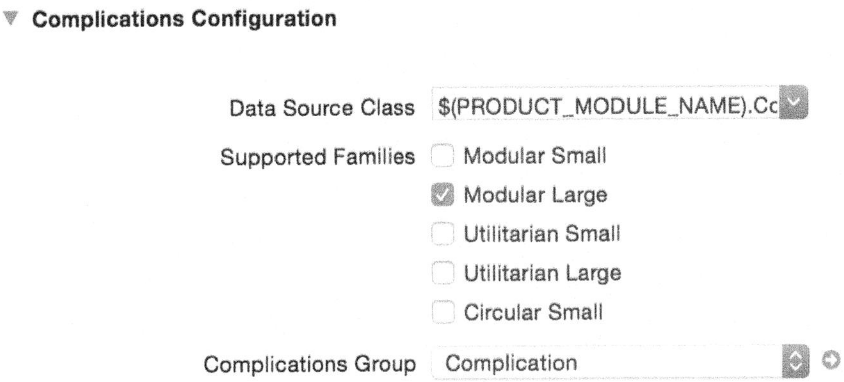

Complications Configuration
Data Source Class
$(PRODUCT_MODULE_NAME).Cc
Supported Families
Modular Small
Modular Large
Utilitarian Small
Utilitarian Large
Circular Small
Complications Group
Complication

Figure 10-42. Enable only modular large complications for this example

Now let's create the data model. It will be similar to what we did in Recipe 10.8, but this time we want to provide train times. For the train type and the train company, we'll create enumerations:

```
enum TrainType : String{
  case HighSpeed = "High Speed"
  case Commuter = "Commuter"
  case Coastal = "Coastal"
}

enum TrainCompany : String{
  case SJ = "SJ"
  case Southern = "Souther"
  case OldRail = "Old Rail"
}
```

 These enumerations are of type `String`, so you can display them on your UI easily without having to write a `switch` statement.

Then we'll define a protocol to which our train object will conform. Protocol-oriented programming offers many possibilities (see Recipe 6.18), so let's do that now:

```
protocol OnRailable{
  var type: TrainType {get}
  var company: TrainCompany {get}
  var service: String {get}
  var departureTime: Date {get}
}

struct Train : OnRailable{
  let type: TrainType
  let company: TrainCompany
  let service: String
  let departureTime: Date
}
```

As we did in Recipe 10.8, we are going to define a data provider. In this example, we create a few trains that depart at specific times with different types of services and from different operators:

```
struct DataProvider{

  func allTrainsForToday() -> [Train]{

    var all = [Train]()

    let now = Date()
```

```
    let cal = Calendar.current
    let unitsArray: [Calendar.Component] = [.year, .month, .day]
    let units = Set(unitsArray)
    var comps = cal.dateComponents(units, from: now)

    // first train
    comps.hour = 6
    comps.minute = 30
    comps.second = 0
    let date1 = cal.date(from: comps)!
    all.append(Train(type: .Commuter, company: .SJ,
      service: "3296", departureTime: date1))

    // second train
    comps.hour = 9
    comps.minute = 57
    let date2 = cal.date(from: comps)!
    all.append(Train(type: .HighSpeed, company: .Southern,
      service: "2307", departureTime: date2))

    // third train
    comps.hour = 12
    comps.minute = 22
    let date3 = cal.date(from: comps)!
    all.append(Train(type: .Coastal, company: .OldRail,
      service: "3206", departureTime: date3))

    // fourth train
    comps.hour = 15
    comps.minute = 45
    let date4 = cal.date(from: comps)!
    all.append(Train(type: .HighSpeed, company: .SJ,
      service: "3703", departureTime: date4))

    // fifth train
    comps.hour = 18
    comps.minute = 19
    let date5 = cal.date(from: comps)!
    all.append(Train(type: .Coastal, company: .Southern,
      service: "8307", departureTime: date5))

    // sixth train
    comps.hour = 22
    comps.minute = 11
    let date6 = cal.date(from: comps)!
    all.append(Train(type: .Commuter, company: .OldRail,
      service: "6802", departureTime: date6))

    return all

}
```

```
}
```

Now let's move to the ComplicationController class of our watch extension. Here we will provide watchOS with the data it needs to display our complication. The first task is to extend Collection so that we can find the next train in the array that the allTrainsForToday() function of DataProvider returns:

```
extension Collection where Iterator.Element : OnRailable {

  func nextTrain() -> Iterator.Element?{
    let now = Date()
    for d in self{
      if now.compare(d.departureTime as Date) == .orderedAscending{
        return d
      }
    }
    return nil
  }

}
```

And we need a data provider in our complication:

```
class ComplicationController: NSObject, CLKComplicationDataSource {

  let dataProvider = DataProvider()

  ...
```

For every train, we need to create a template that watchOS can display on the screen. All templates are of type CLKComplicationTemplate, but don't initialize that class directly. Instead, create a template of type CLKComplicationTemplateModular LargeStandardBody that has a header, two lines of text with the second line being optional, and an optional image. The header will show constant text (see Figure 10-41), so instantiate it with type CLKSimpleTextProvider. For the first line of text, you want to show how many minutes away the next train is, so that will require a text provider of type CLKRelativeDateTextProvider as we talked about before.

The initializer for CLKRelativeDateTextProvider takes in a parameter of type CLK RelativeDateStyle that defines the way the given date has to be shown. In our example, we use CLKRelativeDateStyle.offset:

```
func templateForTrain(_ train: Train) -> CLKComplicationTemplate{
  let template = CLKComplicationTemplateModularLargeStandardBody()
  template.headerTextProvider = CLKSimpleTextProvider(text: "Next train")

  template.body1TextProvider =
    CLKRelativeDateTextProvider(date: train.departureTime as Date,
      style: .offset,
      units: NSCalendar.Unit.hour.union(.minute))
```

```
let secondLine = "\(train.service) - \(train.type)"

template.body2TextProvider = CLKSimpleTextProvider(text: secondLine,
  shortText: train.type.rawValue)

return template
}
```

 The second line of text we are providing has a shortText alternative. If the watch UI has no space to show our secondLine text, it
will show the shortText alternative.

We are going to need to provide timeline entries (date plus template) for every train
as well, so let's create a helper method for that:

```
func timelineEntryForTrain(_ train: Train) -> CLKComplicationTimelineEntry{
  let template = templateForTrain(train)
  return CLKComplicationTimelineEntry(date: train.departureTime as Date,
    complicationTemplate: template)
}
```

When we are asked for the first and the last date of the data we provide, we read our
data provider's array of trains and return the first and the last train's dates,
respectively:

```
func getTimelineStartDate(for complication: CLKComplication,
  withHandler handler: @escaping (Date?) -> Void) {
    handler(dataProvider.allTrainsForToday().first!.departureTime as Date)
}
```

```
func getTimelineEndDate(for complication: CLKComplication,
  withHandler handler: @escaping (Date?) -> Void) {
    handler(dataProvider.allTrainsForToday().last!.departureTime)
}
```

We want to allow the user to be able to time travel so that she can see the next train as
she changes the time with the digital crown. Also, as our data is not particularly sensitive, we'll allow viewing this data on the lock screen:

```
func getSupportedTimeTravelDirections(
  for complication: CLKComplication,
  withHandler handler: @escaping (CLKComplicationTimeTravelDirections) -> Void) {
    handler([.forward, .backward])
}
```

```
func getPrivacyBehavior(for complication: CLKComplication,
  withHandler handler: @escaping (CLKComplicationPrivacyBehavior) -> Void) {
    handler(.showOnLockScreen)
}
```

Regarding time travel, when asked for trains after and before a certain time, our code should go through all the trains and filter out the times we don't want displayed, as we did in Recipe 10.8:

```
func getTimelineEntries(for complication: CLKComplication,
  before date: Date, limit: Int,
  withHandler handler: @escaping (([CLKComplicationTimelineEntry]?) -> Void)) {

    let entries = dataProvider.allTrainsForToday().filter{
      date.compare($0.departureTime as Date) == .orderedDescending
    }.map{
      self.timelineEntryForTrain($0)
    }

    handler(entries)
}

func getTimelineEntries(for complication: CLKComplication,
  after date: Date, limit: Int,
  withHandler handler: @escaping (([CLKComplicationTimelineEntry]?) -> Void)) {

    let entries = dataProvider.allTrainsForToday().filter{
      date.compare($0.departureTime as Date) == .orderedAscending
    }.map{
      self.timelineEntryForTrain($0)
    }

    handler(entries)

}
```

When the getCurrentTimelineEntryForComplication(_:withHandler:) method is called on our delegate, we get the next train's timeline entry and return it:

```
func getCurrentTimelineEntry(for complication: CLKComplication,
  withHandler handler: @escaping ((CLKComplicationTimelineEntry?) -> Void)) {

    if let train = dataProvider.allTrainsForToday().nextTrain(){
      handler(timelineEntryForTrain(train))
    } else {
      handler(nil)
    }

}
```

Because we provide data until the end of today, we ask watchOS to ask us for new data tomorrow:

```
func getNextRequestedUpdateDate(handler: @escaping (Date?) -> Void) {
  handler(Date.endOfToday());
}
```

Last but not least, we provide our placeholder template:

```
func getPlaceholderTemplate(for complication: CLKComplication,
  withHandler handler: @escaping (CLKComplicationTemplate?) -> Void) {
    if let data = dataProvider.allTrainsForToday().nextTrain(){
      handler(templateForTrain(data))
    } else {
      handler(nil)
    }
}
```

We already saw an example of our app showing the next train (see Figure 10-41), but our app can also participate in time travel (see Figure 10-43). The user can use the digital crown on the watch to move forward or backward and see the next available train at the new time.

Figure 10-43. Moving our complication backward in time

10.10 Displaying Dates in Complications

Problem

You want to display Date instances in your complications.

Solution

To solve this problem, use an instance of the CLKDateTextProvider class, which is a subclass of CLKTextProvider, as your text provider.

> We will use CLKComplicationTemplateModularLargeColumns (a modular large template) for this recipe, so configure your watch target to provide only large modular templates (see Figure 10-42).

Discussion

Let's develop a modular large complication that provides us with the name and the date of the next three public holidays (see Figure 10-44). We are not formatting the date ourselves. We leave it to watchOS to decide how to display the date by using an instance of CLKDateTextProvider.

Figure 10-44. The next three public holidays, with their names and dates

Just as in Recipes 10.8 and 10.9, we are going to add a new class to our watch app called DataProvider. In there, we are going to program all the holidays this year. Let's start off by defining what a Holiday object looks like:

```
protocol Holidayable{
  var date: Date {get}
  var name: String {get}
}

struct Holiday : Holidayable{
  let date: Date
  let name: String
}
```

In our data provider class, we start off by defining some holiday names:

```
struct DataProvider{

  private let holidayNames = [
    "Father's Day",
    "Mother's Day",
    "Bank Holiday",
    "Nobel Day",
    "Man Day",
    "Woman Day",
```

```
  "Boyfriend Day",
  "Girlfriend Day",
  "Dog Day",
  "Cat Day",
  "Mouse Day",
  "Cow Day",
]

private func randomDay() -> Int{
  return Int(arc4random_uniform(20) + 1)
}
```

. . .

Then we move on to providing our instances of Holiday:

```
func allHolidays() -> [Holiday]{

  var all = [Holiday]()

  let now = Date()
  let cal = Calendar.current
  let unitsArray: [Calendar.Component] = [.year, .month, .day]
  let units = Set(unitsArray)
  var comps = cal.dateComponents(units, from: now)

  var dates = [Date]()

  for month in 1...12{
    comps.day = randomDay()
    comps.month = month
    dates.append(cal.date(from: comps)!)
  }

  var i = 0
  for date in dates{
    all.append(Holiday(date: date, name: holidayNames[i]))
    i += 1
  }

  return all

}
```

It's worth noting that the allHolidays() function we just wrote simply goes through all months inside this calendar year and sets the day of the month to a random day. So we will get 12 holidays, one in each month, at a random day inside that month.

Over to our ComplicationController. When we get asked later when we would like to provide more data or updated data to watchOS, we are going to ask for 10 minutes in the future. So if our data changes, watchOS will have a chance to ask us for updated information:

```
extension Date{
  func plus10Minutes() -> Date{
    return addingTimeInterval(10 * 60)
  }
}
```

Because the template we are going to provide allows a maximum of three items, we would like to have methods on `Array` to return the second and the third items inside the array, just like the prebuilt `first` property that the class offers:

```
extension Array{
  var second : Iterator.Element?{
    return count >= 1 ? self[1] : nil
  }
  var third : Iterator.Element?{
    return count >= 2 ? self[2] : nil
  }
}
```

`DataProvider`'s `allHolidays()` method returns 12 holidays. How about extending the built-in array type to always give us the next three holidays? It would have to read today's date, go through the items in our array, compare the dates, and give us just the upcoming three holidays:

```
func minimum<T : Comparable>(_ items: T...) -> T{
  var result = items[0]
  for value in items{
    if value < result{
      result = value
    }
  }
  return result
}

extension Collection where Iterator.Element : Holidayable {

  // may contain less than three holidays
  func nextThreeHolidays() -> Array<Self.Iterator.Element>{

    let now = Date()

    let orderedArray = Array(self.filter{
      now.compare($0.date as Date) == .orderedAscending
    })

    let result = Array(orderedArray[0..<minimum(orderedArray.count, 3)])

    return result
  }

}
```

Now we start defining our complication:

```
class ComplicationController: NSObject, CLKComplicationDataSource {

  let dataProvider = DataProvider()

  ...
```

We need a method that can take in a Holiday object and give us a template of type CLKComplicationTemplate for that. Our specific template for this recipe is of type CLKComplicationTemplateModularLargeColumns. This template is like a 3×3 table. It has three rows and three columns (see Figure 10-44). If we are at the end of the year and we have no more holidays, we return a template that is of type CLKComplication TemplateModularLargeStandardBody and tell the user that there are no more upcoming holidays. Note that both templates have the words "ModularLarge" in their name. Because we have specified in our target setting that we support only modular large templates (see Figure 10-42), this example can return only templates that have those words in their name:

```
func templateForHoliday(_ holiday: Holiday) -> CLKComplicationTemplate{

  let next3Holidays = dataProvider.allHolidays().nextThreeHolidays()

  let headerTitle = "Next 3 Holidays"

  guard next3Holidays.count > 0 else{
    let template = CLKComplicationTemplateModularLargeStandardBody()
    template.headerTextProvider = CLKSimpleTextProvider(text: headerTitle)
    template.body1TextProvider = CLKSimpleTextProvider(text: "Sorry!")
    return template
  }

  let dateUnits = NSCalendar.Unit.month.union(.day)
  let template = CLKComplicationTemplateModularLargeColumns()

  // first holiday
  if let firstHoliday = next3Holidays.first{
    template.row1Column1TextProvider =
      CLKSimpleTextProvider(text: firstHoliday.name)
    template.row1Column2TextProvider =
      CLKDateTextProvider(date: firstHoliday.date, units: dateUnits)
  }

  // second holiday
  if let secondHoliday = next3Holidays.second{
    template.row2Column1TextProvider =
      CLKSimpleTextProvider(text: secondHoliday.name)
    template.row2Column2TextProvider =
      CLKDateTextProvider(date: secondHoliday.date, units: dateUnits)
  }
```

```
// third holiday
if let thirdHoliday = next3Holidays.third{
  template.row3Column1TextProvider =
    CLKSimpleTextProvider(text: thirdHoliday.name)
  template.row3Column2TextProvider =
    CLKDateTextProvider(date: thirdHoliday.date, units: dateUnits)
}

return template
}
```

We need to provide a timeline entry (date plus template) for our holidays as well:

```
func timelineEntryForHoliday(_ holiday: Holiday) ->
  CLKComplicationTimelineEntry{
    let template = templateForHoliday(holiday)
    return CLKComplicationTimelineEntry(date: holiday.date as Date,
                                  complicationTemplate: template)
}
```

And provide the first and last holidays:

```
func getTimelineStartDate(for complication: CLKComplication,
                    withHandler handler: @escaping (Date?) -> Void) {
  handler(dataProvider.allHolidays().first!.date as Date)
}

func getTimelineEndDate(for complication: CLKComplication,
                    withHandler handler: @escaping (Date?) -> Void) {
  handler(dataProvider.allHolidays().last!.date)
}
```

We'll also support time travel and provide our content on the lock screen, because it is not private:

```
func getSupportedTimeTravelDirections(
  for complication: CLKComplication,
  withHandler handler: @escaping (CLKComplicationTimeTravelDirections) -> Void) {
  handler([.forward, .backward])
}

func getPrivacyBehavior(
  for complication: CLKComplication,
  withHandler handler: @escaping (CLKComplicationPrivacyBehavior) -> Void) {
  handler(.showOnLockScreen)
}
```

Now let's give watchOS information about previous and upcoming holidays:

```
func getTimelineEntries(
  for complication: CLKComplication,
  before date: Date, limit: Int,
  withHandler handler: @escaping (([CLKComplicationTimelineEntry]?) -> Void)) {
```

```
  let entries = dataProvider.allHolidays().filter{
    date.compare($0.date as Date) == .orderedDescending
    }.map{
      self.timelineEntryForHoliday($0)
  }

  handler(entries)
}

func getTimelineEntries(
  for complication: CLKComplication,
  after date: Date, limit: Int,
  withHandler handler: @escaping ((([CLKComplicationTimelineEntry]?) -> Void)) {

  let entries = dataProvider.allHolidays().filter{
    date.compare($0.date as Date) == .orderedAscending
    }.map{
      self.timelineEntryForHoliday($0)
  }

  handler(entries)

}
```

Last but not least, we'll ensure that our app provides the upcoming three holidays when asked to provide them *now*:

```
func getCurrentTimelineEntry(
  for complication: CLKComplication,
  withHandler handler: @escaping ((CLKComplicationTimelineEntry?) -> Void)) {

  if let first = dataProvider.allHolidays().nextThreeHolidays().first{
    handler(timelineEntryForHoliday(first))
  } else {
    handler(nil)
  }

}

func getNextRequestedUpdateDate(handler: @escaping (Date?) -> Void) {
  handler(Date().plus10Minutes());
}

func getPlaceholderTemplate(
  for complication: CLKComplication,
  withHandler handler: @escaping (CLKComplicationTemplate?) -> Void) {
  if let holiday = dataProvider.allHolidays().nextThreeHolidays().first{
    handler(templateForHoliday(holiday))
  } else {
    handler(nil)
  }
}
```

See Also

Recipe 10.11

10.11 Displaying Times in Complications

Problem

You want to display a time on your watch UI and want it to look good regardless of available space on the watch.

Solution

Provide your time (in the form of a `Date`) to an instance of `CLKTimeTextProvider` and use it inside a template (see Figure 10-45). Here, our large modular complication in the center of the screen is showing the next pause that we can take at work, which happens to be a coffee pause.

Figure 10-45. The time is displayed on the screen using an instance of CLKTime-TextProvider

 In this recipe, we are going to rely a lot on what we covered in Recipe 10.8 and other complication recipes in this chapter. I suggest reading Recipe 10.8 at least to get an idea of how our data provider works. Otherwise, you will still be able to read this recipe; however, I will skip over some details that I've already explained in Recipe 10.8.

Discussion

This recipe uses a large modular template, so make sure that your project is set up for that (see Figure 10-42). Here, we want to build an app that shows the different breaks or pauses that the user can take at work, and when they occur—for instance, when the first pause is after they get to work, when lunch happens, when the next pause between lunch and dinner is, and when it's time to stop for dinner.

So, we have breaks at work and we need to define them. Create a Swift file in your watch extension and call it *DataProvider*. In there, define your break:

```
import Foundation

protocol Pausable{
  var name: String {get}
  var date: Date {get}
}

struct PauseAtWork : Pausable{
  let name: String
  let date: Date
}
```

Now in your `DataProvider` structure, create four pauses that the user can take at work at different times and provide them as an array:

```
struct DataProvider{

  func allPausesToday() -> [PauseAtWork]{

    var all = [PauseAtWork]()

    let now = Date()
    let cal = Calendar.current

    let unitsArray: [Calendar.Component] = [.year, .month, .day]
    let units = Set(unitsArray)

    var comps = cal.dateComponents(units, from: now)
    comps.calendar = cal
    comps.minute = 30

    comps.hour = 11
    all.append(
      PauseAtWork(name: "Coffee", date: comps.date!))

    comps.minute = 30
    comps.hour = 14
    all.append(
      PauseAtWork(name: "Lunch", date: comps.date!))

    comps.minute = 0
```

```
        comps.hour = 16
        all.append(
          PauseAtWork(name: "Tea", date: comps.date!))

        comps.hour = 17
        all.append(
          PauseAtWork(name: "Dinner", date: comps.date!))

        return all

    }

}
```

Here we obtain the current date and time and then go from coffee break in the morning to dinner in the evening, adding each pause to the array. The method is called allPausesToday(), and we are going to invoke it from our watch complication.

Before, we created a protocol called Pausable and now we have all our pauses in an array. When we are asked to provide a template for the next pause to show in the complication, we have to get the current time and find the pause whose time is after the current time. So let's bundle that up by extending Collection like we have done in other recipes in this chapter:

```
extension Collection where Iterator.Element : Pausable {

  func nextPause() -> Self.Iterator.Element?{
    let now = Date()

    for pause in self{
      if now.compare(pause.date as Date) == .orderedAscending{
        return pause
      }
    }

    return nil
  }

}
```

In our complication now, we instantiate our data provider:

```
class ComplicationController: NSObject, CLKComplicationDataSource {

  let dataProvider = DataProvider()

    ...
```

For every pause that we want to display to the user (see Figure 10-45), we need to provide a template of type CLKComplicationTemplate to the runtime. We never instantiate that class directly. Instead, we return an instance of a subclass of that class.

In this particular example, we display an instance of CLKComplicationTemplateModu larLargeTallBody. However, if there are no more pauses to take at work (e.g., if the time is 21:00 and the user is no longer at work), we display a placeholder to tell the user there are no more pauses. The template for that is of type CLKComplication TemplateModularLargeStandardBody. The difference between the two templates is visible if you read their names. We set the time on our template by setting the body TextProvider property of our CLKComplicationTemplateModularLargeTallBody instance:

```swift
func templateForPause(_ pause: PauseAtWork) -> CLKComplicationTemplate{

  guard let nextPause = dataProvider.allPausesToday().nextPause() else{
    let template = CLKComplicationTemplateModularLargeStandardBody()
    template.headerTextProvider = CLKSimpleTextProvider(text: "Next Break")
    template.body1TextProvider = CLKSimpleTextProvider(text: "None")
    return template
  }

  let template = CLKComplicationTemplateModularLargeTallBody()
  template.headerTextProvider = CLKSimpleTextProvider(text: nextPause.name)
  template.bodyTextProvider =
    CLKTimeTextProvider(date: nextPause.date as Date)

  return template
}
```

We also have to provide some of the other delegate methods of CLKComplicationData Source, such as the timeline entry (date plus template) for every pause that the user can take at work, and we need to support time travel for this example. On top of that, our information is not sensitive, so when asked whether we want to display our complication on the lock screen, we happily say yes:

```swift
func timelineEntryForPause(_ pause: PauseAtWork) ->
  CLKComplicationTimelineEntry{
    let template = templateForPause(pause)
    return CLKComplicationTimelineEntry(date: pause.date as Date,
                                       complicationTemplate: template)
}

func getSupportedTimeTravelDirections(
  for complication: CLKComplication,
  withHandler handler: @escaping (CLKComplicationTimeTravelDirections) -> Void) {
  handler([.forward, .backward])
}

func getPrivacyBehavior(
  for complication: CLKComplication,
  withHandler handler: @escaping (CLKComplicationPrivacyBehavior) -> Void) {
  handler(.showOnLockScreen)
}
```

When asked the beginning and end range of dates for our complications, we will return the dates for the first and the last pause that the user can take at work *today*. Remember, in this complication, we will return *all* the pauses for the current. When the time comes to display the pauses to take at work tomorrow, we will provide a whole set of new pauses:

```
func getTimelineStartDate(for complication: CLKComplication,
                          withHandler handler: @escaping (Date?) -> Void) {
  handler(dataProvider.allPausesToday().first!.date as Date)
}

func getTimelineEndDate(for complication: CLKComplication,
                        withHandler handler: @escaping (Date?) -> Void) {
  handler(dataProvider.allPausesToday().last!.date)
}
```

When the runtime calls the `getTimelineEntries(for:before:limit:withHandler:)` method, provide all the pauses that are available *before* the given date:

```
func getTimelineEntries(
  for complication: CLKComplication,
  before date: Date, limit: Int,
  withHandler handler: @escaping (([CLKComplicationTimelineEntry]?) -> Void)) {

  let entries = dataProvider.allPausesToday().filter{
    date.compare($0.date as Date) == .orderedDescending
    }.map{
      self.timelineEntryForPause($0)
  }

  handler(entries)
}
```

Similarly, when the `getTimelineEntries(for:after:limit:withHandler:)` method is called, return all the available pauses *after* the given date:

```
func getTimelineEntries(
  for complication: CLKComplication,
  after date: Date, limit: Int,
  withHandler handler: @escaping (([CLKComplicationTimelineEntry]?) -> Void)) {

  let entries = dataProvider.allPausesToday().filter{
    date.compare($0.date as Date) == .orderedAscending
    }.map{
      self.timelineEntryForPause($0)
  }

  handler(entries)

}
```

In the `getCurrentTimelineEntry(for:withHandler:)` method, we will be asked to provide the template for the current data (the next pause) to show on the screen. We already have a method on `Collection` called `nextPause()`, so let's use that to provide a template to watchOS:

```
func getCurrentTimelineEntry(
  for complication: CLKComplication,
  withHandler handler: @escaping ((CLKComplicationTimelineEntry?) -> Void)) {

  if let pause = dataProvider.allPausesToday().nextPause(){
    handler(timelineEntryForPause(pause))
  } else {
    handler(nil)
  }

}
```

Because in a typical watch app our data would probably come from a backend, we would like the runtime to ask us for up-to-date information as soon as possible, but not too soon. So let's do that after 10 minutes:

```
func getNextRequestedUpdateDate(handler: @escaping (Date?) -> Void) {
  handler(Date().plus10Minutes());
}
```

Last but not least, we also need to provide a placeholder template when the user is adding our complication to her watch face:

```
func getPlaceholderTemplate(
  for complication: CLKComplication,
  withHandler handler: @escaping (CLKComplicationTemplate?) -> Void) {
  if let pause = dataProvider.allPausesToday().nextPause(){
    handler(templateForPause(pause))
  } else {
    handler(nil)
  }
}
```

See Also

Recipe 10.10

10.12 Displaying Time Intervals in Complications

Problem

You want to display today's meetings on your watchOS UI, together with a time interval (start date–end date). For example, if it's brunch time, the screen should show the description and location of where you are going to have brunch, along with the time interval of the brunch (see Figure 10-46).

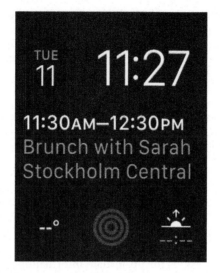

Figure 10-46. Meeting with start and end times

Solution

Use an instance of `CLKTimeIntervalTextProvider` as your text provider (see Figure 10-46).

This recipe is an extension of others we've already looked at, particularly Recipes 10.10 and 10.11.

Discussion

Let's say that we want to have an app that shows us all our meetings today. Every meeting has the following properties:

- Start and end times (the time interval)
- Name (e.g., "Brunch with Sarah")
- Location

Because text providers of type `CLKSimpleTextProvider` accept a short text in addition to the full text, we also have a short version of the location and the name. For instance, the location can be "Stockholm Central Train Station," whereas the short version of this could be "Central Station" or even "Centralen" in Swedish, which means "the center." So let's define this meeting object:

```
protocol Timable{
  var name: String {get}
  var shortName: String {get}
  var location: String {get}
  var shortLocation: String {get}
  var startDate: Date {get}
  var endDate: Date {get}
  var previous: Timable? {get}
}

struct Meeting : Timable{
  let name: String
  let shortName: String
  let location: String
  let shortLocation: String
  let startDate: Date
  let endDate: Date
  let previous: Timable?
}
```

Create a Swift file in your project called *DataProvider*. Put all the meetings for today in there and return an array:

```
struct DataProvider{

  func allMeetingsToday() -> [Meeting]{

    var all = [Meeting]()

    let oneHour: TimeInterval = 1 * 60.0 * 60

    let now = Date()
    let cal = Calendar.current
    let unitsArray: [Calendar.Component] = [.year, .month, .day]
    let units = Set(unitsArray)
    var comps = cal.dateComponents(units, from: now)
    comps.calendar = cal
    comps.minute = 30

    comps.hour = 11
    let meeting1 = Meeting(
      name: "Brunch with Sarah", shortName: "Brunch",
      location: "Stockholm Central", shortLocation: "Central",
      startDate: comps.date!,
      endDate: comps.date!.addingTimeInterval(oneHour), previous: nil)
    all.append(meeting1)

    comps.minute = 30
    comps.hour = 14
    let meeting2 = Meeting(
      name: "Lunch with Gabriella", shortName: "Lunch",
      location: "At home", shortLocation: "Home",
      startDate: comps.date!,
```

```
      endDate: comps.date!.addingTimeInterval(oneHour),
      previous: meeting1)
   all.append(meeting2)

   comps.minute = 0
   comps.hour = 16
   let meeting3 = Meeting(
     name: "Snack with Leif", shortName: "Snack",
     location: "Flags Cafe", shortLocation: "Flags",
     startDate: comps.date!,
     endDate: comps.date!.addingTimeInterval(oneHour),
     previous: meeting2)
   all.append(meeting3)

   comps.hour = 17
   let meeting4 = Meeting(
     name: "Dinner with Family", shortName: "Dinner",
     location: "At home", shortLocation: "Home",
     startDate: comps.date!,
     endDate: comps.date!.addingTimeInterval(oneHour),
     previous: meeting3)
   all.append(meeting4)

   return all

  }

}
```

In your complication class, extend `Collection` so that it can return the upcoming meeting:

```
extension Collection where Iterator.Element : Timable {

  func nextMeeting() -> Self.Iterator.Element?{
    let now = Date()

    for meeting in self{
      if now.compare(meeting.startDate as Date) == .orderedAscending{
        return meeting
      }
    }

    return nil
  }

}
```

I have extended `Collection`, but only if the items are `Timable`. I explained this technique in Recipe 6.18.

In your complication handler, create an instance of the data provider:

```
class ComplicationController: NSObject, CLKComplicationDataSource {

  let dataProvider = DataProvider()

  ...
```

Our template is of type `CLKComplicationTemplateModularLargeStandardBody`, which has a few important properties that we set as follows:

`headerTextProvider`
Shows the time range for the meeting.

`body1TextProvider`
Shows the name of the meeting.

`body2TextProvider`
Shows the location of the meeting.

To display the time range of the meeting, instantiate `CLKTimeIntervalTextProvider`:

```
func templateForMeeting(_ meeting: Meeting) -> CLKComplicationTemplate{

  let template = CLKComplicationTemplateModularLargeStandardBody()

  guard let nextMeeting = dataProvider.allMeetingsToday().nextMeeting() else{
    template.headerTextProvider = CLKSimpleTextProvider(text: "Next Break")
    template.body1TextProvider = CLKSimpleTextProvider(text: "None")
    return template
  }

  template.headerTextProvider =
    CLKTimeIntervalTextProvider(start: nextMeeting.startDate as Date,
                                end: nextMeeting.endDate as Date)

  template.body1TextProvider =
    CLKSimpleTextProvider(text: nextMeeting.name,
                          shortText: nextMeeting.shortName)

  template.body2TextProvider =
    CLKSimpleTextProvider(text: nextMeeting.location,
                          shortText: nextMeeting.shortLocation)

  return template
}
```

Using this method, you can also create timeline entries (date plus template). In this example, we set every new event's start date to the end date of the previous event (if it is available). That way, as soon as the current ongoing meeting ends, the next meeting shows up on the list:

```
func timelineEntryForMeeting(
    _ meeting: Meeting) -> CLKComplicationTimelineEntry{
    let template = templateForMeeting(meeting)

    let date = meeting.previous?.endDate ?? meeting.startDate
    return CLKComplicationTimelineEntry(date: date as Date,
                                        complicationTemplate: template)
}
```

 If the event has no previous events, its timeline entry date will be its start date, instead of the end date of the previous event.

Let's also participate in time travel and show our content on the lock screen as well:

```
func getSupportedTimeTravelDirections(
    for complication: CLKComplication,
    withHandler handler: @escaping (CLKComplicationTimeTravelDirections) -> Void) {
    handler([.forward, .backward])
}

func getPrivacyBehavior(
    for complication: CLKComplication,
    withHandler handler: @escaping (CLKComplicationPrivacyBehavior) -> Void) {
    handler(.showOnLockScreen)
}
```

Then we have to provide the date range for which we have available meetings. The start of the range is the start date of the first meeting, and the end date is the end date of the last meeting:

```
func getTimelineStartDate(for complication: CLKComplication,
                          withHandler handler: @escaping (Date?) -> Void) {
    handler(dataProvider.allMeetingsToday().first!.startDate as Date)
}

func getTimelineEndDate(for complication: CLKComplication,
                        withHandler handler: @escaping (Date?) -> Void) {
    handler(dataProvider.allMeetingsToday().last!.endDate)
}
```

We'll also be asked to provide all the available meetings before a certain date, so let's do that:

```
func getTimelineEntries(
  for complication: CLKComplication,
  before date: Date, limit: Int,
  withHandler handler: @escaping (([CLKComplicationTimelineEntry]?) -> Void)) {

  let entries = dataProvider.allMeetingsToday().filter{
    date.compare($0.startDate as Date) == .orderedDescending
    }.map{
      self.timelineEntryForMeeting($0)
  }

  handler(entries)
}
```

Similarly, we have to provide all our available meetings after a given date:

```
func getTimelineEntries(
  for complication: CLKComplication,
  after date: Date, limit: Int,
  withHandler handler: @escaping (([CLKComplicationTimelineEntry]?) -> Void)) {

  let entries = dataProvider.allMeetingsToday().filter{
    date.compare($0.startDate as Date) == .orderedAscending
    }.map{
      self.timelineEntryForMeeting($0)
  }

  handler(entries)

}
```

Last but not least, we'll provide our placeholder template, the template for now, and the next time we would like watchOS to ask us for updated information:

```
func getCurrentTimelineEntry(
  for complication: CLKComplication,
  withHandler handler: @escaping ((CLKComplicationTimelineEntry?) -> Void)) {

  if let meeting = dataProvider.allMeetingsToday().nextMeeting(){
    handler(timelineEntryForMeeting(meeting))
  } else {
    handler(nil)
  }

}

func getNextRequestedUpdateDate(handler: @escaping (Date?) -> Void) {
  handler(Date().plus10Minutes());
}

func getPlaceholderTemplate(
  for complication: CLKComplication,
  withHandler handler: @escaping (CLKComplicationTemplate?) -> Void) {
```

```
  if let pause = dataProvider.allMeetingsToday().nextMeeting(){
    handler(templateForMeeting(pause))
  } else {
    handler(nil)
  }
}
```

We coded the `plus10Minutes()` method on `Date` in Recipe 10.10.

10.13 Recording Audio in Your Watch App

Problem

You want to allow your users to record audio while inside your watch app, and you want to get access to the recorded audio.

Solution

To enable users to record audio in your watch app, use the `presentAudioRecorderController(withOutputURL:preset:options:completion:)` method of your `WKInterfaceController` class to present a system dialog that can take care of audio recording. To dismiss the dialog, use the `dismissAudioRecordingController()` method of your controller.

The `options` parameter of `presentAudioRecorderControllerWithOutputURL(_:preset:options:completion:)` accepts a dictionary that can contain the following keys:

`WKAudioRecorderControllerOptionsActionTitleKey`
:   This key, of type `String`, will be the title of our recorder.

`WKAudioRecorderControllerOptionsAlwaysShowActionTitleKey`
:   This key, of type `NSNumber`, contains a `Bool` value that dictates whether the title should always be shown on the recorder.

`WKAudioRecorderControllerOptionsAutorecordKey`
:   This key, of type `NSNumber`, contains a `Bool` value to indicate whether recording should begin automatically when the dialog is presented.

`WKAudioRecorderControllerOptionsMaximumDurationKey`
:   This key, of type `NSNumber`, contains a `TimeInterval` value to dictate the maximum duration of the audio content.

Discussion

For this recipe, we are going to create a watch app whose UI looks like that shown in Figure 10-47. It holds a label to show the current status (started recording, failed recording, etc.) and a button that, when pressed, will show the recording dialog.

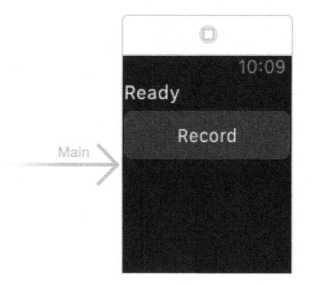

Figure 10-47. Label for status and button to record

Hook the label up to your code with the name `statusLbl`. Then hook your record button to your interface under a method named `record()`. Your interface code should look like this now:

```
class InterfaceController: WKInterfaceController {

  @IBOutlet var statusLbl: WKInterfaceLabel!

  ...
```

Define the URL where your recording will be saved:

```
var url: URL{
  let fm = FileManager()
  let url = try! fm.url(for: .musicDirectory,
                     in: FileManager.SearchPathDomainMask.userDomainMask,
                     appropriateFor: nil, create: true)
    .appendingPathComponent("recording")
  return url
}
```

Also, because the completion block of your recording screen might not get called on the main thread, create a variable that can set the text inside the status label on the main thread:

```
var status = ""{
  willSet{
    DispatchQueue.main.async{
      self.statusLbl.setText(newValue)
    }
  }
}
```

Next, construct your options for when the record button is pressed:

```
let oneMinute: TimeInterval = 1 * 60

let yes = NSNumber(value: true)
let no = NSNumber(value: false)

let options = [
  WKAudioRecorderControllerOptionsActionTitleKey : "Audio Recorder",
  WKAudioRecorderControllerOptionsAlwaysShowActionTitleKey : yes,
  WKAudioRecorderControllerOptionsAutorecordKey : no,
  WKAudioRecorderControllerOptionsMaximumDurationKey : oneMinute
] as [AnyHashable : Any]
```

Last but not least, present your audio recorder to the user and then set the status accordingly:

```
presentAudioRecorderController(
  withOutputURL: url,
  preset: WKAudioRecorderPreset.wideBandSpeech,
  options: options){
    success, error in

    defer{
      self.dismissAudioRecorderController()
    }

    guard success && error == nil else{
      self.status = "Failed to record"
      return
    }

    self.status = "Successfully recorded"

}
```

10.14 Playing Local and Remote Audio and Video in Your Watch App

Problem

You want to play audio or video files, whether they are saved locally or online.

Solution

Use the `presentMediaPlayerControllerWithURL(_:options:completion:)` instance method of your interface controller (`WKInterfaceController`). Close the media player with the `dismissMediaPlayerController()` method.

Discussion

The first parameter to this method is just the URL from which the media must be loaded. The `options` parameter is a dictionary that can have the following keys:

`WKMediaPlayerControllerOptionsAutoplayKey`

A Boolean value (wrapped inside an `NSNumber` instance) that dictates whether the media should autoplay when it is opened. This is set to `false` by default.

`WKMediaPlayerControllerOptionsStartTimeKey`

The number of seconds (of type `TimeInterval`) into the media where you want to start it.

`WKMediaPlayerControllerOptionsVideoGravityKey`

A value of type `WKVideoGravity` (place its raw integer value in your dictionary) that dictates the scaling of the video. You can, for instance, specify `WKVideoGravity.ResizeAspectFill`.

`WKMediaPlayerControllerOptionsLoopsKey`

A Boolean value (wrapped inside `NSNumber`) that specifies whether the media should loop automatically. The default is `false`.

For this recipe, you are going to create a UI similar to that in Recipe 10.13 (see Figure 10-47). The UI looks like Figure 10-48.

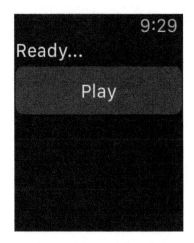

Figure 10-48. Label to show the current status, and a button to start the playback

Hook up the label to an outlet called `statusLbl` and the action of the button to a method called `play()`. Then create a variable in your code called `status` of type `String`, just as you did in Recipe 10.13. In the `play()` method, first construct your URL:

```
guard let url = URL(string: "http://localhost:8888/video.mp4") else{
  status = "Could not create url"
  return
}
```

I am running MAMP (the free version) on my computer and I'm hosting a video called *video.mp4*. You can download lots of public domain files by just searching online.

You want the media player to do the following:

- Autoplay the video.
- Loop the video.
- Resize the video so that it fills the entire screen.
- Start at 4 seconds into the video.

So, construct the options dictionary as follows:

```
let gravity = WKVideoGravity.resizeAspectFill.rawValue

let options = [
  WKMediaPlayerControllerOptionsAutoplayKey : NSNumber(value: true),
  WKMediaPlayerControllerOptionsStartTimeKey : 4.0 as TimeInterval,
```

```
    WKMediaPlayerControllerOptionsVideoGravityKey : gravity,
    WKMediaPlayerControllerOptionsLoopsKey : NSNumber(value: true),
    ] as [AnyHashable : Any]
```

Now start the media player and handle any possible errors:

```
presentMediaPlayerController(with: url, options: options) {
    didPlayToEnd, endTime, error in

    self.dismissMediaPlayerController()

    if let error = error{
        self.status = "Error occurred \(error)"
        return
    }

    if didPlayToEnd{
        self.status = "Played to end of the file"
    } else {
        self.status = "Did not play to end of file. End time = \(endTime)"
    }

}
```

CHAPTER 11

Contacts

The Contacts framework is for those who want to import, show, select, modify, and save contacts on a user's iOS device. This framework is fully compatible with Swift's lingo and is very easy to work with. At the heart of the Contacts framework is the `CNContact` object, which represents a contact. You get access to the Contacts database using the `CNContactStore` class.

Every time you want to access the address book, whether you are trying to create a new contact or fetch an existing one, you need to ensure that you have sufficient access to the address book. You can check your access privileges using the `authoriza tionStatus(for:)` class method of your contact store. This method takes in one parameter of type `CNEntityType`. You can pass the value of `Contacts` to this method, for instance, to ask for access to the user's contacts. If you do not have access, you can use the `requestAccess(for:completionHandler:)` method of your contact store to request access.

The concept of a *partial contact* is important enough to cover now as well. A partial contact is a contact whose properties have not all been fetched from the store yet. For instance, perhaps you can fetch only a contact's first and last name, not her profile photo or email addresses. This is a partial contact. A partial contact's other information—such as email addresses—that has not been fetched yet can later be fetched from the store using her identifier (part of the `CNContact` object).

Some of the classes that are part of the Contacts framework have immutable and mutable flavors. An example is the `CNContact` and `CNMutableContact` classes. The former is a contact that you have fetched from the store and just use in your app, while the latter is a contact that you have created in your app and want to save into the store.

Contact objects on iOS are thread-safe. I suggest that you do all your fetch operations on a background thread. Fetch the contacts in the background and safely display your contacts on your UI by accessing the same contact objects on the main thread.

 In this chapter, it's best to always reset the contents of your address book on the simulator by resetting the simulator before testing the code in each recipe, unless I've explicitly specified not to. This is just to make sure that every recipe is working with a clear state of the address book database. You can find the Contacts app on your simulator. It should look like Figure 11-1 in a clear state.

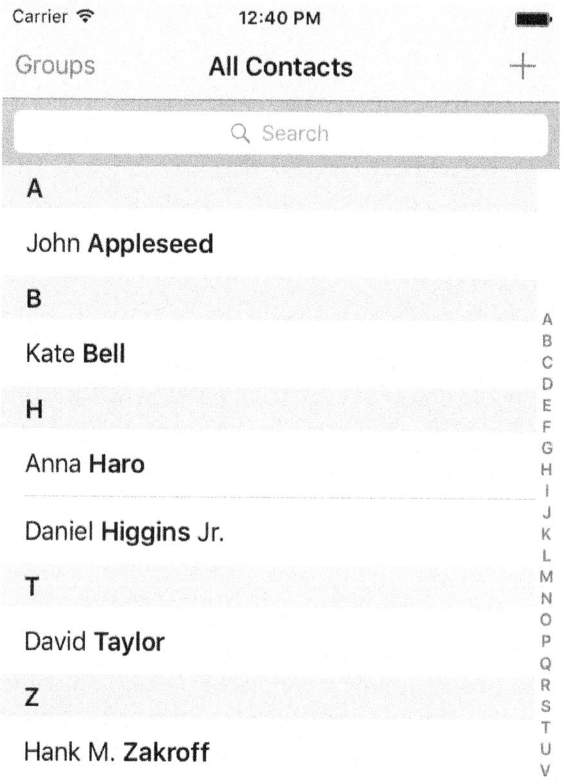

Carrier 📶	12:40 PM	🔋

Groups **All Contacts** +

🔍 Search

A

John **Appleseed**

B

Kate **Bell**

H

Anna **Haro**

Daniel **Higgins** Jr.

T

David **Taylor**

Z

Hank M. **Zakroff**

Figure 11-1. Clean state of the Contacts app on the simulator

11.1 Creating Contacts

Problem

You want to insert a new contact into the Contacts database.

Solution

Follow these steps:

1. Request access to the database if you don't already have it.
2. Create an instance of the CNMutableContact class.
3. Set its various properties, such as givenName, middleName, and familyName.
4. Instantiate CNSaveRequest, call the addContact(_:toContainerWithIdenti fier:) method on it, and pass your contact to it. Set the container ID to nil.
5. Once you have the request, execute it on your store instance using execute(_:).

Discussion

Create a single view app and first ask for permission to access contacts on the user's device:

```
// this is a separate helper class
public final class ContactAuthorizer{

  public class func authorizeContacts(completionHandler
    : @escaping (_ succeeded: Bool) -> Void){

    switch CNContactStore.authorizationStatus(for: .contacts){
    case .authorized:
      completionHandler(true)
    case .notDetermined:
      CNContactStore().requestAccess(for: .contacts){succeeded, err in
        completionHandler(err == nil && succeeded)
      }
    default:
      completionHandler(false)
    }

  }

}

// put this in your app delegate
func application(
  _ application: UIApplication,
  didFinishLaunchingWithOptions
  launchOptions: [UIApplicationLaunchOptionsKey : Any]? = nil) -> Bool {

  ContactAuthorizer.authorizeContacts {succeeded in
    if succeeded{
      self.createContact()
    } else{
      print("Not handled")
    }
```

```
  }
    return true
}
```

After we get the permission here, we're calling the `createContact()` method that we are just about to code. Also, we're using a property on the class that is our instance of the contact store:

```
var store = CNContactStore()
```

In the `createContact()` method, first let's create the basics of the contact object with the name and such:

```
let fooBar = CNMutableContact()
fooBar.givenName = "Foo"
fooBar.middleName = "A."
fooBar.familyName = "Bar"
fooBar.nickname = "Fooboo"
```

Then we set the profile photo:

```
// profile photo
if let img = UIImage(named: "apple"),
  let data = UIImagePNGRepresentation(img){
  fooBar.imageData = data
}
```

 I've included a profile photo that I can use in the app. You don't have to do that if you don't want to. This code will work even if you don't have a profile photo by jumping over this section if the image cannot be found.

Now we're going to set the user's phone numbers by setting an array of `CNLabeled Value` on the `phoneNumbers` property of the contact object. Labeled values are instances of the aforementioned class and can have a label and a value. The label is a string such as `CNLabelHome` or `CNLabelWork`, and the value, in the case of a phone number, is an instance of the `CNPhoneNumber` class:

```
// set the phone numbers
let homePhone = CNLabeledValue(label: CNLabelHome,
                               value: CNPhoneNumber(stringValue: "123"))
let workPhone = CNLabeledValue(label: CNLabelWork,
                               value: CNPhoneNumber(stringValue: "567"))
fooBar.phoneNumbers = [homePhone, workPhone]
```

We'll then set the email addresses for this person by manipulating the `emailAd dresses` property of the contact. This property also accepts an array of `CNLabeled Value`. The values of this labeled object are the email addresses, as string objects:

```
// set the email addresses
let homeEmail = CNLabeledValue(label: CNLabelHome,
                               value: "foo@home" as NSString)
let workEmail = CNLabeledValue(label: CNLabelWork,
                               value: "bar@home" as NSString)
fooBar.emailAddresses = [homeEmail, workEmail]
```

Next up, let's write some information in this contact about her job using the job Title, organizationName, and departmentName properties:

```
// job info
fooBar.jobTitle = "Chief Awesomeness Manager (CAM)"
fooBar.organizationName = "Pixolity"
fooBar.departmentName = "IT"
```

After that, we'll set the Facebook and Twitter profiles of this user. We do that by setting the value of the socialProfiles array on the contact. This array takes items of type CNLabeledValue, and the value of each one of these labeled objects should be of type CNSocialProfile. We can set the service for each of the profiles using constants such as the following:

- CNSocialProfileServiceFacebook
- CNSocialProfileServiceTwitter
- CNSocialProfileServiceLinkedIn
- CNSocialProfileServiceFlickr

```
// social media
let facebookProfile = CNLabeledValue(label: "Facebook", value:
  CNSocialProfile(
    urlString: nil, username: "foobar",
    userIdentifier: nil, service: CNSocialProfileServiceFacebook))

let twitterProfile = CNLabeledValue(label: "Twitter", value:
  CNSocialProfile(
    urlString: nil, username: "foobar",
    userIdentifier: nil, service: CNSocialProfileServiceTwitter))

fooBar.socialProfiles = [facebookProfile, twitterProfile]
```

We're also going to set some instant messaging information for our contact, such as her Skype and AIM information. To do this, we need to set the value of the instantMessageAddresses property, which takes in an array of, you guessed it, CNLabeledValue. Each of these values should be of type CNInstantMessageAddress, and the service inside each message address object can be a string such as:

- CNInstantMessageServiceSkype
- CNInstantMessageServiceAIM
- CNInstantMessageServiceMSN

- CNInstantMessageServiceYahoo

```
// instant messaging
let skypeAddress = CNLabeledValue(label: "Skype", value:
  CNInstantMessageAddress(username: "foobar",
                         service: CNInstantMessageServiceSkype))
let aimAddress = CNLabeledValue(label: "AIM", value:
  CNInstantMessageAddress(username: "foobar",
                         service: CNInstantMessageServiceAIM))
fooBar.instantMessageAddresses = [skypeAddress, aimAddress]
```

We can also set some notes on our contact using the note property, which is just a string:

```
// some additional notes
fooBar.note = "Some additional notes"
```

Next, we need to set the birthday property. This is a property of type DateCompo nents:

```
// birthday
var birthday = DateComponents()
birthday.year = 1980
birthday.month = 9
birthday.day = 27
fooBar.birthday = birthday
```

Every contact also has a property named dates that can contain dates such as the user's anniversary. This is an array of CNLabeledValue objects. We can set the anniversary for this user as follows:

```
// anniversary
let anniversaryDate = NSDateComponents()
anniversaryDate.month = 6
anniversaryDate.day = 13

let anniversary = CNLabeledValue(label: "Anniversary",
                                value: anniversaryDate)

fooBar.dates = [anniversary]
```

 We don't set a year for the anniversary because an anniversary is a repeating event.

We're finally done with our contact and can save her into the contact store:

```
// saving the contact to the contact store
let request = CNSaveRequest()
request.add(fooBar, toContainerWithIdentifier: nil)
```

```
do{
  try store.execute(request)
  print("Successfully stored the contact")
} catch let err{
  print("Failed to save the contact. \(err)")
}
```

 If you run this code *n* times on the same device, you will get *n* of the same contacts. The Contacts database does not prevent multiple saves on the same contact. They become different contacts eventually. It is our responsibility to avoid this.

And now our contact appears in the list (Figure 11-2).

Carrier 📶   2:35 PM   📶 🔋

❮ All Contacts   Edit

Foo A. Bar
"Fooboo"
Chief Awesomeness Manager (CAM) -
IT
Pixolity

home   📞
1 (23)

work   📞
567

FaceTime   📹

home
foo@home

work
bar@home

birthday
September 27, 1980

Anniversary
June 13

Facebook
foobar

Figure 11-2. The new contact in all its glory

11.2 Searching for Contacts

Problem

You want to search the contacts available on a device.

Solution

There are various ways of fetching contacts from a store. Here are some of them, in no particular order:

`unifiedContacts(matching:keysToFetch:)` *method of* `CNContactStore`
   This allows you to fetch all contacts that match a certain predicate.

`enumerateContacts(with:usingBlock:)` *method of* `CNContactStore`
   This allows you to enumerate through all contacts that match a fetch request. The fetch request can have a predicate if you want it to. Otherwise, you can use this method with a request object that does *not* have a predicate, in order to fetch *all* contacts.

`unifiedContact(withIdentifier:keysToFetch:)` *method of* `CNContactStore`
   This fetches only a single contact with a given identifier, if it can find one. Use this method to fetch properties for a partially fetched contact.

 The term "unified contacts" is iOS's way of showing that the contact objects that we get are intelligently merged from different sources, if available. If you have "Foo Bar" in your contacts and then you sign into Facebook with its iOS app and bring your Facebook contacts into your phone, and you have "Foo Bar" on Facebook as well, iOS will merge that contact for you into one contact. Foo Bar is now a unified contact.

Discussion

Let's have a look at a few examples. First, let's write some code that will find anybody in your address book whose name matches "John". Start by creating a predicate using the `predicateForContactsMatchingName(_:)` class method of the `CNContact` class:

```
let predicate = CNContact.predicateForContacts(matchingName: "john")
```

Then you are going to specify that you need the first and last names of the contacts that match that name:

```
let toFetch = [CNContactGivenNameKey as NSString, CNContactFamilyNameKey
               as NSString]
```

Once that is done, use the `unifiedContacts(matching:keysToFetch:)` method of the contact store to fetch the contacts matching your predicate. Go through all the matching contacts and print the first and last name of each alongside its `identifier` property:

```
do{
  let contacts = try store.unifiedContacts(
    matching: predicate, keysToFetch: toFetch)

  for contact in contacts{
    print(contact.givenName)
    print(contact.familyName)
    print(contact.identifier)
  }

} catch let err{
  print(err)
}
```

To ensure that I am doing the search on a background thread, I've wrapped this code inside `OperationQueue().addOperation(_:)`. I suggest that you do the same.

Every contact object has a handy property called `identifier`. This identifier usually looks like a UUID. If you keep an identifier to a contact, you can always refetch that contact using the `unifiedContact(withIdentifier:keysToFetch:)` method of `CNContactStore`. You do not have to explicitly fetch the `identifier` property of a contact. This identifier is fetched whether you want it or not, for every contact that you get from a store. So you can omit that in your `keysToFetch`.

Let's look at another example. This time you are going to do the same thing that you did in the previous example, but instead use the `CNContactFetchRequest` class mixed with the `enumerateContacts(with:usingBlock:)` method of `CNContactStore` to achieve the same results.

First, specify what properties in the contacts you are interested in reading:

```
let toFetch = [CNContactGivenNameKey as NSString, CNContactFamilyNameKey
               as NSString]
```

Next, construct your fetch request using these properties:

```
let request = CNContactFetchRequest(keysToFetch: toFetch)
request.predicate = CNContact.predicateForContacts(matchingName: "john")
```

Then fetch the contacts with the aforementioned method:

```
do{
  try store.enumerateContacts(with: request) {
    contact, stop in
    print(contact.givenName)
    print(contact.familyName)
    print(contact.identifier)
  }
} catch let err{
  print(err)
}
```

The block that you pass to this method has two parameters. The first is the contact. The second is a Boolean *pointer* that you can set to `true` whenever you want to exit this enumeration. You can do that like this:

```
stop.memory = true
```

How about looking at another example. Let's say that you want to fetch all contacts whose name is similar to "Foo." You then want to find out whether they have a profile photo. If they do, you will refetch those contacts and get their profile photos. The purpose of this exercise is to show you that if you are interested in contacts with photos, it is best to first see whether they have photos, and only if they do fetch their profile photos. Start by defining the keys that you want to fetch and asking for a key that tells you whether a contact has a photo:

```
var toFetch = [CNContactImageDataAvailableKey as NSString]
```

Then define your predicate:

```
let predicate = CNContact.predicateForContacts(matchingName: "foo")
```

Next, find all contacts that match your predicate:

```
let contacts = try store.unifiedContacts(matching: predicate,
                        keysToFetch: toFetch)
```

 The previous statement must be wrapped inside a do{}catch{} block; otherwise, it won't compile. I am not writing that statement here in the book because I want to explain the code step by step. If I paste the do{}catch{}, I'll have to paste the whole code in a gigantic block and that's not very good.

Now that you have your contacts, go through them and find only the ones that *do* have an image:

```
for contact in contacts{
  guard contact.imageDataAvailable else{
    continue
  }

  ...
```

The CNContact class offers an isKeyAvailable(_:) method that returns true or false depending on whether or not a given key is available for access on a contact. So here you are going to ask whether your contacts have images (the CNContactImageDa taKey key), and if they do, you are going to read the image:

```
//have we fetched image data?
if contact.isKeyAvailable(CNContactImageDataKey){
  print(contact.givenName)
  print(contact.identifier)
  if let imageData = contact.imageData,
    let image = UIImage(data: imageData){
    print(image)
  }
}
else {

  ...
```

 This example is for demonstration purposes—none of your contacts at this point will have images because you have not fetched the images yet in your original fetch request. The primary goal here is to teach you how to use the isKeyAvailable(_:) method.

If the contacts don't have their image data available at this point (which they won't!), you will use the identifier of each one of them and refetch them, but this time specifying that you need the image data as well:

```
else {
  toFetch += [CNContactImageDataKey as NSString,
             CNContactGivenNameKey as NSString]
  do{
    let contact = try store.unifiedContact(
      withIdentifier: contact.identifier, keysToFetch: toFetch)
    print(contact.givenName)

    if contact.isKeyAvailable(CNContactImageDataKey),
      let imageData = contact.imageData,
      let image = UIImage(data: imageData){
      print(image)
    }
    print(contact.identifier)
  } catch let err{
    print(err)
  }
}
```

And that's it, really. If you have the identifier of a contact, you can fetch that contact quite easily, as we saw. Now let's say that you do have this identifier saved somewhere inside your app and you want to directly fetch that contact. You do that using the `unifiedContact(withIdentifier:keysToFetch:)` method of the contact store:

```
OperationQueue().addOperation{[unowned store] in
  let id = "AECF6A0E-6BCB-4A46-834F-1D8374E6FE0A:ABPerson"
  let toFetch = [CNContactGivenNameKey as NSString,
    CNContactFamilyNameKey as NSString]

  do{

    let contact = try store.unifiedContact(withIdentifier: id,
                                 keysToFetch: toFetch)

    print(contact.givenName)
    print(contact.familyName)
    print(contact.identifier)

  } catch let err{
    print(err)
  }
}
```

See Also

Recipe 11.1

11.3 Updating Contacts

Problem

You have an existing contact whose properties you want to update.

Solution

Call the `mutableCopy()` method of your `CNContact` class. This will give you an instance of `CNMutableContact`. Once you have a mutable contact, you can change her properties as you would with a contact of type `CNContact`. Once done editing, instantiate `CNSaveRequest`, issue the `updateContact(_:)` method on it, and pass your mutable contact to that method. Now that you have the request object, pass it to the `execute(_:)` method of your store to update the contact.

Discussion

Let's check out an example. Let's say that we want to find a contact named "John" (using the steps outlined in Recipe 11.2) and then add a new email address to his contact information, in case it's not already set. Figure 11-3 shows the contact we will change. The contact comes prefilled in your iOS simulator, with only one work email address. We are going to add another work email to this list:

```
OperationQueue().addOperation{[unowned store] in
  let predicate = CNContact.predicateForContacts(matchingName: "john")
  let toFetch = [CNContactEmailAddressesKey as NSString]

  do{
    let contacts = try store.unifiedContacts(matching: predicate,
                                             keysToFetch: toFetch)

    guard contacts.count > 0 else{
      print("No contacts found")
      return
    }

    // only do this to the first contact matching our criteria
    guard let contact = contacts.first else{
      return
    }

    ...
```

Carrier 🖗	4:27 PM	▬▶
❮ All Contacts		Edit

JA **John Appleseed**

mobile
(888) 555-5512

home
(888) 555-1212

work
John-Appleseed@mac.com

Figure 11-3. Current state of the contact

 We are only adding this new email to the *first* contact that matches our criteria.

Now we have a contact object that matches our criteria. Let's see whether he already has this email address, and bail out if he does:

```
let newEmail = "newemail@work.com"

for email in contact.emailAddresses{
  if email.value as String == newEmail{
    print("This contact already has this email")
    return
  }
}
```

Now that we are sure he didn't have this email address already in the list, we will add it:

```
let john = contact.mutableCopy() as! CNMutableContact

let emailAddress = CNLabeledValue(label: CNLabelWork,
                                  value: "newemail@work.com" as NSString)

john.emailAddresses.append(emailAddress)

let req = CNSaveRequest()
req.update(john)

try store.execute(req)

print("Successfully added an email")
```

Now if we look at our contact in the list, we can see the new email address added (see Figure 11-4).

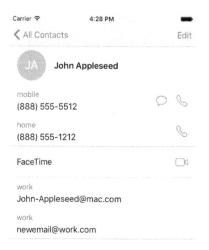

Figure 11-4. The new email address is added to our contact

Another example would be to go through all our contacts and fetch all their notes. If there is no note set for a contact, we'll set up a dummy note and save that contact back into the database. We can therefore use the CNContactNoteKey key in our fetch request as shown here:

```
OperationQueue().addOperation{[unowned store] in
  let keys = [CNContactNoteKey as NSString]
  let req = CNContactFetchRequest(keysToFetch: keys)
  do{
    try store.enumerateContacts(with: req){contact, stop in
      if contact.note.characters.count == 0{

        let updated = contact.mutableCopy() as! CNMutableContact
        updated.note = "Some note"
        let req = CNSaveRequest()
        req.update(updated)
        do{
          try store.execute(req)
          print("Successfully added a note")
        } catch let err{
          print(err)
        }
      }
    }
  } catch let err{
    print(err)
  }
}
```

As another example, we can go through all the contacts on the device by fetching their given name (CNContactGivenNameKey) and last name (CNContactFamilyName Key). Then we can look at these names and find any characters in them that are *not* letters (numbers, punctuation), and remove those illegal characters. First let's read the contacts and their first names and last names, and also define what we consider illegal characters:

```
OperationQueue().addOperation{[unowned store] in
  let keys = [CNContactGivenNameKey as NSString,
    CNContactFamilyNameKey as NSString]
  let req = CNContactFetchRequest(keysToFetch: keys)
  do{
    try store.enumerateContacts(with: req){contact, stop in

      let illegalCharacters = CharacterSet.letters
        .inverted

      let first = NSString(string: contact.givenName)
      let last = NSString(string: contact.familyName)

      ...
```

Then we find out whether the first or the last names have any illegal characters:

```
let foundIllegalCharactersInFirstName =
  first.rangeOfCharacter(from: illegalCharacters).location
    != NSNotFound

let foundIllegalCharactersInLastName =
  last.rangeOfCharacter(from: illegalCharacters).location
    != NSNotFound
```

If any illegal characters were found in either the first or the last name, we remove them and then save the contact back into the database:

```
if foundIllegalCharactersInFirstName ||
  foundIllegalCharactersInLastName{

  let cleanFirstName =
    (first.components(separatedBy: illegalCharacters)
      as NSArray).componentsJoined(by: "")

  let cleanLastName =
    (last.components(separatedBy: illegalCharacters)
      as NSArray).componentsJoined(by: "")


  let newContact = contact.mutableCopy() as! CNMutableContact
  let req = CNSaveRequest()
  newContact.givenName = cleanFirstName
  newContact.familyName = cleanLastName
  req.update(newContact)

  do{
    try store.execute(req)
    print("Successfully removed illegal characters from contact")
  } catch let err{
    print(err)
  }

}
```

See Also

Recipe 11.1

11.4 Deleting Contacts

Problem

You want to delete a contact on a device.

Solution

Follow these steps:

1. Find your contact using what you learned in Recipe 11.2.
2. Instantiate an object of type CNSaveRequest.
3. Issue the deleteContact(_:) function on the request and pass your mutable contact to it.
4. Execute your request using the execute(_:) method of your contact store.

 Deleting a contact from a store is irreversible. I suggest that you test your code on the simulator first and, if possible, ask the users first whether they allow a contact to be deleted.

Discussion

Let's have a look at an example. We want to find all contacts named John and then delete the first one that we find (I am not showing an alert asking the user whether this is OK or not, because that's not the focus of this recipe—I suggest that you do so, though):

```
OperationQueue().addOperation{[unowned store] in
  let predicate = CNContact.predicateForContacts(matchingName: "john")
  let toFetch = [CNContactEmailAddressesKey as NSString]

  do{

    let contacts = try store.unifiedContacts(matching: predicate,
                                             keysToFetch: toFetch)

    guard contacts.count > 0 else{
      print("No contacts found")
      return
    }

    // only do this to the first contact matching our criteria
    guard let contact = contacts.first else{
      return
    }

    let req = CNSaveRequest()
    let mutableContact = contact.mutableCopy() as! CNMutableContact
    req.delete(mutableContact)

    do{
      try store.execute(req)
      print("Successfully deleted the user")
```

```
      } catch let e{
        print("Error = \(e)")
      }

  } catch let err{
     print(err)
  }
}
```

See Also

Recipe 11.7

11.5 Formatting Contact Data

Problem

You want to present a local contact's name and postal address in a localized and read-able way, regardless of the current language on the user's device.

Solution

Use an instance of the `CNContactFormatter` or the `CNPostalAddressFormatter` class. The former one can easily be used to format the contact's name, and the latter is self-explanatory.

Discussion

The `CNContactFormatter` class allows you to format the name of any contact, according to the localization settings of the current device. For instance, in some languages, the last name of a person may be mentioned first. You can use the `string(from:style:)` function of this method to get the full name.

 You must fetch the full name of a contact from the store for this class to work at all. Otherwise, you might get an exception.

We can build on Recipe 11.2 by writing a simple extension on `CNContactStore` that allows us to fetch the first contact that it finds with a given name. I've named this method `firstUnifiedContactMatching(name:toFetch:output:)`, and it calls my output block when it finds the contact or if an error occurs. You don't have to know the full implementation of this method because you already know how you can fetch a contact with a given name.

So, let's look at an example where we fetch a contact from the store and print his full name to the console:

```
let toFetch =
  CNContactFormatter.descriptorForRequiredKeys(for: .fullName)

store.firstUnifiedContactMatching(name: "john", toFetch: [toFetch]){
  guard let contact = $0 else{
    return
  }

  guard let name = CNContactFormatter().string(from: contact) else{
    return
  }

  print("The name of the contact is \(name)")

}
```

Note that I am using the `descriptorForRequiredKeys(for:)` class method of the `CNContactFormatter` class to get an object of type `CNKeyDescriptor` and then pass the results to `firstUnifiedContactMatching(name:toFetch:output:)` when fetching the contact. The aforementioned method of `CNContactFormatter` tells the system what properties of the contact to fetch—in this case, all the properties that are required for the full name, including the first, middle, and last names.

Now imagine that we want to find a contact's localized phonetic name. A phonetic name is the name of a person written as it is pronounced, rather than how the name is spelled. For instance, a person's name might be Julian, but in Swedish, because the J is pronounced as "you," this name would be pronounced as "you-lian." So "you-lian" is the phonetic equivalent of the name "Julian" in Swedish. These phonetic names are very useful for Siri. A Swedish speaker will ask Siri to phone up "you-lian" and Siri will have no idea who that is unless the phonetic name has been set for that user.

Create a contact in your list. Set his first name to "Julian" and last name to "Julianson." Then tap the "add field" button at the bottom of the contact creation screen and add the phonetic first and last name fields to the contact (see Figure 11-5).

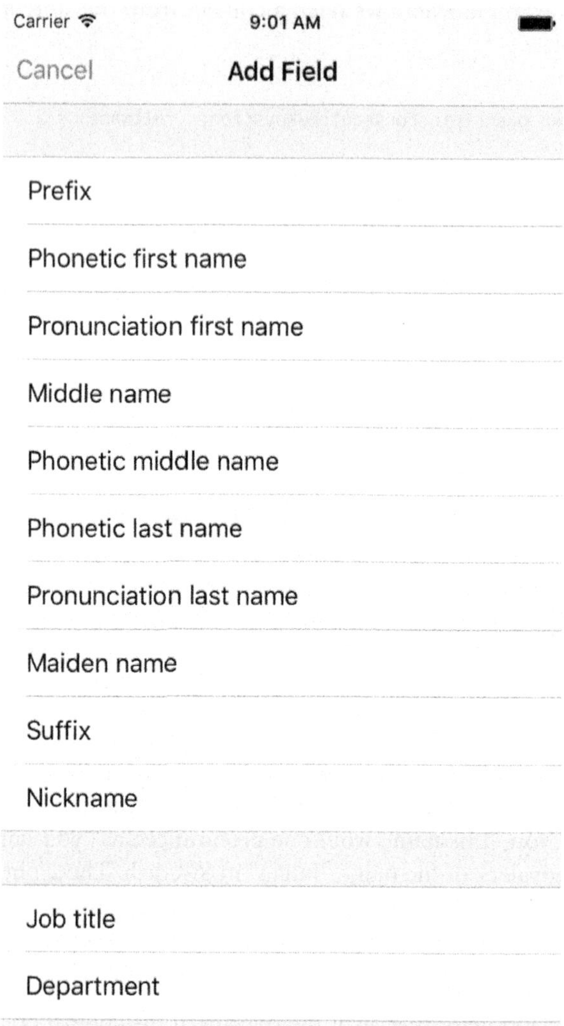
Carrier
9:01 AM
Cancel
Add Field
Prefix
Phonetic first name
Pronunciation first name
Middle name
Phonetic middle name
Phonetic last name
Pronunciation last name
Maiden name
Suffix
Nickname
Job title
Department

Figure 11-5. Add the phonetic first name and last name fields to your new contact

Set the phonetic first name to "Youlian" and the phonetic last name to "Youlianson," so your contact looks like Figure 11-6.

Figure 11-6. Your contact's phonetic name is also displayed, if set

Let's now look at an example where we fetch the phonetic name of a contact and then format it according to the localization on the current device. First, we need to find the fields in the contact store for phonetic name. We do that using the `descriptor ForRequiredKeys(for:)` class method of `CNContactFormatter`, this time passing the value of `phoneticFullName` to it. Because the `string(from:style:)` class method of the `CNContactFormatter` class by default reads the full name, and not the phonetic full name, we will have to start using the `string(from:style:)` instance method of this class instead. The last parameter to this function allows us to pass a style of type `CNContactFormatterStyle` that can be set to `FullName` or `phoneticFullName`:

```
let style = CNContactFormatterStyle.phoneticFullName

let toFetch =
  CNContactFormatter.descriptorForRequiredKeys(for: style)

store.firstUnifiedContactMatching(name: "julian", toFetch: [toFetch]){

  guard let contact = $0 else{
    return
  }

  guard let name = CNContactFormatter
    .string(from: contact, style: style) else{
      return
  }

  print("The phonetic name of the contact is \(name)")

}
```

Aside from getting the localized full name of a contact, you can also get her address information, again properly localized, using the `CNPostalAddressFormatter` class. Follow these steps:

1. Fetch your contact, making sure to include the `CNContactPostalAddressesKey` key.
2. Get the address from the contact using the `postalAddresses` property of `CNContact`. This will give you a value of type `CNLabeledValue`. Get the `value` of this labeled value and cast it to `CNPostalAddress`.
3. Instantiate `CNPostalAddressFormatter`.
4. Pass the postal address to the `string(from:)` method of your postal address formatter to get the formatted address:

```
let toFetch = [CNContactPostalAddressesKey as NSString]

store.firstUnifiedContactMatching(name: "john", toFetch: toFetch){
  guard let contact = $0 else{
    return
  }

  guard let firstAddress = contact.postalAddresses.first else{
    print("no postal address could be found")
    return
  }

  let formatter = CNPostalAddressFormatter()
  let formattedAddress = formatter.string(from: firstAddress.value)

  print("The address is \(formattedAddress)")

}
```

11.6 Picking Contacts with a Prebuilt System UI

Problem

You want to use a built-in system dialog to allow your users to pick contacts from their contact store.

Solution

Use an instance of the `CNContactPickerViewController` class inside the `ContactsUI` framework.

 Instances of the `CNContactPickerViewController` class cannot be pushed to the stack. They need to be presented modally. Use the `present(_:animated:completion:)` method of your view or navigation controller to display the contact picker modally.

Discussion

Let's say that you want to allow the user to pick a contact. You will then attempt to read the phone numbers from that contact. Instances of the CNContactPickerView Controller class have a property called delegate of type CNContactPickerDelegate.

Some of the interesting methods in this delegate are:

contactPickerDidCancel(_:)
> This gets called when the user cancels their request to pick a contact.

contactPicker(_:didSelectContact:)
> This gets called when the user picks a contact from the list.

In this example, we want to allow the user to pick a contact, whereupon we will read all the phone numbers from that contact. Place a button in your storyboard and hook that button to a method in your code called pickaContact(). In that code, we present a simple contact picker:

```
let controller = CNContactPickerViewController()

controller.delegate = self

navigationController?.present(controller,
                      animated: true, completion: nil)
```

> All this should be done inside a view controller that conforms to CNContactPickerDelegate.

Then, when the user picks a contact, just print out all the phone numbers from that contact, if any, to the console:

```
func contactPickerDidCancel(_ picker: CNContactPickerViewController) {
  print("Cancelled picking a contact")
}

func contactPicker(_ picker: CNContactPickerViewController,
               didSelectContact contact: CNContact) {

  print("Selected a contact")

  if contact.isKeyAvailable(CNContactPhoneNumbersKey){
    // this is an extension I've written on CNContact
    contact.printPhoneNumbers()
  } else {
    /*
      TOOD: partially fetched, use what you've learned in this chapter to
```

```
    fetch the rest of this contact
    */
    print("No phone numbers are available")
  }

}
```

 The printPhoneNumbers() function is a custom extension on CNContact that I've written. You don't have to know the implementation of that function, as it's not relevant to this recipe. You already know how to do this using what you learned in Recipe 11.2.

In this example, we are looking for contacts with phone numbers, but the user is allowed to pick any contact, even if that contact has no phone numbers. How do we remedy this? A property called predicateForEnablingContact of type NSPredicate, on instances of CNContactPickerViewController, allows us to specify which contacts should be enabled and which ones should be disabled. Here we can create a predicate that checks the @count of the phoneNumbers property. Also, for fun, let's say that we only want to allow contacts whose names start with "John" to be selectable (see Figure 11-7):

```
let controller = CNContactPickerViewController()

controller.delegate = self

controller.predicateForEnablingContact =
  NSPredicate(format:
    "phoneNumbers.@count > 0 && givenName BEGINSWITH 'John'",
            argumentArray: nil)

navigationController?.present(controller,
                             animated: true, completion: nil)
```

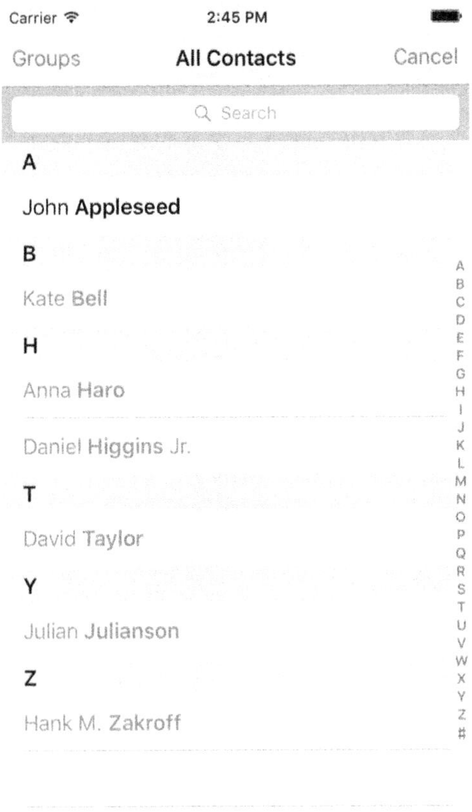

Figure 11-7. Only people whose names start with "John" and who have at least one phone number are retrieved

The `predicateForEnablingContact` property disables all contacts who do not pass the predicate, so that the user won't even be able to select those contacts. There is another property on `CNContactPickerViewController` that does something more interesting: `predicateForSelectionOfContact`. The contacts that pass this predicate will be selectable by the user so that when the user taps such a contact, the controller is dismissed and we get access to the contact object. The contacts that do not pass this predicate will still be selectable, but upon selection, their details will be shown to the user using the system UI. They won't be returned to our app:

```
let controller = CNContactPickerViewController()

controller.delegate = self

controller.predicateForSelectionOfContact =
```

```
  NSPredicate(format:
    "phoneNumbers.@count > 0",
            argumentArray: nil)

navigationController?.present(controller,
                      animated: true, completion: nil)
```

CNContactPickerViewController has another funky property—predicateForSelec
tionOfProperty—that dictates which property for any contact the user should be
able to pick. If you want to allow the user to pick a specific property—say the first
phone number—of any contact to be passed to your app, you also have to implement
the contactPicker(_:didSelectContactProperty:) method of the CNContactPick
erDelegate protocol. Let's write sample code that allows the user to pick any contact
as long as that contact has at least one phone number, and then to pick the first phone
number of that contact to be returned to our app:

```
let controller = CNContactPickerViewController()

controller.delegate = self

controller.predicateForEnablingContact =
  NSPredicate(format:
    "phoneNumbers.@count > 0",
            argumentArray: nil)

controller.predicateForSelectionOfProperty =
  NSPredicate(format: "key == 'phoneNumbers'", argumentArray: nil)

navigationController?.present(controller,
                      animated: true, completion: nil)
```

Then we'll provide an implementation of the contactPicker(_:didSelectContact
Property:) method:

```
func contactPicker(_ picker: CNContactPickerViewController,
               didSelect contactProperty: CNContactProperty) {

  print("Selected a property")

}
```

In addition to all of this, you can also allow the user to pick multiple contacts. Do
that by implementing the contactPicker(_:didSelectContacts:) method of the
CNContactPickerDelegate protocol (see Figure 11-8):

```
func contactPicker(_ picker: CNContactPickerViewController,
               didSelect contacts: [CNContact]) {
  print("Selected \(contacts.count) contacts")
}

// allows multiple selection mixed with contactPicker:didSelectContacts:
```

```
func example5(){
  let controller = CNContactPickerViewController()

  controller.delegate = self

  navigationController?.present(controller,
                            animated: true, completion: nil)
}
```

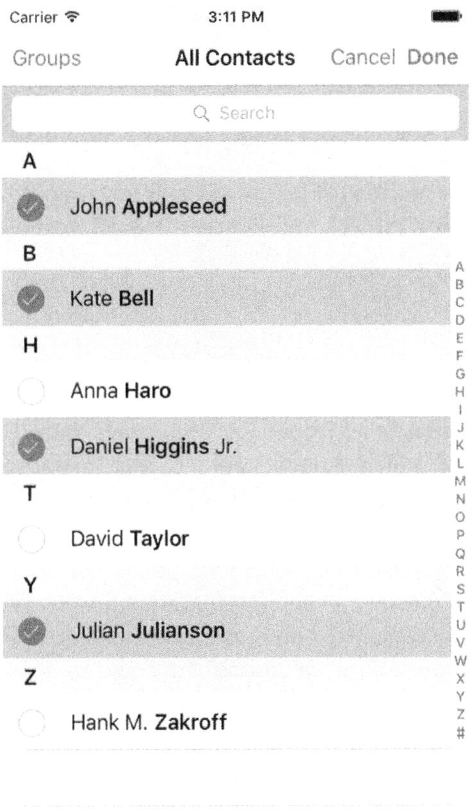

Figure 11-8. The user is able to select multiple contacts at the same time and return to our app at the end

See Also

Recipe 11.8

11.7 Creating Contacts with a Prebuilt System UI

Problem

You want to specify some basic information for a new contact and let a system UI and the user take care of the creation of this contact.

Solution

Follow these steps:

1. Create an instance of CNContactStore and ask for permission to use the store (see Recipe 11.1).
2. Create a contact of type CNMutableContact and put your default values in it. This is an optional step. You might want the user to create a whole new contact on her own, with no predefined values from your side.
3. Instantiate an object of type CNContactViewController using the forNewContact initializer and pass your contact to it.
4. Set the contactStore property of this view controller to a valid contact store instance.
5. Optionally, set the delegate property of this view controller to a valid delegate object that conforms to the CNContactViewControllerDelegate protocol.

Discussion

Recipe 11.1 covers how to create a contact programmatically. What if you have some basic information about a contact, or no information at all, and you want your user to supply the rest of the information? Of course, you could create a UI to allow the user to do that, but why do so if the SDK already comes with a prebuilt UI called CNContactViewController?

You can simply push an instance of the CNContactViewController class on to your navigation controller. When you become the delegate of this view controller, a delegate method named contactViewController(_:didCompleteWith:) will get called if the user cancels or accepts the contact creation. Use this method to dismiss (pop) the contact view controller:

```
func contactViewController(_ viewController: CNContactViewController,
                          didCompleteWith contact: CNContact?) {

  guard let nc = navigationController else {return}

  // whatever happens, pop back to our view controller
  defer{nc.popViewController(animated: true)}
```

```
guard let contact = contact else{
  print("The contact creation was cancelled")
  return
}

print("Contact was created successfully \(contact)")
}
```

Let's look at a simple example now. Create a simple contact with some basic information and then ask the user to complete the creation process:

```
let contact = CNContact().mutableCopy() as! CNMutableContact
contact.givenName = "Anthony"
contact.familyName = "Appleseed"

let controller = CNContactViewController(forNewContact: contact)
controller.contactStore = store
controller.delegate = self

navigationController?
  .pushViewController(controller, animated: true)
```

The user will see a UI similar to Figure 11-9.

Carrier 🗢	4:48 PM	🔋
Cancel	**New Contact**	Done

add photo — Anthony

Appleseed

Company

⊕ add phone

⊕ add email

Figure 11-9. The New Contact system UI is displayed, asking the user to finish off or cancel the contact creation

 The contact that you pass to the aforementioned initializer of CNContactViewController is optional. If you pass nil, the New Contact dialog that the user sees will be empty and the user will have to fill out every field in the UI.

See Also

Recipe 11.4

11.8 Displaying Contacts with a Prebuilt System UI

Problem

You want to use a built-in system UI to display an existing contact's information.

Solution

Use the `forContact` initializer of the `CNContactViewController` class and pass this method an instance of the `CNContact` that you want to display.

Discussion

Sometimes you might want to display information for a particular contact but don't want to write the whole UI yourself. Why would you? It's a lot of work to display *all* the information. That's where you can use the `CNContactViewController` class again.

This example uses my custom `firstUnifiedContactMatch ing(name:toFetch:output:)` method to fetch an existing contact. You learned about the implementation of this method in Recipe 11.2.

So this is what you are going to do: fetch a contact whose name matches "John" and display his information on the screen. Make sure that you fetch all the required keys for your contact. Otherwise, the controller won't be able to display the contact's information. You can get the list of required keys by calling the `descriptorForRequired Keys()` class function of the `CNContactViewController` class:

```
let toFetch = [CNContactViewController.descriptorForRequiredKeys()]
store.firstUnifiedContactMatching(name: "john", toFetch: toFetch){

  guard let contact = $0 else{
    print("No contact was found")
    return
  }

  let controller = CNContactViewController(for: contact)
  controller.contactStore = self.store
  controller.allowsEditing = false

  controller.displayedPropertyKeys =
    [CNContactEmailAddressesKey, CNContactPostalAddressesKey]
```

```
self.navigationController?
    .pushViewController(controller, animated: true)
```

}

By default, when a contact is displayed, the contact controller allows the user to edit that contact. You can disable that behavior by setting the allowsEditing property of the controller to false. Also bear in mind that you have to set the contactStore property of the controller to the same store from where you fetched your contact.

There is another interesting property on the controller: displayedPropertyKeys. As its name implies, it allows you to pass a series of contact property keys that have to be displayed. Other properties will be hidden. I have, in our code, enabled only email and postal addresses. The results are shown in Figure 11-10. Some other information, such as full name, is shown by default.

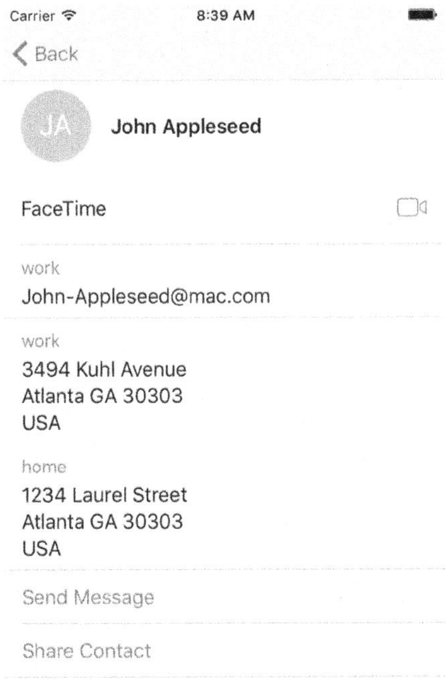

Figure 11-10. Displaying a contact

See Also

Recipe 11.6

CHAPTER 12

Extensions

Apple increased the number of extensions that we developers can write in the new iOS. One of the hot extensions that everybody seems to be talking about is the Safari Content Blocker, which allows developers to specify which URLs or resources should get blocked in Safari tabs.

Extensions are separate binaries that sit inside your app's bundle. They usually have their own naming convention and are contained in reserved folders inside your app bundle. It's best not to mention what they are called on disk, because Apple can change that at any time without us knowing. Because extensions sit in their own folders and have their own bundles, they do *not* share the same physical space as their container app. But, through some work, they *can* access the container app's resources, such as images and text.

12.1 Creating Safari Content Blockers

Problem

You want to create a content blocker that the user can add to her Safari browser for blocking specific web content.

Solution

Use the Safari Content Blocker extension.

Discussion

This is something I am very excited about. You can ignore the long list of content blockers popping up on the App Store every day from now on.

This is how the Apple blocker works. When you create an app, you can add a Safari Content Blocker extension to it. In that extension, you define the rules for your content blocking (whether you want to block images, stylesheets, etc.). The user can then, after opening your app at least once, go into the settings on her device and enable your content blocker. From now on, if she visits a web page that your content blocker applies to, she will see only the content that passes your filters.

Let's create a simple single view controller app and then add a new target to the app. On the target selection screen, under the iOS main section, choose Application Extension and then choose the Content Blocker Extension (see Figure 12-1).

Choose a template for your new target:				
iOS				
Application	Action	Content Blocker	Custom	Document
Framework & Library	Extension	Extension	Keyboard	Provider
Application Extension				
Apple Watch				
Test	Photo Editing	Share Extension	Shared Links	Spotlight Index
watchOS	Extension		Extension	Extension
Application				
Framework & Library				
OS X	17			
Application				
Framework & Library	Today			
Application Extension	Extension			
Test				
System Plug-in	Content Blocker Extension			
Other	This template builds a Safari Content Blocker application extension.			

Cancel   Previous   Next

Figure 12-1. Adding a new Content Blocker extension to an existing app

Give any name that you want to your extension. It doesn't really matter so much for this exercise.

Now go to the new extension's new file called *blockerList.json* and place the following content in it:

```
[
  {
    "action": {
      "type": "block"
    },
    "trigger": {
      "url-filter": ".*",
      "resource-type" : ["image"],
      "if-domain" : ["edition.cnn.com"]
    }
  }
]
```

Even though there is a specific type of formatting to this file, I think you can just read this as I've written it and understand what it is doing. It is blocking all images that are under the *edition.cnn.com* domain name. Now head to your app delegate and import the `SafariServices` framework. Every time you change your content blocker, you will have to go to the Settings application on the simulator and turn it off and on again so that the simulator understands that the extension is updated. We are now going to write a piece of code that automates that for us:

```
func applicationDidBecomeActive(_ application: UIApplication) {

  // TODO: replace this with your own content blocker's identifier
  let id = "se.pixolity.Creating-Safari-Content-Blockers.Image-Blocker"
  SFContentBlockerManager.reloadContentBlocker(withIdentifier: id) {error in
    guard error == nil else {
      // an error happened, handle it
      print("Failed to reload the blocker")
      return
    }
    print("Reloaded the blocker")
  }
}
```

Then reset your simulator and run your app. Send your app to the background, open Safari on the simulator, and type in **cnn.com**. This will redirect you to *http://edition.cnn.com/* (at the time of this writing). Safari will hit the filter we wrote and discard all the images. The results will be lovely. (Well, I don't know whether a website without images is lovely or not, but it's what we set out to do.)

A user can always enable or disable a content blocker. To do that, you can go to the Settings app on your device and in the search field type in **blocker**. Then tap the Content Blockers item that pops up (see Figure 12-2).

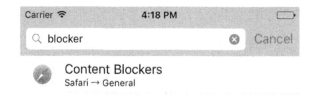

Figure 12-2. Searching for "blocker" will allow you to go directly to the Content Blockers settings section of Safari

From there, you can enable or disable available Safari content blockers (see Figure 12-3).

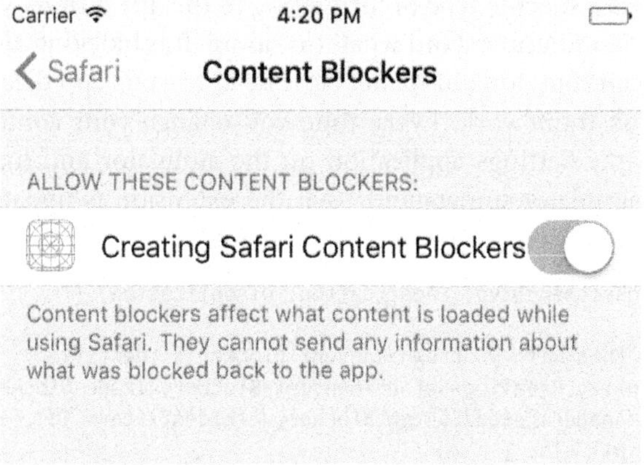

Figure 12-3. Our app is shown in the list of content blockers as the only available application as of now

Now that you have seen an example, let me bug you with some more details on that JSON file. That file contains an array of dictionaries with various configurations that you can enter. This book would grow very large if I thoroughly described everything there, so I will simply explain the options for each field through some pseudo-JSON code:

```
[
  {
    "action": {
      "type": "block" | "block-cookies" | "css-display-none",
      "selector" : This is a CSS selector that the action will be applied to
    },
    "trigger": {
      "url-filter": "this is a filter that will be applied on the WHOLE url",
      "url-filter-is-case-sensitive" : same as url-filter but case sensitive,
      "resource-type" : ["image" | "style-sheet" | "script" | "font" | etc],
```

```
      "if-domain" : [an array of actual domain names to apply filter on],
      "unless-domain" : [an array of domain names to exclude from filter],
      "load-type" : "first-party" | "third-party"
    }
  }
]
```

Armed with this knowledge, let's do some more experiments. Let's now block all a tags in *macrumors.com*:

```
{
  "action": {
    "type": "css-display-none",
    "selector" : "a"
  },
  "trigger": {
    "url-filter": ".*",
    "if-domain" : ["macrumors.com"]
  }
}
```

 I have no affiliation with nor any hate toward MacRumors—I find that website quite informative, actually. Check it out for yourself. I am using this website as an example only, and I am *not* suggesting that content on the website is worthy of blocking.

Or how about removing the a tag at the top of the *macrumors.com* homepage that has an id attribute equal to logo?

```
{
  "action": {
    "type": "css-display-none",
    "selector" : "a[id='logo']"
  },
  "trigger": {
    "url-filter": ".*",
    "if-domain" : ["macrumors.com"]
  }
}
```

Now let's have a look at another example. Let's start blocking all images on all websites except for *reddit.com*:

```
{
  "action": {
    "type": "block"
  },
  "trigger": {
    "url-filter": ".*",
    "resource-type" : ["image"],
    "unless-domain" : ["reddit.com"]
```

```
    }
}
```

Or how about blocking all elements of type a that have an href attribute on Apple's website?

```
{
  "action": {
    "type": "css-display-none",
    "selector" : "a[href]"
  },
  "trigger": {
    "url-filter": ".*",
    "if-domain" : ["apple.com"]
  }
}
```

See Also

Recipe 12.2

12.2 Creating Shared Links for Safari

Problem

You want to display your own links inside Safari's shared links on users' devices.

Solution

Add the new Shared Links Extension target to your existing app and code the extension. It is prepopulated, so you don't really have to do much.

Discussion

Shared links are like bookmarks, but lead to content defined in your app or a website. The links are visible inside Safari on iOS when the user taps the Bookmarks button and then the Shared Links icon. To get started, create a single view controller project and then add a new target to your project. On the target selection screen, under the iOS main section, choose Application Extension and then choose the Shared Links Extension (see Figure 12-4).

Choose a template for your new target:

iOS
  Application
  Framework & Library
  Application Extension
  Apple Watch
  Test
watchOS
  Application
  Framework & Library
OS X
  Application
  Framework & Library
  Application Extension
  Test
  System Plug-in
Other

Action Extension	Content Blocker Extension	Custom Keyboard	Document Provider
Photo Editing Extension	Share Extension	Shared Links Extension	Spotlight Index Extension
Today Extension			

Shared Links Extension

This template builds a Safari Shared Links application extension.

Cancel   Previous   **Next**

Figure 12-4. Creating a new Shared Links extension in Xcode

I suggest that you also add some proper icons to your app's bundle, because your app's icon will also appear in the list of shared links when iOS shows your shared link. You can just do a Google search for "public domain icon" and find some really awesome icons that you can use in your app. Also make sure to add a simple icon to your Shared Links extension, because our code will show this icon in the list. Your extension's icon will appear on the left side of the link and your app icon at the top right (see Figure 12-5).

Figure 12-5. The shared link's icon appears on the left and the app's icon in the upper-right corner

Then head to the new file called *RequestHandler.swift* that has been created in your extension. Xcode has already populated this file with all the code that you need to display your shared link. All you need to do is uncomment the line that starts with `exten sionItem.attachments`, load your extension's icon, and attach it to the extension item like so:

```
import Foundation

class RequestHandler: NSObject, NSExtensionRequestHandling {

  func beginRequest(with context: NSExtensionContext) {
    let extensionItem = NSExtensionItem()

    extensionItem.userInfo = [
      "uniqueIdentifier": "uniqueIdentifierForSampleItem",
      "urlString": "http://reddit.com/r/askreddit",
      "date": Date()
    ]

    extensionItem.attributedTitle = NSAttributedString(string: "Reddit")

    extensionItem.attributedContentText = NSAttributedString(
      string: "AskReddit, one of the best subreddits there is")

    guard let img = Bundle.main.url(forResource: "ExtIcon",
      withExtension: "png") else {
        context.completeRequest(returningItems: nil, completionHandler: nil)
        return
    }

    extensionItem.attachments = [NSItemProvider(contentsOf: img)!]

    context.completeRequest(returningItems: [extensionItem],
                       completionHandler: nil)
  }

}
```

Run your code and then open Safari on the device. Navigate to the Bookmarks button and then Shared Links to see your link displayed (Figure 12-6).

Figure 12-6. Your shared link is displayed in the list

The user can also subscribe to or unsubscribe from various shared link providers by tapping the Subscriptions button (see Figure 12-7).

Figure 12-7. The user can subscribe to or unsubscribe from shared links providers right in Safari

See Also

Recipe 12.1

12.3 Maintaining Your App's Indexed Content

Problem

You want to know when iOS is about to delete your indexed items and you would like to be able to provide new content to the search index.

This is an extension to the search capability explained in Recipe 13.2.

Solution

Add a Spotlight Index extension to your app and update the index right in your extension (see Figure 12-8).

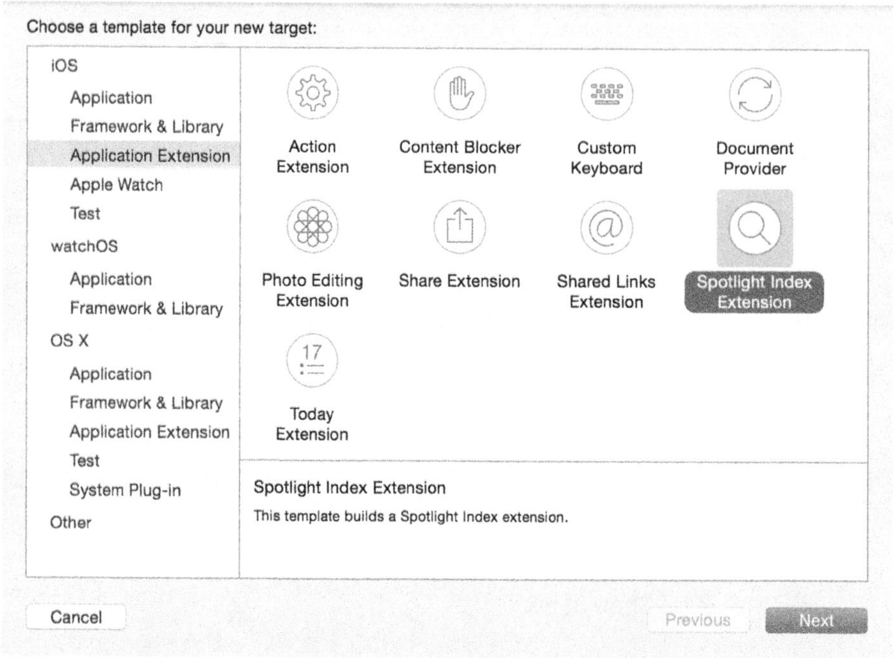

Figure 12-8. Adding a Spotlight Index extension will allow you to reindex your app's searchable content

Discussion

Every now and then, iOS has to clean up the search index on a device. When this happens, apps that have provided searchable content will be given a chance to reindex their items. To get started, create a Spotlight Index extension as shown in Figure 12-8. I've given mine the name of `Reindex`. It's up to you what you want to name your extension. Now you will get a class called `IndexRequestHandler` in your extension. It offers two methods:

- `searchableIndex(_:reindexAllSearchableItemsWithAcknowledgementHandler:)`
- `searchableIndex(_:reindexSearchableItemsWithIdentifiers:acknowledgementHandler:)`

The first method gets called when you are asked to reindex *all* your previously indexed items. This can happen if the index is corrupted on the device and you are asked to reindex all of your content. The second method will be called on your extension if you have to index specific items with the given identifiers. You will be given a function called an *acknowledgment handler* to call when you are done indexing again.

 In both of these methods, the first parameter that you are given is an index into which you have to index your items. Use that index instead of the default index.

Here is an example. Let's define a protocol that dictates what indexable items have to look like:

```
protocol Indexable{
  var id: String {get set}
  var title: String {get set}
  var description: String {get set}
  var url: URL? {get set}
  var thumbnail: UIImage? {get set}
}
```

And then a structure that conforms to our protocol:

```
struct Indexed : Indexable{
  // Indexable conformance
  var id: String
  var title: String
  var description: String
  var url: URL?
  var thumbnail: UIImage?
}
```

Later on we are going to go through an array of Indexed instances, grab all the IDs, and put those in an array. Then, when we are asked by iOS to index certain items with given IDs, we can just find the IDs in our array and then find the associated indexed items using the IDs. For this, we can use protocol extensions on sequence types (I wrote about this in Recipe 6.18):

```
extension Sequence where Iterator.Element : Indexable{
  func allIds() -> [String]{
    var ids = [String]()
    for (_, v) in self.enumerated(){
      ids.append(v.id)
    }
    return ids
  }
}
```

And now the juicy part—our extension. We construct an array of indexed items:

```
lazy var indexedItems: [Indexed] = {

  var items = [Indexed]()
  for n in 1...10{
    items.append(
      Indexed(id: "id \(n)", title: "Item \(n)",
              description: "Description \(n)", url: nil, thumbnail: nil))
  }
  return items

}()
```

When we are asked to reindex all our items, we just go through this array and reindex them (see Recipe 13.2):

```
override func searchableIndex(_ searchableIndex: CSSearchableIndex,
  reindexAllSearchableItemsWithAcknowledgementHandler
  acknowledgementHandler: @escaping () -> Void) {

    for _ in indexedItems{
      // TODO: you can index the item here
    }

    // call this handler once you are done
    acknowledgementHandler()
}
```

When we are asked to reindex only specific items with given identifiers, we use our sequence type extension to find all the IDs of our indexed items. Then we search through these IDs for the IDs that iOS gave us. Should we find a match, we will reindex that item. Code for reindexing is not shown here, but Recipe 13.2 shows you how to do it:

```
override func searchableIndex(_ searchableIndex: CSSearchableIndex,
  reindexSearchableItemsWithIdentifiers identifiers: [String],
  acknowledgementHandler: @escaping () -> Void) {

    // get all the identifiers strings that we have
    let ourIds = indexedItems.allIds()

    // go through the items that we have and look for the given ID
    var n = 0
    for i in identifiers{
      if let index = ourIds.index(of: i){
        let _ = indexedItems[index]
        // TODO: reindex this item
      }
      n += 1
    }

    acknowledgementHandler()
}
```

CHAPTER 13

Web and Search

iOS brings with it some really exciting functionality, such as indexing content inside your app as searchable content on an iOS device. Even better, you can contribute to iOS's public search index so that your searchable content appears on devices that don't even have your app installed. That's pretty cool, don't you agree? In this chapter, we'll have a look at all these great features.

13.1 Continuing a Spotlight Search Within Your App

Problem

You are already indexing your app content in Spotlight (more recipes on that in this chapter), but you also want to allow the user to continue the search from Spotlight directly in your app (see Figure 13-1).

Figure 13-1. The "Search in App" button at the upper right lets you search within the host application

Solution

Follow these steps:

1. Add the `CoreSpotlightContinuation` key to your *Info.plist* file with a Boolean value of `YES`. This will allow your app to take part in Spotlight search continuation.
2. Index your searchable items, as you will learn in Recipe 13.2.

3. Implement the `application(_:willContinueUserActivityWithType:)` method of your app delegate.
4. In this method, see whether the given activity type is `CSQueryContinuation ActionType`. If yes, return `true`; otherwise, return `false` (or, if you have other activity types to process, look at those as well before returning `false`).
5. Implement the `application(_:continue:restorationHandler:)` method in your app delegate.
6. In this method, look at the incoming activity (of type `NSUserActivity`) and see whether you can find the `kCSSearchQueryString` key inside the `userInfo` property of the user activity. The value of this key should be of type `String` and be nonempty for search continuation. If this value is a nonempty `String` object, your user has chosen to continue her search inside your app and you have access to her search query in Spotlight through the value of the `kCSSearchQueryString` key.

Discussion

Let's implement a sample application. First, add the `CoreSpotlightContinuation` key to your *Info.plist* file with a Boolean value of YES. After you've done that, create a method within your app delegate that will index an item in Spotlight. This is explained in detail in a separate recipe in this chapter (Recipe 13.2), so I won't explain it here:

```
func indexItems(){

  CSSearchableIndex.default().deleteAllSearchableItems {error in

    guard error == nil else {
      print("Error happened while deleting the index")
      return
    }

    let attributes =
      CSSearchableItemAttributeSet(itemContentType: kUTTypeImage as String)
    attributes.title = "Foo Bar"
    attributes.contentDescription = "Just some description"
    attributes.keywords = ["foo", "bar"]

    let item = CSSearchableItem(uniqueIdentifier: "foobar",
                                domainIdentifier: "se.pixolity",
                                attributeSet: attributes)

    CSSearchableIndex.default().indexSearchableItems([item]){error in
      if let error = error {
        print("Failed to index the item \(error)")
      } else {
        print("Indexed the item successefully")
```

```
      }
    }

  }

}
```

We'll invoke this method when the application has finished running, so that we have an item indexed in Spotlight:

```
func application(
  _ application: UIApplication,
  didFinishLaunchingWithOptions
  launchOptions: [UIApplicationLaunchOptionsKey: Any]?) -> Bool {

  indexItems()

  return true
}
```

We should then tell iOS when our application can and cannot handle an activity. The activity of type `String` will be handed to us in the `application(_:willContinueUserActivityWithType:)` method of our app delegate, and the return value of this function, of type `Bool`, determines whether we can or cannot handle the activity:

```
func application(
  _ application: UIApplication,
  willContinueUserActivityWithType userActivityType: String) -> Bool {

  if userActivityType == .CSQueryContinuationActionType{
    return true
  } else {
    return false
  }

}
```

Last but not least, we need to implement the `application(_:continue:restorationHandler:)` method in our app delegate and look at the incoming user activity's userInfo property:

```
func application(_ application: UIApplication,
  continue userActivity: NSUserActivity,
  restorationHandler: @escaping ([Any]?) -> Void) -> Bool {

  guard let query =
    userActivity.userInfo?[String.CSSearchQueryString] as? String,
    query.characters.count > 0 else {
      return false
  }

  print("The query is \(query)")
```

```
    return true
```

}

If you want to give your users a smooth entry point into your app as a result of search, you will need to ensure that the page inside your app that relates to the user's searched item appears almost immediately in front of the user. That is to say, you will need to remove all activities that are irrelevant to the user's search and keep initial processing to a minimum to ensure a smooth transition from Spotlight into your app.

For instance, imagine that you have written an application where users can search through a database of hotels and find information, photos, and many other details about a hotel. Now, if the user goes through Spotlight to find a hotel that your application has information about and taps on that hotel, they should land directly on the hotel's information page. So in this case, you wouldn't want to download your whole database or even its index and photos and other unnecessary information. Instead, you would directly display the hotel's information page, ensuring that your application processes and opens as fast as possible for the user.

See Also

Recipe 13.2

13.2 Making Your App's Content Searchable

Problem

You want the user to be able to search within the contents *inside* your app, from iOS's search functionality (see Figure 13-2).

Solution

First, you will need to construct an object of type `CSSearchableItemAttributeSet`. This will represent the metadata for any one item that you want to index in the search. Then you'll construct an instance of the `CSSearchableItem` class with your metadata and expiration date, plus some other properties that you will see soon. You index an item using the `CSSearchableIndex` class. You'll get a completion block that will let you know whether or not things went well.

Figure 13-2. iOS has improved search functionality

Discussion

You have to keep quite a few things in mind when indexing items in the local device search functionality. I'll walk you through them one by one. Always keep this index in a useful state. Don't index stuff that you don't need, and make sure you delete the old items. You can specify an expiration date for your content, so I suggest that you always do that.

Let's look at an example. Start by including the two required frameworks that you are going to use:

```
import CoreSpotlight
import MobileCoreServices
```

Then delete all existing indexed items using the `deleteAllSearchableItems(comple tionHandler:)` method of the `CSSearchableIndex` class. This method takes in a closure that gives you an optional error. Check this error if you want to find out whether something went wrong:

```
// delete the existing indexed items
CSSearchableIndex.default()
  .deleteAllSearchableItems {err in
    if let err = err{
```

```
        print("Error in deleting \(err)")
    }
}
```

Now instantiate your metadata of type CSSearchableItemAttributeSet and give it a title, description, path and URL, keywords, and a thumbnail:

```
let attr = CSSearchableItemAttributeSet(
  itemContentType: kUTTypeText as String)

attr.title = "My item"
attr.contentDescription = "My description"
attr.path = "http://reddit.com"
attr.contentURL = URL(string: attr.path!)!
attr.keywords = ["reddit", "subreddit", "today", "i", "learned"]


if let url = Bundle(for: type(of: self))
  .url(forResource: "Icon", withExtension: "png"){
    attr.thumbnailData = try? Data(contentsOf: url)
}
```

Then create the actual searchable item of type CSSearchableItem and set its expiration date 20 seconds into the future:

```
// searchable item
let item = CSSearchableItem(
  uniqueIdentifier: attr.contentURL!.absoluteString,
  domainIdentifier: nil, attributeSet: attr)

let cal = Calendar.current

// our content expires in 20 seconds
item.expirationDate = cal.date(from: cal
  .dateComponents(in: cal.timeZone, from:
    Date().addingTimeInterval(20)))
```

Finally, use the indexSearchableItems(_:) method of the CSSearchableIndex class to index the item that you just created. You can index an array of items, but you have just one item, so index that for now:

```
// now index the item
CSSearchableIndex.default()
  .indexSearchableItems([item]) {err in
    guard err == nil else{
      print("Error occurred \(err!)")
      return
    }

    print("We successfully indexed the item. Will expire in 20 seconds")

}
```

When the user taps your item in the results list, your app will be opened and iOS will call the `application(_:continue:restorationHandler:)` method on your app delegate. In this method, you have to do a few things:

1. Check the activity type that is given to you and make sure it is `CSSearchableItem ActionType`. The aforementioned method gets called under various circumstances—for example, with Handoff—so you have to make sure you are responding only to activities that concern indexed items.
2. Check the `userInfo` property of the activity and read the value of the `CSSearch ableItemActivityIdentifier` key from it. This should be the identifier for your indexed item:

```swift
func application(_ application: UIApplication,
  continue userActivity: NSUserActivity,
    restorationHandler: @escaping ([Any]?) -> Void) -> Bool {

  guard userActivity.activityType == CSSearchableItemActionType,
    let id = userActivity
      .userInfo?[CSSearchableItemActivityIdentifier] as? String
    else{
      return false
  }

  // now we have access to the ID of the activity, and that is the URL
  print(id)

  return true

}
```

Run your code and then send your app to the background. Open a search in your iPhone, search for the item that you just indexed (see Figure 13-3).

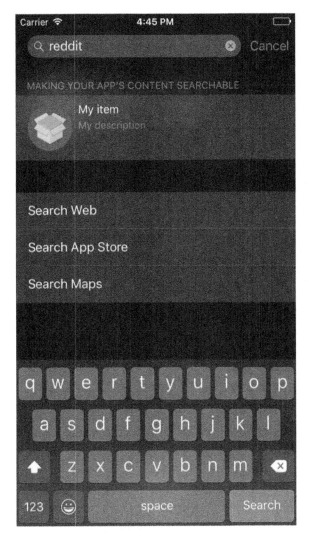

Figure 13-3. Your item is listed in the search results

See Also

Recipe 13.1

13.3 Making User Activities Searchable

Problem

You want to allow user activities inside your app to be searchable. User activities are of type NSUserActivity.

Solution

Use the isEligibleForSearch and eligibleForPublicIndexing properties of the NSUserActivity class to mark your activities as searchable.

Discussion

Let's say that the user is inside your app and is editing the text inside a text field. You start a user activity and want the user to be able to search for this activity in her home screen, then continue with that activity later. Start with the UI. Drop a text field and a text view on your view controller to make it look like Figure 13-4.

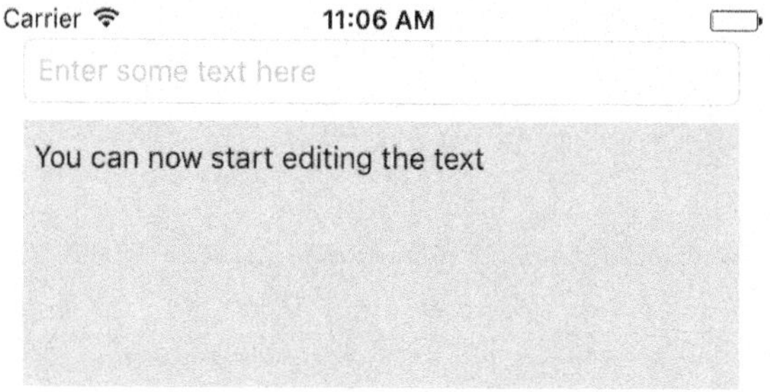

Figure 13-4. Put a text field and a text view on your UI

The text field will allow the user to enter whatever text she wants, and you will use the text view to write log messages so that you (and the user) know what is going on under the hood of your app. Hook these up to your code. I've named the text field textField and the text view status. Also set the delegate of your text field to your view controller, because you are going to want to know when the text field becomes active and inactive. That lets you update the user activity accordingly.

Make your view controller conform to the UITextFieldDelegate and NSUserActivityDelegate protocols and implement the user activity delegate methods:

```
func userActivityWasContinued(_ userActivity: NSUserActivity) {
  log("Activity was continued")
}
```

```
func userActivityWillSave(_ userActivity: NSUserActivity) {
  log("Activity will save")
}
```

This handy method allows you to log messages into your text view:

```
func log(_ t: String){
  DispatchQueue.main.async {
    self.status.text = t + "\n" + self.status.text
  }
}
```

You also need another method that can read the content of your text field and, if it's nil, give you an empty string:

```
func textFieldText() -> String{
  if let txt = self.textField.text{
    return txt
  } else {
    return ""
  }
}
```

Then create your user activity as a lazy variable and mark it as searchable:

```
// TODO: change this ID to something relevant to your app
let activityType = "se.pixolity.Making-User-Activities-Searchable.editText"
let activityTxtKey = "se.pixolity.Making-User-Activities-Searchable.txt"

lazy var activity: NSUserActivity = {
  let a = NSUserActivity(activityType: self.activityType)
  a.title = "Text Editing"
  a.isEligibleForHandoff = true
  a.isEligibleForSearch = true
  // do this only if it makes sense
  // a.isEligibleForPublicIndexing = true
  a.delegate = self
  a.keywords = ["txt", "text", "edit", "update"]

  let att = CSSearchableItemAttributeSet(
    itemContentType: kUTTypeText as String)
  att.title = a.title
  att.contentDescription = "Editing text right in the app"
  att.keywords = Array(a.keywords)

  if let u = Bundle.main.url(forResource: "Icon", withExtension: "png"){
    att.thumbnailData = try? Data(contentsOf: u)
  }
  a.contentAttributeSet = att

  return a
}()
```

Make sure that you import the CoreSpotlight and MobileCore Services frameworks.

Once your text field becomes active, mark the activity as the current one:

```
func textFieldDidBeginEditing(_ textField: UITextField) {
  log("Activity is current")
  userActivity = activity
  activity.becomeCurrent()
}

func textFieldDidEndEditing(_ textField: UITextField) {
  log("Activity resigns being current")
  activity.resignCurrent()
  userActivity = nil
}
```

When the text field's content changes, mark that the user activity needs to be updated:

```
func textField(_ textField: UITextField,
  shouldChangeCharactersIn range: NSRange,
    replacementString string: String) -> Bool {

  activity.needsSave = true

  return true

}
```

A method in your view controller named `updateUserActivityState(_:)` gets called periodically when the current activity needs to be updated. Here you get the chance to update the user info dictionary of the activity:

```
override func updateUserActivityState(_ a: NSUserActivity) {

  log("We are asked to update the activity state")

  a.addUserInfoEntries(
    from: [self.activityTxtKey : self.textFieldText()])

  super.updateUserActivityState(a)

}
```

That's it, really. Now when the user starts writing text in the text field and then sends the app to the background, she will be able to search for the activity that she had started right on her home screen and then continue where she left off. I will not cover the details of handling the request to continue the user activity, because they are not new APIs.

See Also

Recipes 13.1, 13.2, and 13.4

13.4 Deleting Your App's Searchable Content

Problem

You have indexed some items in Spotlight and you would like to get rid of that now.

Solution

Use a combination of the following methods on CSSearchableIndex:

- deleteAllSearchableItems(completionHandler:)
- deleteSearchableItems(withDomainIdentifiers:completionHandler:)
- deleteSearchableItems(withIdentifiers:completionHandler:)

Discussion

Let's have a look at an example. Say that you have already indexed some items (see Recipe 13.2) and you want to delete that content. The first step is to get a handle to the CSSearchableIndex class:

```
let identifiers = [
  "com.yourcompany.etc1",
  "com.yourcompany.etc2",
  "com.yourcompany.etc3"
]

let i = CSSearchableIndex(name: Bundle.main.bundleIdentifier!)
```

Then use the fetchLastClientState(_:completionHandler:) method on the index to get the latest application state that you submitted to the index. After that, you can begin deleting the items inside the identifiers array by using the beginIndex Batch() function on the index. Then use the deleteSearchableItems(withIdentifi ers:completionHandler:) function, which returns a completion handler. This handler will return an optional error that dictates whether the deletion went OK or not. Once you are done, end the batch updates on the index with the endBatch(with ClientState:completionHandler:) method:

```
i.fetchLastClientState {clientState, err in
  guard err == nil else{
    print("Could not fetch last client state")
    return
  }
```

```
let state: Data
if let s = clientState{
  state = s
} else {
  state = Data()
}

i.beginBatch()

i.deleteSearchableItems(withIdentifiers: identifiers) {err in
  if let e = err{
    print("Error happened \(e)")
  } else {
    print("Successfully deleted the given identifiers")
  }
}
i.endBatch(withClientState: state, completionHandler: {err in
  guard err == nil else{
    print("Error happened in ending batch updates = \(err!)")
    return
  }
  print("Successfully batch updated the index")
})

}
```

The content identifiers that I've put in the identifiers array are just an example. I don't know what identifiers you'll want to use, but make sure that you update this array before attempting to delete the existing indexed items.

See Also

Recipe 13.3

CHAPTER 14

Multitasking

iOS has some really cool multitasking functionalities on select devices, such as the latest iPads. One of these functionalities is *PiP*, or Picture in Picture. In this chapter, we'll have a look at some of these exciting features.

14.1 Supporting Split Views

Problem

You would like your universal app on an iPad to allow a side-by-side view. That is to say that you would like the user to be able to drag another completely different app onto the right side of the screen while your app is running, consuming a portion of the screen and forcing your application to resize its contents to fit the smaller screen.

Solution

The easiest solution to supporting side-by-side views is to create your project with the latest version of Xcode, which by default ensures that your app will have split view enabled on larger displays (such as the iPad).

Split view occurs when the user who is running your app slides the right edge of the display toward the left, at which point a drawer of available apps that support split view appears on the screen in a vertically scrollable list (see Figure 14-1). Then the user can choose one of the available apps and tap it, at which point the chosen app is opened and starts consuming the right side of the screen's real estate. There will then be a bar visible between the app running on the right side and your app on the left side. This bar can be dragged further to the left to give more space to the app on the right or further to the right to give more space to the app on the left.

Figure 14-1. The split view is now enabled in your app, which is on the lefthand side (empty for now), and the available apps that support split view are shown in the list on the righthand side; when the user chooses one, that app will be opened

 Split views are available only on devices that have enough screen real estate and device resources, such as memory, for this functionality. The iPad Pro is an example of such a device that allows split views.

If you, however, have an old project that you would like to support split screen for, follow these steps:

1. Add a file to your project called *LaunchScreen.storyboard* (see Figure 14-2). This will replace your launch screen static images. You will then have to set it as your launch screen storyboard in your project settings (General tab), under the App Icons and Launch Images section.

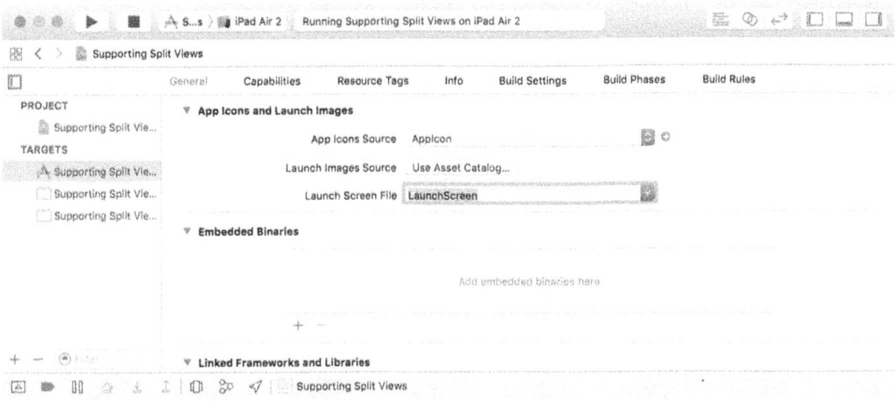

Figure 14-2. Adding LaunchScreen.storyboard as your app's dynamic launch screen

2. Set the base SDK for your project to the latest SDK available in the latest Xcode version.

3. In your *Info.plist* file, under the `UISupportedInterfaceOrientations~ipad` key, declare that you support all orientations. You can also do this on the General tab of your target in Xcode, under the Deployment Info section.

4. Ensure that the `UIRequiresFullScreen` key in your *plist* is either removed or, if it exists and you want to keep it, has the value of `NO`.

Discussion

Split view is a great feature, and as a developer you of course would like to support it in your apps. However, you need to ensure that your UI components work correctly with different size classes and screen orientations.

For instance, let's say that you want to add a view of type `UIView` to your app's main view and you would like it to be resizable so that when split view is fired up, your view gets resized correctly. You then have to think about the width, height, and horizontal and vertical positioning of this view. Assuming that it will fill up the whole screen, you can add the proper constraints to this view in either IB, or in code. Let's look at the code:

```
import UIKit

class ViewController: UIViewController {

  override func viewDidLoad() {
    super.viewDidLoad()

    let newView = UIView()
    newView.backgroundColor = .orange
```

```
newView.translatesAutoresizingMaskIntoConstraints = false

view.addSubview(newView)

newView.leadingAnchor.constraint(equalTo:
    view.leadingAnchor).isActive = true

newView.trailingAnchor.constraint(equalTo:
    view.trailingAnchor).isActive = true

newView.topAnchor.constraint(equalTo: view.topAnchor).isActive = true
newView.bottomAnchor.constraint(equalTo: view.bottomAnchor).isActive = true

    }

}
```

You can create the same constraints in IB by simply dragging a new view instance on top of your view controller and then, from the Resolve Auto Layout Issues section in IB, choosing "Reset to Suggested Constraints" while you have selected your newly created view.

14.2 Adding Picture in Picture Playback Functionality

Problem

You want to let a user shrink a video to occupy a portion of the screen, so that she can view and interact with other content in other apps.

Solution

I'll break the process down into small and digestible steps:

1. You need a view that has a layer of type `AVPlayerLayer`. This layer will be used by a view controller to display the video.
2. Instantiate an item of type `VPlayerItem` that represents the video.
3. Take the player item and place it inside an instance of `AVPlayer`.
4. Assign this player to your view's layer player object. (Don't worry if this sounds confusing. I'll explain it soon.)
5. Assign this view to your view controller's main view and issue the `play()` function on the player to start normal playback.
6. Using key-value observing (KVO), listen to changes to the `currentItem.status` property of your player and wait until the status becomes `ReadyToPlay`, at which point you will create an instance of the `AVPictureInPictureController` class.

7. Start a KVO listener on the `pictureInPicturePossible` property of your controller. Once this value becomes `true`, let the user know that she can now go into Picture in Picture mode.

8. Now, when the user presses a button to start Picture in Picture, read the value of `pictureInPicturePossible` from your controller for safety's sake, and if it checks out, call the `startPictureInPicture()` function on the controller to start the Picture in Picture eventually.

Discussion

Picture in Picture is finally here. Let's get started! Armed with what you learned in this recipe's Solution, begin by defining your view. Create a view class and call it `Pip View`. Go into the *PipView.swift* file and start by importing the right frameworks:

```
import Foundation
import UIKit
import AVFoundation
```

Then define what a "pippable" item is. It is any type that has a PiP layer and a PiP player:

```
protocol Pippable{
  var pipLayer: AVPlayerLayer{get}
  var pipLayerPlayer: AVPlayer? {get set}
}
```

Extend `UIView` to make it pippable:

```
extension UIView : Pippable{

  var pipLayer: AVPlayerLayer{
    get{return layer as! AVPlayerLayer}
  }

  // shortcut into pipLayer.player
  var pipLayerPlayer: AVPlayer?{
    get{return pipLayer.player}
    set{pipLayer.player = newValue}
  }

  open public func awakeFromNib() {
    super.awakeFromNib()
    backgroundColor = .black

  }

}
```

Last but not least for this view, change the view's layer class to `AVPlayerLayer`:

```
class PipView : UIView{

  override class var layerClass: AnyClass{
    return AVPlayerLayer.self
  }

}
```

Go to your view controller's storyboard and change the main view's class to `PipView`. Also embed your view controller in a navigation controller and put two bar button items on the nav bar, namely:

- Play (give it a play button style)
- PiP (by pressing this the user will enable PiP; disable this button by default and hook it to an outlet in your code)

You'll end up with something like Figure 14-3.

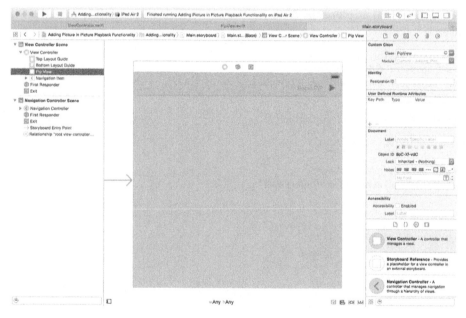

Figure 14-3. Your view controller should look like this

Hook up the two buttons to your view controller's code. The play button will be hooked to a method called `play()` and the PiP button to `beginPip()`. Now head to your view controller and import some frameworks you'll need:

```
import UIKit
import AVKit
```

```
import AVFoundation
import SharedCode
```

Define the KVO context for watching the properties of your player:

```
private var kvoContext = 0
let pipPossible = "pictureInPicturePossible"
let currentItemStatus = "currentItem.status"
```

Then your view controller becomes pippable:

```
protocol PippableViewController{
  var pipView: PipView {get}
}
extension ViewController : PippableViewController{
  var pipView: PipView{
    return view as! PipView
  }
}
```

If you want to, you can define your view controller as conformant to AVPictureInPictureControllerDelegate to get delegate messages from the PiP view controller.

Next, define a property for the PiP button on your view controller so that you can enable this button when PiP is available:

```
@IBOutlet var beginPipBtn: UIBarButtonItem!
```

You also need a player of type AVPlayer. Don't worry about its URL; you will set it later:

```
lazy var player: AVPlayer = {
  let p = AVPlayer()
  p.addObserver(self, forKeyPath: currentItemStatus,
    options: .new, context: &kvoContext)
  return p
}()
```

Now define the PiP controller and the video URL. As soon as the URL is set, construct an asset to hold the URL, place it inside the player, and set the player on your view's layer:

```
var pipController: AVPictureInPictureController?

var videoUrl: URL? = nil{
  didSet{
    if let u = videoUrl{
      let asset = AVAsset(url: u)
      let item = AVPlayerItem(asset: asset,
        automaticallyLoadedAssetKeys: ["playable"])
```

```
      player.replaceCurrentItem(with: item)
      pipView.pipLayerPlayer = player
    }
  }
}
```

You also need a method that returns the URL of the video you are going to play. I've embedded a public domain video into my app and it resides in my app bundle. Check out this book's GitHub repo for sample code:

```
var embeddedVideo: URL?{
  return Bundle.main.url(forResource: "video", withExtension: "mp4")
}
```

You need to determine whether PiP is supported by calling the isPictureInPicture Supported() class method of the AVPictureInPictureController class:

```
func isPipSupported() -> Bool{
  guard AVPictureInPictureController.isPictureInPictureSupported() else{
    // no PiP
    return false
  }

  return true
}
```

When you start the PiP controller, you also need to make sure that the audio plays well even though the player is detached from your app. For that, you have to set your app's audio playback category:

```
func setAudioCategory() -> Bool{
  // set the audio category
  do{
    try AVAudioSession.sharedInstance().setCategory(
      AVAudioSessionCategoryPlayback)
    return true
  } catch {
    return false
  }
}
```

When PiP playback is available, you can finally construct your PiP controller with your player's layer. Remember, if the layer is not ready yet to play PiP, constructing the PiP view controller will fail:

```
func startPipController(){
  pipController = AVPictureInPictureController(playerLayer: pipView.pipLayer)
  guard let controller = pipController else{
    return
  }

  controller.addObserver(self, forKeyPath: pipPossible,
```

```
    options: .new, context: &kvoContext)
}
```

Write the code for `play()` now. You don't have to check for availability of PiP just because you want to play a video:

```
@IBAction func play() {
  guard setAudioCategory() else{
    alert("Could not set the audio category")
    return
  }

  guard let u = embeddedVideo else{
    alert("Cannot find the embedded video")
    return
  }

  videoUrl = u
  player.play()

}
```

As soon as the user presses the PiP button, if the `pictureInPicturePossible()` method of your PiP controller returns `true`, start PiP:

```
@IBAction func beginPip() {

  guard isPipSupported() else{
    alert("PiP is not supported on your machine")
    return
  }

  guard let controller = pipController else{
    alert("Could not instantiate the pip controller")
    return
  }

  controller.addObserver(self, forKeyPath: pipPossible,
    options: .new, context: &kvoContext)

  if controller.isPictureInPicturePossible{
    controller.startPictureInPicture()
  } else {
    alert("Pip is not possible")
  }

}
```

Last but not least, listen for KVO messages:

```
override func observeValue(
  forKeyPath keyPath: String?,
  of object: Any?, change: [NSKeyValueChangeKey : Any]?,
```

```
context: UnsafeMutableRawPointer?) {

  guard context == &kvoContext else{
    return
  }

  if keyPath == pipPossible{
    guard let possibleInt = change?[NSKeyValueChangeKey.newKey]
      as? NSNumber else{
        beginPipBtn.isEnabled = false
        return
    }

    beginPipBtn.isEnabled = possibleInt.boolValue

  }

  else if keyPath == currentItemStatus{

    guard let statusInt = change?[NSKeyValueChangeKey.newKey] as? NSNumber,
      let status = AVPlayerItemStatus(rawValue: statusInt.intValue),
      status == .readyToPlay else{
        return
    }

    startPipController()

  }

}
```

Give this a go on an iPad Air 2 or a similar device that has PiP support.

14.3 Handling Low Power Mode and Providing Alternatives

Problem

You want to know whether the device is in low power mode and want to be updated on the status of this mode as the user changes it.

Solution

To determine if the device is in low power mode, read the value of the `low PowerModeEnabled` property of your process (of type `NSProcessInfo`), and listen to `NSProcessInfoPowerStateDidChangeNotification` notifications to find out when this state changes.

Discussion

Low power mode is a feature that Apple has placed inside iOS so that users can preserve battery whenever they wish to. For instance, if you have 10% battery while some background apps are running, you can save power by:

- Disabling background apps
- Reducing network activity
- Disabling automatic mail pulls
- Disabling animated backgrounds
- Disabling visual effects

And that's what low power mode does. In Figure 14-4, low power mode is disabled because there is a good amount of battery left on this device. Should the battery reach about 10%, the user will automatically be asked to enable low power mode.

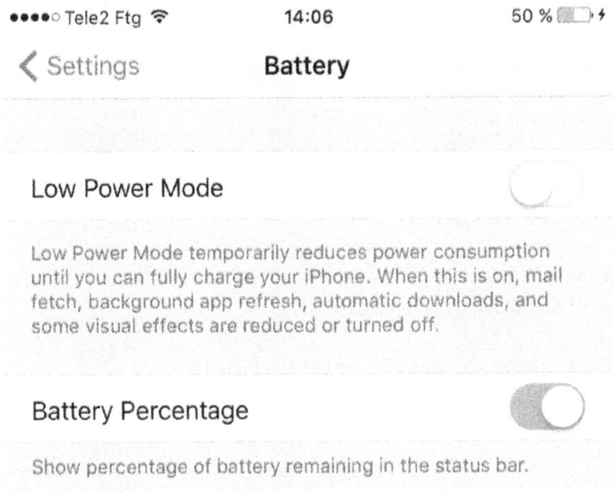

Figure 14-4. Low power mode in the Settings app

Let's create an app that wants to download a URL but won't do so when low power mode is enabled. Instead, the app will defer the download until this mode is disabled. We'll start by listening to `NSProcessInfoPowerStateDidChangeNotification` notifications:

```
override func viewDidLoad() {
  super.viewDidLoad()

  NotificationCenter.default.addObserver(
    self,
    selector: #selector(powerModeChanged(_:)),
    name: NSNotification.Name.NSProcessInfoPowerStateDidChange, object: nil)

  downloadNow()

}
```

Our custom downloadNow() method has to avoid downloading the file if the device is in low power mode:

```
func downloadNow(){

  guard let url = URL(string: "http://localhost:8888/video.mp4"),
    !processInfo.isLowPowerModeEnabled else{
      return
  }

  // do the download here
  print(url)

  mustDownloadVideo = false

}
```

Last but not least, we write the powerModeChanged(_:) method that we have hooked to our notification:

```
import UIKit

class ViewController: UIViewController {

  var mustDownloadVideo = true
  let processInfo = ProcessInfo.processInfo

  @objc func powerModeChanged(_ notif: Notification){

    guard mustDownloadVideo else{
      return
    }

    downloadNow()

  }

  ...
```

CHAPTER 15

Maps and Location

In this chapter, we will have a look at some awesome updates to the MapKit and Core Location frameworks.

15.1 Customizing the Map View with System Buttons

Problem

Instead of letting your map view display the compass or user tracking buttons (as it does by default), you want to place these buttons somewhere else in your application's UI.

Solution

Follow these steps:

1. For the user tracking button, create an instance of `MKUserTrackingButton` that inherits from `UIView`. You can then add this view to another view in your view hierarchy. Alternatively you can create an instance of `UIBarButtonItem` using its `UIBarButtonItem(customView:)` method, which lets you place the bar button on a navigation item. In the Discussion, we'll show an example that uses a `UIBar ButtonItem`.

2. For the compass button, create an instance of the `MKCompassButton` class that also inherits from the `UIView` class. To display it, you have the same options as for the user tracking button.

3. Set the `mapType` property of your map view to `mutedStandard`, of type `MKMapType`, so that the map view itself does not show the standard buttons and views.

4. Set the value of the `showsCompass` property of your map view to `false`, so that the map view does not show its own compass button.

The resulting map view and navigation bar are shown in Figure 15-1.

Figure 15-1. Map with compass and user tracking buttons in navigation bar

Discussion

Let's have a look at an example. Here we:

1. Place a map view on our view controller.

2. Ensure that the map view covers the entire view controller.
3. Embed our view controller inside a navigation controller.
4. Connect our map view to an outlet called `mapView` inside the view controller's code.

Don't forget to import the `MapKit` framework. Our first lines follow:

```
import UIKit
import MapKit

class ViewController: UIViewController {

  @IBOutlet weak var mapView: MKMapView!

  //the rest of our code will be placed here...
```

Now we are going to write a computed property for our view controller that returns an instance of `MKUserTrackingButton` wrapped inside an instance of `UIBarButton Item`:

```
var trackingButton: UIBarButtonItem{
  let button = MKUserTrackingButton(mapView: self.mapView)
  return UIBarButtonItem(customView: button)
}
```

Similarly, for the tracking button, we write a computed property for our view controller that returns an instance of `MKCompassButton` wrapped inside an instance of `UIBar ButtonItem`:

```
var compassButton: UIBarButtonItem{
  let button = MKCompassButton(mapView: self.mapView)
  button.compassVisibility = .visible
  return UIBarButtonItem(customView: button)
}
```

As our view controller's view loads up, we will then place these bar button items on our navigation bar:

```
override func viewDidLoad() {
  super.viewDidLoad()

  mapView.mapType = .mutedStandard
  mapView.showsCompass = false
  navigationItem.rightBarButtonItem = trackingButton
  navigationItem.leftBarButtonItem = compassButton

}
```

Keep in mind that both `MKCompassButton` and `MKUserTrackingButton` are views of type `UIView`, and not instances of `UIBarButtonItem`. We wrapped them inside instances of `UIBarButtonItem` in this recipe so that we could place them inside our navigation bar. If you want to put the buttons in another view instead of the navigation bar, you can use the view's `addSubview(_:)` function.

15.2 Displaying System Annotations on the Map

Problem

You want to display customizable annotations on the map view.

Solution

Follow these steps:

1. Import `MapKit` in your code.
2. Write an annotation class that conforms to `NSObject` and `MKAnnotation`.
3. Hold a reference to your coordinates in an object of type `CLLocationCoordinate2D`, which has a latitude and longitude.
4. Instantiate your annotation class from the `CLLocationCoordinate2D` object.
5. Invoke the `register(_:forAnnotationViewWithReuseIdentifier:)` function of your map view with an identifier of type `MKMapViewDefaultAnnotationViewReuseIdentifier` and an annotation view class of type `MKMarkerAnnotationView.self`.
6. Invoke the `addAnnotation(_:)` function of your map view to add your annotation object to the map view.
7. Ensure that you are the delegate of your map view by setting the `delegate` property of your map view either in IB or in code.
8. Implement the `mapView(_:viewFor:)` delegate function of `MKMapViewDelegate`. From there, return an instance of the `MKMarkerAnnotationView` class for your annotations.

A sample annotated map is shown in Figure 15-2.

Figure 15-2. A map with an annotation view we added from our application

Discussion

We'll start with Xcode. Place a map view on your view controller and ensure that it covers the entire screen. Set the `delegate` property of the map view to your view controller and then connect the map view to an outlet in your view controller called `map View`.

We will now write a class that conforms to `NSObject` and `MKAnnotation`, so it can represent our annotation objects:

```
class Annotation: NSObject, MKAnnotation{

  var coordinate: CLLocationCoordinate2D
  var title: String?
  var subtitle: String?

  init (coordinate: CLLocationCoordinate2D,
        title: String?,
        subtitle: String?){

    self.coordinate = coordinate
    self.title = title
    self.subtitle = subtitle

    super.init()

  }

}
```

Now we are going to define a location, of type `CLLocationCoordinate2D`, with a latitude and longitude. I have chosen to show a locality called Löttorp, which is in the south of Sweden on a little island called Öland, but you can change this latitude and longitude to any other valid value that you desire:

```
extension CLLocationCoordinate2D{

  static var southOfSweden: CLLocationCoordinate2D{
    return CLLocationCoordinate2D(latitude: 57.166096, longitude: 16.993009)
  }

}
```

Now that we have the coordinates, we can turn it into an instance of `Annotation` using a title and subtitle of our choice:

```
extension CLLocationCoordinate2D{

  func annotation(withTitle title: String?, subTitle: String?) -> Annotation{
    return Annotation(coordinate: self, title: title, subtitle: subTitle)
  }

}
```

We start in our view controller by ensuring that we are conforming to the `MKMapView Delegate` protocol and that we have a reference to our map view that is placed on the storyboard:

```
class ViewController: UIViewController, MKMapViewDelegate {

  @IBOutlet weak var mapView: MKMapView!
```

```
// the rest of our code will be placed here soon...
```

The next step is to ensure that we are registering `MKMarkerAnnotationView` as the default annotation view in our map view. Then we create an annotation of type `Annotation` (our own class) and add that annotation to our map view:

```
override func viewDidLoad() {
  super.viewDidLoad()

  mapView.register(
    MKMarkerAnnotationView.self,
    forAnnotationViewWithReuseIdentifier:
    MKMapViewDefaultAnnotationViewReuseIdentifier)

  let southOfSweden =
    CLLocationCoordinate2D.southOfSweden.annotation(
      withTitle: "Löttorp", subTitle: "Centrum")

  mapView.addAnnotation(southOfSweden)

}
```

Last but not least, we will instantiate `MKMarkerAnnotationView` in the `mapView(_:viewFor:)` delegate function:

```
func mapView(_ mapView: MKMapView,
             viewFor annotation: MKAnnotation) -> MKAnnotationView? {

  guard let view = mapView.dequeueReusableAnnotationView(
    withIdentifier: MKMapViewDefaultAnnotationViewReuseIdentifier) as?
    MKMarkerAnnotationView else {return nil}

  view.animatesWhenAdded = true
  view.titleVisibility = .adaptive
  view.subtitleVisibility = .adaptive

  return nil
}
```

See Also

Recipe 15.3

15.3 Clustering Annotations for a Clutter-Free Map

Problem

You have too many annotations to display on the map and you would like to cut down on the superfluous icons, which do not contribute to the user's understanding.

Solution

Follow these steps:

1. Subclass MKAnnotation. In your subclass, store a property of type String? that will be the identifier by which you can group your annotations on the map.
2. When you display annotation views on the map, such as annotation views of type MKMarkerAnnotationView, set their clusteringIdentifier property to the aforementioned String? property.

 This recipe is based on what you learned in Recipe 15.2. I suggest that you read that recipe before digging deeper into this one.

Discussion

Annotation views of type MKAnnotationView, including the MKMarkerAnnotation View class, have a property called clusteringIdentifier of type String?. When you provide this property to your annotation views, if the user zooms out of the map view so that they can see more content, iOS will attempt to group your annotation views with the same clustering identifier so that a single annotation view represents all the views that are close together.

For instance, if you have 100 annotations to place in New York, all very close to each other, and the user has zoomed out of the map to see New York, Philadelphia, and Washington DC, in the same map view, it's not very attractive to display 100 pins just on New York, which by this time is probably the size of a peanut. For this reason, you can provide a clustering identifier to your annotation views, which iOS will use to attempt to cluster your annotation views into groups based on the amount of zooming that the user has done. Instead of, for example, 100 annotation views, the user sees only one. As the user then zooms into the map, more and more of the annotation views pop up.

Let's extend what we learned in Recipe 15.2 and add a new property called cluster ingIdentifier, of type String?, to our annotation object:

```
import UIKit
import MapKit

class Annotation: NSObject, MKAnnotation{

  var coordinate: CLLocationCoordinate2D
  var title: String?
  var subtitle: String?
```

```
let clusteringIdentifier: String?

//more of our implementation will follow here shortly
```

Since we have added this new property to our class, we need to change our initializer to account for this new property:

```
init (coordinate: CLLocationCoordinate2D,
      title: String? = nil,
      subtitle: String? = nil,
      clusteringIdentifier: String? = nil){

  self.coordinate = coordinate
  self.title = title
  self.subtitle = subtitle
  self.clusteringIdentifier = clusteringIdentifier

  super.init()

}
```

For the sake of simplicity, in this recipe we are not going to use the title and subtitle properties, but we need the coordinate and the clusteringIdentifier properties. So let's create a convenience initializer that takes in a latitude and longitude, which it can use to construct the coordinate property, along with taking in the clustering identifier:

```
convenience init (lat: CLLocationDegrees,
                  long: CLLocationDegrees,
                  clusteringIdentifier: String){
  self.init(
    coordinate:CLLocationCoordinate2D(latitude: lat, longitude: long),
    title: nil,
    subtitle: nil,
    clusteringIdentifier: clusteringIdentifier
  )

}
```

In our view controller, we are going to define three groups of annotations, each group having eight annotation objects and each annotation in the same group being very close to the others.

I have chosen the south of Sweden as a destination for these annotations: specifically, a place called Borgholm, which is a very small town on an island belonging to Sweden called Öland. So let's first define eight annotation objects in our map view, all having the same clustering identifier:

```
class ViewController: UIViewController, MKMapViewDelegate {

  @IBOutlet weak var mapView: MKMapView!
```

```
private var firstGroupOfAnnotations: [Annotation]{
  let id = "Borgholm Center"
  return [
    Annotation(lat: 56.878785, long: 16.648149, clusteringIdentifier: id),
    Annotation(lat: 56.882349, long: 16.651926, clusteringIdentifier: id),
    Annotation(lat: 56.883193, long: 16.654673, clusteringIdentifier: id),
    Annotation(lat: 56.879536, long: 16.653299, clusteringIdentifier: id),
    Annotation(lat: 56.879254, long: 16.657419, clusteringIdentifier: id),
    Annotation(lat: 56.877472, long: 16.655359, clusteringIdentifier: id),
    Annotation(lat: 56.879348, long: 16.660852, clusteringIdentifier: id),
    Annotation(lat: 56.878316, long: 16.653643, clusteringIdentifier: id)
  ]
}

//the rest of our view controller code will follow here shortly...
```

These annotations are all in the center of this little town, with an identifier equal to *Borgholm Center* as you can see. Now we are going to group eight more annotations with another identifier, in the same town, but not in the center:

```
private var secondGroupOfAnnotations: [Annotation]{
  let id = "Borgholm"
  return [
    Annotation(lat: 56.879629, long: 16.662569, clusteringIdentifier: id),
    Annotation(lat: 56.880286, long: 16.664629, clusteringIdentifier: id),
    Annotation(lat: 56.879348, long: 16.662569, clusteringIdentifier: id),
    Annotation(lat: 16.662569, long: 16.661024, clusteringIdentifier: id),
    Annotation(lat: 56.883100, long: 16.669950, clusteringIdentifier: id),
    Annotation(lat: 56.879067, long: 16.666002, clusteringIdentifier: id),
    Annotation(lat: 56.878222, long: 16.664114, clusteringIdentifier: id),
    Annotation(lat: 56.877847, long: 16.663599, clusteringIdentifier: id),
  ]
}
```

Last but not least, we'll create a third group of annotations that are in the suburbs of this little town:

```
private var thirdGroupOfAnnotations: [Annotation]{
  let id = "Borgholm Suburbs"
  return [
    Annotation(lat: 56.874564, long: 16.661196, clusteringIdentifier: id),
    Annotation(lat: 56.875408, long: 16.662741, clusteringIdentifier: id),
    Annotation(lat: 56.878504, long: 16.667204, clusteringIdentifier: id),
    Annotation(lat: 56.877191, long: 16.666346, clusteringIdentifier: id),
    Annotation(lat: 56.876534, long: 16.667547, clusteringIdentifier: id),
    Annotation(lat: 56.876253, long: 16.666002, clusteringIdentifier: id),
    Annotation(lat: 56.878129, long: 16.671152, clusteringIdentifier: id),
    Annotation(lat: 56.877284, long: 16.667376, clusteringIdentifier: id),
  ]
}
```

Now we have three groups of annotations, and every annotation in a group shares an identifier with the rest of the annotations in the same group. So if we add these annotations to our map and then zoom out far enough, we should only see 3 annotations on the map instead of 24. But let's add these annotations to the map first:

```
override func viewDidLoad() {
  super.viewDidLoad()

  mapView.register(
    MKMarkerAnnotationView.self,
    forAnnotationViewWithReuseIdentifier:
    MKMapViewDefaultAnnotationViewReuseIdentifier)

  mapView.addAnnotations(firstGroupOfAnnotations)
  mapView.addAnnotations(secondGroupOfAnnotations)
  mapView.addAnnotations(thirdGroupOfAnnotations)

}
```

Next we'll provide annotation views for these annotations, and then set the annotation view's clusteringIdentifier to the clusteringIdentifier property of our Annotation class, instances of which we created in our firstGroupOfAnnotations, secondGroupOfAnnotations, and thirdGroupOfAnnotations private properties:

```
func mapView(_ mapView: MKMapView,
             viewFor annotation: MKAnnotation) -> MKAnnotationView? {

  guard let annotation = annotation as? Annotation else {return nil}

  guard let view = mapView.dequeueReusableAnnotationView(
    withIdentifier: MKMapViewDefaultAnnotationViewReuseIdentifier) as?
    MKMarkerAnnotationView else {return nil}

  view.animatesWhenAdded = true
  view.titleVisibility = .adaptive
  view.subtitleVisibility = .adaptive
  view.clusteringIdentifier = annotation.clusteringIdentifier

  return nil
}
```

Let's run the application and then zoom a little bit into Öland, just far enough to be able to see Borgholm (see Figure 15-3). Here we can see three clusters of annotations.

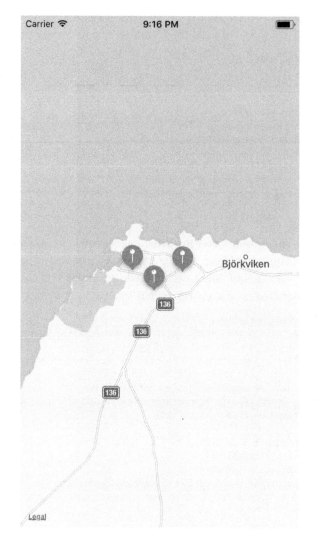

Figure 15-3. Three circular red annotations, each holding eight annotations

As we zoom into the map, more and more annotations pop up here and there, under the clusters (see Figure 15-4).

Figure 15-4. More annotations pop up as we zoom further into the map

See Also

Recipe 15.2

15.4 Displaying a Specific Location on the Map

Problem

You have a latitude and a longitude of a location on Earth that you would like to display as a pin on the map.

Solution

Follow these steps:

1. Import MapKit as a framework into your project.
2. Create a class that conforms to both NSObject and MKAnnotation. Conforming to the MKAnnotation protocol requires defining its variables—particularly coordinate, title, and subtitle—and methods. Instances of classes that conform to MKAnnotation can be added to the map view via its addAnnotation(_:) method.
3. For the map to know where to set the visible region that the user actually sees, instead of seeing the entire map of the Earth, instantiate MKCoordinateSpan with a latitude delta and longitude delta of type double. The smaller the deltas, the closer the camera is to the Earth.
4. Instantiate MKCoordinateRegion with the location you want to be the center of the map, and pass the coordinate span instance that you created in the previous step to the coordinate region.
5. Call the addAnnotation(_:) method of your map view to set the annotation at the right spot.
6. Call the setRegion(_:animated:) method of your map view to set the visible region of your map.

Discussion

Let's have a look at an example. Create a single view application in Xcode and open the *Main.storyboard* file in Interface Builder. From the Object Library, drag and drop a map view onto your view controller and make sure it covers the entire screen (Figure 15-5). Also connect the reference outlet of the map view to a variable in your view controller called mapView.

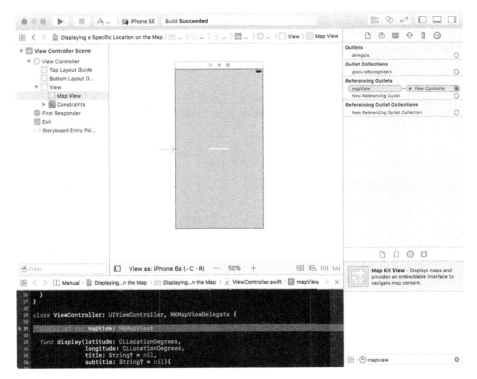

Figure 15-5. *The map view is placed on the view controller and covers the entire screen*

Following this recipe's Solution, now create an `Annotation` instance that conforms to both `NSObject` and `MKAnnotation`:

```swift
import UIKit
import MapKit

class Annotation : NSObject, MKAnnotation{
  let coordinate: CLLocationCoordinate2D
  let title: String?
  let subtitle: String?

  init(latitude: CLLocationDegrees, longitude: CLLocationDegrees,
      title: String?, subtitle: String?){
    self.coordinate = CLLocationCoordinate2D(latitude: latitude,
                                             longitude: longitude)
    self.title = title
    self.subtitle = subtitle
  }

}
```

Since the `Annotation` class now has references to the coordinates, and coordinates are required to find the region that has to be displayed, you can extend this class to return the region of type `MKCoordinateRegion`:

```
extension Annotation{
  var region: MKCoordinateRegion{
    let span = MKCoordinateSpan(latitudeDelta: 0.05, longitudeDelta: 0.05)
    return MKCoordinateRegion(center: coordinate, span: span)
  }
}
```

Now start with the definition of the view controller:

```
class ViewController: UIViewController {

  @IBOutlet var mapView: MKMapView!


  ...
```

You can then code a method that takes in a latitude, longitude, title, and subtitle for a pin to be displayed on the screen, instantiates the annotation, and adds that annotation to the map:

```
func display(latitude: CLLocationDegrees,
             longitude: CLLocationDegrees,
             title: String? = nil,
             subtitle: String? = nil){

  let annotation = Annotation(latitude: latitude,
                              longitude: longitude,
                              title: title,
                              subtitle: subtitle)

  mapView.addAnnotation(annotation)

  mapView.setRegion(annotation.region, animated: false)

}
```

Now you can simply call this function and display, for instance, a pin where Stockholm's Central Station is:

```
override func viewDidLoad() {
  super.viewDidLoad()

  let stockholmCentralStation = (lat: 59.330139, long: 18.058155)

  display(latitude: stockholmCentralStation.lat,
          longitude: stockholmCentralStation.long,
          title: "Central Station",
          subtitle: "Stockholm")

}
```

Experiment a little bit with the latitude and longitude delta values of the region instance of type MKCoordinateRegion, and see how decreasing this value zooms the map more into the center. Also, change the latitude and the longitude and see how that affects where the point is displayed.

See Also

Recipe 15.2

15.5 Requesting the User's Location a Single Time

Problem

You want an optimized and energy-efficient way of requesting the current location of the user only once.

Solution

You will need to use the requestLocation() method of the CLLocationManager class. The new location will be sent to your location manager's locationManager(_:did UpdateLocations:) delegate method. Errors will be reported by location Manager(_:didFailWithError:). You can make only one request to this method at any given time. A new request will cancel the previous one.

Discussion

Place a button on your interface inside IB and hook it up to a method in your code called requestLocation(). Then go into your *Info.plist* file and set the value of the NSLocationWhenInUseUsageDescription key to a valid string that explains to the user why you want to get her location. You will also have to import the CoreLocation framework and make your view controller conform to CLLocationManagerDelegate.

Implement a variable in your view controller to represent the location manager:

```
lazy var locationManager: CLLocationManager = {
  let manager = CLLocationManager()
  manager.delegate = self
  manager.desiredAccuracy = kCLLocationAccuracyNearestTenMeters
  return manager
}()
```

When your button is pressed, request access to the user's location. This request sends the user's location to your app only when it is in the foreground. As soon as your app is sent to the background, iOS stops delivering location updates to you:

```
@IBAction func requestLocation() {

  locationManager.requestWhenInUseAuthorization()

}
```

Then wait for the user to accept or reject the request. If everything is going smoothly, request the user's location:

```
func locationManager(_ manager: CLLocationManager,
  didChangeAuthorization status: CLAuthorizationStatus) {

    if case .authorizedWhenInUse = status{
      manager.requestLocation()
    } else {
      // TODO: we didn't get access, handle this
    }

}
```

Last but not least, wait for the location-gathering mechanism to fail or succeed:

```
func locationManager(_ manager: CLLocationManager,
  didUpdateLocations locations: [CLLocation]) {
    // TODO: now you have access to the location--do your work
}

func locationManager(_ manager: CLLocationManager,
  didFailWithError error: Error) {
  // TODO: handle the error
}
```

See Also

Recipe 15.6

15.6 Requesting the User's Location in the Background

Problem

You want to receive updates on the user's location while your app is in the background. Being a good iOS citizen, you won't ask for this unless you *really* need it for the *main* functionality of your app.

Solution

Set the allowsBackgroundLocationUpdates property of your location manager to true and ask for location updates using the requestAlwaysAuthorization() function.

Discussion

When linked against the latest iOS SDK, apps that want to ask for a user's location when they're in the background have to set the allowsBackgroundLocationUpdates property of their location manager to true. Let's have a look at an example. Start a single view controller app, place a button on your UI in IB, and give it a title similar to "Request background location updates." Then hook it to a method in your view controller and name the method requestBackgroundLocationUpdates(). In your *Info.plist* file, set the string value of the NSLocationAlwaysUsageDescription key and make sure that it explains exactly why you want to access the user's location even in the background. Then go into the Capabilities section of your target, and under Background Modes, enable "Location updates" (see Figure 15-6).

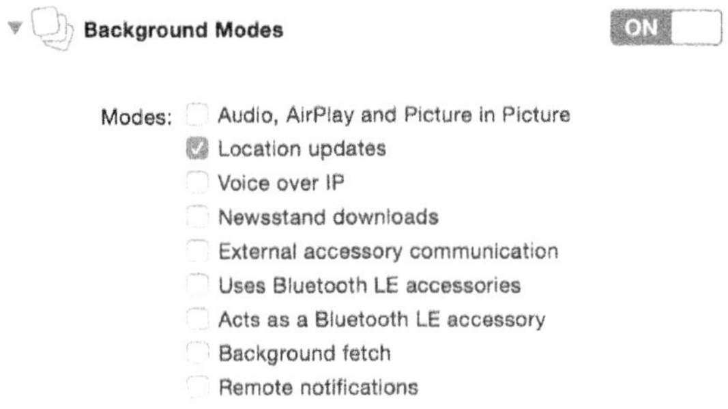

Figure 15-6. Enabling location updates in Background Modes in your project

Now import CoreLocation in your code and make your view controller conformant to CLLocationManagerDelegate. Create your location manager and make sure that the allowsBackgroundLocationUpdates property is set to true:

```
lazy var locationManager: CLLocationManager = {
  let m = CLLocationManager()
  m.delegate = self
  m.desiredAccuracy = kCLLocationAccuracyNearestTenMeters
  m.allowsBackgroundLocationUpdates = true
  return m
}()
```

When the user presses the button, ask for location updates:

```
@IBAction func requestBackgroundLocationUpdates() {
  locationManager.requestAlwaysAuthorization()
}
```

Wait until the user accepts the request and then start looking for location updates:

```
func locationManager(
  _ manager: CLLocationManager,
```

```
  didChangeAuthorization status: CLAuthorizationStatus) {

  if case CLAuthorizationStatus.authorizedAlways = status{
    manager.startUpdatingLocation()
  }

}
```

Last but not least, implement the usual location manager methods to get to know when the user's location has changed:

```
func locationManager(_ manager: CLLocationManager,
                     didUpdateLocations locations: [CLLocation]) {
  // TODO: now you have access to the location--do your work

}

func locationManager(_ manager: CLLocationManager,
                     didFailWithError error: Error) {
  // TODO: handle the error
}
```

See Also

Recipe 15.5

15.7 Customizing the Tint Color of Pins on the Map

Problem

You want to set the tint color of pin annotations on your map manually.

Solution

Use the `pinTintColor` property of the `MKPinAnnotationView` class.

Discussion

Let's check out an example. Create a single view controller project and dump a map view on top of your view. Make sure that you set the delegate of this map view to your view controller. Also link it to a variable named `map` in your view controller.

In the view controller, we are going to create annotations with reusable identifiers, so let's use the color as the ID:

```
import Foundation
import UIKit

public extension UIColor{
  final func toString() -> String{
```

```
    var red = 0.0 as CGFloat
    var green = 0.0 as CGFloat
    var blue = 0.0 as CGFloat
    var alpha = 0.0 as CGFloat
    getRed(&red, green: &green, blue: &blue, alpha: &alpha)

    return "\(Int(red))\(Int(green))\(Int(blue))\(Int(alpha))"
  }
}
```

Now create the annotation:

```
import Foundation
import MapKit

public class Annotation : NSObject, MKAnnotation{
  public var coordinate: CLLocationCoordinate2D
  public var title: String?
  public var subtitle: String?

  public init(coordinate: CLLocationCoordinate2D,
    title: String, subtitle: String){
    self.coordinate = coordinate
    self.title = title
    self.subtitle = subtitle
  }

}
```

Ensure that your view controller conforms to the MKMapViewDelegate protocol, define the location that you want to display on the map, and create an annotation for it:

```
let color = UIColor(red: 0.4, green: 0.8, blue: 0.6, alpha: 1.0)
let location = CLLocationCoordinate2D(latitude: 59.33, longitude: 18.056)

lazy var annotations: [MKAnnotation] = {
  return [Annotation(coordinate: self.location,
                     title: "Stockholm Central Station",
                     subtitle: "Stockholm, Sweden")]
}()
```

When your view appears on the screen, add the annotation to the map:

```
 override func viewDidAppear(_ animated: Bool) {
  super.viewDidAppear(animated)

  map.removeAnnotations(annotations)
  map.addAnnotations(annotations)

}
```

And when the map view asks for an annotation view for your annotation, return an
annotation view with the custom color (see Figure 15-7):

```
func mapView(_ mapView: MKMapView,
             viewFor annotation: MKAnnotation) -> MKAnnotationView? {

  let view: MKPinAnnotationView
  if let v = mapView.dequeueReusableAnnotationView(
    withIdentifier: color.toString()), v is MKPinAnnotationView{
    view = v as! MKPinAnnotationView
  } else {
    view = MKPinAnnotationView(annotation: annotation,
                              reuseIdentifier: color.toString())
  }

  view.pinTintColor = color

  return view

}
```

Figure 15-7. Our custom-color pin is displayed on the map

See Also

Recipe 15.2

15.8 Providing Detailed Pin Information with Custom Views

Problem

When the user taps an annotation in a map, you want to display details for that annotation in a view.

Solution

Set the `detailCalloutAccessoryView` property of your `MKAnnotationView` instances to a valid `UIView` instance.

Discussion

Create your project following the steps outlined in Recipe 15.7. In this recipe, we're going to reuse a lot of code from the aforementioned recipe, *except* for the implementation of the `mapView(_:viewForAnnotation:)` delegate method of our view controller. Instead, we are going to construct instances here of `MKAnnotationView` and then set the detail callout accessory view:

```
func mapView(
  _ mapView: MKMapView,
  viewForAnnotation annotation: MKAnnotation) -> MKAnnotationView? {

  let view: MKAnnotationView
  if let v = mapView
    .dequeueReusableAnnotationView(withIdentifier: identifier){
    // reuse
    view = v
  } else {
    // create a new one
    view = MKAnnotationView(annotation: annotation,
                            reuseIdentifier: identifier)

    view.canShowCallout = true

    if let img = UIImage(named: "Icon"){
      view.detailCalloutAccessoryView = UIImageView(image: img)
    }

    if let extIcon = UIImage(named: "ExtIcon"){
      view.image = extIcon
    }
  }

  return view
```

```
}
```

Figure 15-8 shows the image of an annotation on a map. The image inside the callout is the detail callout accessory view.

Figure 15-8. Annotation with detail callout accessory

 I am using two public domain images in this recipe. You also can find public domain images on Google.

See Also

Recipes 15.2 and 15.7

15.9 Displaying Traffic, Scale, and Compass Indicators on the Map

Problem

You want to display traffic as well as the little compass and scale indicators on the map view.

Solution

Set the following properties of your map view to `true`:

- `showsCompass`
- `showsTraffic`
- `showsScale`

Discussion

Place a map view on your view and set the appropriate constraints on it so that it stretches across the width and height of your view controller's view. This is really optional, but useful so the user can see the map view properly on all devices. Then follow the steps outlined in Recipe 15.7 to place an annotation on the map. Write code similar to the following in a method such as `viewDidLoad()`:

```
map.showsCompass = true
map.showsTraffic = true
map.showsScale = true
```

The results will be similar to those shown in Figure 15-9. The scale is shown on the top left and the compass on the top right. You have to rotate the map for the compass to appear.

Figure 15-9. Map with scale, compass, and traffic indicators

See Also

Recipe 15.10

15.10 Providing an ETA for Transit Transport Type

Problem

You want your app to provide routing options to users when they are in the iOS Maps app.

Solution

You will need to mark your app as a routing app and construct an instance of the `MKDirectionsRequest` class. Set the `transportType` property of that request to `Transit` and send your request to Apple to calculate an estimated time of arrival (ETA), using the `calculateETA(completionHandler:)` method of the `MKDirections` class.

 We use GeoJSON files (*https://tools.ietf.org/html/rfc7946*) here, so be sure to read the spec for that format before proceeding with this recipe.

Discussion

Create a single view application. Then head to the Capabilities tab in Xcode, enable the Maps section, and mark the routing options that you believe your app will be able to provide (see Figure 15-10). I've enabled everything for demonstration purposes, but you probably wouldn't want to enable *all* of these in your app.

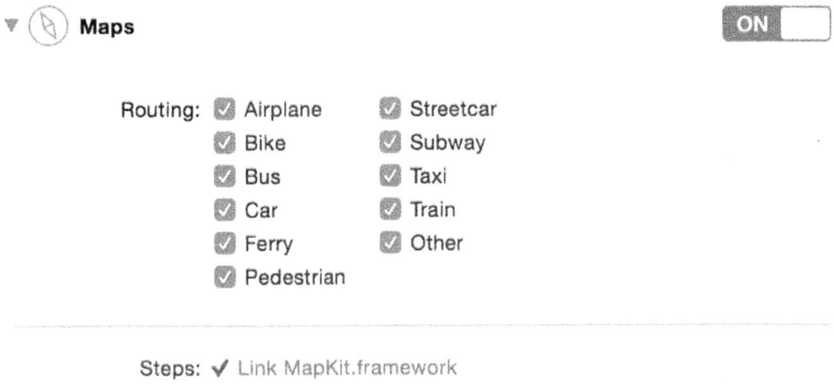

Figure 15-10. Transportation routing options

Create a new *Directions.geoJson* file in your app and then head over to GeoJson.io (*http://geojson.io/*) to create the polygon that defines your routing coverage area. Then copy and paste the generated content and place it in the aforementioned file in your project. Now go and edit your target's scheme. Under Run and then Options, find the Routing App Coverage File section and select your file (see Figure 15-11).

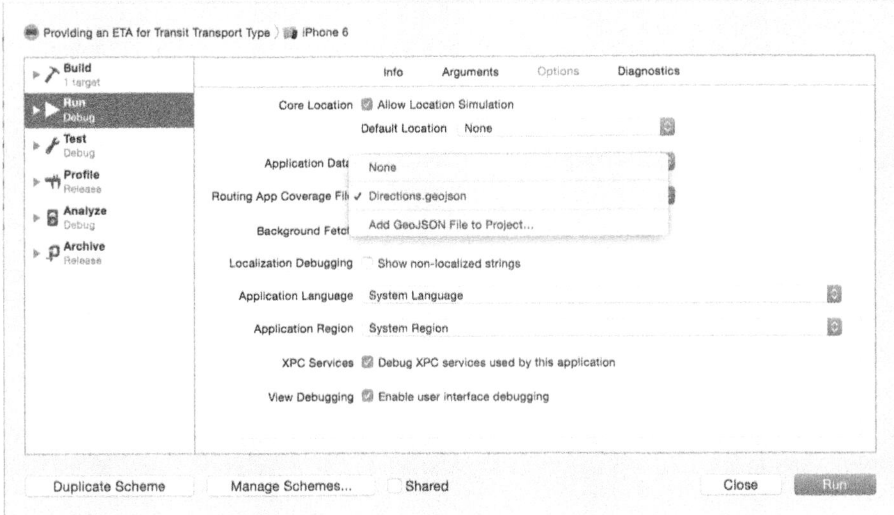

Figure 15-11. Select the routing coverage file for your project

You can always go to GeoJSONLint (*http://geojsonlint.com/*) to validate your GeoJSON files.

This will allow the Maps app to open your app whenever the user asks for transit
information in the iOS Maps app. Now code the `application(_:openURL:options:)`
method of your app delegate and handle the routing request there:

```
func application(_ app: UIApplication,
                open url: URL,
                options:
    [UIApplicationOpenURLOptionsKey : Any] = [:]) -> Bool {

    guard MKDirectionsRequest.isDirectionsRequest(url) else{
        return false
    }

    // now we have the URL
    let req = MKDirectionsRequest(contentsOf: url)

    guard req.source != nil && req.destination != nil else{
        return false
    }

    req.transportType = .transit
    req.requestsAlternateRoutes = true

    let dir = MKDirections(request: req)

    dir.calculateETA {response, error in
        guard let resp = response, error == nil else{
            // handle the error
            print(error!)
            return
        }

        print("ETA response = \(resp)")

    }

    return true

}
```

Now open the Maps app and ask for directions from one location to another. If the
Maps app can't handle the request, it will show a little View Routing Apps button.
Even if the Maps app isn't able to show the routing options, the user can always press
the little navigation button to open alternative routing apps (see Figure 15-12). Your
app will be displayed in the list of routing apps if the user asks for a routing option

you support, and if the starting and stopping points are within the shape you defined in your GeoJSON file. When the user opens your app, your app delegate will be informed and will calculate an ETA.

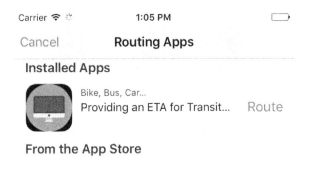

Figure 15-12. Our app, displayed in the list of routing apps

See Also

Recipe 15.9

15.11 Launching the iOS Maps App in Transit Mode

Problem

You want to launch iOS's Maps app in transit mode.

Solution

When calling the `openMaps(with:launchOptions:)` class method of `MKMapItem`, in the options collection, set the value of the `MKLaunchOptionsDirectionsModeKey` key to `MKLaunchOptionsDirectionsModeTransit`.

Discussion

Let's create a single view controller app and place a button on the view controller to open a map. Set the title of this button to something like "Open Maps app in transit mode." Then hook it up to your view controller. For every coordinate of type `CLLocationCoordinate2D`, you have to create an instance of `MKPlacemark` and then, from the placemark, create an instance of `MKMapItem`.

Here is the source map item:

```
let srcLoc = CLLocationCoordinate2D(latitude: 59.328564,
                                    longitude: 18.061448)
let srcPlc = MKPlacemark(coordinate: srcLoc, addressDictionary: nil)
let src = MKMapItem(placemark: srcPlc)
```

Followed by the destination map item:

```
let desLoc = CLLocationCoordinate2D(latitude: 59.746148,
                                    longitude: 18.683281)
let desPlc = MKPlacemark(coordinate: desLoc, addressDictionary: nil)
let des = MKMapItem(placemark: desPlc)
```

 You can use the Get Latitude and Longitude website (*http://www.latlong.net/*) to find the latitude and longitude of any point on the map.

Now you can launch the app, in transit mode, with the source and the destination points:

```
let options = [
  MKLaunchOptionsDirectionsModeKey : MKLaunchOptionsDirectionsModeTransit
]

MKMapItem.openMaps(with: [src, des], launchOptions: options)
```

See Also

Recipes 15.9 and 15.10

15.12 Showing Maps in Flyover Mode

Problem

You want to display your maps in a flyover state, where the regions on the map are translated onto a 3D globe, rather than a 2D flattened map.

Solution

Set the `mapType` property of your `MKMapView` to either `hybridFlyover` or `satelliteFlyover`.

Discussion

The flyover mode of a map view represents the map as if it were on a globe, rather than flat. Keep that in mind when placing a camera on the map to show to the user.

Start off with a single view controller app. Place a map view on your view and hook it up to your code. I've named mine `map`. When your view gets loaded, make sure that your map type is one of the aforementioned flyover modes:

```
map.mapType = .satelliteFlyover
map.showsBuildings = true
```

Then, when your view appears on the screen, set the camera on your map:

```
let loc = CLLocationCoordinate2D(latitude: 59.328564,
                                 longitude: 18.061448)

let altitude: CLLocationDistance = 500
let pitch: CGFloat = 45
let heading: CLLocationDirection = 90

let c = MKMapCamera(
  lookingAtCenter: loc,
  fromDistance: altitude, pitch: pitch, heading: heading)

map.setCamera(c, animated: true)
```

Run this code on a real device (this doesn't work very well on the simulator) and you'll get a display along the lines of Figure 15-13.

Figure 15-13. The Stockholm Central Station is shown here under satellite flyover mode

CHAPTER 16

UI Testing

Apple added quite a good framework for UI testing in the latest Xcode. This is so much fun, I am sure you are going to enjoy writing UI tests. UI tests go hand in hand with accessibility, so knowing a bit about that is very useful, if not necessary.

When you are debugging accessibility-enabled apps on the simulator, you may want to use a really handy dev tool that comes with Xcode: the Accessibility inspector (Figure 16-1). You can find it by right-clicking Xcode's icon in the Dock and choosing Open Developer Tool, then Accessibility Inspector. The Accessibility inspector allows you to move your mouse over items on the screen and get information about their accessibility properties, such as their values, identifiers, and so on. I suggest that you use this program whenever you want to figure out the identifiers, labels, and values of UI components on your views.

In this chapter, we will have a look at how to write UI tests and evaluate the results. We will use Xcode's automated UI tests and also write some tests by hand.

16.1 Preparing Your Project for UI Testing

Problem

You have an existing app or want to create a new app, and you want to ensure that you have some UI testing capabilities built into your app so that you can get started writing UI tests.

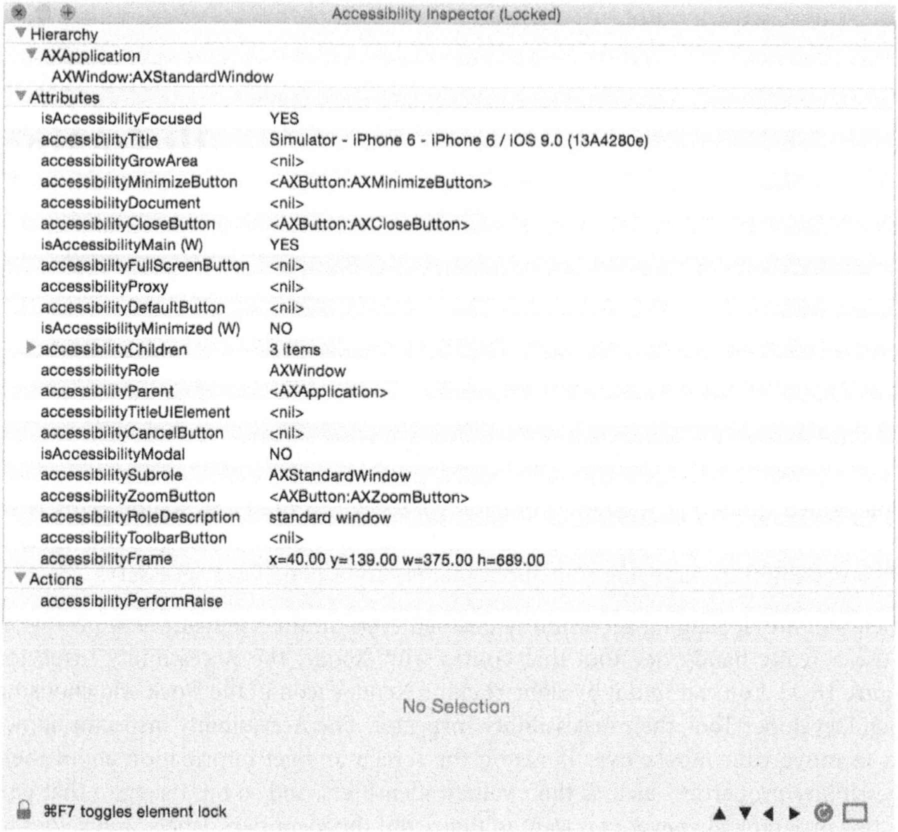

Accessibility Inspector (Locked)	

▼ Hierarchy
  ▼ AXApplication
    AXWindow:AXStandardWindow
▼ Attributes

isAccessibilityFocused	YES
accessibilityTitle	Simulator - iPhone 6 - iPhone 6 / iOS 9.0 (13A4280e)
accessibilityGrowArea	\<nil\>
accessibilityMinimizeButton	\<AXButton:AXMinimizeButton\>
accessibilityDocument	\<nil\>
accessibilityCloseButton	\<AXButton:AXCloseButton\>
isAccessibilityMain (W)	YES
accessibilityFullScreenButton	\<nil\>
accessibilityProxy	\<nil\>
accessibilityDefaultButton	\<nil\>
isAccessibilityMinimized (W)	NO
▶ accessibilityChildren	3 items
accessibilityRole	AXWindow
accessibilityParent	\<AXApplication\>
accessibilityTitleUIElement	\<nil\>
accessibilityCancelButton	\<nil\>
isAccessibilityModal	NO
accessibilitySubrole	AXStandardWindow
accessibilityZoomButton	\<AXButton:AXZoomButton\>
accessibilityRoleDescription	standard window
accessibilityToolbarButton	\<nil\>
accessibilityFrame	x=40.00 y=139.00 w=375.00 h=689.00

▼ Actions
  accessibilityPerformRaise

No Selection

🔒 ⌘F7 toggles element lock   ▲ ▼ ◀ ▶ ⊚ ▢

Figure 16-1. The Accessibility inspector showing information for a button on the screen, in the simulator

Solution

If you have an existing project, simply add a new UI Test target to your project. If you are creating a new project from scratch, you can add a UI Test target during the creation process.

Discussion

If you are starting a new app from scratch, upon setting your project's properties, you will be given a chance to create a UI testing target (see Figure 16-2). Enable the "Include UI Tests" option.

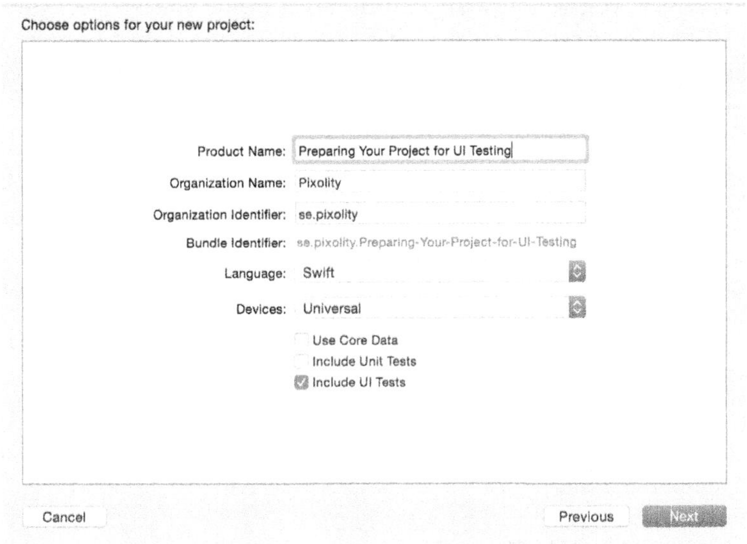

Figure 16-2. Enabling the Include UI Tests option in Xcode's new project sheet

If you have an existing project and want to add a new UI testing target to it, create a new target. On the templates screen, under iOS, choose Test; then choose Cocoa Touch UI Testing Bundle (see Figure 16-3).

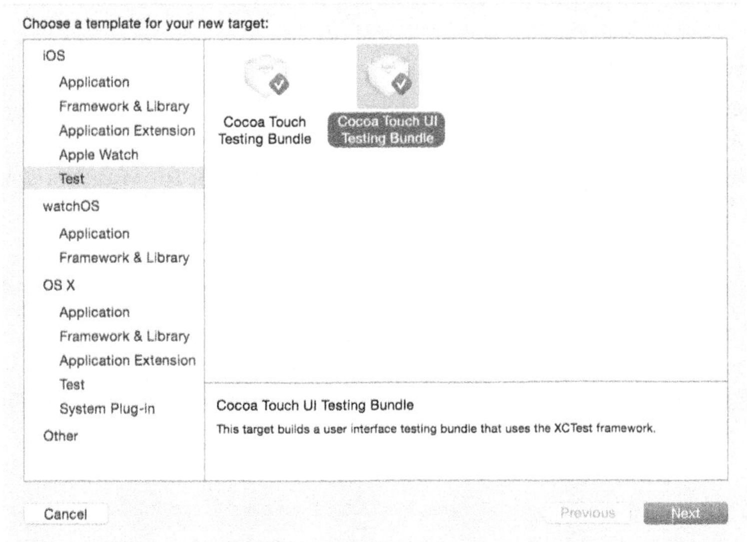

Figure 16-3. Adding a new UI testing bundle to your existing app

On the next screen, you will be asked which target inside your project you want to create the UI testing target. Make sure that you choose the right target on. You can change this later if you want from the properties of your UI Test target (see Figure 16-4).

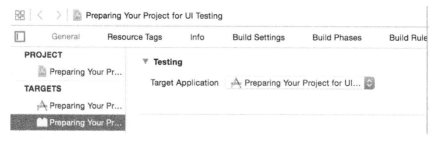

Figure 16-4. You can change the target to which your UI tests are attached even after the creation of your UI Test target

16.2 Automating UI Test Scripts

Problem

You want Xcode to generate most, if not all, of your UI testing code. You can write more UI testing code in Swift, but it would be useful to take advantage of what Xcode gives you for free.

Solution

Use the new Record button in Xcode when you are in your UI testing target's code (the red circle near the upper-left corner of Figure 16-5). This will really be handy if you want to automatically get all your UI test code written for you (but sometimes you'll still have to write some yourself).

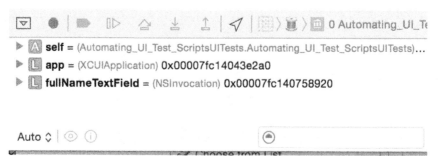

Figure 16-5. The little circular Record button in the debugger section of Xcode's window automatically gets UI test code

You can write all your UI tests in pure Swift code. No more mucking around with JavaScript. Jeez, isn't that a relief?!

Discussion

Let's say that you have a UI that looks similar to that shown in Figure 16-6. In this UI, the user is allowed to enter some text in the text field at the top of the screen. Once she is done, she can just press the Capitalize button and the code will translate her input into its equivalent capitalized string and place it in the label at the bottom.

| Carrier 🗼 | 4:36 PM | ⬜› |

Hello, World

Capitalize

HELLO, WORLD

Figure 16-6. Sample UI with text fields and button

I assume that you have arranged these UI components inside a storyboard. In the Identity inspector in IB, set the accessibility labels of your text field to "Full Name," your button to "Capitalize," and your label to "Capitalized String." Now hook up your text field and your label to your code under the names of `lbl` and `txtField` as I've done (this just makes understanding the code easier; you can name them what you want). Then hook the action of your button to your code. I've named this action method `capitalize()`. Now when the user presses the button, we read the text and capitalize it:

```
@IBAction func capitalize() {
  guard let txt = txtField.text, txt.characters.count > 0 else{
    return
  }
  lbl.text = txt.uppercased()
  lbl.accessibilityValue = lbl.text
}
```

Now head over to the main Swift file for your UI tests and you should see a simple empty method, usually named `testExample()`. Put your cursor inside that method and then press the Record button. Xcode will open your app and you will be able to interact with your app as you would normally. Acting as a user would be expected to act, select the text field by tapping it and then type some text in it, like "Hello, World!" Finally, press the Capitalize button. Xcode will generate a test that looks more or less like:

```
let app = XCUIApplication()
let fullNameTextField = app.textFields["Full Name"]
fullNameTextField.tap()
fullNameTextField.typeText(enteredString)
app.buttons["Capitalize"].tap()
```

We have a problem, Watson! We now need to make sure that the capitalized text inside our label is correctly capitalized. How can we do that in Xcode and get Xcode to generate the code for us? Well, the answer is: we can't! This is a logical task that you cannot automate with Xcode, so let's do it ourselves. In the app object, there is a property called staticTexts. We can get our label from there:

```
let lbl = app.staticTexts["Capitalized String"]
```

This will give us an item of type XCUIElement. Just so you know, the app object is of type XCUIApplication. Every element has a value property that is an optional value of type AnyObject. For our label, this is going to contain a string. So let's read its value as a string and then compare it with the string that we expect it to be:

```
let app = XCUIApplication()
let fullNameTextField = app.textFields["Full Name"]
fullNameTextField.tap()
fullNameTextField.typeText(enteredString)
app.buttons["Capitalize"].tap()
```

 I took the opportunity to put the entered and expected strings inside string objects so that we don't have to write them multiple times.

Now press the little Play button next to your test method and let Xcode do its thing. You should now see that the text has succeeded if everything went well.

See Also

Recipes 16.1 and 16.3

16.3 Testing Text Fields, Buttons, and Labels

Problem

You want to create UI tests to work with instances of UITextField, UIButton, and UILabel.

Solution

All the aforementioned items are instances of type XCUIElement. That means that you can work with some really cool properties of them in UI testing, such as the following:

- exists
- title
- label
- enabled
- frame
- debugDescription
- descendantsMatchingType(_:)
- childrenMatchingType(_:)

The last two in the list are a bit more advanced, so we won't work with them until later in this chapter when we discuss queries.

Discussion

Let's say that you have a label and a button. When the button is pressed, you want to hide the label (by setting its hidden property to true). You now want to write a UI test to see whether the desired effect actually happens. I assume that you've already set up your UI and you've given accessibility labels of "Button" to the button and "Label" to the label.

 I recommend working as much as possible in Xcode's automated recording system, where you can just interact with your UI as normal and then let Xcode write your UI test code for you. This is the approach I take, not only in this recipe but in all other recipes in this book where appropriate.

From within your UI testing target code, press the Record UI Test button (see Figure 16-5). The code that you'll get will be similar to this:

```
let app = XCUIApplication()
app.buttons["Button"].tap()
```

You can see that the app object has a property called buttons that returns an array of all buttons that are on the screen. That itself is awesome, in my opinion. Then the tap() method is called on your button. You want to find the label now:

```
let lbl = app.staticTexts["Label"]
```

As you can see, the app object has a property called staticTexts that is an array of labels. Any label, anywhere. That's really cool and powerful too. Regardless of where your label is and who its parent is, this property will return that label. Now you want to find whether that label is on the screen:

```
XCTAssert(lbl.exists == false)
```

You can, of course, also read the value of a text field. You can also use the debugger to inspect the `value` property of a text field element using the `po` command. You can find all text fields that are currently on the screen using the `textFields` property of the app that you instantiated with `XCUIApplication()`.

Here is an example where I try to find a text field on the screen with a specific accessibility label that I have set in my storyboard:

```
let app = XCUIApplication()

let txtField = app.textFields["MyTextField"]
XCTAssert(txtField.exists)
XCTAssert(txtField.value != nil)

let txt = txtField.value as! String

XCTAssert(txt.characters.count > 0)
```

See Also

Recipe 16.1

16.4 Finding UI Components

Problem

You want to be able to find your UI components, wherever they are, using simple to complex queries.

Solution

Construct queries of type `XCUIElementQuery`. Link these queries together to create even more complicated queries and find your UI elements.

The `XCUIElement` class conforms to the `XCUIElementTypeQueryProvider` protocol. I am not going to waste space here and copy/paste Apple's code in that protocol, but if you have a look at it yourself, you'll see that it is made out of a massive list of properties (`groups`, `windows`, `dialogs`, `buttons`, etc.).

Here is how I recommend going about finding your UI elements using this knowledge:

1. Instantiate your app with `XCUIApplication()`.

2. Refer to the windows property of the app object to get all the windows in the app as a query object of type XCUIElementQuery.
3. Now that you have a query object, use the childrenMatchingType(_:) method to find children inside this query.

Let's say that you have a simple view controller. Inside that view controller's view, you dump another view, and inside that view you dump a button so that your view hierarchy looks something like Figure 16-7.

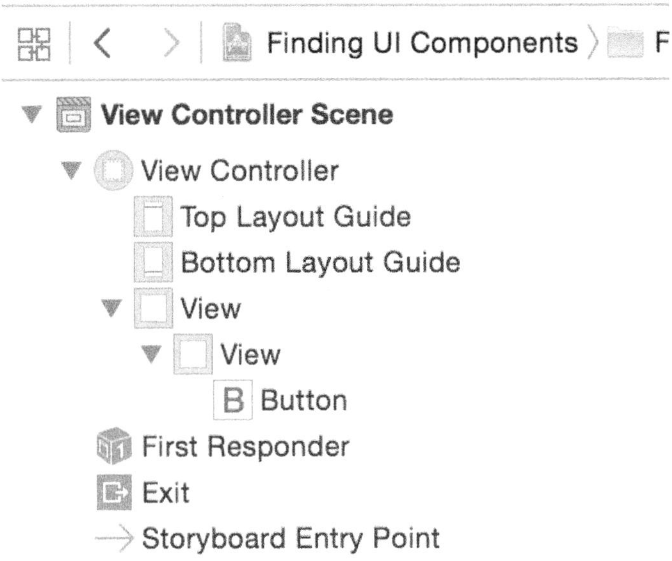

Figure 16-7. Hierarchy of views in this sample app

You created this hierarchy by placing a view inside the view controller's view, and placing a button inside that view. We are now going to try to find that button and tap it:

```
let app = XCUIApplication()
let view = app.windows.children(matching: .other)
let innerView = view.children(matching: .other)
let btn = innerView.children(matching: .button).element(boundBy: 0)
XCTAssert(btn.exists)
btn.tap()
```

Discussion

We can rewrite the code that we wrote just now in a more direct and compact way using the descendantsMatchingType(_:) method:

```
let app = XCUIApplication()

let btn = app.windows.children(matching: .other)
  .descendants(matching: .button).element(boundBy: 0)

XCTAssert(btn.exists)
btn.tap()
```

Here we are looking at the children of all our windows that are of type Unknown (view) and then finding a button inside them, wherever that button may be and in whichever subview it may have been bundled up. Can this be written in a simpler way? You betcha:

```
let app = XCUIApplication()

let btn = app.windows.children(matching: .other)
  .descendants(matching: .button).element(boundBy: 0)

XCTAssert(btn.exists)
btn.tap()
```

 The buttons property of our app object is a query that returns all the buttons that are descendants of any window inside the app. Isn't that awesome?

Those of you with a curious mind are probably thinking, "Can this be written in a more *complex* way?" Well, yes, I am glad you asked:

```
let app = XCUIApplication()

let btn = app.windows.children(matching: .other)
  .descendants(matching: .button).element(boundBy: 0)

XCTAssert(btn.exists)
btn.tap()
```

Here we first find the main view inside the view controller that is on the screen. Then we find *all* views that have a button inside them as a first child using the awesome containingType(_:identifier:) method. Once we have all the views that have buttons in them, we find the first button inside the first view and then tap it.

Now let's take the same view hierarchy, but this time we will use predicates of type NSPredicate to find our button. There are two handy methods on XCUIElementQuery that we can use to find elements with predicates:

- element(matching predicate: NSPredicate) -> XCUIElement
- matching(_ predicate: NSPredicate) -> XCUIElementQuery

The first method will find *an* element that matches a given predicate (so your result has to be unique), and the second method finds *all* elements that match a given predicate. Now we can find a button inside our UI with a specific title:

```
let app = XCUIApplication()

let btns = app.buttons.matching(
  NSPredicate(format: "title like[c] 'Button'"))

XCTAssert(btns.count >= 1)

let btn = btns.element(boundBy: 0)

XCTAssert(btn.exists)
```

We can also write a test script that goes through all the disabled buttons on our UI:

```
let app = XCUIApplication()

let btns = app.buttons.matching(
  NSPredicate(format: "title like[c] 'Button'"))

XCTAssert(btns.count &gt;= 1)

let btn = btns.element(boundBy: 0)

XCTAssert(btn.exists)
```

See Also

Recipe 16.1

16.5 Long-Pressing on UI Elements

Problem

You want to be able to simulate long-pressing on a UI element using UI tests.

Solution

Use the `pressForDuration(_:)` method of `XCUIElement`.

Discussion

Create a single view app and, when your view gets loaded, add a long gesture recognizer to the view. The following code waits until the user long-presses the view for 5 seconds:

```
override func viewDidLoad() {
  super.viewDidLoad()
```

```
view.isAccessibilityElement = true

let gr = UILongPressGestureRecognizer(target: self,
  action: #selector(handleLongPress))

gr.minimumPressDuration = 5

view.addGestureRecognizer(gr)
```

}

The gesture recognizer is hooked to a method. In this method, we will show an alert controller and ask the user for her name. Once she has answered the question and pressed the save button on the alert, we will set the entered value as the accessibility value of our view so that we can read it in our UI tests:

```
@objc func handleLongPress(){
  let c = UIAlertController(title: "Name", message: "What is your name?",
    preferredStyle: .alert)

  c.addAction(UIAlertAction(title: "Cancel", style: .destructive,
    handler: nil))

  c.addAction(UIAlertAction(title: "Save", style: .destructive){
    action in

    guard let fields = c.textFields, fields.count == 1 else{
      return
    }

    let txtField = fields[0]
    guard let txt = txtField.text, txt.characters.count > 0 else{
      return
    }

    self.view.accessibilityValue = txt

  })

  c.addTextField {txt in
    txt.placeholder = "Foo Bar"
  }

  present(c, animated: true, completion: nil)

}
```

Now let's go to our UI test code and do the following:

1. Get an instance of our app.
2. Find our view object with the childrenMatchingType(_:) method of our app.

3. Call the `pressForDuration(_:)` method on it.
4. Call the `typeText(_:)` method of our app object and find the save button on the dialog.
5. Programmatically press the save button using the `tap()` method.
6. Check the value of our view against the value that we entered earlier. They should match.

Here's the code:

```
let app = XCUIApplication()
let view = app.windows.children(matching: .other).element(boundBy: 0)
view.press(forDuration: 5)

XCTAssert(app.alerts.count > 0)

let text = "Foo Bar"
app.typeText(text)

let alert = app.alerts.element(boundBy: 0)
let saveBtn = alert.descendants(matching: .button).matching(
  NSPredicate(format: "title like[c] 'Save'")).element(boundBy: 0)

saveBtn.tap()

XCTAssert(view.value as! String == text)
```

 I highly recommend that you always start by using the automatically recorded and written UI tests that Xcode can create for you. This will give you insight into how you can find your UI elements better on the screen. Having said that, Xcode isn't always so intelligent about finding the UI elements.

See Also

Recipes 16.1 and 16.2

16.6 Typing Inside Text Fields

Problem

You would like to write UI tests for an app that contains text fields. You want to be able to activate a text field, type some text in it, deactivate it, and then run some tests on the results, or a combination of the aforementioned scenarios.

Solution

Follow these steps:

1. Find your text field with the `textFields` property of your app or one of the other methods mentioned in Recipe 16.4.
2. Call the `tap()` method on your text field to activate it.
3. Call the `typeText(_:)` method on the text field to type whatever text you want.
4. Call the `typeText(_:)` method of your app with the value of `XCUIKeyboardKey.return` as the parameter. This will simulate pressing the Enter key on the keyboard. (You may want to check out other `XCUIKeyboardKey` constant values, such as `XCUIKeyboardKey.space` or `XCUIKeyboardKey.command`.)
5. Once you are done, read the `value` property of your text field element as a `String` and do your tests on that.

Discussion

Create a single view app and place a text field on the UI. Set the accessibility label of that text field to "myText." Set your text field's delegate as your view controller and make your view controller conform to `UITextFieldDelegate`. Then implement the notoriously redundant delegate method named `textFieldShouldReturn(_:)` so that pressing the Return key on the keyboard will dismiss the keyboard from the screen:

```
import UIKit

class ViewController: UIViewController, UITextFieldDelegate {

  func textFieldShouldReturn(_ textField: UITextField) -> Bool {
    textField.resignFirstResponder()
    return true
  }

}
```

Then, inside your UI tests, write code similar to what I suggested in this recipe's Solution section:

```
let app = XCUIApplication()
let myText = app.textFields["myText"]
myText.tap()

let text1 = "Hello, World!"

myText.typeText(text1)
myText.typeText(XCUIKeyboardKey.delete.rawValue)
app.typeText(XCUIKeyboardKey.return.rawValue)

XCTAssertEqual((myText.value as! String).characters.count,
  text1.characters.count - 1)
```

16.7 Swiping on UI Elements

Problem

You want to simulate swiping on various UI components in your app.

Solution

Use the various swipe methods on XCUIElement, such as the following:

- swipeUp()
- swipeDown()
- swipeRight()
- swipeleft()

Discussion

Let's set our root view controller to a table view controller and program the table view controller so that it shows 10 hardcoded cells inside it:

```
import UIKit

class ViewController: UITableViewController {

  let id = "c"

  lazy var items: [String] = {
    return (0..<10).map{"Item \($0)"}
  }()

  override func tableView(_ tableView: UITableView,
    numberOfRowsInSection section: Int) -> Int {
    return items.count
  }

  override func tableView(_ tableView: UITableView,
    cellForRowAt indexPath: IndexPath) -> UITableViewCell {

      let c = tableView.dequeueReusableCell(withIdentifier: id,
        for: indexPath)

      c.textLabel!.text = items[(indexPath as NSIndexPath).row]

      return c

  }

  override func tableView(_ tableView: UITableView,
    commit editingStyle: UITableViewCellEditingStyle,
```

```
forRowAt indexPath: IndexPath) {

  items.remove(at: (indexPath as NSIndexPath).row)
  tableView.deleteRows(at: [indexPath],
    with: .automatic)

}

}
```

With this code, the user can swipe left on any cell and then press the Delete button to delete that cell. Let's test this in our UI test. This is what you'll need to do:

1. Get the handle to the app.
2. Using the `cells` property of the app object, first count to make sure there are initially 10 items in the table view.
3. Then find the fifth item and swipe left on it with the `swipeLeft()` method.
4. After that, find the Delete button using the `buttons` property of the app object and tap on it with the `tap()` method.
5. Finally, assert that the cell was deleted for sure by making sure the cell's count is now 9 instead of 10:

```
let app = XCUIApplication()
let cells = app.cells
XCTAssertEqual(cells.count, 10)
app.cells.element(boundBy: 4).swipeLeft()
app.buttons["Delete"].tap()
XCTAssertEqual(cells.count, 9)
```

16.8 Tapping UI Elements

Problem

You want to be able to simulate various ways of tapping UI elements when writing your UI tests.

Solution

Use one or a combination of the following methods of the `XCUIElement` class:

- `tap()`
- `doubleTap()`
- `twoFingerTap()`

Double-tapping is two taps, with one finger. The two-finger tap is
one tap, but with two fingers.

Discussion

Create a single view app and then add a gesture recognizer to the view that sets the
accessibility of the view whenever two fingers have been tapped on the view:

```
import UIKit

class ViewController: UIViewController {

  @objc func handleTap(){
    view.accessibilityValue = "tapped"
  }

  override func viewDidLoad() {
    super.viewDidLoad()

    view.isAccessibilityElement = true
    view.accessibilityValue = "untapped"
    view.accessibilityLabel = "myView"

    let tgr = UITapGestureRecognizer(
      target: self, action: #selector(handleTap))

    tgr.numberOfTapsRequired = 1
    tgr.numberOfTouchesRequired = 2
    view.addGestureRecognizer(tgr)

  }

}
```

Now our UI tests will do a two-finger tap on the view and check its value before and
after to make sure it checks out:

```
let app = XCUIApplication()
let view = app.descendants(matching: .other)["myView"]

XCTAssert(view.exists)
XCTAssert(view.value as! String == "untapped")

view.twoFingerTap()

XCTAssert(view.value as! String == "tapped")
```

See Also

Recipes 16.1 and 16.4

CHAPTER 17

Core Motion

Apple has finally brought some long-awaited features into the Core Motion framework. It's especially exciting that the same capabilities, or some version of them, are also available on the Apple Watch. This is great news for us developers because we can program for the watch in a more native way, rather than reading this data from the user's iPhone and sending it to the watch with Bluetooth.

There are a couple of key terms I'll be using throughout this chapter that you need to know about:

Cadence

I use a cadence sensor on my bicycle. It helps me figure out how many times I spin my pedals, which can be crucial knowledge. Think about riding downhill on a bicycle, at a 45-degree angle, for 20 minutes out of a total 40-minute bike ride. Without accounting for cadence your total calories burned and effort will be miscalculated because you might not even have pedaled when going downhill. The watch actually includes a cadence sensor for *running*.

Pace

This is a ratio, dividing the time you have been moving by the distance. If you're counting in meters, for instance, your pace might be 0.5 seconds per meter, meaning that you travelled 1 meter in half a second.

iOS devices can provide pace and cadence information when it's available from the pedometer. Some pedometers might not have this information available. You can call the isPaceAvailable() class function of CMPedometer to check whether pace information is available. Similarly, you can call the isCadenceAvailable() class method of CMPedometer to determine whether cadence information is available.

Import the Core Motion framework into your project before attempting to run the code we write in this chapter.

17.1 Querying Pace and Cadence Information

Problem

You want to get cadence and pace information from the pedometer on an iOS device.

Solution

Follow these steps:

1. Find out whether cadence and pace are available.
2. Call the `startUpdates(from:withHandler:)` function of `CMPedometer`.
3. In your handler block, read the `currentPace` and `currentCadence` properties of the incoming optional `CMPedometerData` object.

Discussion

Let's check out an example:

```
guard CMPedometer.isCadenceAvailable() &&
  CMPedometer.isPaceAvailable() else{
    print("Pace and cadence data are not available")
    return
}

let oneWeekAgo = Date(timeIntervalSinceNow: -(7 * 24 * 60 * 60))
pedometer.startUpdates(from: oneWeekAgo) {data, error in

  guard let pData = data, error == nil else{
    return
  }

  if let pace = pData.currentPace{
    print("Pace = \(pace)")
  }

  if let cadence = pData.currentCadence{
    print("Cadence = \(cadence)")
  }

}
```

```
// remember to stop the pedometer updates with stopPedometerUpdates()
// at some point
```

 When you finish querying pedometer data, always remember to call the stopPedometerUpdates()function on your instance of CMPedometer.

17.2 Recording and Reading Accelerometer Data

Problem

You want iOS to accumulate some accelerometer data for a specific number of seconds and then batch-update your app with all the accelerometer data in one go.

Solution

Follow these steps:

1. Call the isAccelerometerRecordingAvailable() class function on the CMSensor Recorder class and abort if it returns false, because that means that accelerometer recording is not available.
2. Instantiate CMSensorRecorder.
3. Call the recordAccelerometer(forDuration:) function on your sensor recorder and pass the number of seconds for which you want to record accelerometer data.
4. Go into a background thread and wait for your data if you want.
5. Call the accelerometerData(from:to:) function on your sensor recorder to get the accelerometer data from a given date to another date. The return value of this function is a CMSensorDataList object, which is enumerable. Each item in this enumeration is of type CMRecordedAccelerometerData.
6. Read the value of each CMRecordedAccelerometerData. You'll have properties like startDate, timestamp, and acceleration, which is of type CMAcceleration.

Discussion

I mentioned that CMSensorDataList is enumerable. That means it conforms to the NSFastEnumeration protocol, but you cannot use the for x in ... syntax on this type of enumerable object. You'll have to make it conform to the Sequence protocol and implement the makeIterator() function like so:

```
extension CMSensorDataList : Sequence{
  public func makeIterator() -> NSFastEnumerationIterator {
```

```
    return NSFastEnumerationIterator(self)
  }
}
```

First, define a lazily allocated sensor recorder. If sensor information is not available, your object won't hang around in the memory:

```
lazy var recorder = CMSensorRecorder()
```

Then check whether sensor information is available:

```
guard CMSensorRecorder.isAccelerometerRecordingAvailable() else {
  print("Accelerometer data recording is not available")
  return
}
```

Next, record the sensor data for a period:

```
let duration = 3.0
recorder.recordAccelerometer(forDuration: duration)
```

Then go to the background and read the data:

```
OperationQueue().addOperation{[unowned recorder] in

  Thread.sleep(forTimeInterval: duration)
  let now = Date()
  let past = now.addingTimeInterval(-(duration))
  guard let data = recorder.accelerometerData(from: past, to: now) else{
    return
  }

  print(data)

}
```

It is important to enumerate the result of accelerometer Data(from:to:) on a non-UI thread, because there may be thousands of data points in the results.

CHAPTER 18

Security

iOS 11 didn't change much with regard to the Security framework. A few things were added, mainly about the keychain. There are also some additions that are about Application Transport Security, or ATS. ATS is now incorporated into iOS, so all apps compiled with the new Xcode, and running under the latest iOS version, will by default use HTTPS for all their network traffic. There are some pros and cons to this: it is good because it strongly encourages the use of secure connections for everything, but sometimes it can be annoying to *force* using a secure connection for everything!

There are also some changes that affect the way we can store values in the keychain, but overall, not much to worry about.

18.1 Supporting Password Autofill with iCloud Keychain

Problem

You have a companion website to your iOS app through which users can register for your service, using their username (or email address) and a password. You would like the users who have registered through the website to be able to log in to your app without having to enter their username and password each time. The app can find these credentials in iCloud, where the user has placed them using Touch ID.

Solution

Follow these steps:

1. Create a file called *apple-app-site-association* and place the following content in it:

```
{
  "webcredentials" : {
    "apps" : ["TEAMID.X.Y.Z"]
```

```
    }
}
```

Where the italicized items are:

TEAMID

> Your iOS app developer team identifier. You can find this identifier on Apple's developer website.

X

> The first part of the reverse domain associated with your company.

Y

> Usually the name of your company.

Z

> Usually the identifier for your app.

An example of this complete formula would be *SO3269D.com.company.myapp*, for instance.

2. Place this file inside the *.well-known* folder located in the root folder of your website. If your website is called *https://website.com/*, for instance, this file will need to be accessible at *https://website.com/.well-known/apple-app-site-association*. Note that your website has to support HTTPS, as this file cannot be reached on HTTP by iOS.
3. While your app's source code is open in Xcode, go to your project's Capabilities section in Xcode and enable the Associated Domains switch.
4. In the Associated Domains section in Xcode, press the + button and add your website's address to the list of domains, as shown in Figure 18-1.

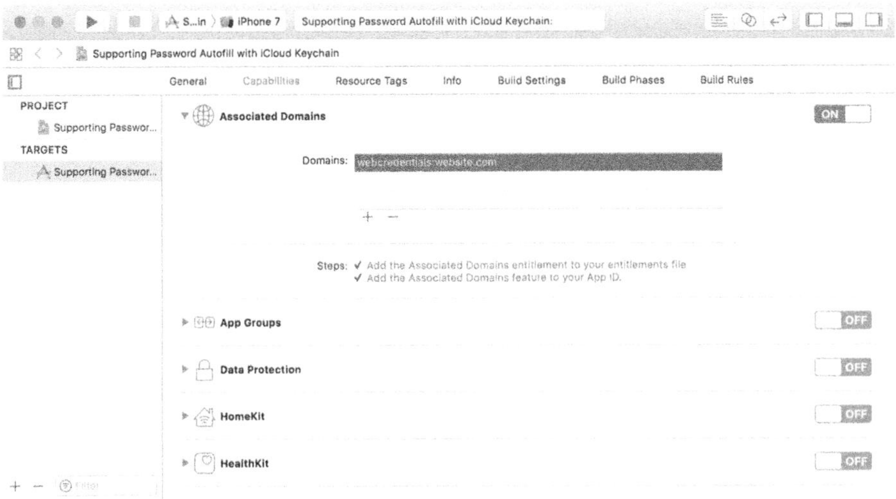

Figure 18-1. We have associated our website address, webcredentials.website.com, with our application

5. In your code, in the username text field of your login screen, set the `textContent Type` property's value to `username`. The `textContentType` property is of type `UITextContentType`.

6. For your password field, set the `textContentType` to `password`, which is again of type `UITextContentType`.

Discussion

When you place the *apple-app-site-association* file in your website's *.well-known* folder inside the root folder of your website, and then enable Associated Domains in your application, iOS attempts to connect to your associated website when running your application and reads the *apple-app-site-association* file. If the app identifier inside this file is equal to the identifier for your application, the security chain is complete. Your app points to your website and your website points to your app! In this way, iOS allows the user to use the same iCloud Keychain credentials that she has saved into iCloud while signing up in your website inside your application, using Touch ID.

You can also set the text content type of your login screen in IB's Attributes Inspector Panel, as shown in Figure 18-2. On the left side of the panel, I have selected the Username text field in the login screen of my app. On the right side, at the top, I have changed the content type to Username. I would then do the same thing with the Password field in the login screen in your app, setting the content type to Password.

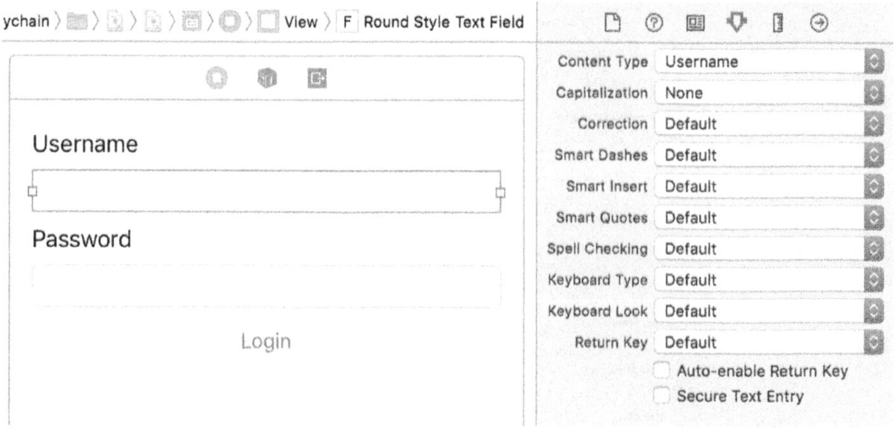

Figure 18-2. Setting the content type for the username in the app's login screen

See Also

Recipe 18.3

18.2 Protecting Your Network Connections with ATS

Problem

You want to control the details about the HTTPS channels through which your network connections go, or use a nonsecure channel (HTTP).

I do not personally suggest using nonsecure connections. However, in some cases, if you are using a backend that does not provide an HTTPS variant, you will eventually be forced to go through HTTP. In this chapter, I'll help you figure out how to do that as well.

Solution

By default, all domain names that you use in your URLs will be going through secure channels. But you can indicate specific exceptions. ATS has a dictionary key in your *Info.plist* file called NSAppTransportSecurity. Under that, you have another dictionary key called NSExceptionDomains. Under this key you can list specific domain names that don't use ATS.

Discussion

If you want to disable ATS entirely so that all your network connections go through channels specified in your code, simply insert the NSAllowsArbitraryLoads key under the `NSExceptionDomains` key. The `NSAllowsArbitraryLoads` key accepts a Boolean value. If set to `true`, your HTTP connections will be HTTP and HTTPS will be HTTPS.

Alternatively, under the `NSExceptionDomains` key, you can specify the name of your domain and set its data type to be a dictionary. Under this dictionary, you can have the following keys:

`NSExceptionAllowsInsecureHTTPLoads`

If set to `true`, allows HTTP loads on the given domain.

`NSIncludesSubdomains`

If set to `true`, includes all the subdomains of the given domain as an exception from ATS.

`NSRequiresCertificateTransparency`

Dictates that the SSL certificate of the given URL has to include certificate-transparency information. Check certificate transparency out on the web for more information.

`NSExceptionMinimumTLSVersion`

This is a key to which you assign a string value to specify the minimum TLS version for the connection. Values can be `TLSv1.0`, `TLSv1.1`, or `TLSv1.2`.

So if you want to disable ATS completely, your *plist* will look like this:

```
<plist version="1.0">
<dict>
        <key>NSExceptionDomains</key>
        <dict>
                <key>NSAllowsArbitraryLoads</key>
                <true/>
        </dict>
</dict>
</plist>
```

How about if you want to have ATS enabled, but not for *mydomain.com* and its subdomains? You can do that as follows, in addition to requesting certificate transparency:

```
<plist version="1.0">
<dict>
<key>NSExceptionDomains</key>
<dict>
        <key>NSAllowsArbitraryLoads</key>
        <false/>
        <key>mydomain.com</key>
        <dict>
                <key>NSExceptionAllowsInsecureHTTPLoads</key>
                <true/>
```

```
            <key>NSIncludesSubdomains</key>
            <true/>
            <key>NSRequiresCertificateTransparency</key>
            <true/>
        </dict>
</dict>
</dict>
</plist>
```

Finally, you can enable ATS *only* for *mydomain.com* as follows:

```
<plist version="1.0">
<dict>
<key>NSExceptionDomains</key>
<dict>
        <key>NSAllowsArbitraryLoads</key>
        <true/>
        <key>mydomain.com</key>
        <dict>
                <key>NSExceptionAllowsInsecureHTTPLoads</key>
                <false/>
                <key>NSIncludesSubdomains</key>
                <true/>
        </dict>
</dict>
</dict>
</plist>
```

18.3 Binding Keychain Items to Passcode and Touch ID

Problem

You want to create a secure item in the keychain that is accessible only if the user has set a passcode on her device *and* has opted in to using the device with Touch ID. So, at least one finger has to have been registered.

Solution

Follow these steps:

1. Create your access control flags with the `SecAccessControlCreateWithFlags()` function.

   Pass the value of `kSecAttrAccessibleWhenPasscodeSetThisDeviceOnly` as the `protection` parameter and the value of `SecAccessControlCreateFlags.touchIDAny` as the `flags` parameter.

2. In your secure dictionary, add a key named `kSecUseAuthenticationUI` and set its value to `kSecUseAuthenticationUIAllow`. This allows the user to unlock the secure key with her device passcode or Touch ID.

3. In your secure dictionary, add a key named `kSecAttrAccessControl` and set its value to the return value of the `SecAccessControlCreateWithFlags()` function that you called earlier.

Discussion

For extra security, you might want to sometimes bind secure items in the keychain to Touch ID and a passcode on a device. As explained in the Solution section, you'll have to first create your access control flags with the `SecAccessControlCreateWith Flags()` function and then proceed to use the `SecItemAdd()` function as you normally would, to add a secure item to the keychain.

The following example saves a password (as a string) into the keychain and binds it to the user's passcode and Touch ID. Start off by creating the access control flags:

```
guard let flags =
  SecAccessControlCreateWithFlags(
    kCFAllocatorDefault,
    kSecAttrAccessibleWhenPasscodeSetThisDeviceOnly,
    SecAccessControlCreateFlags.touchIDAny, nil) else{
      print("Could not create the access control flags")
      return
}
```

Then define the data that you want to store in the keychain:

```
let password = "some string"

guard let data = password.data(using: String.Encoding.utf8) else{
  print("Could not get data from string")
  return
}
```

The next step is to create the dictionary that you need to pass to the `SecItemAdd()` function later with all your flags:

```
let service = "onlinePasswords"

let attrs = [
  kSecClass.str() : kSecClassGenericPassword.str(),
  kSecAttrService.str() : service,
  kSecValueData.str() : data,
  kSecUseAuthenticationUI.str() : kSecUseAuthenticationUIAllow.str(),
  kSecAttrAccessControl.str() : flags,
  ]
```

Last but not least, asynchronously add the item to the keychain:

```
OperationQueue().addOperation{
  guard SecItemAdd(attrs, nil) == errSecSuccess else{
    print("Could not add the item to the keychain")
```

```
    return
  }

  print("Successfully added the item to keychain")
}
```

Earlier, we used the value of SecAccessControlCreateFlags.touchIDAny in the flags parameter of the SecAccessControlCreateWithFlags() function to specify that we need Touch ID to be enabled on the current device before our secure item can be read. There is another value in SecAccessControlCreateFlags that you might find useful: touchIDCurrentSet. If you use this value, your secure item will still require Touch ID, but it will be invalidated by a change to the current set of enrolled Touch ID fingers. If the user adds a new finger to Touch ID or removes an existing one, your item will be invalidated and won't be readable.

See Also

Recipe 18.1

18.4 Opening URLs Safely

Problem

You want to find out whether an app on the user's device can open a specific URL.

Solution

Follow these steps:

1. Define the key of LSApplicationQueriesSchemes in your *plist* file as an array.
2. Under that array, define your URL schemes as strings. These are the URL schemes that you want your app to be able to open.
3. In your app, issue the canOpenUrl(_:) method on your shared app.
4. If you can open the URL, do so it using the open(_:options:completionHan dler:) method of the shared app.
5. If you cannot open the URL, offer an alternative to your user if possible.

Discussion

In iOS, previously, apps could issue a canOpenUrl(_:) call to find out whether there was another application on the device that could open a particular URL. For instance, you could call this method to find out whether it was possible to open *instagram://app* (see "iPhone Hooks" in the Instagram Developer Documentation (*https://instagram.com/developer/mobile-sharing/iphone-hooks/*)). If so, you would know that Instagram is installed on the user's device. The information gathered using this technique was then used for marketing, among other things.

In the latest iOS, you need to use the *plist* file to define the URLs that you want to be able to open or to check whether URLs can be opened. If you define too many APIs or unrelated APIs, your app might get rejected. If you try to open a URL that you have not defined in the *plist*, you will get a failure. You can use canOpenUrl(_:) to check whether you can access a URL before trying to open it: the method returns true if you have indicated that you can open that kind of URL, and false otherwise.

Let's check out an example. First, try to find out whether you can open the Instagram app on the user's device:

```
guard let url = URL(string: "instagram://app"),
  UIApplication.shared.canOpenURL(url) else{
    return
}
```

Now that you know you can open the URL proceed to do so:

```
UIApplication.shared.open(url){succeeded in
  if succeeded{
    print("Successfully opened Instagram")
  } else {
    print("Could not open Instagram")
  }
}
```

Then go into the *plist* file and tell iOS that you want to open URL schemes starting with "instagram":

```
<plist version="1.0">
<array>
      <string>instagram</string>
</array>
</plist>
```

18.5 Authenticating the User with Touch ID and Timeout

Problem

You want to ask the user for permission to read secure content in the keychain. This includes setting a timeout after which you will no longer have access.

Solution

Follow these steps:

1. Create your access control flags with `SecAccessControlCreateWithFlags()`, as you saw in Recipe 18.3.
2. Instantiate a context object of type `LAContext`.
3. Set the `touchIDAuthenticationAllowableReuseDuration` property of your context to `LATouchIDAuthenticationMaximumAllowableReuseDuration`, so your context will lock out only after the maximum allowed number of seconds.
4. Call the `evaluateAccessControl(_:operation:localizedReason:)` method on your context to get access to the access control.
5. If you gain access, create your keychain request dictionary and include the `kSecUseAuthenticationContext` key. The value of this key will be your context object.
6. Use the `SecItemCopyMatching()` function with your dictionary to read a secure object with the given access controls.

Discussion

Whenever you write an item to the keychain, you can do so with access controls as we saw in Recipe 18.3. So, assume that your item requires Touch ID. If you want to read that item now, you need to request permission to do so. First, define your context and the reason why you want to read the item:

```
let context = LAContext()
let reason = "To unlock previously stored security phrase"
```

Then define your access controls as before:

```
guard let flags =
  SecAccessControlCreateWithFlags(
    kCFAllocatorDefault,
    kSecAttrAccessibleWhenPasscodeSetThisDeviceOnly,
    SecAccessControlCreateFlags.touchIDAny, nil) else{
      print("Could not create the access control flags")
      return
}
```

Also specify how long you can get access for. After this time passes, the user will be forced to use Touch ID again to unlock the context:

```
context.touchIDAuthenticationAllowableReuseDuration =
LATouchIDAuthenticationMaximumAllowableReuseDuration
```

Last but not least, gain access to the given access controls and read the item if possible:

```
context.evaluateAccessControl(
  flags,
  operation: LAAccessControlOperation.useItem,
  localizedReason: reason) {[unowned context] succ, err in
```

```
guard succ && err == nil else {
  print("Could not evaluate the access control")
  if let e = err {
    print("Error = \(e)")
  }
  return
}

print("Successfully evaluated the access control")

let service = "onlinePasswords"

let attrs = [
  kSecClass.str() : kSecClassGenericPassword.str(),
  kSecAttrService.str() : service,
  kSecUseAuthenticationUI.str() : kSecUseAuthenticationUIAllow.str(),
  kSecAttrAccessControl.str() : flags,
  kSecReturnData.str() : kCFBooleanTrue,
  kSecUseAuthenticationContext.str() : context,
  ] as NSDictionary

// now attempt to use the attrs with SecItemCopyMatching

print(attrs)

}
```

The operation argument of the evaluateAccessControl(_:operation:localized Reason:) method takes in a value of type LAAccessControlOperation that indicates the type of operation you want to perform. Some of the values that you can use are useItem, createItem, createKey, and useKeySign.

See Also

Recipe 18.3

Last but not least, instantiate the voice synthesizer, of type AVSpeechSynthesizer, and ask it to speak out the voice object:

```
let alex = AVSpeechSynthesizer()
alex.delegate = self
alex.speak(toSay)
```

19.2 Downloading and Preparing Remote Media for Playback

Problem

You have some remote assets, such as sound files, and would like to download them, even if in the background. Along the way, you want to provide real-time feedback on the download process.

Solution

Follow these steps:

1. Create an instance of AVURLAsset with the URL to your asset.
2. Use the background(withIdentifier:) class method on URLSessionConfiguration to create a background session configuration.
3. Create a session of type AVAssetDownloadURLSession and pass your configuration to it.
4. Construct the URL where your asset has to be downloaded onto the disk.
5. Use the makeAssetDownloadTask(asset:destinationURL:options) method of your session to create a download task of type AVAssetDownloadTask.
6. Call the resume() method on your task to start the task.
7. Conform to the AVAssetDownloadDelegate protocol to get events from your task.

All the classes discussed here whose names start with "AV" are in the AVFoundation framework, so make sure to import it.

Discussion

Let's imagine that you have an *.mp4* file that you want to download and play back in your app. First set up your view controller:

```
import UIKit
import AVFoundation

class ViewController: UIViewController, AVAssetDownloadDelegate {

  let url = URL(string: "http://localhost:8888/video.mp4")!
  let sessionId = "com.mycompany.background"
  let queue = OperationQueue()
  var task: AVAssetDownloadTask?
  var session: AVAssetDownloadURLSession?

  ...
```

 I have used MAMP to start a local server on my machine and am hosting the file *video.mp4* on my own computer, hence the URL that you are seeing. You can and probably should change this URL to a point to valid media file that AVFoundation can handle, like *.mov* or *.mp4*.

Now define some of the delegate methods defined in `AVAssetDownloadDelegate` and `URLSessionTaskDelegate`:

```
func urlSession(_ session: URLSession, task: URLSessionTask,
              didCompleteWithError error: Error?) {
  // code this
}

func urlSession(_ session: URLSession,
              assetDownloadTask: AVAssetDownloadTask,
              didLoad timeRange: CMTimeRange,
              totalTimeRangesLoaded loadedTimeRanges: [NSValue],
              timeRangeExpectedToLoad: CMTimeRange) {
  // code this
}

func urlSession(_ session: URLSession,
              assetDownloadTask: AVAssetDownloadTask,
              didResolve resolvedMediaSelection: AVMediaSelection) {

}
```

Next, create an asset by its URL. At the same time, tell the system that you don't want cross-site references to be resolved using a dictionary with a key equal to `AVURLAssetReferenceRestrictionsKey` and value of `AVAssetReferenceRestrictions.forbidCrossSiteReference`:

```
let options = [AVURLAssetReferenceRestrictionsKey :
  AVAssetReferenceRestrictions.forbidCrossSiteReference.rawValue]

let asset = AVURLAsset(url: url, options: options)
```

Now it's time to create the configuration object, of type `URLSessionConfiguration`:

```
let config = URLSessionConfiguration
  .background(withIdentifier: sessionId)
```

Then create the session, of type `AVAssetDownloadURLSession`:

```
let session = AVAssetDownloadURLSession(
  configuration: config,
  assetDownloadDelegate: self, delegateQueue: queue)

self.session = session
```

 Be sure to keep a reference to the session, and to the task that you are going to create next. This is so you can refer to them later and cancel or reuse them if necessary.

And last but not least, construct the task and start it:

```
guard let task = session.makeAssetDownloadTask(
  asset: asset,
  assetTitle: "Asset title",
  assetArtworkData: nil,
  options: nil) else {
    print("Could not create the task")
    return
}

self.task = task

task.resume()
```

19.3 Enabling Spoken Audio Sessions

Problem

You have an ebook reading app (or similar app) and would like to enable a specific audio session that allows your app's audio to be paused—but another app is playing back voice on top of yours (such as an app that provides navigation information with voice).

Solution

Follow these steps:

1. First, you will need to go through the available audio session categories inside the `availableCategories` property of your audio session and find `AVAudioSession CategoryPlayback`.
2. Then go through the values inside the `availableModes` property of your audio session (of type `AVAudioSession`). If you cannot find `AVAudioSessionMode SpokenAudio`, exit gracefully.
3. If you find the `AVAudioSessionModeSpokenAudio` mode, set your audio category to `AVAudioSessionCategoryPlayback` using the `setCategory(_:with:)` method of the audio session.
4. Activate your session with the `setActive(_:with:)` method of your audio session.

Discussion

Suppose you are developing an ebook app and have a Read button in the UI that the user presses to ask the app to read the contents of the book out loud. For this you can use the `AVAudioSessionModeSpokenAudio` audio session mode, but you have to check first whether that mode exists. To find out, use the `availableModes` property of your audio session.

Let's look at an example. First, look for the `AVAudioSessionCategoryPlayback` category and the `AVAudioSessionModeSpokenAudio` mode:

```
guard session.availableCategories.filter(
  {$0 == AVAudioSessionCategoryPlayback}).count == 1 &&
  session.availableModes.filter(
    {$0 == AVAudioSessionModeSpokenAudio}).count == 1 else{
      print("Could not find the category or the mode")
      return
}
```

After you confirm that the category and mode are available, set the category and mode and then activate your audio session:

```
do{
  try session.setCategory(AVAudioSessionCategoryPlayback,
                    with:
    AVAudioSessionCategoryOptions.interruptSpokenAudioAndMixWithOthers)

  try session.setMode(AVAudioSessionModeSpokenAudio)

  try session.setActive(true, with:
    AVAudioSessionSetActiveOptions.notifyOthersOnDeactivation)

} catch let err{
  print("Error = \(err)")
}
```

CHAPTER 20

UI Dynamics

UI Dynamics allow you to create very nice effects on your UI components, such as gravity and collision detection. Let's say that you have two buttons on the screen that the user can move around. You could create opposing gravity fields on them so that they repel each other and cannot be dragged into each other. Or, for instance, you could provide a more dynamic UI by creating a turbulence field under all your UI components so that they move around automatically ever so slightly (or through a noise field, as described in Recipe 20.4) even when the user is not interacting with them. All of this is possible with the tools that Apple has given you in UIKit. You don't have to use any other framework to dig into UI Dynamics.

One of the basic concepts in UI Dynamics is an *animator*. Animator objects, which are of type `UIDynamicAnimator`, hold together and orchestrate all the effects. For instance, if you have collision detection and gravity effects, the animator decides how the pull on an object through gravity will work hand in hand with the collision detection around the edges of your reference view.

Reference views are like canvases where all your animations happen. Effects are added to views and then added to an animator, which itself is placed on a reference view. In other words, the reference view is the canvas and the views on your UI (buttons, lables, etc.) will have effects.

20.1 Adding a Radial Gravity Field to Your UI

Problem

You want to add a radial gravity field to your UI, with animations.

Solution

Use the `radialGravityFieldWithPosition(_:)` class method of `UIFieldBehavior` and add this behavior to a dynamic animator of type `UIDynamicAnimator`.

Discussion

A typical gravity behavior pulls items in a given direction. A radial gravity field has a center and a region in which everything is drawn to the center, just like gravity on Earth, whereby everything is pulled toward the core of this sphere.

For this recipe, we'll design a UI like Figure 20-1. The gravity is at the center of the main view and the orange view is affected by it.

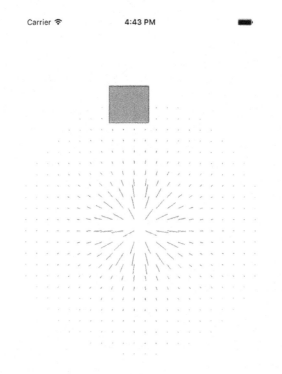

Figure 20-1. A main view and another view that is an orange square

Note that the gravity field here is not linear. We would like this gravity field to repel the orange view, instead of pulling it toward the core, and we would like the user to be able to pan this orange view around the screen and release it to see how the gravity affects the view at that point in time (think about pan gesture recognizers).

To begin, create a single view app that has no navigation bar and then go into IB and add simple colorful view to your main view. Color it orange(ish), and link it to your view controller under the name orangeView (see Figure 20-2).

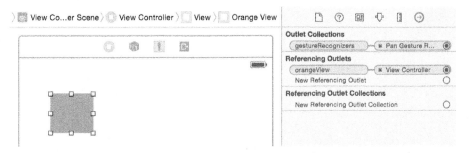

Figure 20-2. Add the orange view on top of the view controller's view and hook it to the view controller's code

Then, from the Object Library, find a pan gesture recognizer (see Figure 20-3) and drop it onto your orange view so that it gets associated with that view. You can find the pan gesture recognizer by typing its name into the Object Library's search field.

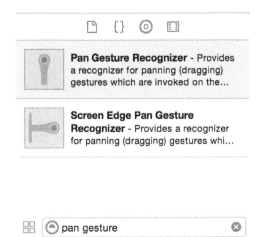

Figure 20-3. Getting the pan gesture recognizer

You should then associate the pan gesture recognizer's code to a method in your code called panning(_:). So now your view controller's header should look like this:

```
import UIKit
import SharedCode

class ViewController: UIViewController {

  @IBOutlet var orangeView: UIView!

  ...
```

 Whenever I write a piece of code that I want to share between various projects, I put it inside a framework that I've written called SharedCode. You can find this framework in the GitHub repo of this book. In this example, I've extended CGSize so that I can find the CGPoint at the center of CGSize like so:

```
import Foundation

extension CGSize{

  public var center: CGPoint{
    return CGPoint(x: width / 2.0, y: height / 2.0)
  }

}
```

Then, in the view controller, create your animator, specifying this view as the reference view:

```
lazy var animator: UIDynamicAnimator = {
  let animator = UIDynamicAnimator(referenceView: self.view)
  animator.isDebugEnabled = true
  return animator
  }()
```

If you are writing this code, you'll notice that you'll get a compiler error saying that the debugEnabled property is not available on an object of type UIDynamicAnimator. That is absolutely right. This is a *debug only* method that Apple has provided to us and which we should only use when debugging our apps. Because this property isn't actually available in the header file of UIDynamicAnimator, we need to create a bridging header (with a bit of Objective-C code) to enable this property. Create your bridging header and then extend UIDynamicAnimator:

```
@import UIKit;

#if DEBUG

@interface UIDynamicAnimator (DebuggingOnly)
@property (nonatomic, getter=isDebugEnabled) BOOL debugEnabled;
@end
```

```
#endif
```

When the orange view is repelled by the reversed radial gravity field, it should collide with the edges of your view controller's view and stay within the bounds of the view:

```
lazy var collision: UICollisionBehavior = {
  let collision = UICollisionBehavior(items: [self.orangeView])
  collision.translatesReferenceBoundsIntoBoundary = true
  return collision
  }()
```

Then create the radial gravity of type `UIFieldBehavior`. Two properties in this class are quite important:

region

> This is of type `UIRegion` and specifies the region covered by this gravity field.

strength

> This is a floating-point value that indicates (if positive) the force by which items get pulled into the gravity field. If you assign a negative value to this property, items get repelled by this gravity field.

Configure the gravity field to consume an area with a radius of 200 points and to repel items:

```
lazy var centerGravity: UIFieldBehavior = {
  let centerGravity =
  UIFieldBehavior.radialGravityField(position: self.view.center)
  centerGravity.addItem(self.orangeView)
  centerGravity.region = UIRegion(radius: 200)
  centerGravity.strength = -1 // repel items
  return centerGravity
  }()
```

When the user rotates the device, recenter the gravity:

```
override func viewWillTransition(to size: CGSize,
  with
  coordinator: UIViewControllerTransitionCoordinator) {

    super.viewWillTransition(to: size,
      with: coordinator)

    centerGravity.position = size.center

}
```

Remember the center property that we added earlier on top of CGSize?

When your view is loaded, add your behaviors to the animator:

```
override func viewDidLoad() {
  super.viewDidLoad()

  animator.addBehavior(collision)
  animator.addBehavior(centerGravity)

}
```

To handle the panning, consider a few things:

- When panning begins, you have to disable your animators so that none of the behaviors have an effect on the orange view.
- When the panning is in progress, you have to move the orange view where the user's finger is pointing.
- When the panning ends, you have to re-enable your behaviors.

All this is accomplished in the following code:

```
@IBAction func panning(_ sender: UIPanGestureRecognizer) {

  switch sender.state{
  case .began:
    collision.removeItem(orangeView)
    centerGravity.removeItem(orangeView)
  case .changed:
    orangeView.center = sender.location(in: view)
  case .ended, .cancelled:
    collision.addItem(orangeView)
    centerGravity.addItem(orangeView)
  default: ()
  }

}
```

20.2 Creating a Linear Gravity Field on Your UI

Problem

You want to create a gravity field that follows a vector on your UI.

Solution

Use the `linearGravityFieldWithVector(_:)` class method of `UIFieldBehavior` to create your gravity field. The parameter to this method is of type `CGVector`. You can provide your own *x* and *y* values for this vector when you construct it. This is now your gravity field, and you can add it to an animator of type `UIDynamicAnimator`.

 I am basing this recipe on Recipe 20.1. There are some things, such as the bridging header to enable debugging, that I mentioned in Recipe 20.1 and won't mention again in this recipe. I might skim over them but won't go into details.

Discussion

Whereas the example we looked at in Recipe 20.1 had a center and a radius, a linear gravity field has a direction only (up, down, right, left, etc.). In this example, we are going to use the exact same UI that we created in Recipe 20.1. So, create the little orange view on your storyboard and link it to an `orangeView` outlet in your code. Add a pan gesture recognizer to it as well and add it to a method called `panning(_:)`.

Right now, your view controller's code should look like this:

```
import UIKit
import SharedCode

class ViewController: UIViewController {

@IBOutlet var orangeView: UIView!

  lazy var animator: UIDynamicAnimator = {
    let animator = UIDynamicAnimator(referenceView: self.view)
    animator.isDebugEnabled = true
    return animator
    }()

  lazy var collision: UICollisionBehavior = {
    let collision = UICollisionBehavior(items: [self.orangeView])
    collision.translatesReferenceBoundsIntoBoundary = true
    return collision
    }()

  ...
```

The next step is to create your linear gravity field:

```
lazy var gravity: UIFieldBehavior = {
  let vector = CGVector(dx: 0.4, dy: 1.0)
  let gravity =
  UIFieldBehavior.linearGravityField(direction: vector)
```

```
  gravity.addItem(self.orangeView)
  return gravity
}()
```

Last but not least, handle the panning and add the effects to the animator (see Recipe 20.1):

```
override func viewDidLoad() {
  super.viewDidLoad()

  animator.addBehavior(collision)
  animator.addBehavior(gravity)

}

@IBAction func panning(_ sender: UIPanGestureRecognizer) {

  switch sender.state{
  case .began:
    collision.removeItem(orangeView)
    gravity.removeItem(orangeView)
  case .changed:
    orangeView.center = sender.location(in: view)
  case .ended, .cancelled:
    collision.addItem(orangeView)
    gravity.addItem(orangeView)
  default: ()
  }

}
```

If you run your app now, you should see an interface similar to Figure 20-4. The linear gravity field pulls all objects down and to the right. This is because in the vector you specified a positive *y*-delta that pulls everything down and a positive *x*-delta that pulls everything to the right. I suggest that you play around with the delta values (of type CGVector) to get a feel for how they affect gravity.

Figure 20-4. Linear gravity acting on an object

You can also go ahead and change some other aspects of your gravity field. For instance, set the `strength` property of the gravity field to 20 and see how much more gravity is applied to your objects. Similarly, play with the `animationSpeed` property of your gravity field to set the animation speed.

20.3 Creating Turbulence Effects with Animations

Problem

You want to simulate turbulence in your animator and have your UI components flail about when they hit the turbulent region.

Solution

Instantiate your turbulence with the `turbulenceFieldWithSmoothness(_:animation Speed:)` class method of `UIFieldBehavior`. Then do the following:

1. Set the `UIFieldBehavior` class's `strength` property according to your needs.
2. Set its `region` property to an instance of `UIRegion`. This defines in which region of the screen your turbulence behavior is effective.
3. Set its `position` property to a `CGPoint` instance in your reference view.

After you are done setting up the turbulence behavior, add it to your animator of type `UIDynamicAnimator`.

Discussion

In this recipe, we'll create an effect very similar to what we got in Recipe 20.2, but also add a turbulence field in the center of the screen. So, when we take our little orange view (see Figure 20-1) and drop it from the top-left corner of the screen, it will fall down (and to the right; see Figure 20-4). But on its way down, it will hit our turbulence field and its movements will be affected.

Set up your gravity field exactly as you did in Recipe 20.2. I won't go through that here again. Then create a turbulence field in the center of the screen with a radius of 200 points:

```
lazy var turbulence: UIFieldBehavior = {
  let turbulence = UIFieldBehavior.turbulenceField(smoothness: 0.5,
    animationSpeed: 60.0)
  turbulence.strength = 12.0
  turbulence.region = UIRegion(radius: 200.0)
  turbulence.position = self.orangeView.bounds.size.center
  turbulence.addItem(self.orangeView)
  return turbulence
}()
```

Make sure to add this field to your animator. When the user is panning with the gesture recognizer (see Recipe 20.1), disable all your behaviors, and re-enable them when the panning is finished:

```
override func viewDidLoad() {
  super.viewDidLoad()

  animator.addBehavior(collision)
  animator.addBehavior(gravity)
  animator.addBehavior(turbulence)

}

@IBAction func panning(_ sender: UIPanGestureRecognizer) {
```

```
switch sender.state{
case .began:
  collision.removeItem(orangeView)
  gravity.removeItem(orangeView)
  turbulence.removeItem(orangeView)
case .changed:
  orangeView.center = sender.location(in: view)
case .ended, .cancelled:
  collision.addItem(orangeView)
  gravity.addItem(orangeView)
  turbulence.addItem(orangeView)
default: ()
}

}
```

Give it a go and see the results for yourself. Drag the orange view to the top-left corner of the screen and drop it. It will be dragged down and to the right, and when it hits the center of the screen (inside a radius of 200 points), it will wiggle around a bit because of turbulence.

20.4 Adding Animated Noise Effects to Your UI

Problem

You want to add a noise field on your UI and have your UI components surf in all directions on this field.

Solution

1. Create a noise field using the `noiseFieldWithSmoothness(_:animationSpeed:)` class method of `UIFieldBehavior`.
2. Add the views you want affected by this noise to the field using its `addItem(_:)` method.
3. Add your noise field to an animator of type `UIDynamicAnimator` (see Recipe 20.1).

> This recipe is based on what you learned in Recipe 20.1—refer back to that recipe if you need a refresher.

Discussion

Noise is great for having an item constantly move around on your reference view in random directions. Have a look at the noise field in Figure 20-5. This noise field is shown graphically on the UI using a UI Dynamics debugging trick.

Figure 20-5. Noise field affecting a square view

The direction of the noise that you see on the field dictates in which direction the field repels the items attached to it. In this case, I've used negative gravity (think of it that way). If you want to limit the effective region of your noise field on your reference view, simply set the `region` property of your field. This is of type `UIRegion`.

Now create your UI exactly as you did in Recipe 20.1. You should have an orange view that is accessible through the `orangeView` property of your view controller. Create a collision detector and an animator using what you learned in the aforementioned recipe. Then go ahead and create your noise field:

```
lazy var noise: UIFieldBehavior = {
  let noise = UIFieldBehavior.noiseField(smoothness: 0.9,
                                         animationSpeed: 1)
  noise.addItem(self.orangeView)
  return noise
}()
```

Add the noise field to your animator:

```
override func viewDidLoad() {
  super.viewDidLoad()
  animator.addBehavior(collision)
  animator.addBehavior(noise)
}
```

Last but not least, handle your pan gesture recognizer's event, so that when the user starts dragging the orange view across the screen your dynamic behaviors will shut down, and as soon as the user is done with dragging, they will come back up:

```
@IBAction func panning(_ sender: UIPanGestureRecognizer) {

  switch sender.state{
  case .began:
    collision.removeItem(orangeView)
    noise.removeItem(orangeView)
  case .changed:
    orangeView.center = sender.location(in: view)
  case .ended, .cancelled:
    collision.addItem(orangeView)
    noise.addItem(orangeView)
  default: ()
  }

}
```

20.5 Creating a Magnetic Effect Between UI Components

Problem

You want to create a magnetic field between two or more UI elements.

Solution

Follow these steps:

1. Create your animator (see Recipe 20.1).
2. Create a collision detector of type `UICollisionBehavior`.
3. Create a magnetic field of type `UIFieldBehavior` using the `magneticField()` class method of `UIFieldBehavior`.
4. Add your magnetic field and collision detector to your animator.

I am basing this recipe on what you learned in Recipes 20.1 and 20.4.

Discussion

Create a UI that looks similar to Figure 20-6.

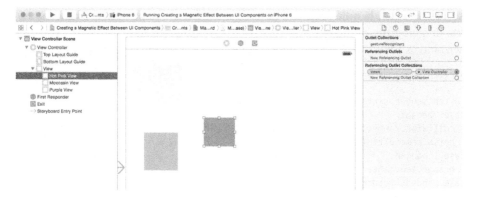

Figure 20-6. Place three colorful views on your UI

Then link all the views to an outlet collection called `views` in your code:

```
class ViewController: UIViewController {

  @IBOutlet var views: [UIView]!

  ...
```

Now that you have an array of views to which you want to apply a noise field and a magnetic field, it's best to extend `UIFieldBehavior` so that you can pass it an array of UI elements instead of one element at a time:

```
extension UIFieldBehavior{
  public func addItems(_ items: [UIDynamicItem]){
    for item in items{
      addItem(item)
```

```
      }
    }
}
```

Also, it's best to extend `UIDynamicAnimator` so that you can add all your behaviors to your animator at once:

```
extension UIDynamicAnimator{
  public func addBehaviors(_ behaviors: [UIDynamicBehavior]){
    for behavior in behaviors{
      addBehavior(behavior)
    }
  }
}
```

Now add a noise and a collision behavior, plus your animator, using what you learned in Recipe 20.4. I won't repeat that code here.

Create a magnetic field and enable it on all your views:

```
lazy var magnet: UIFieldBehavior = {
  let magnet = UIFieldBehavior.magneticField()
  magnet.addItems(self.views)
  return magnet
}()
```

Last but not least, add your behaviors to the animator:

```
var behaviors: [UIDynamicBehavior]{
  return [collision, noise, magnet]
}

override func viewDidLoad() {
  super.viewDidLoad()
  animator.addBehaviors(behaviors)
}
```

Run the app and see the results for yourself (see Figure 20-7).

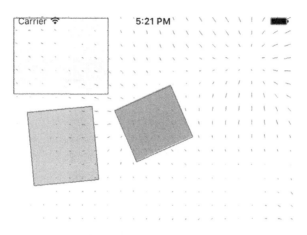

Figure 20-7. The magnetic field causes all the views to attract one another

20.6 Designing a Velocity Field on Your UI

Problem

You want to apply force, following a vector, onto your UI components.

Solution

Follow these steps:

1. Create an animator of type `UIDynamicAnimator` (see Recipe 20.1).
2. Create a collision detector of type `UICollisionBehavior`.
3. It's best to also have gravity or other forces applied to your field (see Recipes 17.1 and 17.2).
4. Create a velocity field using the `UIFieldBehavior` class's `velocityFieldWithVector(_:)` method and supply a vector of type `CGVector`.
5. Set the `position` property of your velocity field to an appropriate point on your reference view.
6. Then set the `region` property of your velocity field to an appropriate region (of type `UIRegion`) of your reference view.
7. Once done, add your behaviors to your animator.

If you haven't yet, I recommend having a look at Recipe 20.1, where I described most of the basics of setting up a scene with gravity and an animator. I won't go into those in detail again.

In this recipe, I am also going to use a few extensions that we coded in Recipe 20.5.

Discussion

A velocity field applies a force toward a given direction to dynamic items, such as UIView instances. In this recipe, we are going to design a field that looks like the field in Recipe 20.5. On top of that, we are going to apply a slight upward and leftbound force that is positioned smack dab in the center of the screen. We'll position an orange view on the main storyboard and have all the forces applied to this poor little guy. We will then place the orange view on top of the reference view so that when we run the app, a few things will happen:

1. The southeast-bound gravity will pull the orange view to the bottom right of the screen.
2. The orange view will keep falling down until it hits the northwest-bound velocity field, at which point the orange view will get uncomfortable and move up and left a bit a few times, and keep falling until it gets out of the velocity field.
3. The orange view will then eventually settle at the bottom right of the view.

Set up your gravity, animator, and collision detector just as you did in Recipe 20.2 (I won't repeat that code). Then set up the velocity field:

```
lazy var velocity: UIFieldBehavior = {
  let vector = CGVector(dx: -0.4, dy: -0.5)
  let velocity = UIFieldBehavior.velocityField(direction: vector)
  velocity.position = self.view.center
  velocity.region = UIRegion(radius: 100.0)
  velocity.addItem(self.orangeView)
  return velocity
}()
```

Then batch up all your forces into one variable that you can give to your animator, using the extension we wrote in Recipe 20.5:

```
var behaviors: [UIDynamicBehavior]{
  return [self.collision, self.gravity, self.velocity]
}

override func viewDidLoad() {
  super.viewDidLoad()
  animator.addBehaviors(behaviors)
}
```

When the user starts panning your orange view around, stop all the forces, then restart them when she is done dragging:

```
@IBAction func panning(_ sender: UIPanGestureRecognizer) {

  switch sender.state{
  case .began:
    collision.removeItem(orangeView)
    gravity.removeItem(orangeView)
    velocity.removeItem(orangeView)
  case .changed:
    orangeView.center = sender.location(in: view)
  case .ended, .cancelled:
    collision.addItem(orangeView)
    gravity.addItem(orangeView)
    velocity.addItem(orangeView)
  default: ()
  }

}
```

20.7 Handling Collisions Between Nonrectangular Views

Problem

You want to create nonrectangular-shaped views in your app, and you want your collision detection to work properly with these views.

Solution

Follow these steps:

1. First, you'll need to subclass `UIView` and override the `collisionBoundsType` variable of type `UIDynamic ItemCollisionBoundsType`. In there, return `UIDynamic ItemCollisionBoundsType.Path`. This makes sure that you have your own Bézier path of type `UIBezierPath`, and you want that to define the edges of your view, which are essentially the edges that your collision detector has to detect.
2. Override the `collisionBoundingPath` variable of type `UIBezierPath` in your view and in there, return the path that defines your view's edges.
3. In your `UIBezierPath`, create the shape you want for your view. The first point in this shape needs to be the center of your shape. You must draw your shape in a convex and counterclockwise manner.
4. Override the `drawRect(_:)` method of your view and draw your path there.
5. Add your behaviors to your new and awesome view and then create an animator of type `UIDynamicAnimator` (see Recipe 20.1).

---

6. Optionally, throw in a noise field as well to create some random movements between your dynamic items (see Recipe 20.4).

 I am going to draw a pentagon view in this recipe. I won't teach how that is drawn because you can find the basic rules of drawing a pentagon online, and that is entirely outside the scope of this book.

Discussion

Here, we are aiming to create a dynamic field that looks like Figure 20-8. The views we'll create are a square and a pentagon. We will have proper collision detection between the two views.

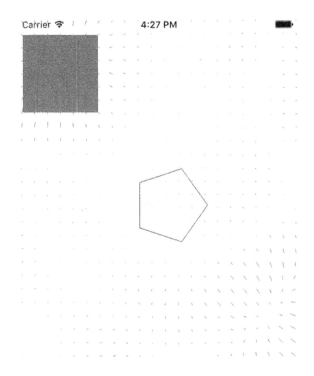

Figure 20-8. Square and pentagon with collision detection

Let's start off by creating a little extension on the StrideThrough structure. You'll see soon, when we code our pentagon view, that we are going to go through five points of the pentagon that are drawn on the circumference of the bounding circle, plot them on the path, and draw lines between them. We will use stride(from:through:by:)

to create the loop. We would like to perform a function over every item in this array of numbers, hence the following extension:

```
extension StrideThrough{
  func forEach(_ f: (Iterator.Element) -> Void){
    for item in self{
      f(item)
    }
  }
}
```

Let's move on to creating a class named PentagonView that subclasses UIView. We want this view to be constructed only by a diameter. This will be the diameter of the bounding circle within which the pentagon will reside. Therefore, we need a diame
ter variable, along with our constructor and perhaps a nice class method constructor for good measure:

```
class PentagonView : UIView{

  private var diameter: CGFloat = 0.0

  class func pentagonViewWithDiameter(_ diameter: CGFloat) -> PentagonView{
    return PentagonView(diameter: diameter)
  }

  init(diameter: CGFloat){
    self.diameter = diameter
    super.init(frame: CGRect(x: 0, y: 0, width: diameter, height: diameter))
  }

  required init?(coder aDecoder: NSCoder) {
    super.init(coder: aDecoder)
  }

  var radius: CGFloat{
    return diameter / 2.0
  }

  ...
```

We need next to create our UIBezierPath. There are five slices inside a pentagon and the angle between each slice, from the center of the pentagon, is 360/5, or 72 degrees. Using this knowledge, we need to be able to, given the center of our pentagon, plot the five points onto the circumference of the bounding circle:

```
func pointFromAngle(_ angle: Double) -> CGPoint{

  let x = radius + (radius * cos(CGFloat(angle)))
  let y = radius + (radius * sin(CGFloat(angle)))
  return CGPoint(x: x, y: y)

}
```

```
lazy var path: UIBezierPath = {
  let path = UIBezierPath()
  path.move(to: self.pointFromAngle(0))

  let oneSlice = (M_PI * 2.0) / 5.0
  let lessOneSlice = (M_PI * 2.0) - oneSlice

  stride(from: oneSlice, through: lessOneSlice, by: oneSlice).forEach{
    path.addLine(to: self.pointFromAngle($0))
  }

  path.close()
  return path
}()
```

That was *the* most important part of this recipe, if you are curious. Once we have the path, we can draw our view using it:

```
override func draw(_ rect: CGRect) {
  guard let context = UIGraphicsGetCurrentContext() else{
    return
  }
  UIColor.clear.setFill()
  context.fill(rect)
  UIColor.yellow.setFill()
  path.fill()
}
```

The next and last step in creating our pentagon view is to override the collision BoundsType and collisionBoundingPath variables:

```
override var collisionBoundsType: UIDynamicItemCollisionBoundsType{
  return .path
}

override var collisionBoundingPath: UIBezierPath{
  let path = self.path.copy() as! UIBezierPath
  path.apply(CGAffineTransform(translationX: -radius, y: -radius))
  return path
}
```

 We are applying a translation transform on our Bézier path before giving it to the collision detector. The reason behind this is that the first point of our path is in the center of our shape, so we need to subtract the *x* and *y* position of the center from the path to translate our path to its actual value for the collision detector to use. Otherwise, the path will be outside the actual pentagon shape. Because the *x* and *y* position of the center of our pentagon *are* in fact the radius of the pentagon and the radius is half the diameter, we provide the radius here to the translation.

Now let's extend `UIView` so that we can add a pan gesture recognizer to it with one line of code. Both the square and our pentagon view will easily get a pan gesture recognizer:

```
extension UIView{
  func createPanGestureRecognizerOn(_ obj: AnyObject){
    let pgr = UIPanGestureRecognizer(
      target: obj, action: #selector(ViewController.panning(_:)))
    addGestureRecognizer(pgr)
  }
}
```

Let's move on to the view controller. Add the following components to the view controller, just as we did in Recipe 20.4:

- An animator of type `UIDynamicAnimator`
- A collision detector of type `UICollisionBehavior`
- A noise field of type `UIFieldBehavior`

Next, we'll bundle the collision detector and the noise field into an array. This lets us add them to our animator faster with the extensions that we created in Recipe 20.5:

```
var behaviors: [UIDynamicBehavior]{
  return [self.collision, self.noise]
}
```

The next step is to create our square view. This one is easy. It is just a simple view with a pan gesture recognizer:

```
lazy var squareView: UIView = {
  let view = UIView(frame: CGRect(x: 0, y: 0, width: 100, height: 100))
  view.createPanGestureRecognizerOn(self)
  view.backgroundColor = UIColor.brown
  return view
  }()
```

Now for the juicy part—the pentagon view! We create it with the constructor of `PentagonView` and then place it in the center of our view:

```
lazy var pentagonView: PentagonView = {
  let view = PentagonView.pentagonViewWithDiameter(100)
  view.createPanGestureRecognizerOn(self)
  view.backgroundColor = UIColor.clear
  view.center = self.view.center
  return view
  }()
```

Then we group the views and add them to our reference view:

```
var views: [UIView]{
  return [self.squareView, self.pentagonView]
}
```

```
override func viewDidLoad() {
  super.viewDidLoad()
  view.addSubview(squareView)
  view.addSubview(pentagonView)
  animator.addBehaviors(behaviors)
}
```

Finally, we handle panning. As soon as the user starts to pan one of our views around, we pause all the behaviors. Once the panning is finished, we re-enable the behaviors:

```
@IBAction func panning(_ sender: UIPanGestureRecognizer) {

  switch sender.state{
  case .began:
    collision.removeItems()
    noise.removeItems()
  case .changed:
    sender.view?.center = sender.location(in: view)
  case .ended, .cancelled:
    collision.addItems(views)
    noise.addItems(views)
  default: ()
  }

}
```

Wrapping up, I want to clarify a few things. We extended UIDynamicAnimator and added the addBehaviors(_:) method to it in Recipe 20.5. In the same recipe, we added the addItems(_:) method to UIFieldBehavior. But in our current recipe, we also need removeItems(), so I think it's best to show that extension again with the new code:

```
extension UIFieldBehavior{
  public func addItems(_ items: [UIDynamicItem]){
    for item in items{
      addItem(item)
    }
  }
  public func removeItems(){
    for item in items{
      removeItem(item)
    }
  }
}
```

You should extend UICollisionBehavior in the exact same way and add the addItems(_:) and removeItems() methods to that class as well.

iMessage Stickers and Apps

We all use messaging capabilities on our iOS devices. This is a bold statement and I have no proof for it, but it's difficult to imagine a person owning an iOS device without having sent or received messages. The main messaging application on iOS is iMessage, but it's not the only messaging option for iOS. You can download and choose among a huge selection of various messaging applications.

iMessage used to be fully closed. That is to say, it lived in its own sandbox (and still does), and did not allow any extensions to be attached to it. But now that has changed, and we developers can finally write our own iMessage extensions that allow even more interactivity to be added to our conversations.

iMessage apps can be of two different types:

Sticker packs

These are a special, unusual kind of app that contain only images, with absolutely no code. You can create this kind of app so users can send the images to one another in iMessage. For instance, if you offer a sticker pack full of heart shapes, users can then download the app and attach those hearts to messages that they or others send. In other words, as the name implies, images can stick to messages!

Full-fledged apps

With this type of iMessage app, you have full control over how your app works. You can do some really fun stuff, which we will review soon. For instance, you can change an existing sticker that was sent previously by one of your contacts, so that you and the person you're chatting with can collaboratively send and receive messages.

21.1 Setting Up a Sticker Pack Application

Problem

You want to create a simple iMessage application that allows your users to send stickers to each other, without writing any code.

Solution

Follow these steps:

1. Open Xcode if it's not already open.
2. Create a new project. In the new project dialog, choose Sticker Pack Application and then click Next (Figure 21-1).

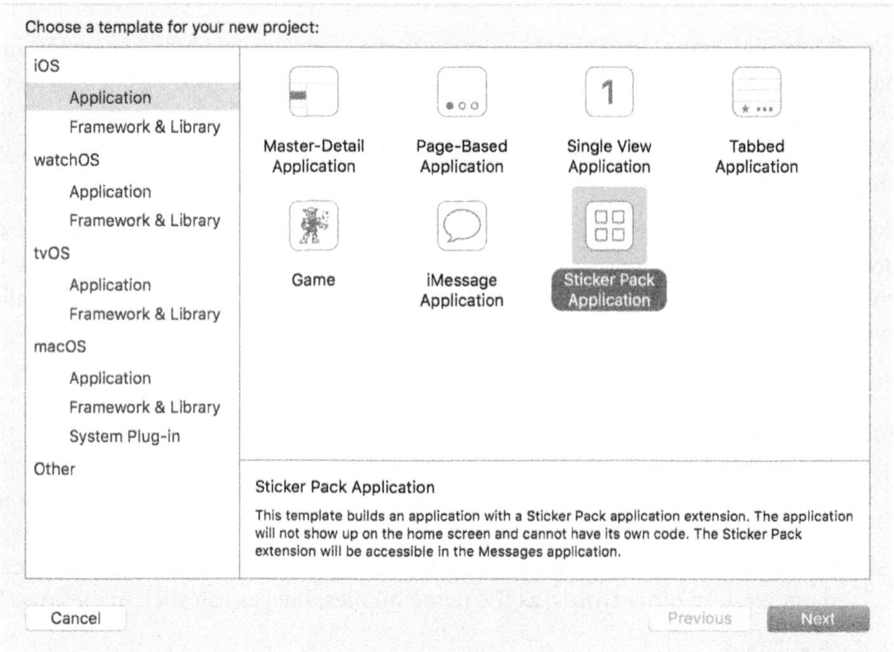

Choose a template for your new project:

iOS				
Application	Master-Detail Application	Page-Based Application	Single View Application	Tabbed Application
Framework & Library				
watchOS	Game	iMessage Application	Sticker Pack Application	
Application				
Framework & Library				

tvOS
Application
Framework & Library

macOS
Application
Framework & Library
System Plug-in

Other

Sticker Pack Application

This template builds an application with a Sticker Pack application extension. The application will not show up on the home screen and cannot have its own code. The Sticker Pack extension will be accessible in the Messages application.

Cancel   Previous   Next

Figure 21-1. Creating a new sticker pack application for iMessage

3. Enter a product name for your project and then click Next (Figure 21-2).

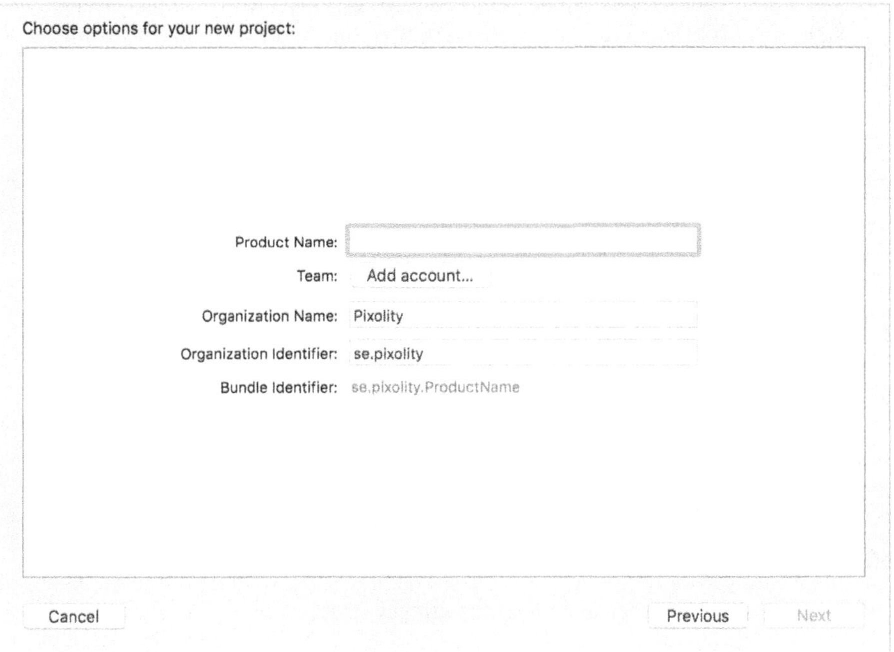

Choose options for your new project:

Product Name:

Team: Add account...

Organization Name: Pixolity

Organization Identifier: se.pixolity

Bundle Identifier: se.pixolity.ProductName

Cancel | Previous | Next

Figure 21-2. Enter your sticker pack application's product name here

4. You will then be asked to save the project somewhere. Choose an appropriate location to save the project to finish this process.

5. You should now see your project opened in Xcode. Click the file named *Stickers.xcstickers* and place your sticker images inside it.

6. After you've completed these steps, test your application on the simulator and then on devices as thoroughly as possible. Once you are happy, you need to code sign and then release your app to the iMessage App Store.

Discussion

With the opening up of iMessage as a platform where developers can build stand-alone apps, Apple has created a new type of store called iMessage App Store, where applications that are compatible with iMessage will show up in the list and users can purchase or download them without cost.

If you create a sticker pack app with no accompanying iOS app, your app shows up only in the iMessage App Store. If you create an iOS app with an accompanying iMessage extension (stickers), your app shows up both in the iOS App Store (for the main iOS app) and in the iMessage App Store (for your iMessage extension).

Your stickers can be PDF, PNG, APNG (PNG with an alpha layer), JPEG, or even (animated) GIF files, but Apple recommends using PNG files for the sake of quality. If you are desperate to create a sticker app but have no images to test with, simply open Finder at */System/Library/CoreServices/CoreTypes.bundle/Contents/Resources/*, then open the ICNS files in that folder with Preview.app, export those ICNS files into PNG files, and drag and drop them into your *Stickers.xcstickers* file in Xcode. Then build and run your project on the simulator.

21.2 Adjusting Sticker Sizes

Problem

You have created a sticker pack application and you want to adjust the size of your stickers in relation to how they appear on the screen.

Solution

Follow these steps in order to change the sticker sizes:

1. While in Xcode, click the *Stickers.xcstickers* file that Xcode created and placed in your project.
2. Open the Attributes inspector in Xcode using Cmd-Alt-4.
3. Locate the Sticker Pack section and then, from the Sticker Size drop-down list in the Attributes inspector and choose between 2 Column, 3 Column, and 4 Column (Figure 21-3).

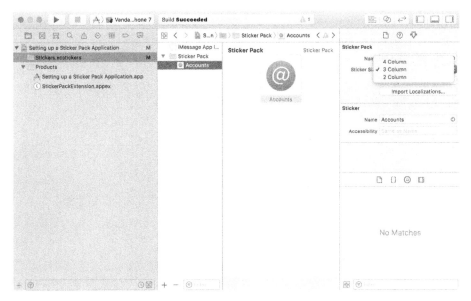

Figure 21-3. Changing the sticker size in the Attributes inspector in Xcode

Discussion

After you ship your sticker applications to the iMessage store and a user downloads them to her device, your stickers appear at a specific size both on the user's device and when sent to the recipient. This size is adjustable—not per sticker, but for the whole sticker pack. All stickers must have the same size.

After you have changed this size, test your app thoroughly on the simulator and on one or more devices before shipping it to the iMessage app store. Ensure that there are no fuzzy edges on your images and that curves look smooth.

See Also

Recipe 21.1

21.3 Building a Full-Fledged iMessage Application

Problem

You want to build a custom iMessage application where you have full control over the presentation of your stickers and how the user interacts with them.

Solution

Create an iMessage application in Xcode by following these steps:

1. Open Xcode if it's not already open.
2. Create a new project. In the template window choose iMessage Application and then click Next (Figure 21-4).

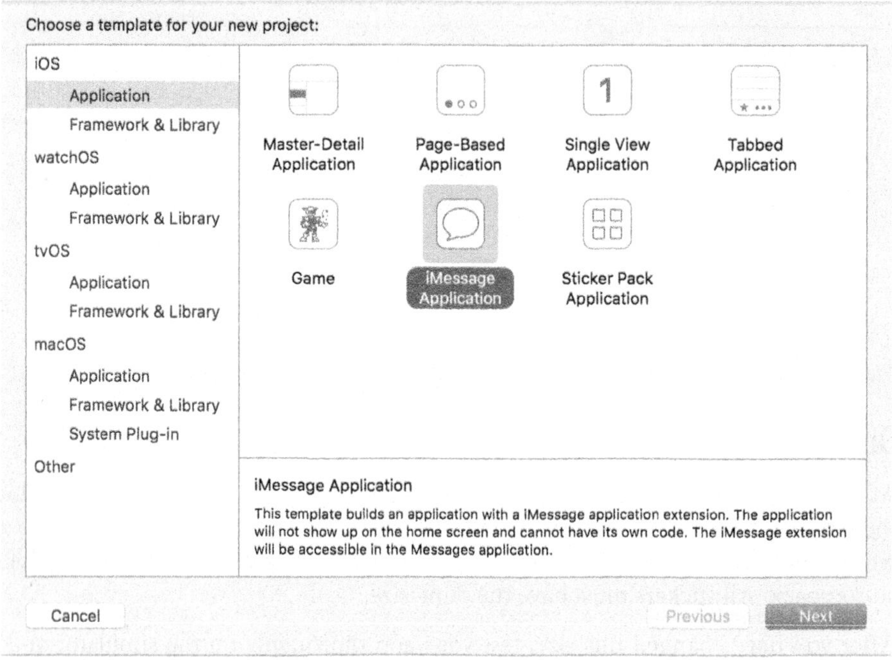

Figure 21-4. Creating a full-fledged iMessage app

3. Enter the product name for your project and then click Next (Figure 21-5). Choose Swift as the language, of course!

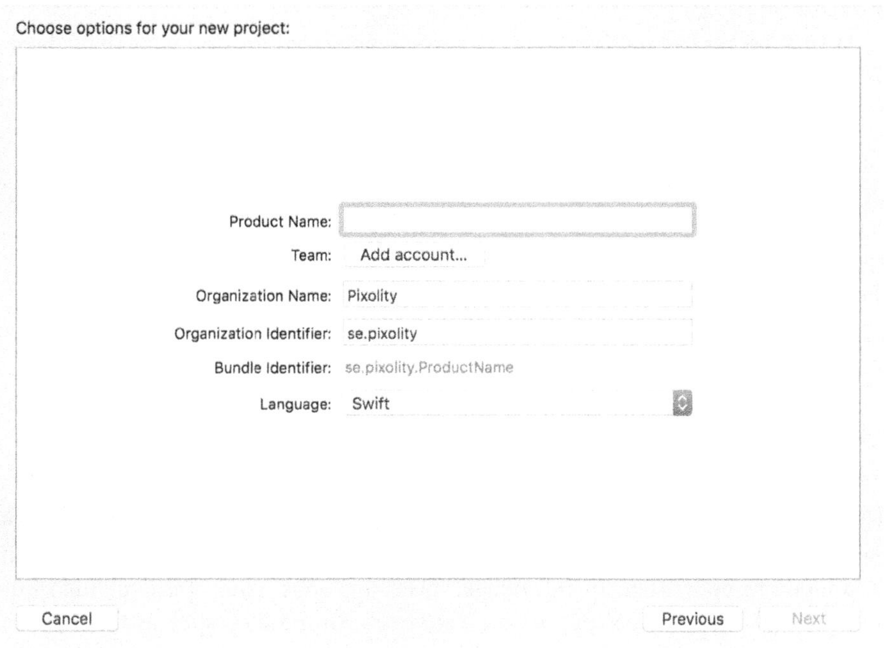

Choose options for your new project:

Product Name:

Team: Add account...

Organization Name: Pixolity

Organization Identifier: se.pixolity

Bundle Identifier: se.pixolity.ProductName

Language: Swift

Cancel   Previous   Next

Figure 21-5. Enter your product name on this screen

4. You will be asked to save your project somewhere. Do so, and then you should see Xcode open up your project.

Discussion

Now that you have created your iMessage app, it's time to learn a bit about what's new in the Messages framework. This framework contains many classes, the most important of which are:

MSMessagesAppViewController
   This is the main view controller of your extension. It gets displayed to users when they open your iMessage application.

MSStickerBrowserViewController
   This is a view controller that gets added to the app view controller and is responsible for displaying your stickers to the user.

MSSticker
   This class encapsulates a single sticker. There is one MSSticker for each sticker in your pack.

`MSStickerView`

Every sticker instance in `MSSticker` has to be placed inside a view to be displayed to the user in the browser view controller. `MSStickerView` is the class for that view.

For the sake of simplicity, for this recipe, hover over */System/Library/CoreServices/ CoreTypes.bundle/Contents/Resources/*, grab the first three ICNS files out of there, and export them, using the Preview app, to your desktop as PNG files with alpha. Later, you will drag and drop them into the *Assets.xcassets* file in your Xcode project under the *MessagesExtension* section—*not* the main app's *Assets.xcassets* file.

When you build an iMessage application as we have just done, your app is separated into two entry points:

- The iOS app entry point with your app delegate and the whole shebang
- The iMessage app extension entry point

This is unlike the sticker pack app that we talked about earlier in this chapter. Sticker pack apps are iMessage apps but have no iOS apps attached to them. Therefore, there is no code to be written. In full-fledged iMessage apps, your app is divided into an iOS app and an iMessage app, so you have two of some files, such as the *Assets.xcassets* file.

Even with custom sticker pack applications, you can build the apps in two different ways:

- Using the existing Messages classes, such as `MSStickerBrowserViewController`, which do the heavy lifting for you
- Using custom collection view controllers that will be attached to your main `MSMessagesAppViewController` instance

This recipe explores the first method, because it is much easier to explain and carry out. Once you have created the main structure of your application as described in this recipe's Solution section, follow these steps to program the actual logic of the app:

1. Drag and drop your PNG stickers into your project's structure, on their own and not in an asset catalog. The reason is that you'll need to find them using their URLs, so you need them to sit on the disk directly.
2. Create a new Cocoa Touch class in your project (Figure 21-6) that will be your `MSStickerBrowserViewController` instance.

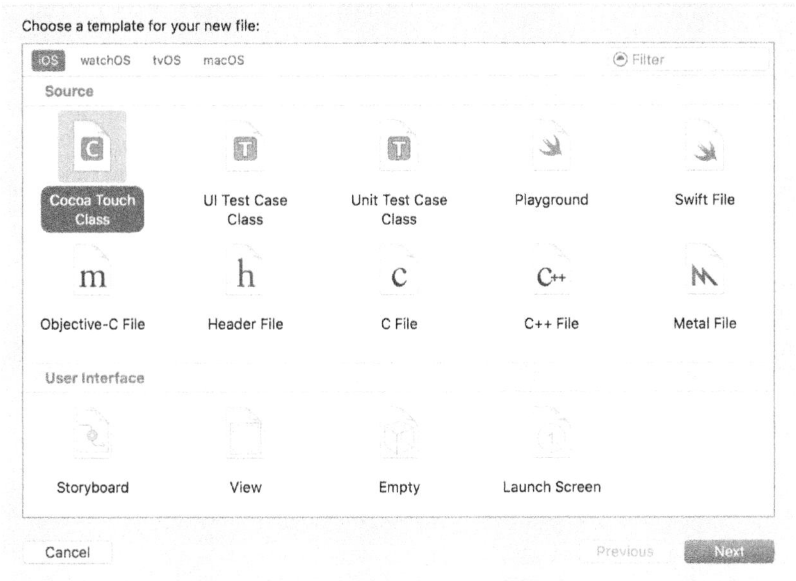

Figure 21-6. Creating a new Cocoa Touch class

3. Give your class the name of `BrowserViewController` (Figure 21-7), ensure it is of type `MSStickerBrowserViewController`, and then click Next.

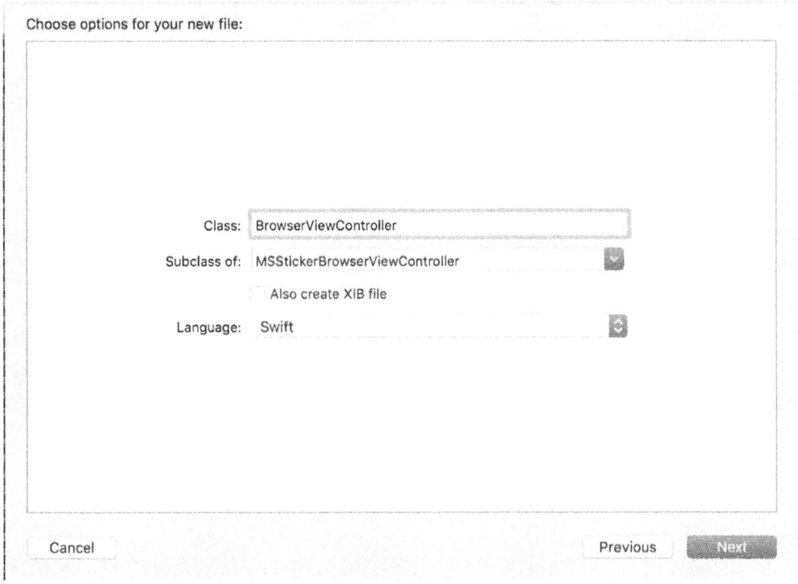

Figure 21-7. Creating your browser view controller

4. Save your file inside your project in the new dialog that appears.

5. Earlier, you added three icons to your project, which you grabbed from */System/ Library/CoreServices/CoreTypes.bundle/Contents/Resources/*. It would be nice if the MSSticker class had an initializer where you could just give it the name of the sticker, instead of the path of the image to which it relates. You can accomplish this by doing a search at runtime in the resources for your app. Create an MSStickerItem enumeration, whose three items match the names of the images you dropped into your project (in my case, Burning, Alert, and Accounts). The extended initializer for MSSticker now accepts an instance of MSStickerItem and uses its name to find the path of the image to apply to the sticker:

```swift
extension MSSticker{

  enum MSStickerItem : String{
    case Burning, Alert, Accounts
  }

  convenience init(item: MSStickerItem) throws{
    try self.init(contentsOfFileURL:
      Bundle.main.url(forResource: item.rawValue, withExtension: "png")!,
              localizedDescription: "")
  }
}
```

6. In the newly created BrowserViewController, create an array of your stickers:

```swift
class BrowserViewController: MSStickerBrowserViewController {

  let stickers = [
    try! MSSticker(item: .Burning),
    try! MSSticker(item: .Alert),
    try! MSSticker(item: .Accounts),
  ]

  ...
```

7. Your instance of MSStickerBrowserViewController has a property called stickerBrowserView of type MSStickerBrowserView, which in turn has a property named dataSource of type MSStickerBrowserViewDataSource?. Your browser view controller by default will become this data source, which means that you need to implement all the nonoptional methods of this protocol, such as numberOfStickers(in:). So let's do that now:

```swift
override func numberOfStickers(in
  stickerBrowserView: MSStickerBrowserView) -> Int {
  return stickers.count
}

override func stickerBrowserView(_ stickerBrowserView: MSStickerBrowserView,
```

```
                                    stickerAt index: Int) -> MSSticker {
    return stickers[index]
}
```

 I'm explicitly unwrapping the optional value of the MSSticker
instance here because I know that those instances exist in my code.
If you are careful with optionals, like I am, in production code, try
to read the values first and then unwrap them only if they exist.

Our browser view controller is done, but how do we display it to the user? Remember
our MSMessagesAppViewController? Well, the answer is through that view controller.
In the viewDidLoad() function of the aforementioned view controller, load your
browser view controller and add it as a child view controller:

```
override func viewDidLoad() {
  super.viewDidLoad()

  let controller = BrowserViewController(stickerSize: .regular)

  controller.willMove(toParentViewController: self)
  addChildViewController(controller)

  if let vcView = controller.view{
    view.addSubview(controller.view)
    vcView.frame = view.bounds
    vcView.translatesAutoresizingMaskIntoConstraints = false
    vcView.leftAnchor.constraint(equalTo: view.leftAnchor).isActive = true
    vcView.rightAnchor.constraint(equalTo: view.rightAnchor).isActive = true
    vcView.topAnchor.constraint(equalTo: view.topAnchor).isActive = true

    vcView.bottomAnchor.constraint(equalTo:
      view.bottomAnchor).isActive = true
  }

  controller.didMove(toParentViewController: self)

}
```

Now press the Run button in Xcode to run your application on the simulator. You
will see a screen similar to Figure 21-8.

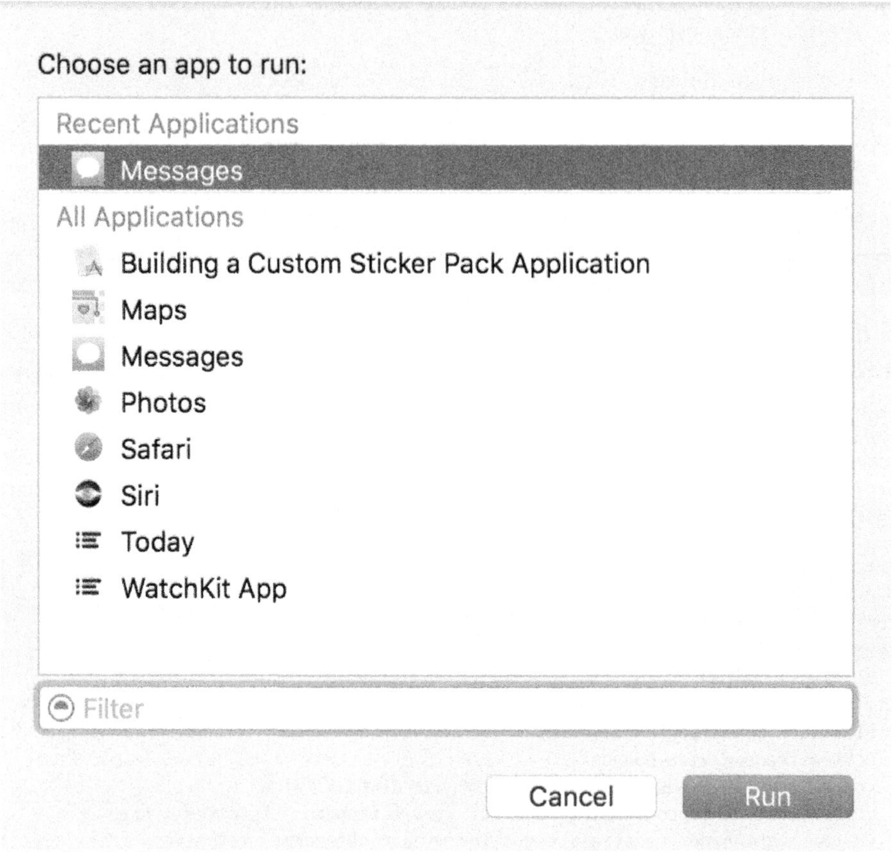

Figure 21-8. Xcode asking you which app on the simulator to attach your app to

In this list, simply choose the Messages app and continue. Once the simulator is running, you can manually open the Messages app, go to an existing conversation that has been placed for you there by the simulator, and press the Apps button on the keyboard. Then choose your app from the list and see your stickers inside the simulator (Figure 21-9).

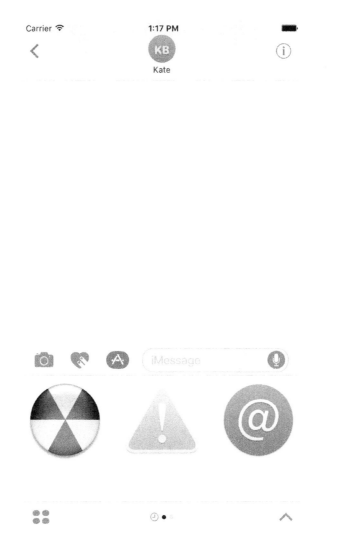

Figure 21-9. Your stickers should be displayed correctly in the iMessage app and can be clicked to be sent to the recipient

See Also

Recipes 21.1 and 21.4

21.4 Adding an iMessage App Extension to an Existing App

Problem

Full-fledged iMessage apps can either stand on their own, without a host iOS app, or be attached to a host iOS app. This recipe shows how to add a new iMessage app extension to an existing app. This in turn allows you to add an iMessage app extension to one of your existing iOS apps so that you can send custom stickers and provide extra functionality to the existing iMessage app.

Solution

Create an iMessage extension and provide the required app icons to it. Follow these steps:

1. Open your project in Xcode.
2. Add a new target of type iMessage extension to your project (Figure 21-10).

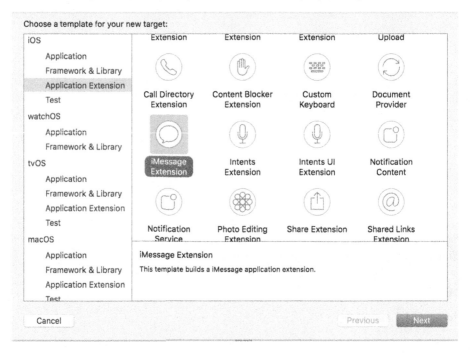

Figure 21-10. Adding an iMessage extension to your app

---

3. On the next screen, enter your extension's product name and other information (Figure 21-11).

Figure 21-11. *Provide a name for the new extension*

4. Then save your new extension to disk and add it to your project.

Discussion

One of the important steps in creating an extension is to add the required icons, so that they appear correctly in the iMessage apps list. Extensions work fine and can be tested without icons, but they will not be accepted to the iMessage App Store without appropriate icons.

See Also

Recipe 21.3

21.5 Utilizing an Expanded View in a Sticker Pack App

Problem

The space that your app gets by default to render itself in an iMessage window is not quite large enough for your purposes and you would like to ask for more space.

Solution

To solve this problem, use the `requestPresentationStyle(_:)` function of the `MSMessagesAppViewController` class to request an expanded view. The parameter that you pass to this function is of type `MSMessagesAppPresentationStyle` and can take the value of either `compact` (the default) or `expanded`.

Discussion

Let's have a look at an example where we put all of this information together to create a functioning application that allows the user to control the size of your rendered app. The user presses a plus button on the interface to expand the extension's view, and can then change the interface back to the compact mode. By default, all extensions launch in the compact mode and can then be changed by the user herself.

Follow these steps to create an iMessage app extension that allows the user to expand its view:

1. Open Xcode and ensure that you have an application with an iMessage extension, as explained in Recipe 21.4.
2. Open your extension's *MainInterface.storyboard* file and then drag a collection view controller and a normal view controller into the scene. Set the collection view controller's class to `StickersViewController` and the normal view controller's class to `ExpandedStickersViewController`. We are going to create these two classes now.
3. Create a new Cocoa Touch class of type `UICollectionViewController` and set its name to `StickersViewController`. Ensure that you don't create an XIB file for it, since its interface is already on your storyboard. Set `StickersViewController` as the storyboard ID of this view controller in the Identity inspector of IB.
4. Next, create another Cocoa Touch class of type `UIViewController` and name it `ExpandedStickersViewController`. Set `ExpandedStickersViewController` as the storyboard ID of this view controller in the Identity inspector of IB.
5. Select your storyboard collection view controller. In the cell that is already created for you in IB, drag and drop an instance of `UIButton`. Set its text to a simple + (plus sign), and then enlarge the font so that it is visible enough for a typical user (Figure 21-12). Also set the reuse identifier of this cell to `Cell` in IB.

Custom Class

Class StickersViewController

Module Current – MessageExt.

Identity

Storyboard ID StickersViewController

Restoration ID

☐ Use Storyboard ID

Figure 21-12. Our collection view Storyboard ID is set along with the creation of the button on our cell

6. Ensure that the button that you placed on your cell has *no* user interactions enabled—otherwise, it will trap all touch events, and we want to trap the touch events through the parent collection view controller. With the button selected, go to the Attributes inspector of IB and deselect the User Interaction Enabled checkbox.

7. Open your *StickersViewController.swift* file and define a protocol for your collection view controller so that any other class can become its delegate. Later, when the user presses the + button on the collection view, you can report this to your delegate object:

```
import UIKit

protocol StickersViewControllerDelegate : class{
  func plusButtonTappedOn(controller: UIViewController)
}

protocol HasStickersDelegate : class{
  weak var delegate: StickersViewControllerDelegate? {get set}
}

class StickersViewController: UICollectionViewController,
  HasStickersDelegate {

  weak var delegate: StickersViewControllerDelegate?

  ...
```

8. Now, provide enough information for the collection view to display your single cell:

```
// we set this to Cell in IB as well, remember?
private let reuseIdentifier = "Cell"

override func numberOfSections(in collectionView: UICollectionView) ->
```

```
        Int {
    return 1
}

override func collectionView(_ collectionView: UICollectionView,
                    numberOfItemsInSection section: Int) -> Int {
    return 1
}

override func collectionView(
  _ collectionView: UICollectionView,
  cellForItemAt indexPath: IndexPath) -> UICollectionViewCell {

    let cell = collectionView.dequeueReusableCell(
      withReuseIdentifier: reuseIdentifier, for: indexPath)

    return cell
}
```

9. And ensure that when the + cell is tapped, you will report it to your delegate:

```
override func collectionView(_ collectionView: UICollectionView,
                    didSelectItemAt indexPath: IndexPath) {
    guard indexPath.row == 0 && indexPath.section == 0 else {return}
    delegate?.plusButtonTappedOn(controller: self)
}
```

10. Now go to the *MessagesViewController.swift* file and define the storyboard identifiers of the two view controllers that you just created:

```
import UIKit
import Messages

struct Identifiers{
static let StickersViewController = "StickersViewController"
static let ExpandedStickersViewController = "ExpandedStickersViewController"
}
```

11. Let's also extend `UIViewController` with a function that allows you to add any
view controller to your Messages app view controller:

```
extension UIViewController{
    func addTo(appViewController host: MSMessagesAppViewController){

        // see if this view controller has a delagete and then set it to
        // the host view controller if yes
        if
          let delegate = host as? StickersViewControllerDelegate,
          let vc = self as? HasStickersDelegate{
          vc.delegate = delegate
        }
```

```
willMove(toParentViewController: host)
host.addChildViewController(self)
view.frame = host.view.bounds
view.translatesAutoresizingMaskIntoConstraints = false
host.view.addSubview(view)
view.leftAnchor.constraint(equalTo: host.view.leftAnchor).isActive = true
    view.rightAnchor.constraint(equalTo: host.view.rightAnchor).isActive
      = true
    view.topAnchor.constraint(equalTo: host.view.topAnchor).isActive
      = true
    view.bottomAnchor.constraint(equalTo:
      host.view.bottomAnchor).isActive = true
    didMove(toParentViewController: host)

  }
}
```

12. Then add a function called loadViewController(forPresentationStyle:) to your MessagesViewController class. In this function, you'll take the incoming presentation style of type MSMessagesAppPresentationStyle and then load either the collection view controller (for compact mode) or the normal view controller (for expanded mode):

```
class MessagesViewController : MSMessagesAppViewController,
StickersViewControllerDelegate {

func loadViewController
  (forPresentationStyle: MSMessagesAppPresentationStyle) -> Bool{

  childViewControllers.forEach{
    $0.willMove(toParentViewController: nil)
    $0.view.removeFromSuperview()
    $0.removeFromParentViewController()
    ($0 as? HasStickersDelegate)?.delegate = nil
  }

  let vcId: String

  switch presentationStyle{
  case .compact:
    vcId = Identifiers.StickersViewController
  case .expanded:
    vcId = Identifiers.ExpandedStickersViewController
  case .transcript:
    return false
  }

  guard let vc = storyboard?
    .instantiateViewController(withIdentifier: vcId) else {return false}
```

```
vc.addTo(appViewController: self)

return true

}

...
```

13. Because you have become the delegate of the collection view controller, you also need to implement its delegate method:

```
func plusButtonTappedOn(controller: UIViewController) {
  let _ = loadViewController(forPresentationStyle: .expanded)
  requestPresentationStyle(.expanded)
}
```

14. You can also load the appropriate view controller based on the reported presentation styles, via methods already defined on MSMessagesAppViewController:

```
override func willBecomeActive(with conversation: MSConversation) {
  // Called when the extension is about to move from the
  // inactive to active state.
  // This will happen when the extension is about to present UI.

  // Use this method to configure the extension and restore previously
  // stored state.

  let _ = loadViewController(forPresentationStyle: .compact)

}

override func willTransition(to presentationStyle:
  MSMessagesAppPresentationStyle) {
  // Called before the extension transitions to a new presentation style.

  // Use this method to prepare for the change in presentation style.
  let _ = loadViewController(forPresentationStyle: presentationStyle)
}

override func didTransition(to presentationStyle:
  MSMessagesAppPresentationStyle) {
  // Called after the extension transitions to a new presentation style.

  // Use this method to finalize any behaviors associated with the
  // change in presentation style.
  let _ = loadViewController(forPresentationStyle: presentationStyle)
}
```

Run your project now on the simulator. You will now see a plus button in the list, as shown in Figure 21-13.

Figure 21-13. The plus button is shown properly in the compact mode of the extension

Once the user taps this button, your extension will request the expanded presentation style (Figure 21-14).

Figure 21-14. The expanded iMessage extension

You can see that the system provides a bar button item on the navigation bar, which, when tapped, will send the extension back to the compact mode.

See Also

Recipe 21.3

21.6 Appending Rich Information to Stickers

Problem

You want to attach extra information, such as a caption, title, and subtitle, to your stickers and messages in an iMessage app.

Solution

Follow these steps:

1. Create an instance of MSMessage.
2. Create a layout object of type MSMessageTemplateLayout and set its properties, such as image and caption.
3. Once the template is ready, set it as the template property of the message object.
4. Send the message to the current conversation using the insert(_:completion Handler:) function of the active conversation object of type MSConversation.

 Your MSMessagesAppViewController instance has a property called activeConversation of type MSConversation?. You can use this optional property to get a reference to your active conversation. Ideally, this property should always be present, but officially it's optional so you can't assume its presence. Always check its value against nil and then handle the situation properly if it is not present.

Discussion

In this recipe we are going to build a new application based on what we discussed in Recipe 21.5. The difference in this recipe is that, when the user presses the + button on our iMessage extension, we will send a prebuilt sticker to the recipient. I have already placed an image called *Accounts.png* inside the image asset catalog of my iMessage extension so that I can open it using an instance of UIImage. You can also do the same thing. I grabbed this image out of the *Accounts.icns* file at */System/ Library/CoreServices/CoreTypes.bundle/Contents/Resources/*.

If you recall from Recipe 21.5, when the + button gets tapped, we call the plusButton TappedOn(controller:) function of our delegate object, which in this case is our instance of MSMessagesAppViewController. In our current recipe, we will rewrite the code in this function so that we create an instance of MSMessage and send it to the recipient. Follow these steps to rewrite this code:

1. Retrieve the current conversation object:

```
func plusButtonTappedOn(controller: UIViewController) {

    guard let conversation = activeConversation else {fatalError()}

    ...
```

2. Retrieve the existing session. If one doesn't exist, create one:

```
let session = conversation.selectedMessage?.session ?? MSSession()
```

3. Instantiate your message object:

```
let message = MSMessage(session: session)
```

4. Create your layout object and assign all its properties to your chosen values:

```
let layout = MSMessageTemplateLayout()
layout.image = messageImage
layout.caption = "Caption"
layout.imageTitle = "Image title"
layout.imageSubtitle = "Image subtitle"
layout.trailingCaption = "Trailing caption"
layout.subcaption = "Subcaption"
layout.trailingSubcaption = "Trailing subcaption"
```

5. Once the layout is ready, insert the message into the conversation:

```
message.layout = layout

conversation.insert(message) {error in
    // empty for now
}
```

When preparing the layout object, we set its `image` property to `messageImage`. This is a custom property I have defined on our instance of `MSMessagesAppViewController`. All it does is call `UIGraphicsImageRenderer` to create an image context, set the background color of the context to black, and then draw the *Accounts.png* file on top of the black background so that the white text that our layout object renders will eventually be visible on the black background:

```
var messageImage: UIImage? {
  guard let image = UIImage(named: "Accounts") else {return nil}
  let rect = image.size.rectWithZeroOrigin

  let renderer = UIGraphicsImageRenderer(bounds: rect)
  return renderer.image {context in
    let bgColor: UIColor = .black
    bgColor.setFill()
    context.fill(rect)
    image.draw(at: .zero)
  }
}
```

Run your code now on the simulator and see the results for yourself (Figure 21-15).

Figure 21-15. Our message, with rich information, is ready to be sent to the recipient

The MSMessageTemplateLayout class has many useful properties, as you have just seen. Let's explore some of them so you understand what they are and what they do:

image: UIImage?
> This is the actual image that will be sent as the message. This is an optional property.

`caption: String?`

If you look closely at Figure 21-15, you will notice that iMessage inserts a little colorful bar at the bottom of your images on which it will render the caption. This is extra information that you can add to your image, of type `String?`.

`subcaption: String?`

This gets rendered underneath the caption, in the additional bar that gets displayed by default by iMessage below the image.

`imageTitle: String?`

The title and the subtitle get rendered at the bottom of the image itself, and they are in a white color, so ensure that your image's background is a color other than white.

`imageSubtitle: String?`

The subtitle that gets rendered underneath the title but still at the bottom-left corner of the image itself.

`trailingCaption: String?`

The trailing caption is displayed on the bottom-right corner.

`trailingSubcaption: String?`

The subcaption gets displayed on the bottom-right corner, underneath the trailing caption.

See Also

Recipe 21.5

21.7 Creating Interactive Conversations with iMessage Apps

Problem

Your iMessage app allows users to send data, such as images or texts, to one another. Inside the active conversation, you would like to allow the recipient of this data to be able to change the data, and send it back, replacing the existing data instead of sending a new message.

Solution

Inside the `MSMessagesAppViewController` instance of your extension, look at the `activeConversation.selectedMessage` property to see whether it's set. If it is, there is a selected message that was previously sent by your iMessage app. Once you find this selected message, use its `url` property to create a mutable instance of the same message.

Discussion

The first message sent by user A to user B with your app will have the `selected Message` property set to `nil` because no previous messages were sent by your app, hence none could be selected. In this case, you can send a new message and set the `url` property of the message to `http://app.com/`. Then, when the recipient receives this message and taps on it, your extension will go into the expanded mode, and there you can find this `selectedMessage` and read its `url` property. You can then compose a new message with new data, images, etc., and set its `url` property to `http://app.com/withnewdata`. Once you send this message, iMessage realizes that you took the selected message and just changed it a little bit. Hence, iMessage will not send a new message, but instead will change the selected message to the new one for both the sender and the receiver.

Let's take what we learned in Recipe 21.6 and change the solution a little bit so that we can create such interactive conversations.

In Recipe 21.6 we have both a compact and an expanded view controller. As explained just now, when the user taps on a message that was previously sent by your app, two things will happen:

- The `willTransition(to:)` function of your `MSMessagesAppViewController` will be called and will change your app to the expanded mode.
- The `activeConversation.selectedMessage` property of your `MSMessagesApp ViewController` will be set to an instance of `MSMessage` that represents the selected message.

Knowing that the app is in expanded mode at this point, we are going to take the same view controller as we did in Recipe 21.6 and change its interface so that there is a button on the screen that looks like Figure 21-16.

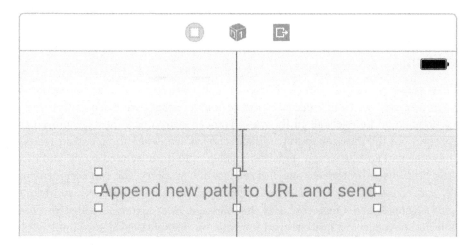

Figure 21-16. Adding an append button to the view controller

We'll hook this button to a new function in our code:

```
import UIKit

class ExpandedStickersViewController: UIViewController, HasStickersDelegate {

  weak var delegate: StickersViewControllerDelegate?

  @IBAction func appendButtonTapped(_ sender: AnyObject) {
    delegate?.plusButtonTappedOn(self)
  }

}
```

 I am utilizing the existing HasStickersDelegate and Stickers ViewControllerDelegate protocols for this view controller because our instance of MSMessagesAppViewController is concerned only with the press of the + button. When MSMessagesApp ViewController traps this pressing of a button, it can read the active conversation's selected message and either send a new one or change the existing one if a selected message is already there.

When the button is tapped on either the compact or the expanded view controller, the plusButtonTappedOn(_:) delegate method will be called in MSMessagesAppView Controller. Here, we are going to look at the selected message to see if it exists and, if it does, determine how many url components it has. So we need a property on the URL class that can count the url components for us:

```
extension URL{
  // counts the number of path components in the URL
  var pathCount: Int{
    let components = NSURLComponents(url: self, resolvingAgainstBaseURL: false)
    return components?.path?
      .components(separatedBy: "/")
      .filter{$0.characters.count > 0}
      .count ?? 0
  }
}
```

For instance, if the URL is *http://app.com/*, this property will return 0 because there is no path component after the domain name. If the URL is *http://app.com/foo*, the property will return 1 because `foo` is the single path component.

What we want to do in the `plusButtonTappedOn(controller:)` delegate method is send the URL of *https://developer.apple.com* to the conversation should there be no previously selected message in the active session. Once the first message is sent in the current session, the recipient can tap it and then append a new path to the URL. The final path that we are going to construct is *library/prerelease/ios/releasenotes/General/WhatsNewIniOS/* appended to *https://developer.apple.com*, so we have a total of six path components to play with. This means six bouncebacks of the same message back and forth between the sender and the recipient.

When *https://developer.apple.com* is sent as the first message, we would like an image to be inside the `MSMessage` instance with the caption "developer.apple.com/," as shown in Figure 21-17.

Figure 21-17. The first message in the conversation refers to developer.apple.com/

Once the recipient gets this message and taps it, the expanded view of our app will be displayed (Figure 21-18).

Figure 21-18. The expanded view of our app is shown after the user taps the selected message, composed by the same app on the sender's side

Upon tapping the button on our expanded view, we will append the next path component, "library/", to the URL and send it over (Figure 21-19).

Figure 21-19. The selected message is changed to the new message with a new caption, indicating the current final path component

Once this new message is sent, the receiver will be able to select it and press the button again on the expanded view to change the message to a new one, with the next path component attached to it (Figure 21-20).

Figure 21-20. The next path component is now attached to the message

So, let's go to the `plusButtonTappedOn(controller:)` delegate method and define our path components:

```
func plusButtonTappedOn(controller: UIViewController) {

  let paths = [
    "library/", "prerelease/", "ios/",
    "releasenotes/", "General/", "WhatsNewIniOS/"
  ]

  ...
```

We will also define the base URL:

```
let base = "developer.apple.com/"
```

We should then find the existing session (or create a new one) and find the active conversation to which we can send or append our messages:

```
guard let conversation = activeConversation else {fatalError()}
let session = conversation.selectedMessage?.session ?? MSSession()
```

We will now construct our URL instance and build a caption for our image:

```
let url: URL
let caption: String?
if let selectedMessageUrl = conversation.selectedMessage?.url{
  let pathCount = selectedMessageUrl.pathCount
  if pathCount < paths.count{
    let lastPath = paths[pathCount]
    url = selectedMessageUrl.appendingPathComponent(lastPath)
    caption = "\(base) (\(lastPath))"
  } else if let lastPath = paths.last {
    url = selectedMessageUrl
    caption = "\(base) (\(lastPath))"
  } else {
    return
  }
} else {
  url = URL(string: "https://\(base)")!
  caption = base
}
```

After this is done, we will create an instance of our `MSMessage` with the session that we previously found and set its layout:

```
let message = MSMessage(session: session)

let layout = MSMessageTemplateLayout()
layout.image = messageImage
layout.caption = caption

message.layout = layout
message.url = url
```

I explained how `messageImage` is implemented in Recipe 21.6.

Last but not least, we will insert this message into the conversation and, once everything is settled, call the `dismiss()` function of our `MSMessagesAppViewController`

---

instance so that if we are in the expanded mode and the user taps the button on the UI, we can close our expanded view so that the user can send the message:

```
conversation.insert(message) {[weak self]error in
  guard let strongSelf = self else {return}
  strongSelf.dismiss()
}
```

Index

About the Author

Vandad Nahavandipoor is currently an iOS developer for TV4 Play in Stockholm. Previously he worked for Lloyds Banking Group in England to deliver their iOS apps to millions of users in the UK. He has led an international team of more than 30 iOS developers, and some of the projects he has overseen include the NatWest and RBS iOS apps running on millions of iPhones and iPads in the UK. Vandad received his BSc and MSc in Information Technology for E-Commerce from the University of Sussex in England.

Vandad's programming experience started when he first learned BASIC on his father's Commodore 64. He then took this experience and applied it on his uncle's computer, running BASIC on DOS. At this point, he found programming for personal computers exciting indeed and moved on to learn Object Pascal. This allowed him to learn Borland Delphi quite easily. He wrote a 400-page book on Borland Delphi and dedicated the book to Borland. From then, he picked up x86 Assembly programming and wrote a hobby 32-bit operating system named Vandior. It wasn't until late 2007 when iOS programming became his main focus.

Colophon

The red-billed tropicbird (*Phaethon aethereus*) is also called the boatswain bird. Tropicbirds look like terns but are not genetically related to them; in fact, tropicbirds have no close living relative species, making them a bit of an evolutionary mystery. The red-billed tropicbird was featured on the Bermudan $50 bill starting in 2009, but it was subsequently replaced by the native white-tailed tropicbird, which has a higher population in Bermuda.

Red-billed tropicbirds are large, with long tails, white bodies, and the eponymous red bill that curves downward. With the tail feathers included, they are almost 40 inches long; a wingspan of one meter balances out their bodies and makes them graceful flyers. They have black markings on their flight feathers and in their eyes. Male and female birds look similar, but males can have longer tails. Red-billed tropicbirds' feet are located very far back on their bodies, so their movements on land are almost comically awkward and occur mostly on their bellies. They are not nimble swimmers either, but they move comfortably through the air over the ocean, where they hover in hopes of catching flying fish. Flying fish appear to be a favorite prey, but tropicbirds will eat other fish and even cephalopods as well.

Red-billed tropicbirds live in places like the Galápagos islands, the Cape Verde islands, the West Indies, and even the Persian Gulf. Despite their preference for warm, tropical waters, a particular single red-billed tropicbird keeps returning to Seal Island in coastal Maine every year. There is a large seabird population in that part of the state, but this individual is the only one of his kind to be found that far north. Some years ago, locals placed a wood decoy carving of a tropicbird out and the inexplicable visitor tried to court and mate with it. The chance of seeing this bird has meant good business for the boat charters that take birdwatchers out to see the puffins and black guillemots that otherwise dominate the local bird scene.

Many of the animals on O'Reilly covers are endangered; all of them are important to the world. To learn more about how you can help, go to *animals.oreilly.com*.

The cover image is from the *Riverside Natural History*. The cover fonts are URW Typewriter and Guardian Sans. The text font is Adobe Minion Pro; the heading font is Adobe Myriad Condensed; and the code font is Dalton Maag's Ubuntu Mono.

Learn from experts.
Find the answers you need.

Sign up for a **10-day free trial** to get **unlimited access** to all of the content on Safari, including Learning Paths, interactive tutorials, and curated playlists that draw from thousands of ebooks and training videos on a wide range of topics, including data, design, DevOps, management, business—and much more.

Start your free trial at:
oreilly.com/safari

(No credit card required.)

CPSIA information can be obtained
at www.ICGtesting.com
Printed in the USA
BVOW09s0352101217
502151BV00003B/4/P